# ZATCH BELL!™

## ZATCH BELL!
### Vol. 10

STORY AND ART BY
**MAKOTO RAIKU**

Translation/David Ury
Touch-up Art & Lettering/Gabe Crate
Design/Izumi Hirayama
Special Thanks/Jessica Villat, Miki Macaluso,
Mitsuko Kitajima, and Akane Matsuo
Editor/Kit Fox

Managing Editor/Annette Roman
Editorial Director/Elizabeth Kawasaki
Editor in Chief/Alvin Lu
Sr. Director of Acquisitions/Rika Inouye
Sr. VP of Marketing/Liza Coppola
Exec. VP of Sales & Marketing/John Easum
Publisher/Hyoe Narita

**Muteki Forugore**
Words and Music by Michihiko Oota, Makoto Raiku and Gyou Yamatoya. Copyright
© 2003 Fujipacific Music Inc. All Rights Administered by Songs Of Windswept
Pacific. All Rights Reserved. Used by Permission.

Printed in the U.S.A.

Published by VIZ Media, LLC
P.O. Box 77010
San Francisco, CA 94107

10 9 8 7 6 5 4 3 2 1
First printing, December 2006

www.viz.com
store.viz.com

 AMHERST PUBLIC LIBRARY
221 SPRING STREET
AMHERST, OHIO 44001

STORY AND ART BY

# MAKOTO RAIKU

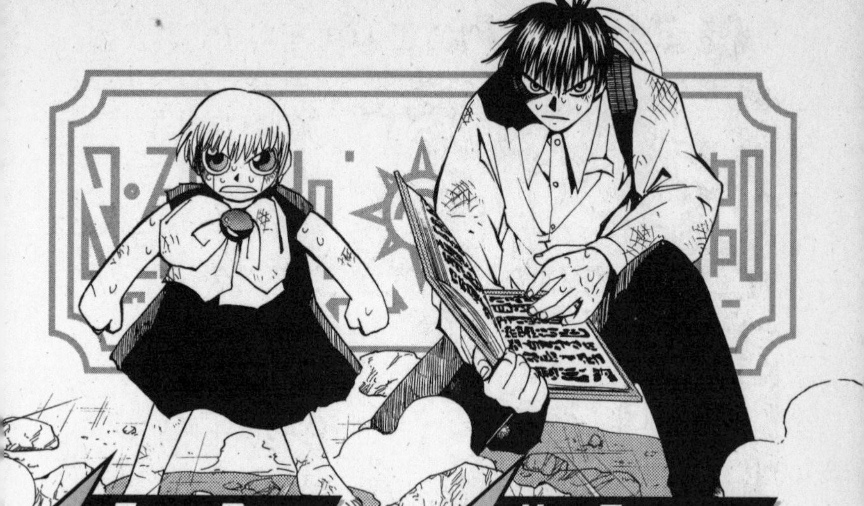

## Zatch Bell

A mamodo who can't remember his past. When Kiyo holds the "Red Book" and reads a spell, lightning bolts shoot from Zatch's mouth. He is fighting to be a "kind king."

## Kiyo Takamine

An aloof student with a keen intellect. The day Kiyo met Zatch, he became the owner of the "Red Book"—and started growing up.

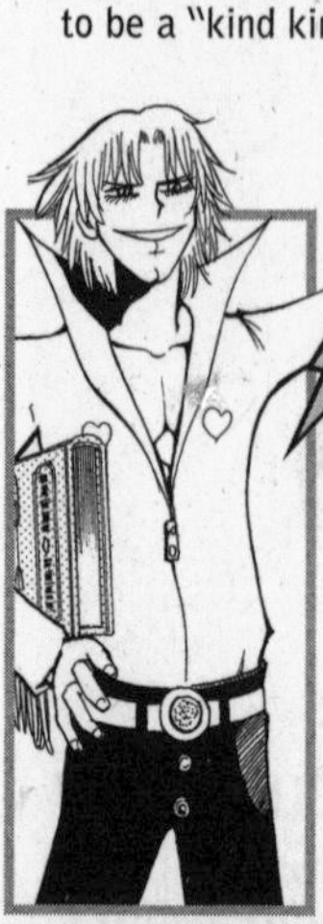

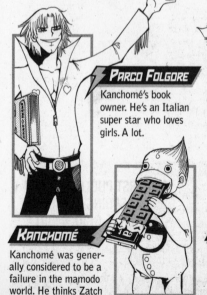

## Parco Folgore

Kanchomé's book owner. He's an Italian super star who loves girls. A lot.

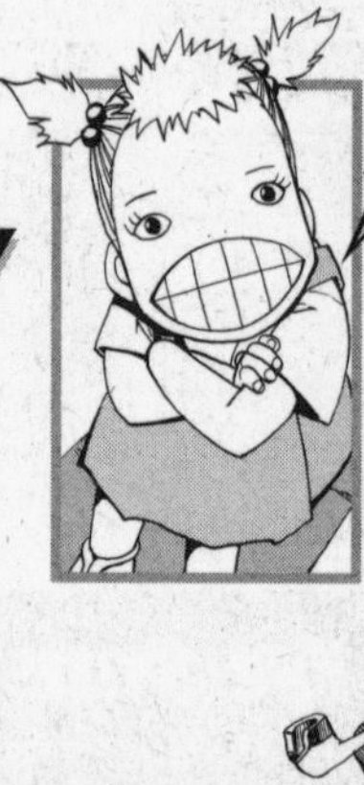

## Naomi

A girl who always picks on Zatch in the park.

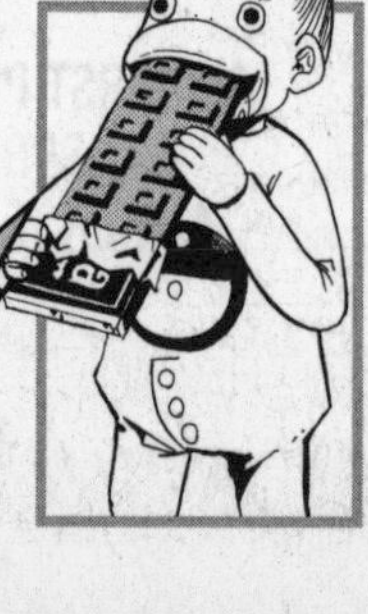

## Kanchomé

Kanchomé was generally considered to be a failure in the mamodo world. He thinks Zatch is his rival.

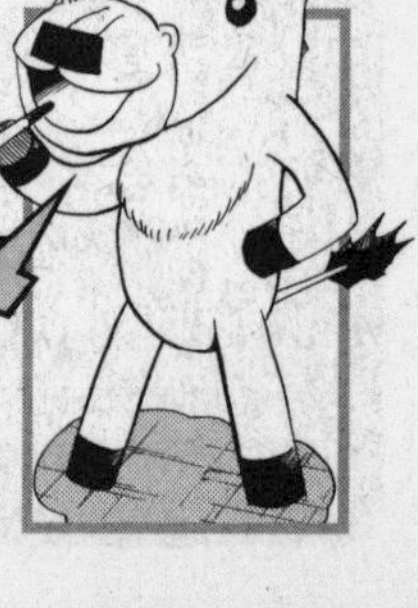

## Ponygon

A mamodo who's staying at Kiyo's house. He hasn't found his partner yet.

## Zatch's Past Opponents

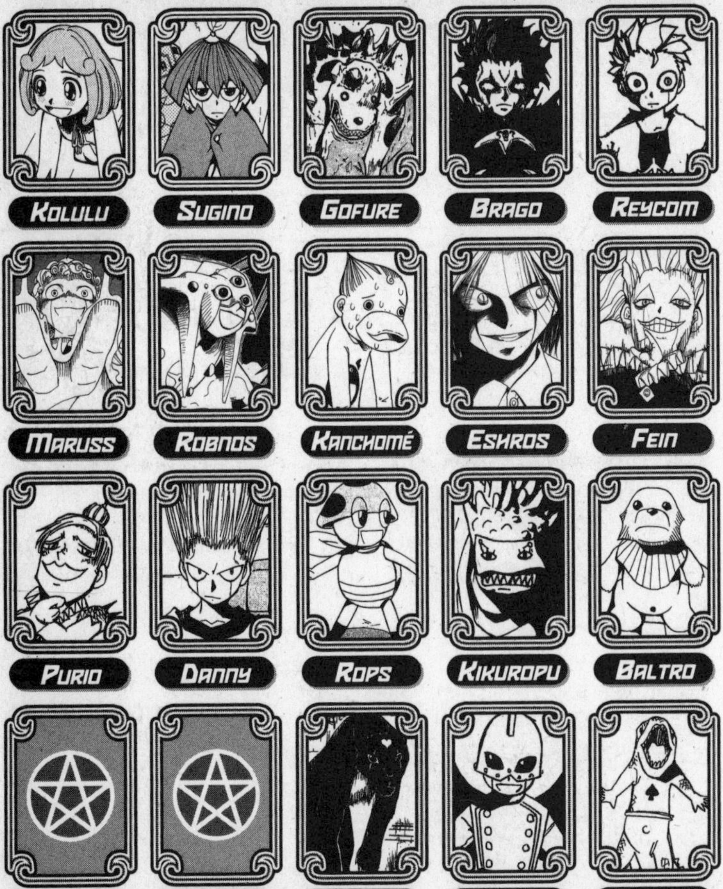
Kolulu
Sugino
Gofure
Brago
Reycom
Maruss
Robnos
Kanchomé
Eshros
Fein
Purio
Danny
Rops
Kikuropu
Baltro
Baransha
Zabas
Zoboron

## The Story Thus Far

The battle to determine who will be the next king of the mamodo world takes place every 1,000 years in the human world. Each mamodo owns a "book" which increases its unique powers, and they must team up with a human in order to fight for their own survival. Zatch is one of 100 mamodo chosen to fight in this battle, and his partner is Kiyo, a junior high school student. The bond between Zatch and Kiyo deepens as they continue to survive through many harsh battles. Zatch swears, "I will fight to become a kind king."

# ZATCH BELL! 10

# CONTENTS

# LEVEL 85: A Reliable Brother

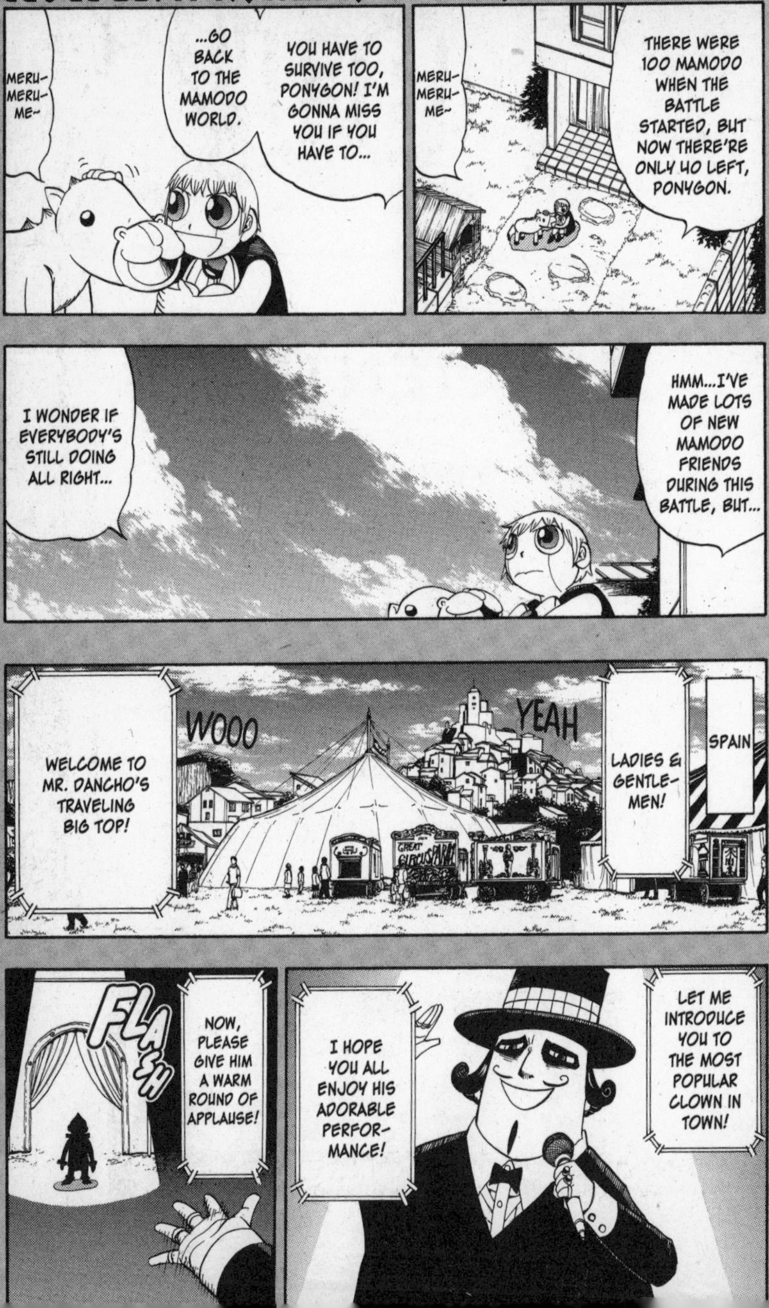
THERE WERE 100 MAMODO WHEN THE BATTLE STARTED, BUT NOW THERE'RE ONLY 40 LEFT, PONYGON.
MERU-MERU-ME~
YOU HAVE TO SURVIVE TOO, PONYGON! I'M GONNA MISS YOU IF YOU HAVE TO...
...GO BACK TO THE MAMODO WORLD.
MERU-MERU-ME~
HMM...I'VE MADE LOTS OF NEW MAMODO FRIENDS DURING THIS BATTLE, BUT...
I WONDER IF EVERYBODY'S STILL DOING ALL RIGHT...
SPAIN
LADIES & GENTLEMEN!
YEAH
WOOO
WELCOME TO MR. DANCHO'S TRAVELING BIG TOP!
GREAT CIRCUS PARK
LET ME INTRODUCE YOU TO THE MOST POPULAR CLOWN IN TOWN!
I HOPE YOU ALL ENJOY HIS ADORABLE PERFORMANCE!
NOW, PLEASE GIVE HIM A WARM ROUND OF APPLAUSE!
FLASH

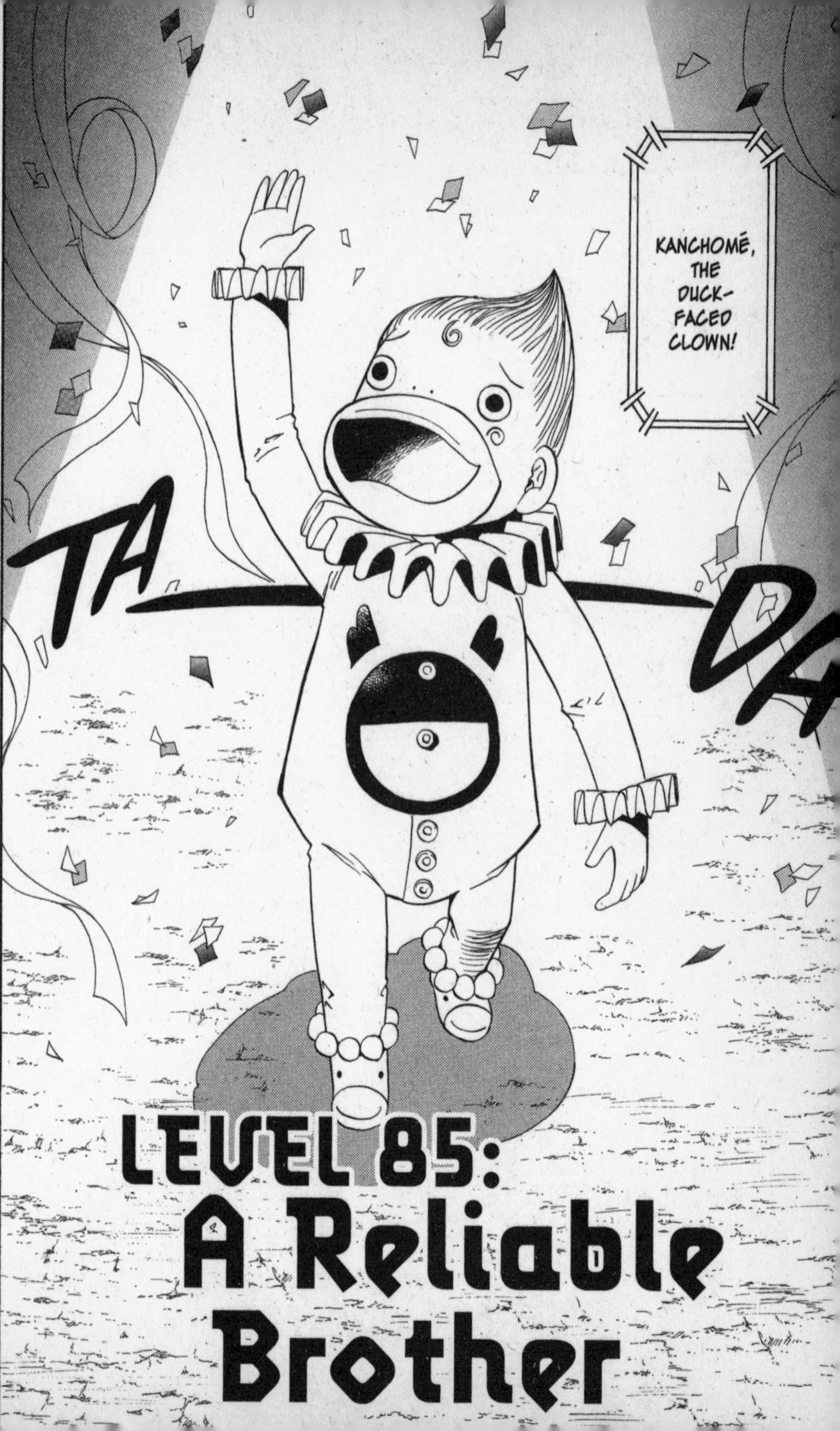
KANCHOMÉ, THE DUCK-FACED CLOWN!
TA—DA

# LEVEL 85: A Reliable Brother

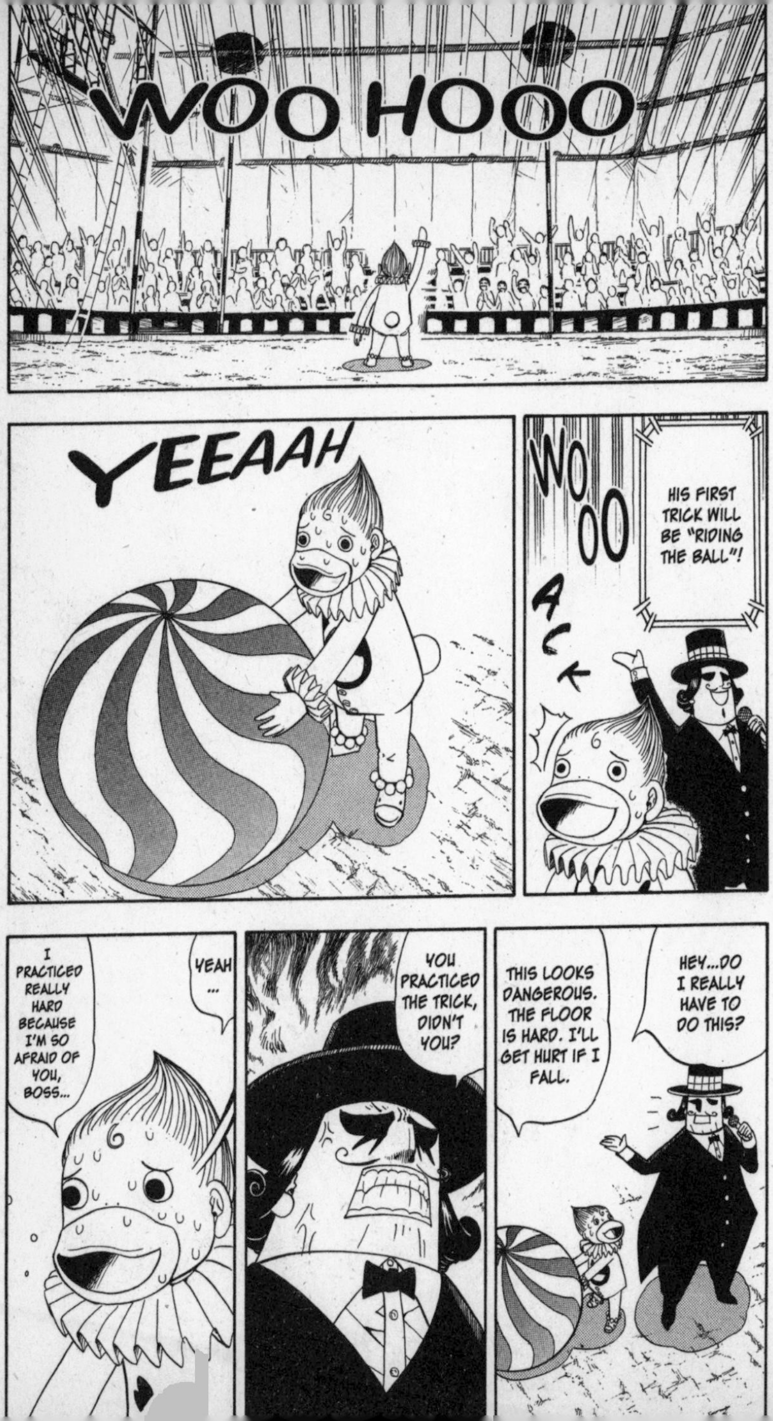
WOO HOOO
HIS FIRST TRICK WILL BE "RIDING THE BALL"!
WOOO
ACK
YEEAAH
HEY...DO I REALLY HAVE TO DO THIS?
THIS LOOKS DANGEROUS. THE FLOOR IS HARD. I'LL GET HURT IF I FALL.
YOU PRACTICED THE TRICK, DIDN'T YOU?
YEAH ...
I PRACTICED REALLY HARD BECAUSE I'M SO AFRAID OF YOU, BOSS...

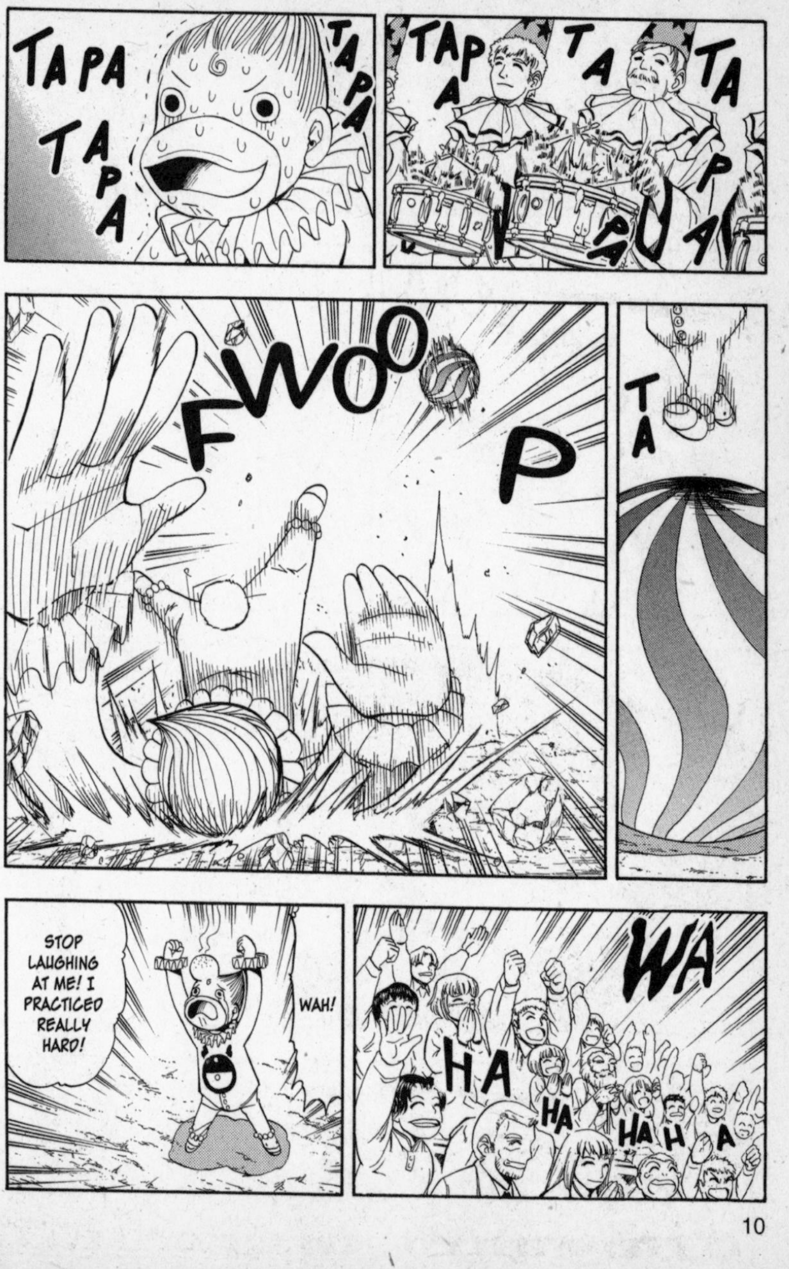
TAPA
TA
TAPA
PA
TAPA
TAPA
TAPA
TAPA
TA
TA
FWOOP
WA
HA
HA
HAHA
HA
STOP LAUGHING AT ME! I PRACTICED REALLY HARD!
WAH!

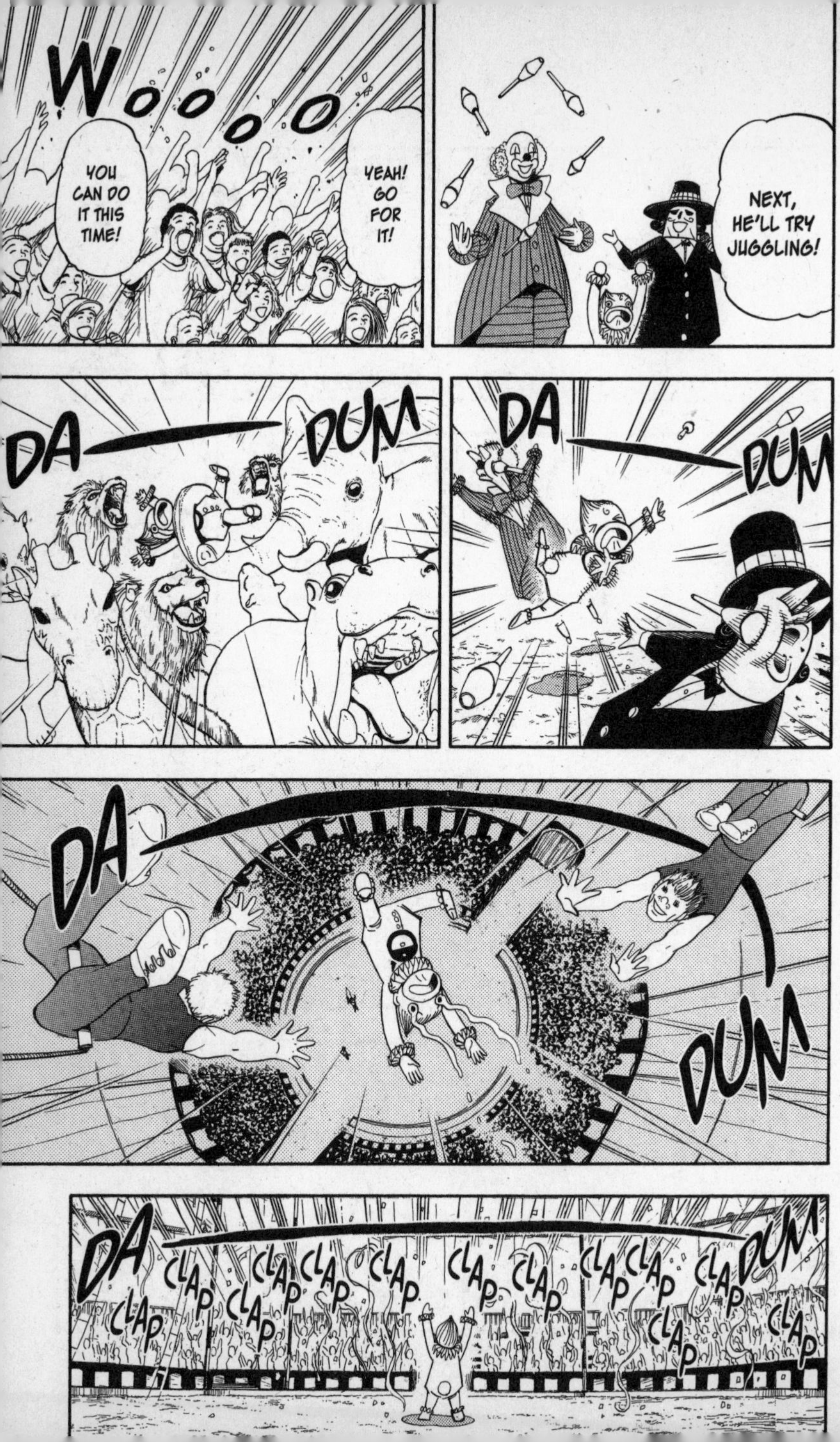
NEXT, HE'LL TRY JUGGLING!
WOOOO
YEAH! GO FOR IT!
YOU CAN DO IT THIS TIME!
DA—DUM
DA—DUM
DA—DUM
DA—DUM
CLAP CLAP CLAP CLAP CLAP CLAP CLAP CLAP CLAP CLAP CLAP CLAP CLAP CLAP CLAP

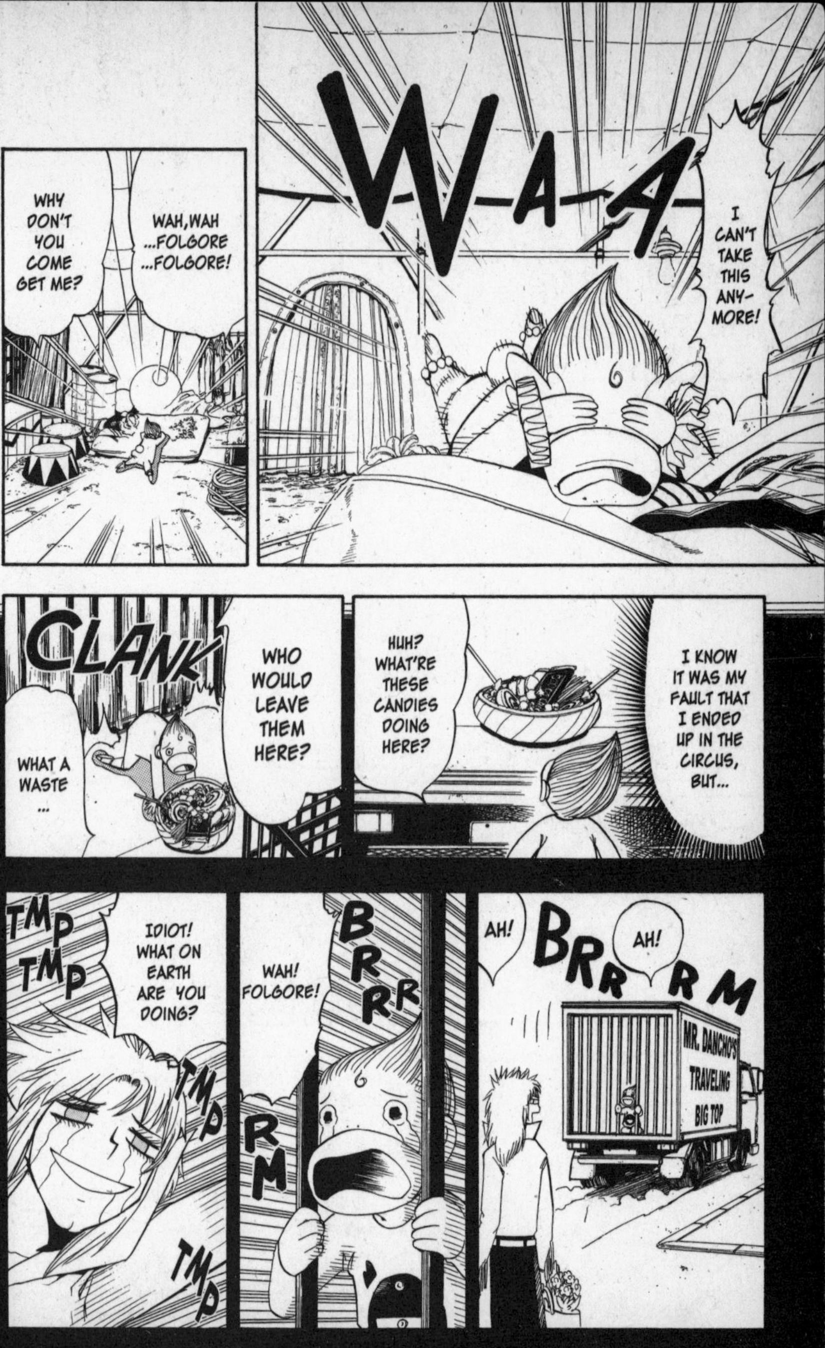
WAA
I CAN'T TAKE THIS ANYMORE!
WAH,WAH ...FOLGORE ...FOLGORE!
WHY DON'T YOU COME GET ME?
I KNOW IT WAS MY FAULT THAT I ENDED UP IN THE CIRCUS, BUT...
HUH? WHAT'RE THESE CANDIES DOING HERE?
CLANK
WHO WOULD LEAVE THEM HERE?
WHAT A WASTE ...
AH!
AH!
BRRR RM
MR. DANCHO'S TRAVELING BIG TOP
BRRR
WAH! FOLGORE!
RM
IDIOT! WHAT ON EARTH ARE YOU DOING?
TMP TMP
TMP
TMP

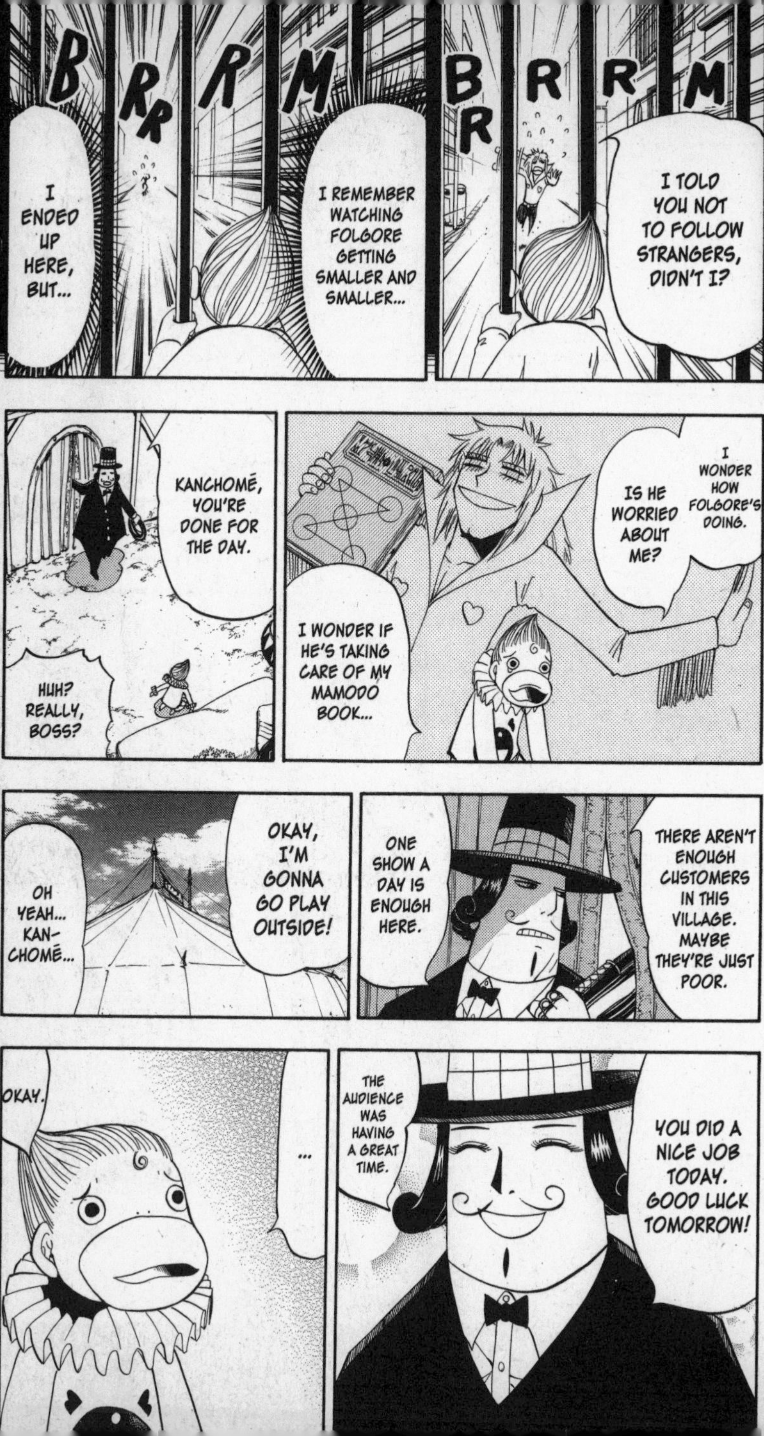
BRRRRM
I TOLD YOU NOT TO FOLLOW STRANGERS, DIDN'T I?
I REMEMBER WATCHING FOLGORE GETTING SMALLER AND SMALLER...
BRRRM
I ENDED UP HERE, BUT...
I WONDER HOW FOLGORE'S DOING.
IS HE WORRIED ABOUT ME?
I WONDER IF HE'S TAKING CARE OF MY MAMODO BOOK...
KANCHOMÉ, YOU'RE DONE FOR THE DAY.
HUH? REALLY, BOSS?
THERE AREN'T ENOUGH CUSTOMERS IN THIS VILLAGE. MAYBE THEY'RE JUST POOR.
ONE SHOW A DAY IS ENOUGH HERE.
OKAY, I'M GONNA GO PLAY OUTSIDE!
OH YEAH... KAN-CHOMÉ...
YOU DID A NICE JOB TODAY. GOOD LUCK TOMORROW!
THE AUDIENCE WAS HAVING A GREAT TIME.
...
OKAY.

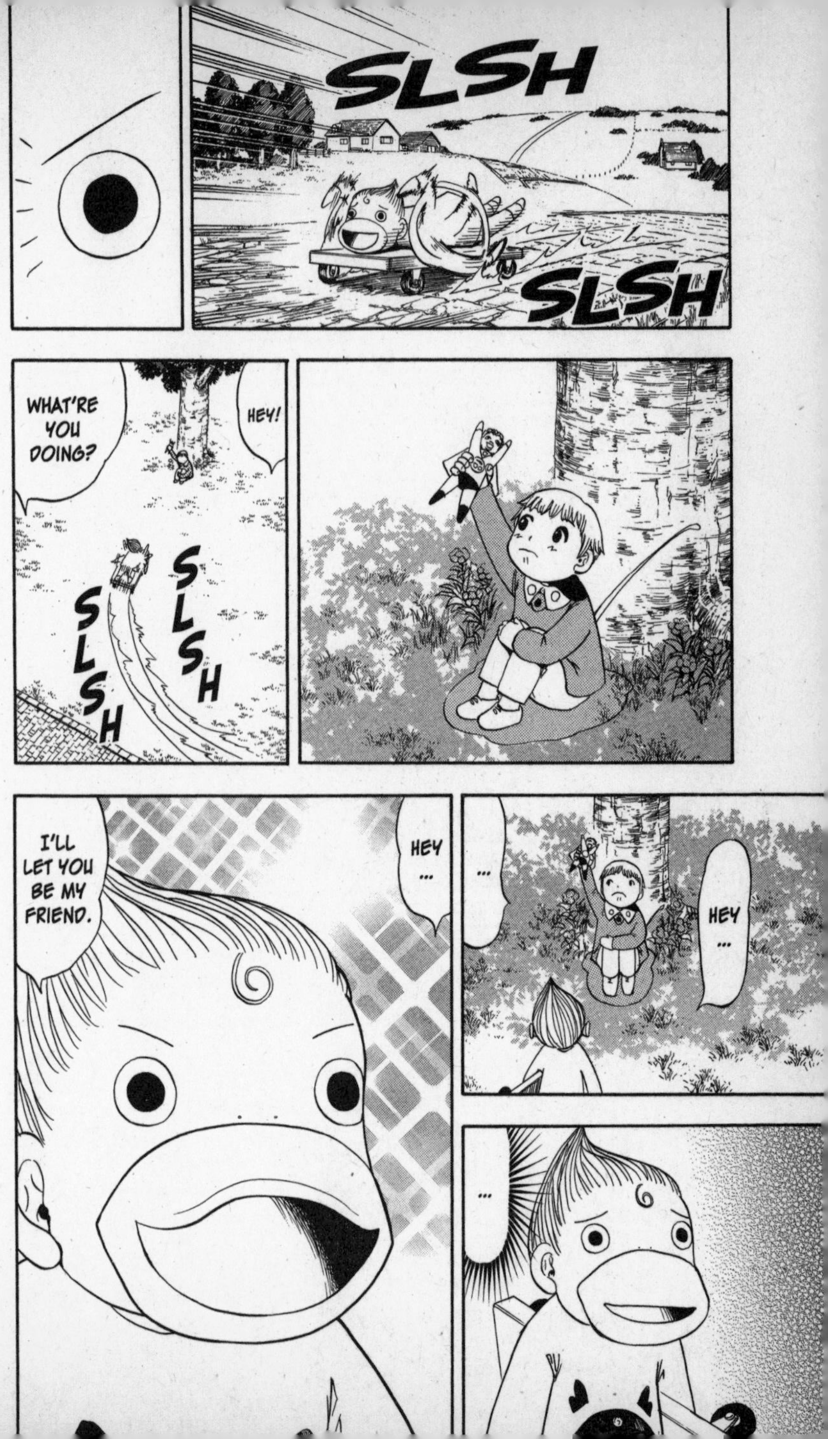
SLSH
SLSH
HEY!
WHAT'RE YOU DOING?
SLSH
SLSH
HEY ...
...
...
HEY ...
I'LL LET YOU BE MY FRIEND.

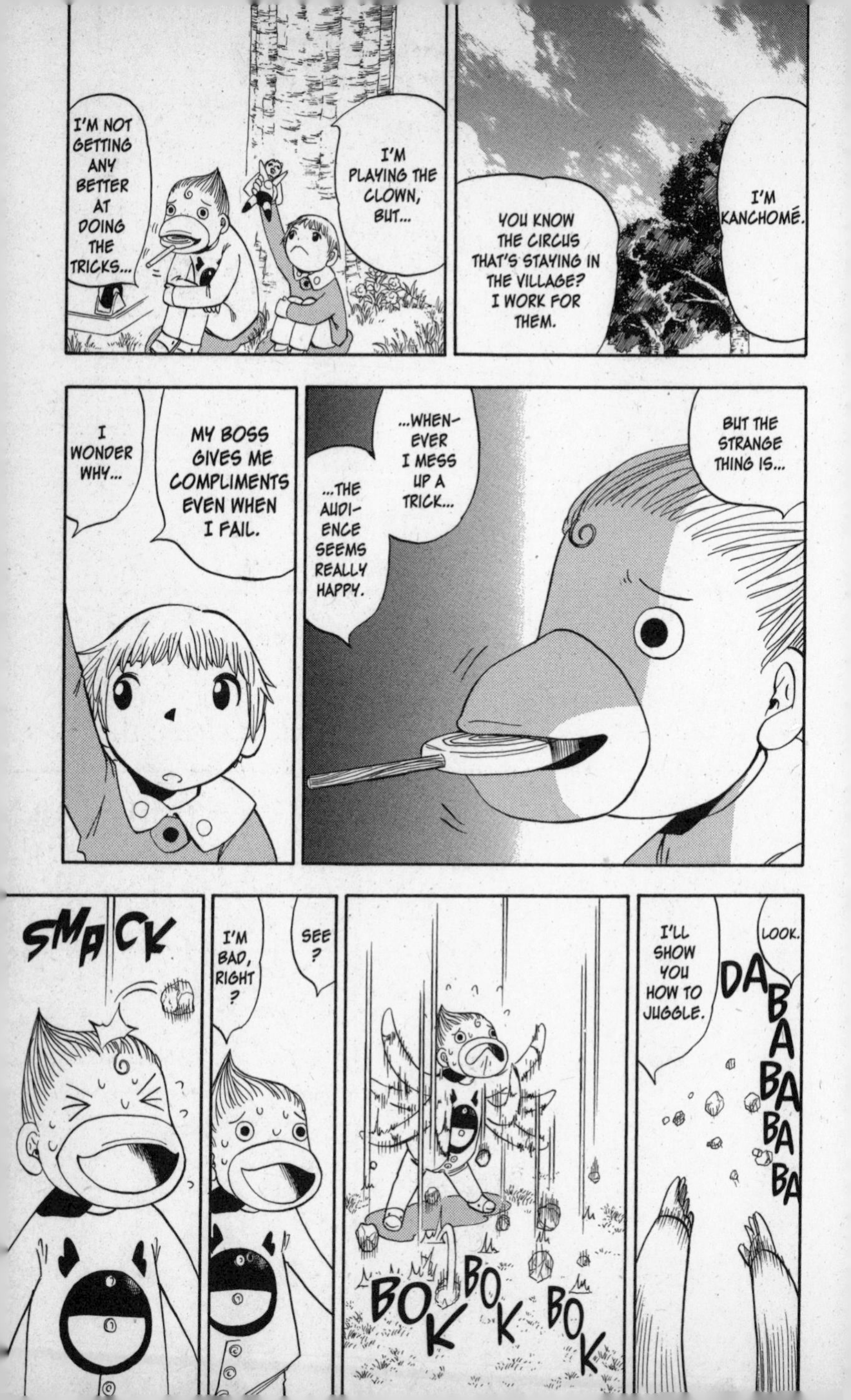
I'M KANCHOMÉ.
YOU KNOW THE CIRCUS THAT'S STAYING IN THE VILLAGE? I WORK FOR THEM.
I'M PLAYING THE CLOWN, BUT...
I'M NOT GETTING ANY BETTER AT DOING THE TRICKS...
BUT THE STRANGE THING IS...
...WHEN-EVER I MESS UP A TRICK...
...THE AUDI-ENCE SEEMS REALLY HAPPY.
MY BOSS GIVES ME COMPLIMENTS EVEN WHEN I FAIL.
I WONDER WHY...
LOOK.
I'LL SHOW YOU HOW TO JUGGLE.
DABABABABA
BOK BOK BOK
SEE?
I'M BAD, RIGHT?
SMACK

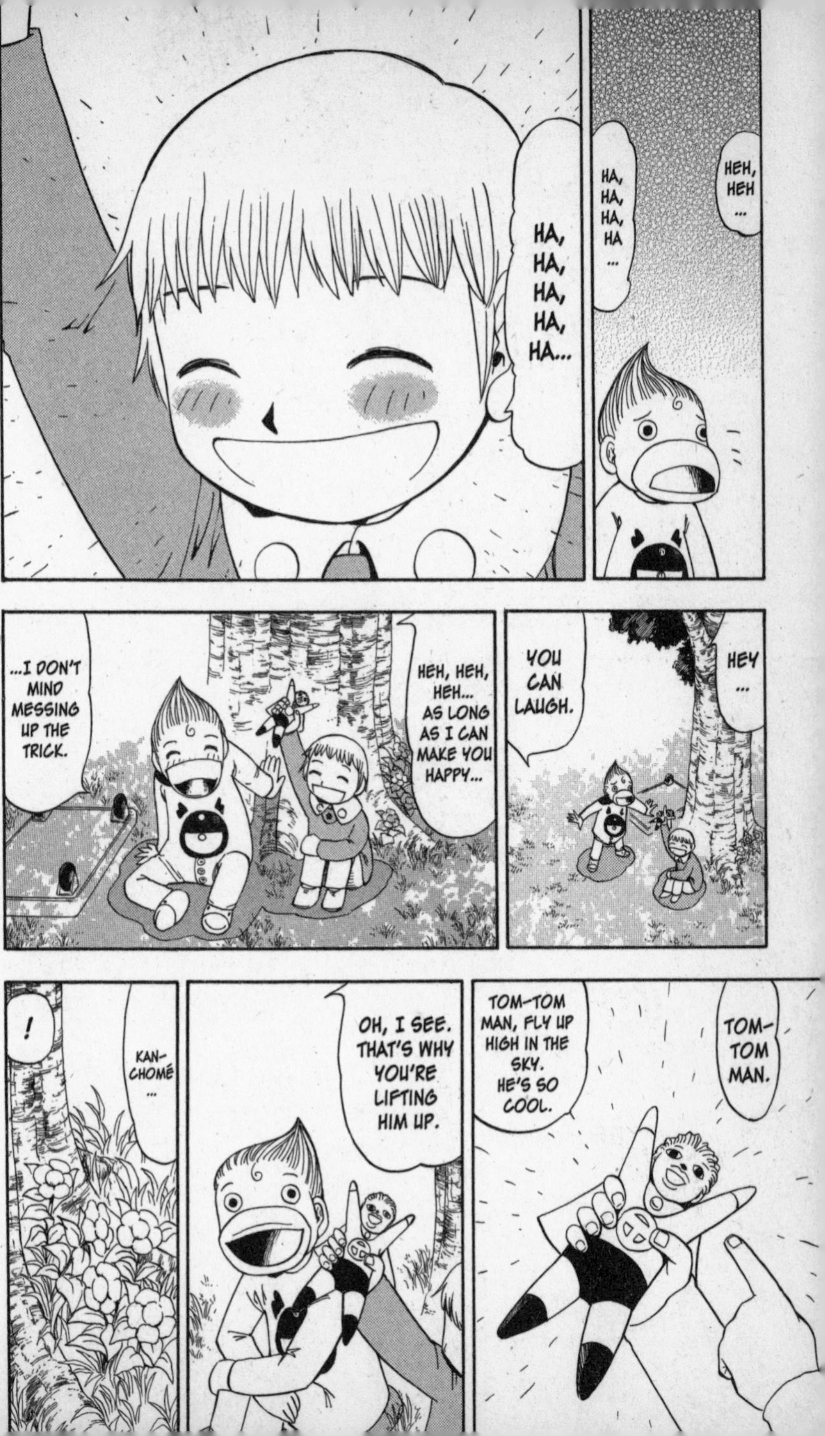
HEH, HEH ...
HA, HA, HA, HA ...
HA, HA, HA, HA, HA...
HEY ...
YOU CAN LAUGH.
HEH, HEH, HEH... AS LONG AS I CAN MAKE YOU HAPPY...
...I DON'T MIND MESSING UP THE TRICK.
TOM-TOM MAN.
TOM-TOM MAN, FLY UP HIGH IN THE SKY. HE'S SO COOL.
OH, I SEE. THAT'S WHY YOU'RE LIFTING HIM UP.
KAN-CHOMÉ ...
!

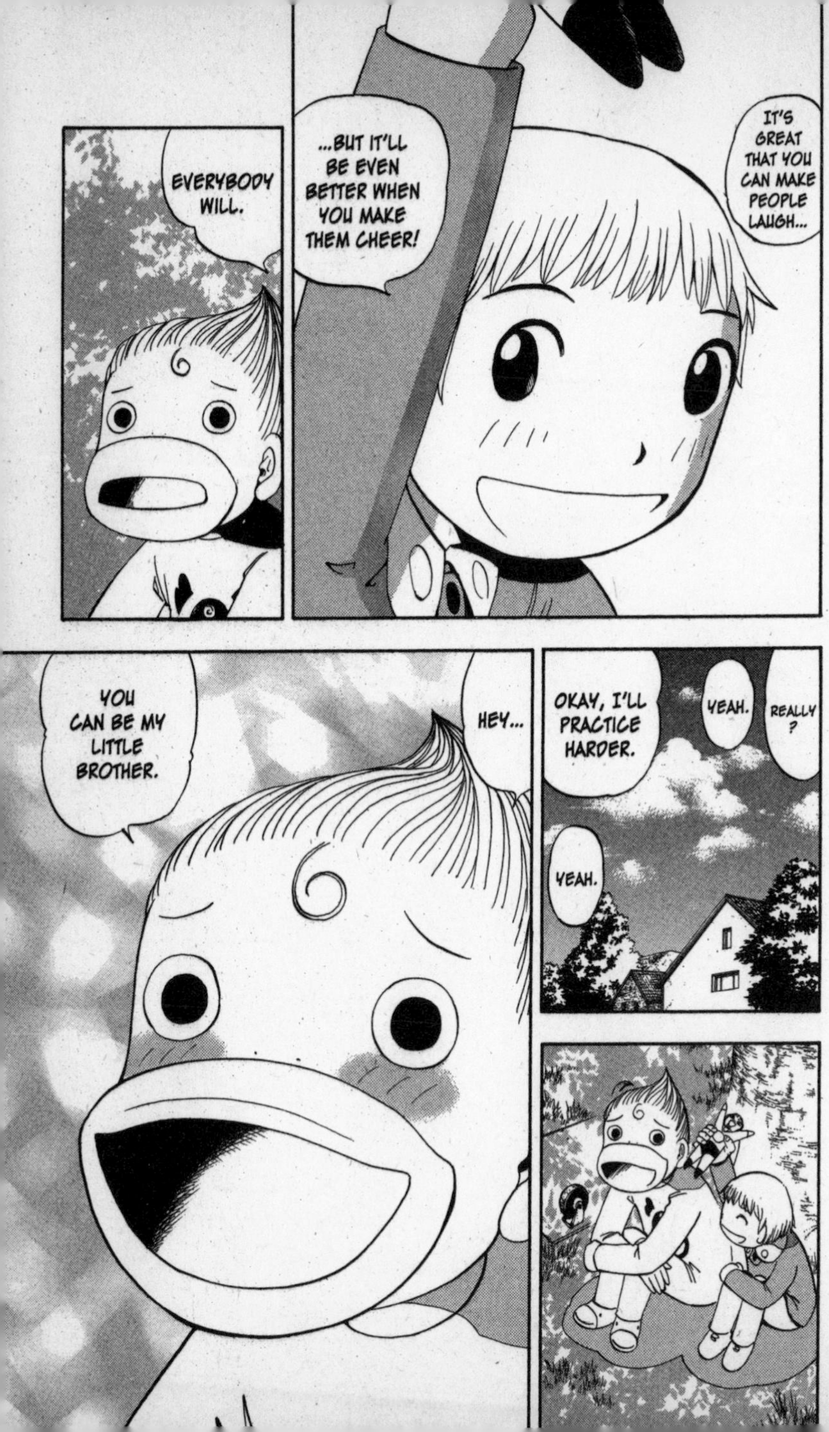
IT'S GREAT THAT YOU CAN MAKE PEOPLE LAUGH...
...BUT IT'LL BE EVEN BETTER WHEN YOU MAKE THEM CHEER!
EVERYBODY WILL.
REALLY?
YEAH.
OKAY, I'LL PRACTICE HARDER.
YEAH.
HEY...
YOU CAN BE MY LITTLE BROTHER.

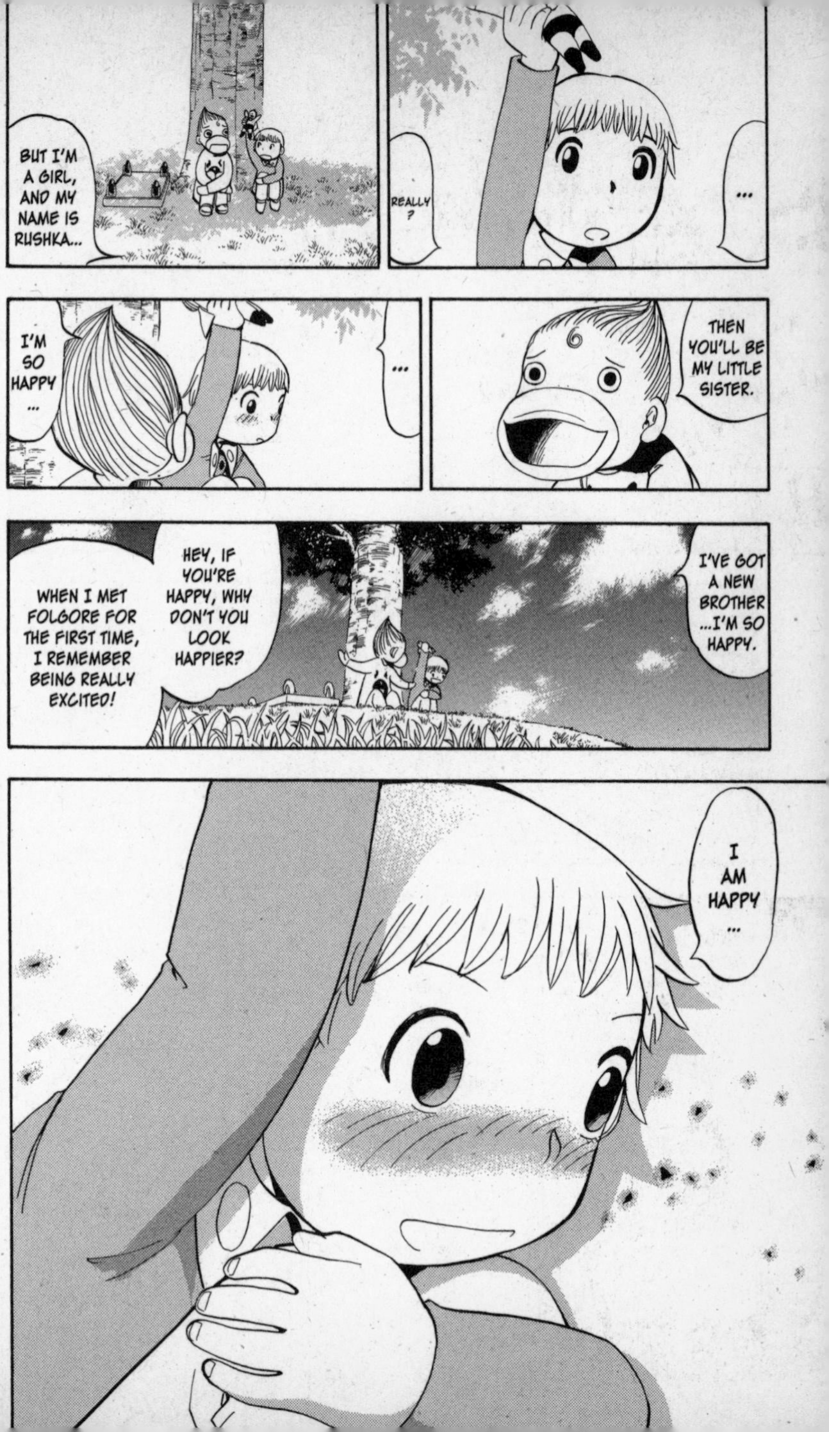
...
REALLY?
BUT I'M A GIRL, AND MY NAME IS RUSHKA...
THEN YOU'LL BE MY LITTLE SISTER.
...
I'M SO HAPPY...
I'VE GOT A NEW BROTHER ...I'M SO HAPPY.
HEY, IF YOU'RE HAPPY, WHY DON'T YOU LOOK HAPPIER?
WHEN I MET FOLGORE FOR THE FIRST TIME, I REMEMBER BEING REALLY EXCITED!
I AM HAPPY...

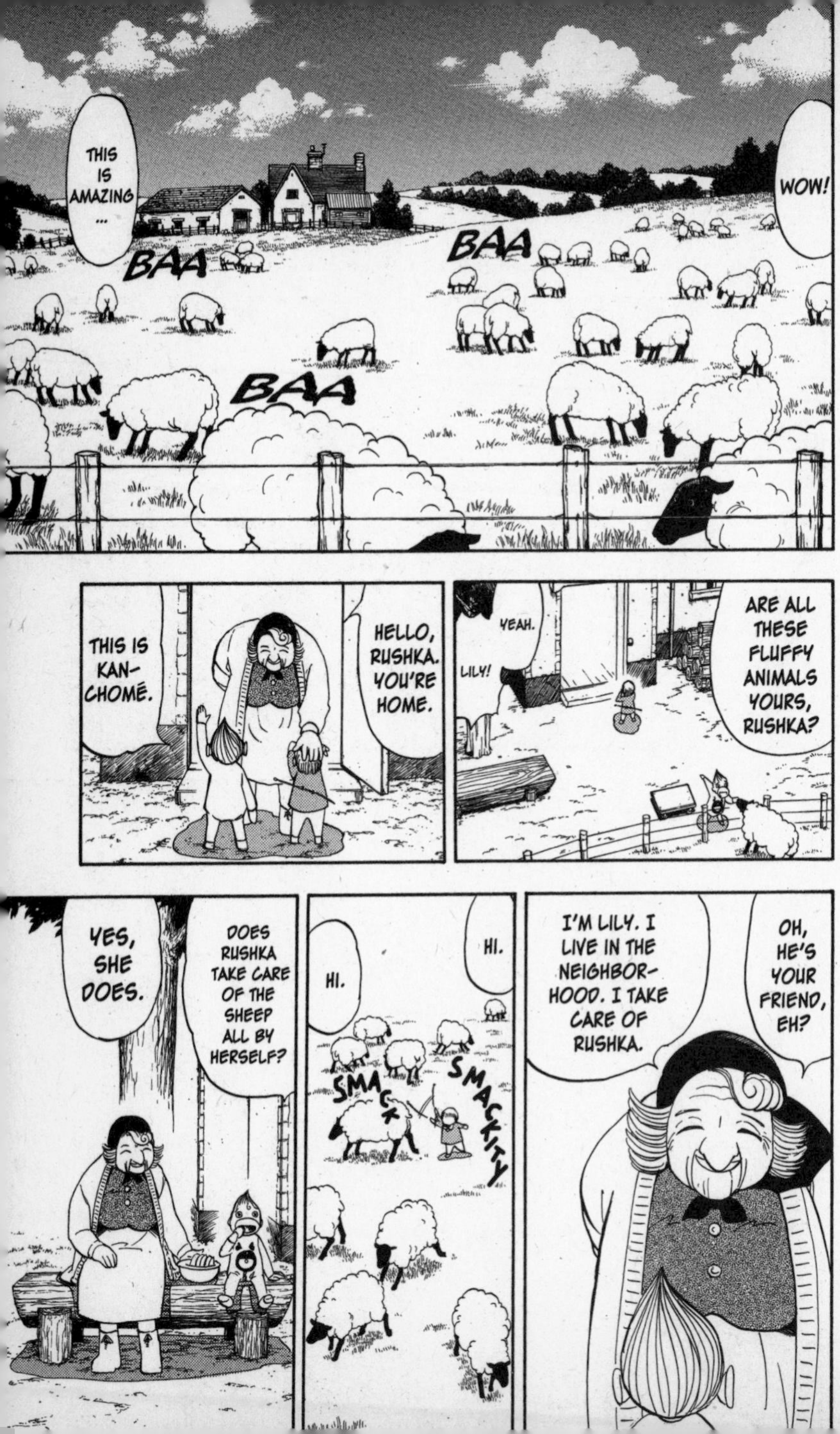
WOW!
BAA
THIS IS AMAZING ...
BAA
BAA
ARE ALL THESE FLUFFY ANIMALS YOURS, RUSHKA?
YEAH.
LILY!
HELLO, RUSHKA. YOU'RE HOME.
THIS IS KANCHOMÉ.
OH, HE'S YOUR FRIEND, EH?
I'M LILY. I LIVE IN THE NEIGHBORHOOD. I TAKE CARE OF RUSHKA.
HI.
HI.
SMACKITY
SMACK
DOES RUSHKA TAKE CARE OF THE SHEEP ALL BY HERSELF?
YES, SHE DOES.

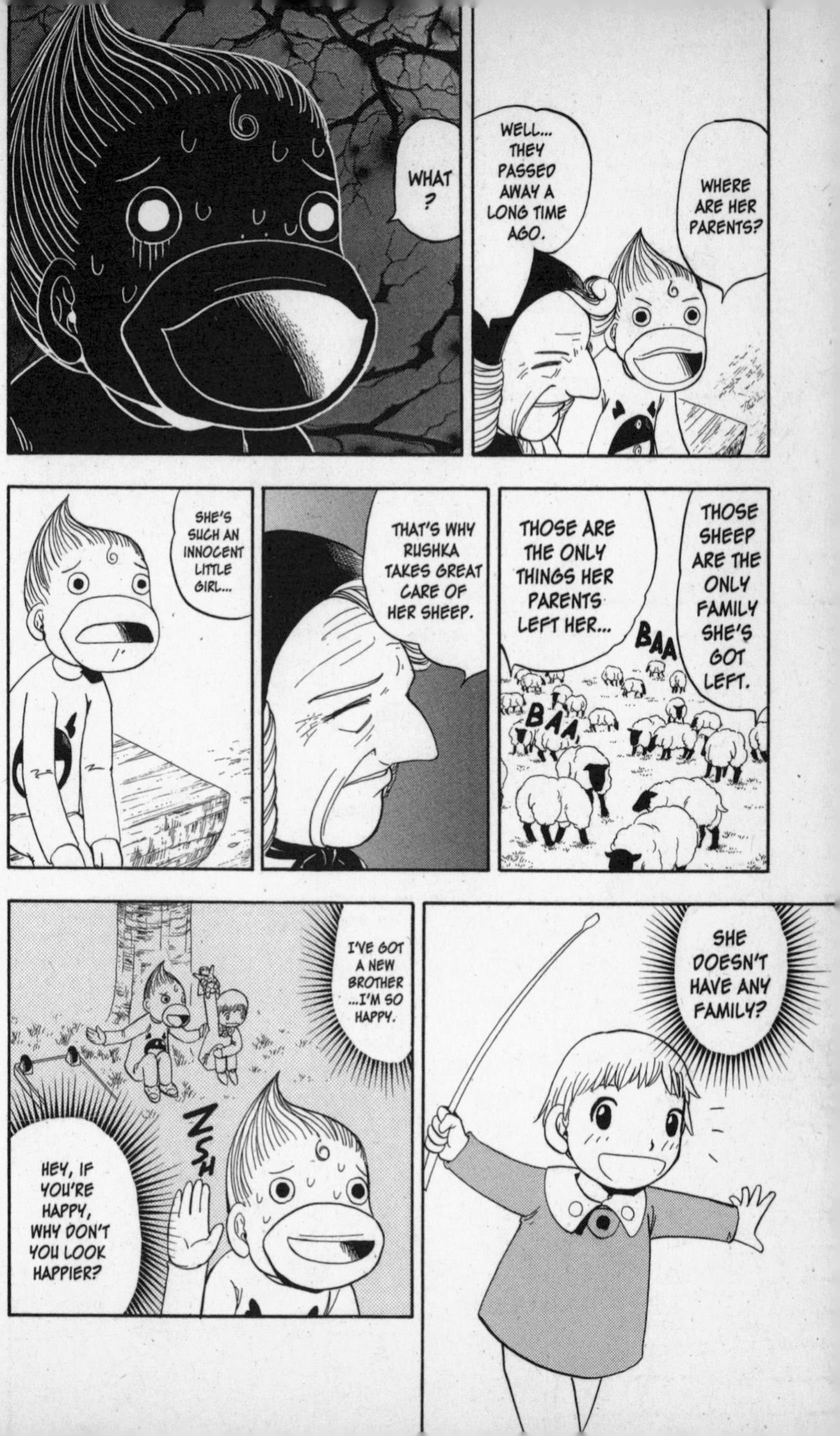
WHERE ARE HER PARENTS?
WELL... THEY PASSED AWAY A LONG TIME AGO.
WHAT?
THOSE SHEEP ARE THE ONLY FAMILY SHE'S GOT LEFT.
THOSE ARE THE ONLY THINGS HER PARENTS LEFT HER...
BAA
BAA
THAT'S WHY RUSHKA TAKES GREAT CARE OF HER SHEEP.
SHE'S SUCH AN INNOCENT LITTLE GIRL...
SHE DOESN'T HAVE ANY FAMILY?
I'VE GOT A NEW BROTHER ...I'M SO HAPPY.
ZSH
HEY, IF YOU'RE HAPPY, WHY DON'T YOU LOOK HAPPIER?

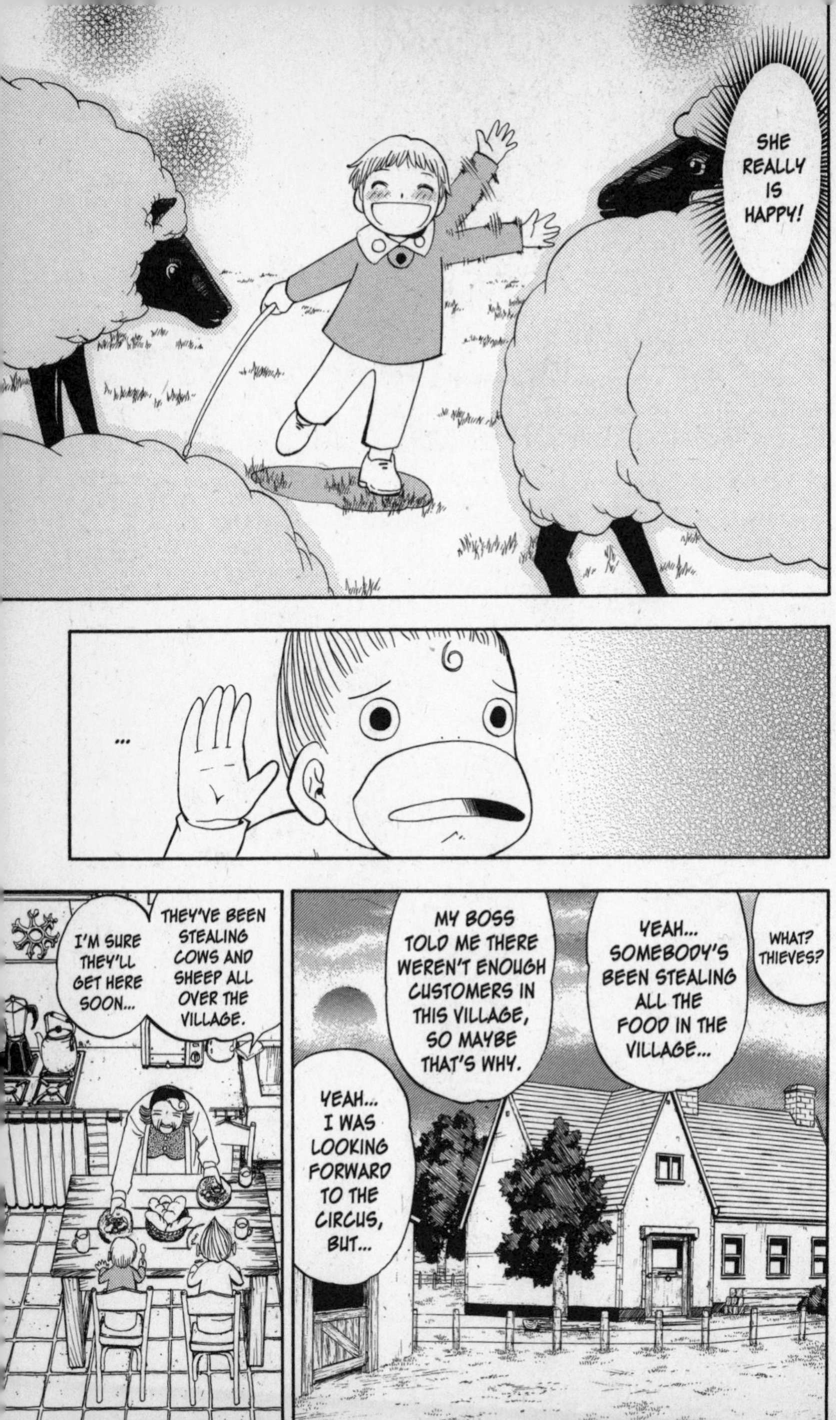
SHE REALLY IS HAPPY!
...
WHAT? THIEVES?
YEAH... SOMEBODY'S BEEN STEALING ALL THE FOOD IN THE VILLAGE...
MY BOSS TOLD ME THERE WEREN'T ENOUGH CUSTOMERS IN THIS VILLAGE, SO MAYBE THAT'S WHY.
YEAH... I WAS LOOKING FORWARD TO THE CIRCUS, BUT...
THEY'VE BEEN STEALING COWS AND SHEEP ALL OVER THE VILLAGE.
I'M SURE THEY'LL GET HERE SOON...

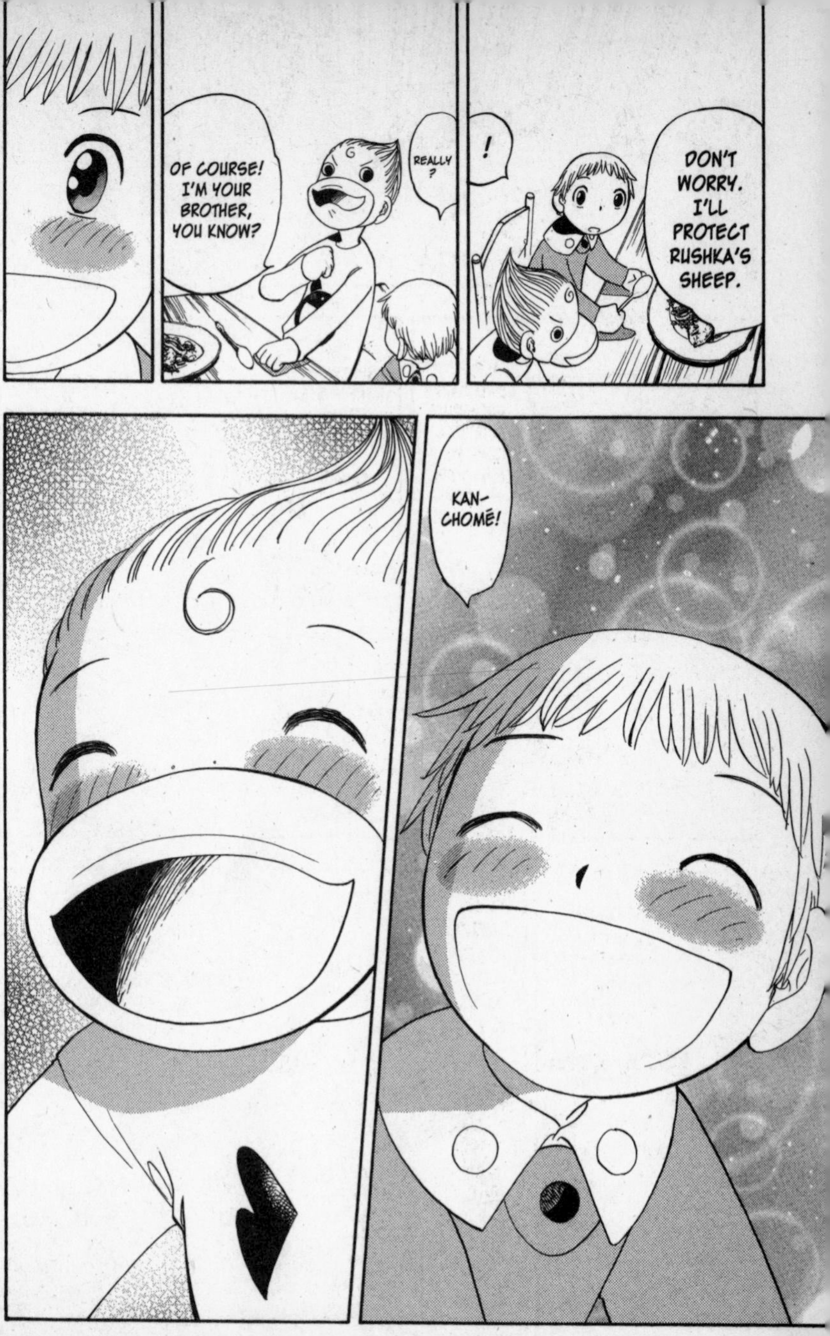
DON'T WORRY. I'LL PROTECT RUSHKA'S SHEEP.
!
REALLY ?
OF COURSE! I'M YOUR BROTHER, YOU KNOW?
KAN-CHOMÉ!

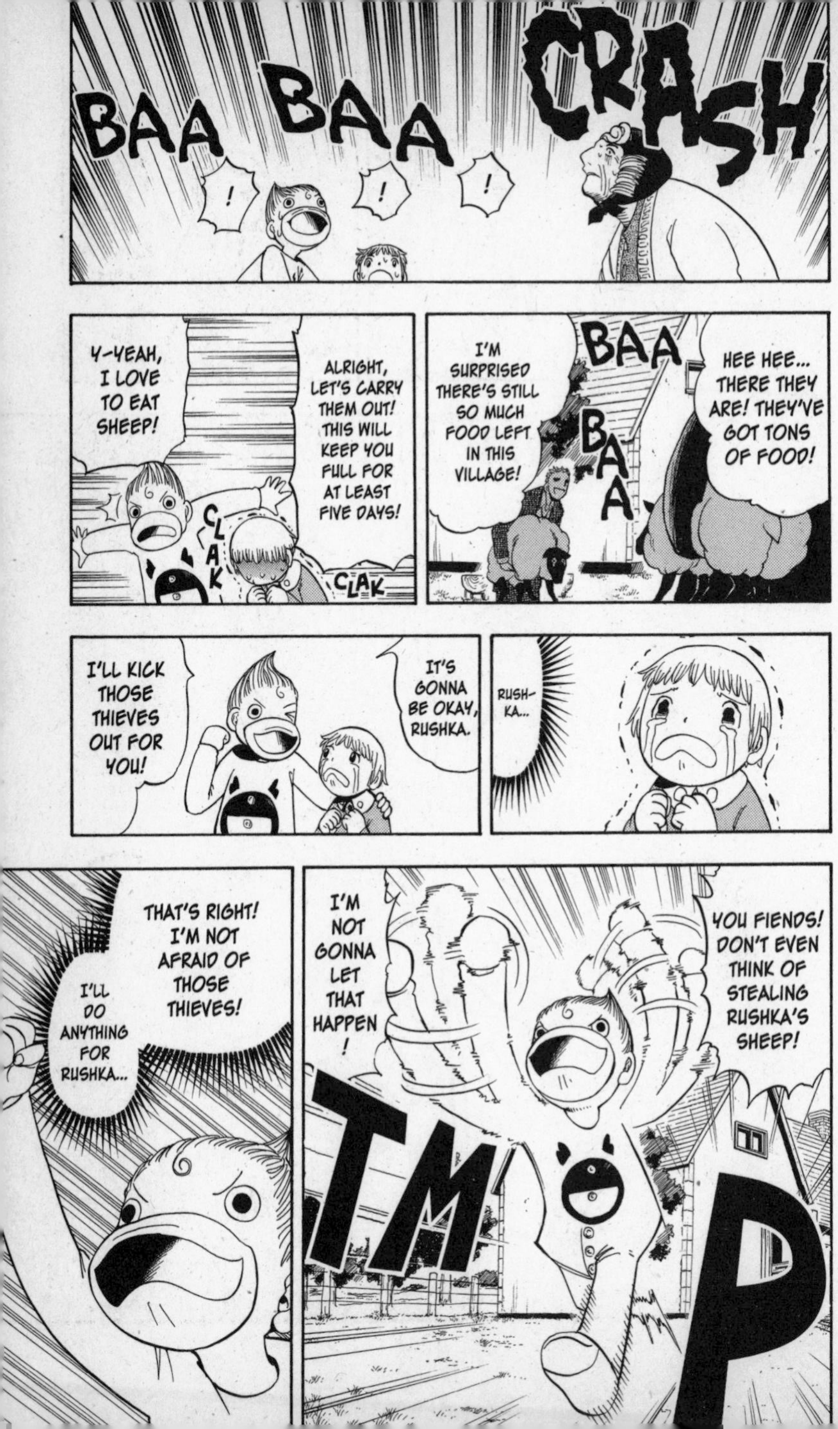
CRASH
BAA
BAA
!
!
!
HEE HEE... THERE THEY ARE! THEY'VE GOT TONS OF FOOD!
BAA
BAA
I'M SURPRISED THERE'S STILL SO MUCH FOOD LEFT IN THIS VILLAGE!
ALRIGHT, LET'S CARRY THEM OUT! THIS WILL KEEP YOU FULL FOR AT LEAST FIVE DAYS!
Y-YEAH, I LOVE TO EAT SHEEP!
CLAK
CLAK
RUSH-KA...
IT'S GONNA BE OKAY, RUSHKA.
I'LL KICK THOSE THIEVES OUT FOR YOU!
YOU FIENDS! DON'T EVEN THINK OF STEALING RUSHKA'S SHEEP!
I'M NOT GONNA LET THAT HAPPEN!
TMP
THAT'S RIGHT! I'M NOT AFRAID OF THOSE THIEVES!
I'LL DO ANYTHING FOR RUSHKA...

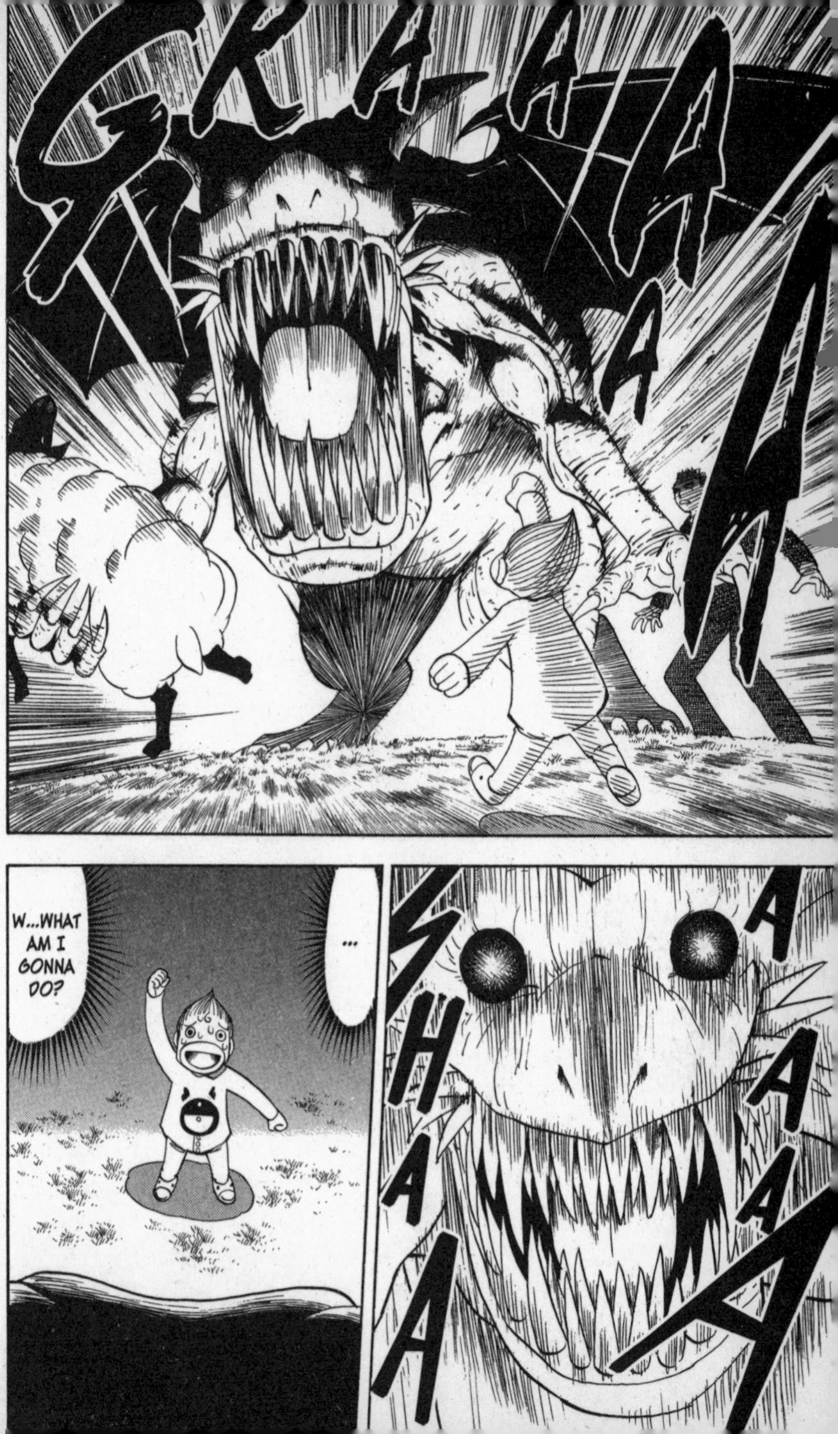
GRAAAAAA
SHAAAAAAAAA
...
W...WHAT AM I GONNA DO?

# LEVEL 86: The Brother's Battle

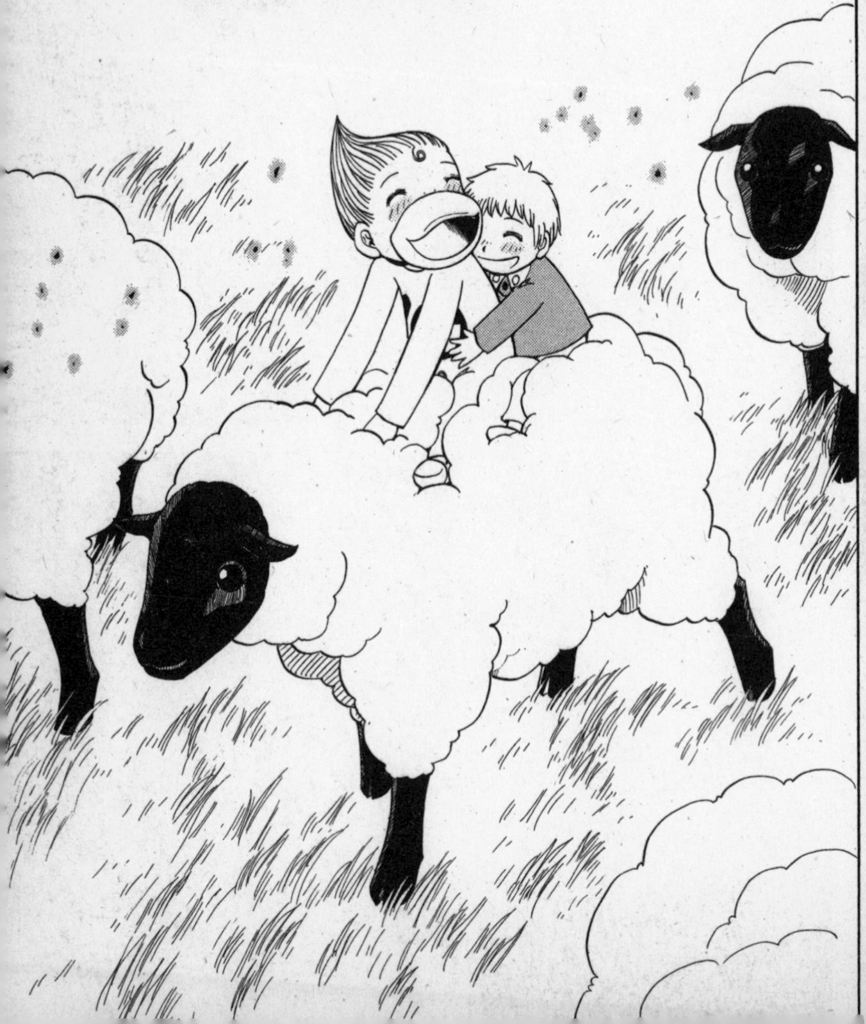

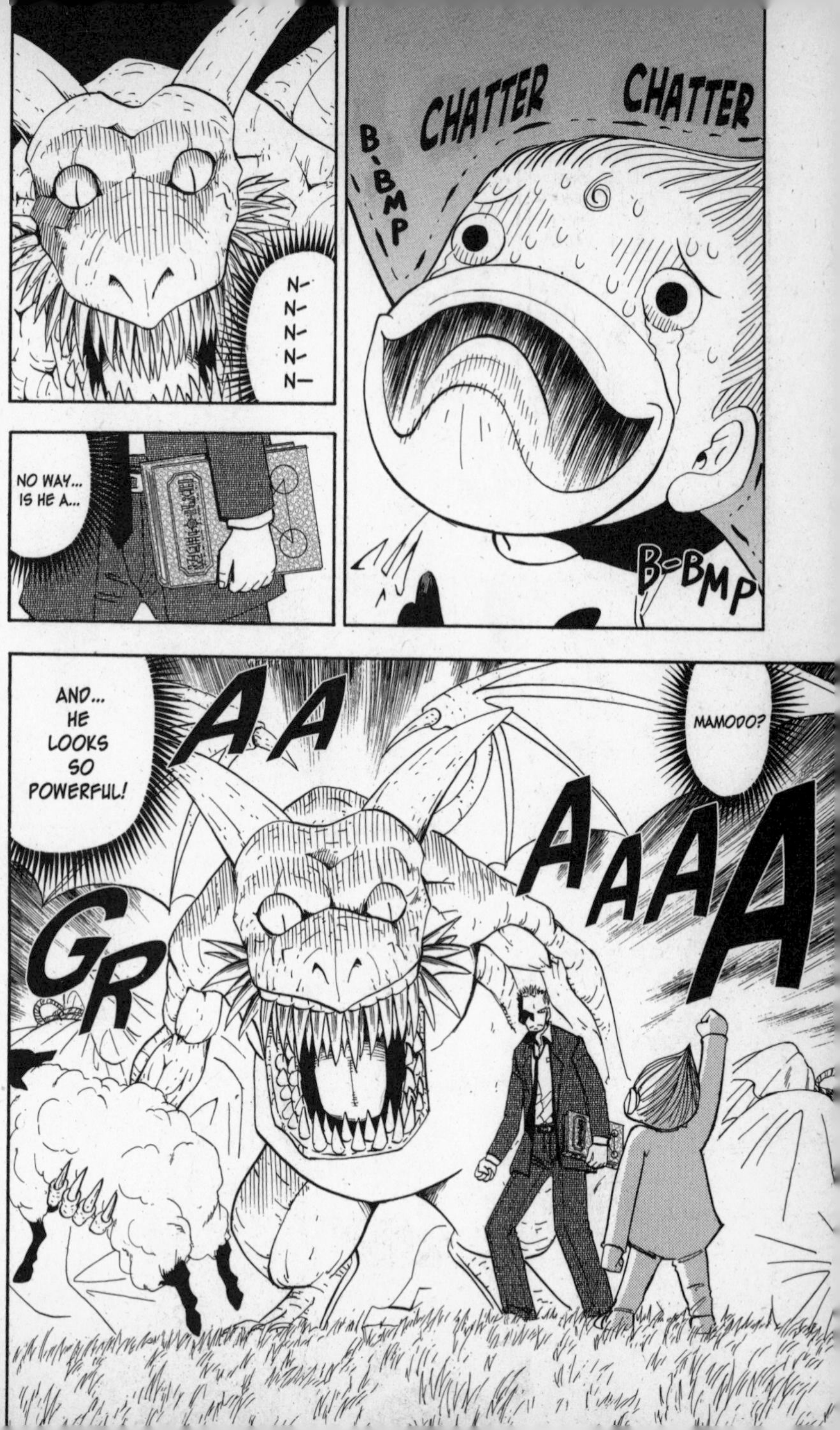
CHATTER CHATTER
B-BMP
B-BMP
N-N-N-N-N-
NO WAY... IS HE A...
MAMODO?
AND... HE LOOKS SO POWERFUL!
GR
AA
AAAAA

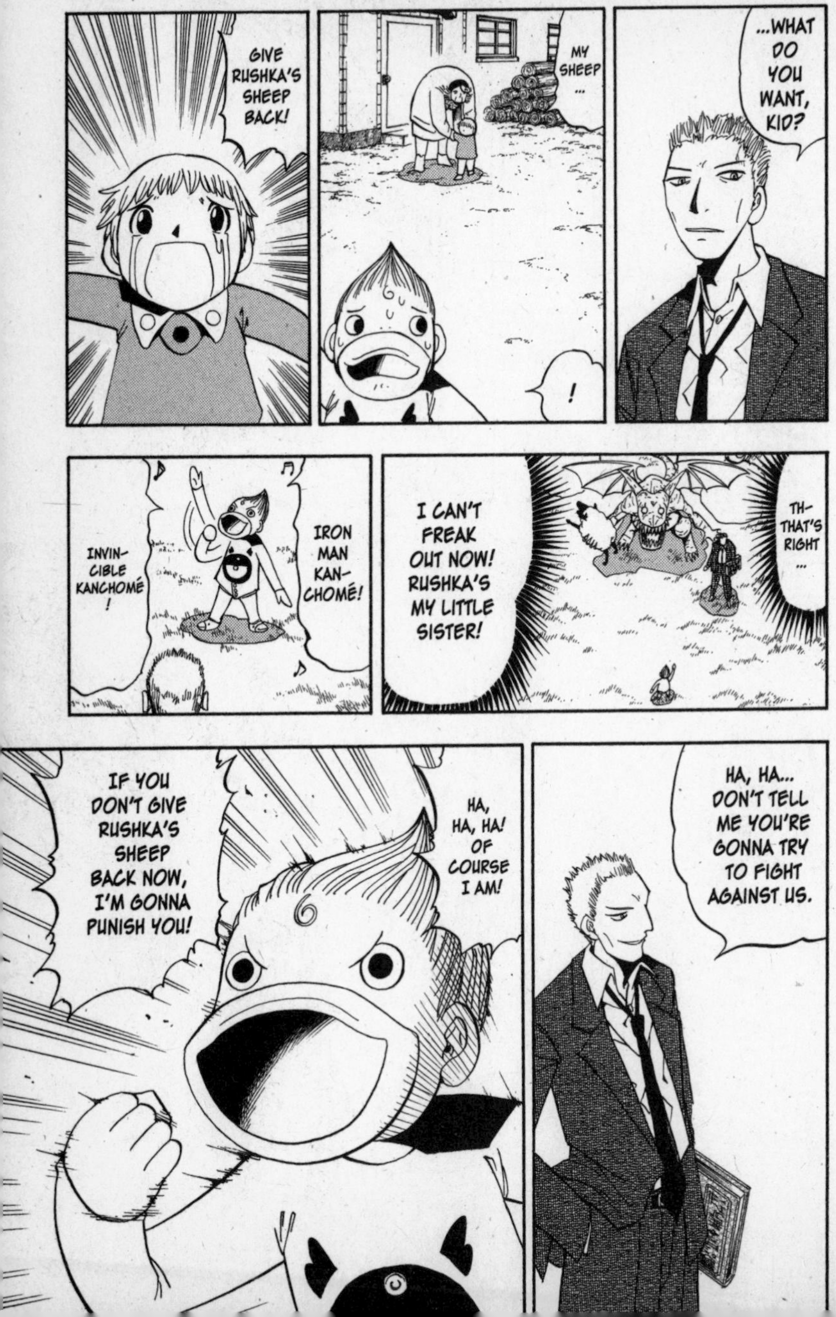
...WHAT DO YOU WANT, KID?
MY SHEEP ...
!
GIVE RUSHKA'S SHEEP BACK!
TH-THAT'S RIGHT ...
I CAN'T FREAK OUT NOW! RUSHKA'S MY LITTLE SISTER!
IRON MAN KAN-CHOMÉ!
INVIN-CIBLE KANCHOMÉ!
HA, HA... DON'T TELL ME YOU'RE GONNA TRY TO FIGHT AGAINST US.
HA, HA, HA! OF COURSE I AM!
IF YOU DON'T GIVE RUSHKA'S SHEEP BACK NOW, I'M GONNA PUNISH YOU!

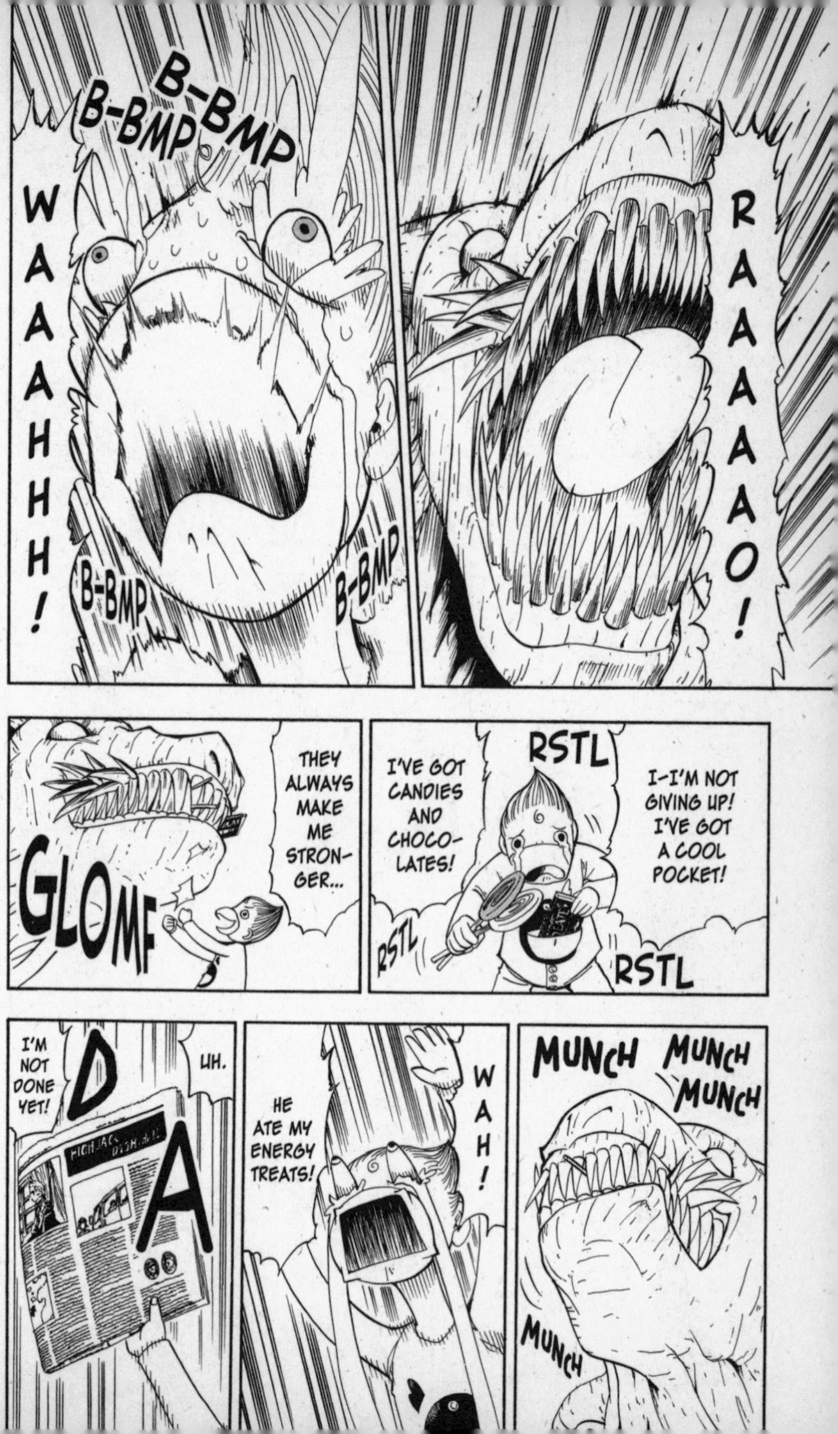
RAAAAAO!
B-BMP
B-BMP
WAAAHHH!
B-BMP
B-BMP
RSTL
I-I'M NOT GIVING UP! I'VE GOT A COOL POCKET!
I'VE GOT CANDIES AND CHOCO-LATES!
RSTL
RSTL
THEY ALWAYS MAKE ME STRON-GER...
GLOMF
MUNCH
MUNCH
MUNCH
MUNCH
WAH!
HE ATE MY ENERGY TREATS!
UH.
I'M NOT DONE YET!
DA

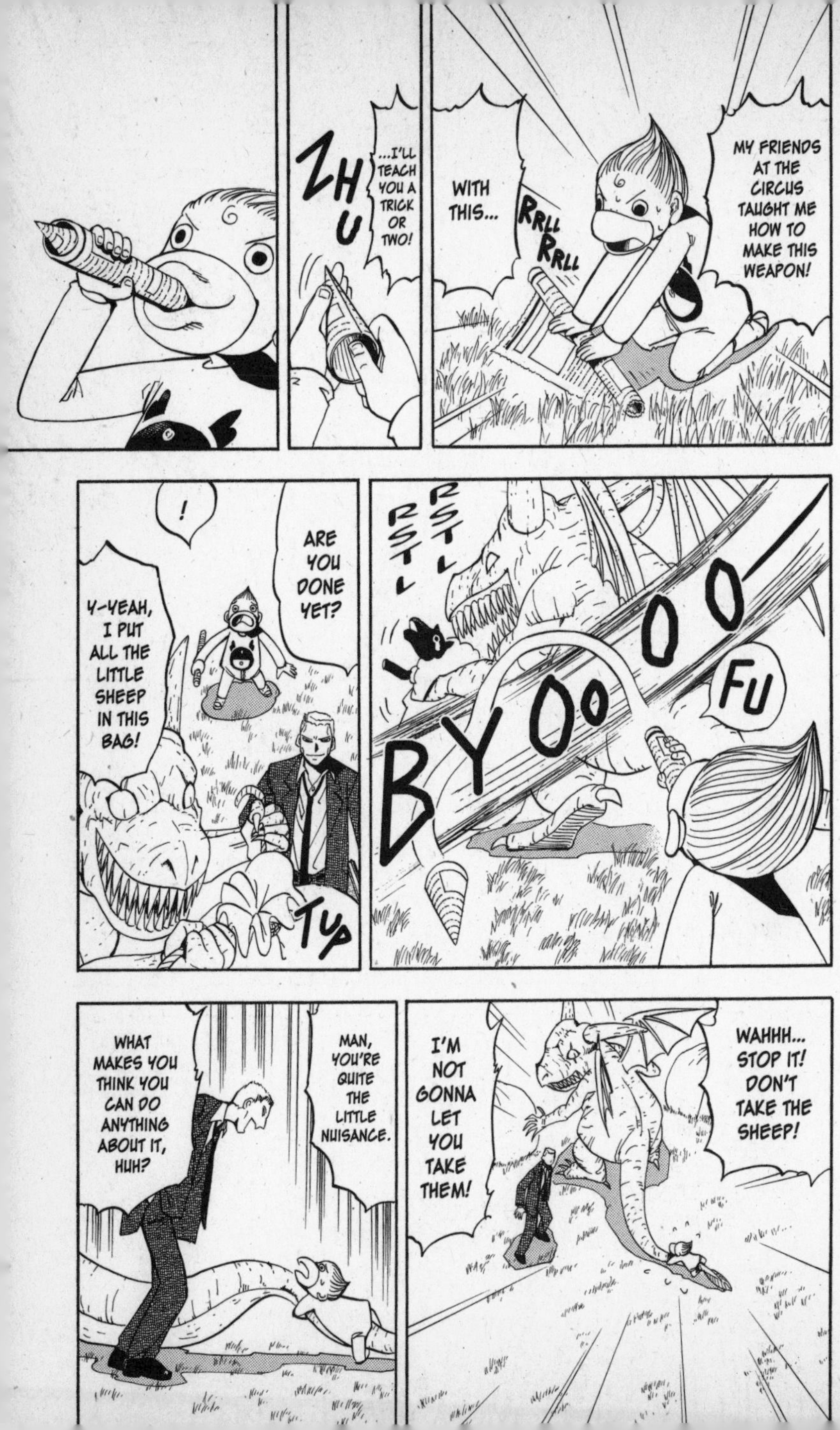
MY FRIENDS AT THE CIRCUS TAUGHT ME HOW TO MAKE THIS WEAPON!
RRLL RRLL
WITH THIS...
...I'LL TEACH YOU A TRICK OR TWO!
ZHU
RSTL RSTL
BYOOOO
FU
ARE YOU DONE YET?
!
Y-YEAH, I PUT ALL THE LITTLE SHEEP IN THIS BAG!
TUP
WAHHH... STOP IT! DON'T TAKE THE SHEEP!
I'M NOT GONNA LET YOU TAKE THEM!
MAN, YOU'RE QUITE THE LITTLE NUISANCE.
WHAT MAKES YOU THINK YOU CAN DO ANYTHING ABOUT IT, HUH?

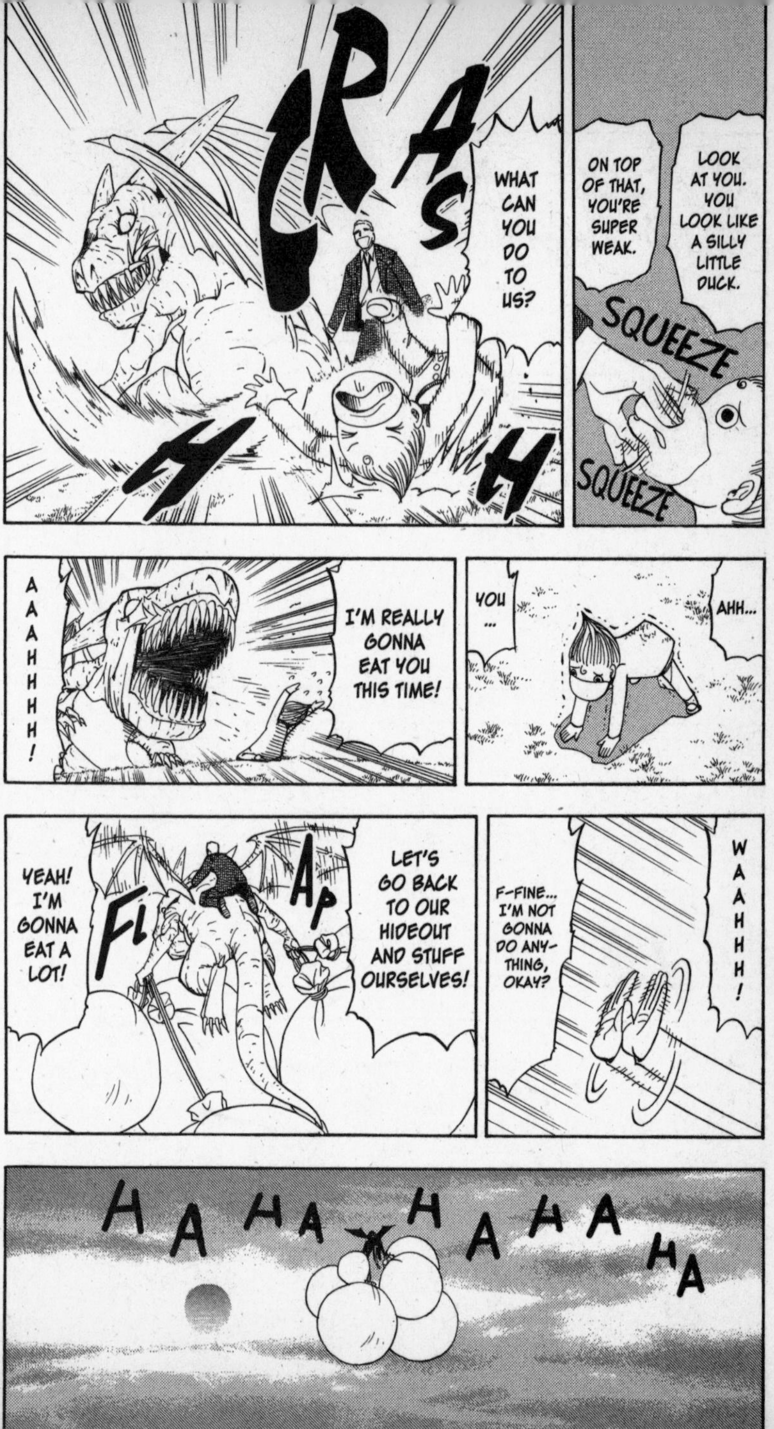
LOOK AT YOU. YOU LOOK LIKE A SILLY LITTLE DUCK.
ON TOP OF THAT, YOU'RE SUPER WEAK.
SQUEEZE
SQUEEZE
CRASH
WHAT CAN YOU DO TO US?
AHH...
YOU ...
I'M REALLY GONNA EAT YOU THIS TIME!
AAAAHHHHH!
WAAHHHH!
F-FINE... I'M NOT GONNA DO ANYTHING, OKAY?
LET'S GO BACK TO OUR HIDEOUT AND STUFF OURSELVES!
FLAP
YEAH! I'M GONNA EAT A LOT!
HA HA HA HA HA HA HA HA

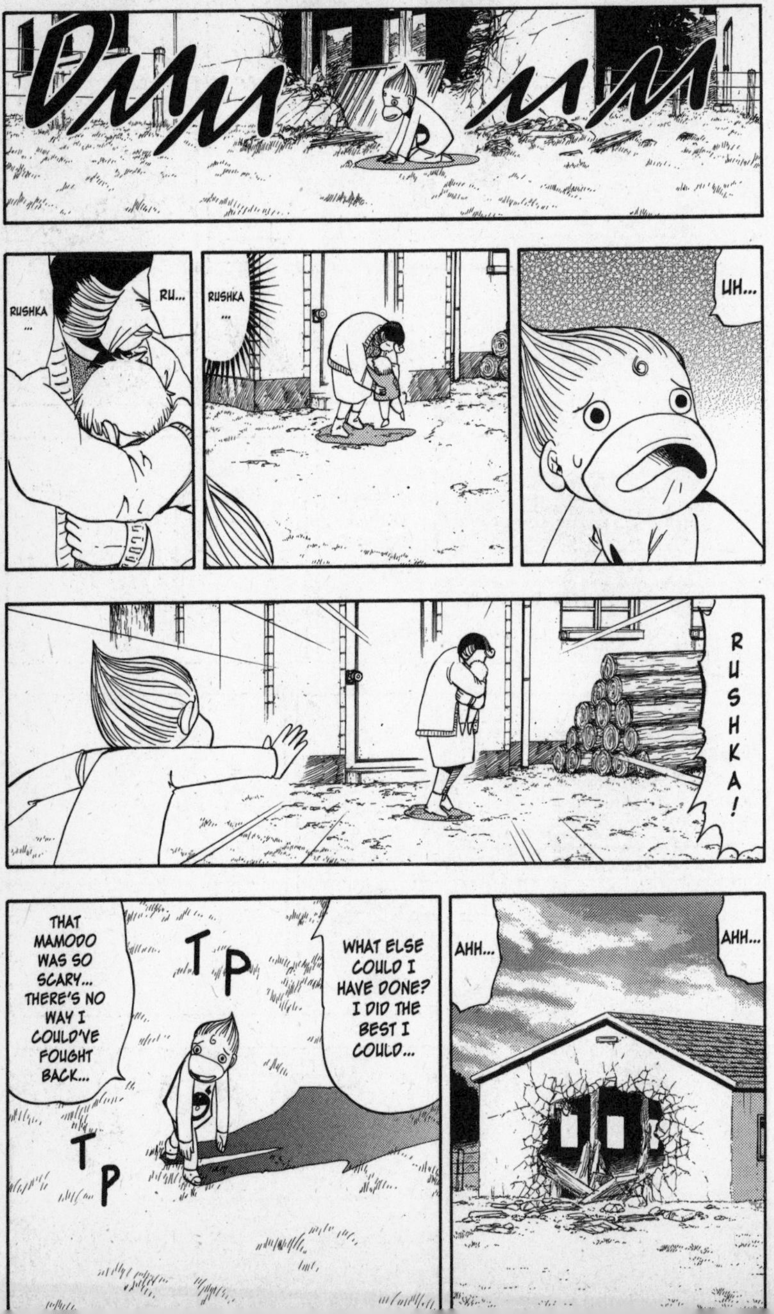
DMMMMM
UH...
RUSHKA ...
RU...
RUSHKA ...
RUSHKA!
AHH...
AHH...
WHAT ELSE COULD I HAVE DONE? I DID THE BEST I COULD...
TP
THAT MAMODO WAS SO SCARY... THERE'S NO WAY I COULD'VE FOUGHT BACK...
TP

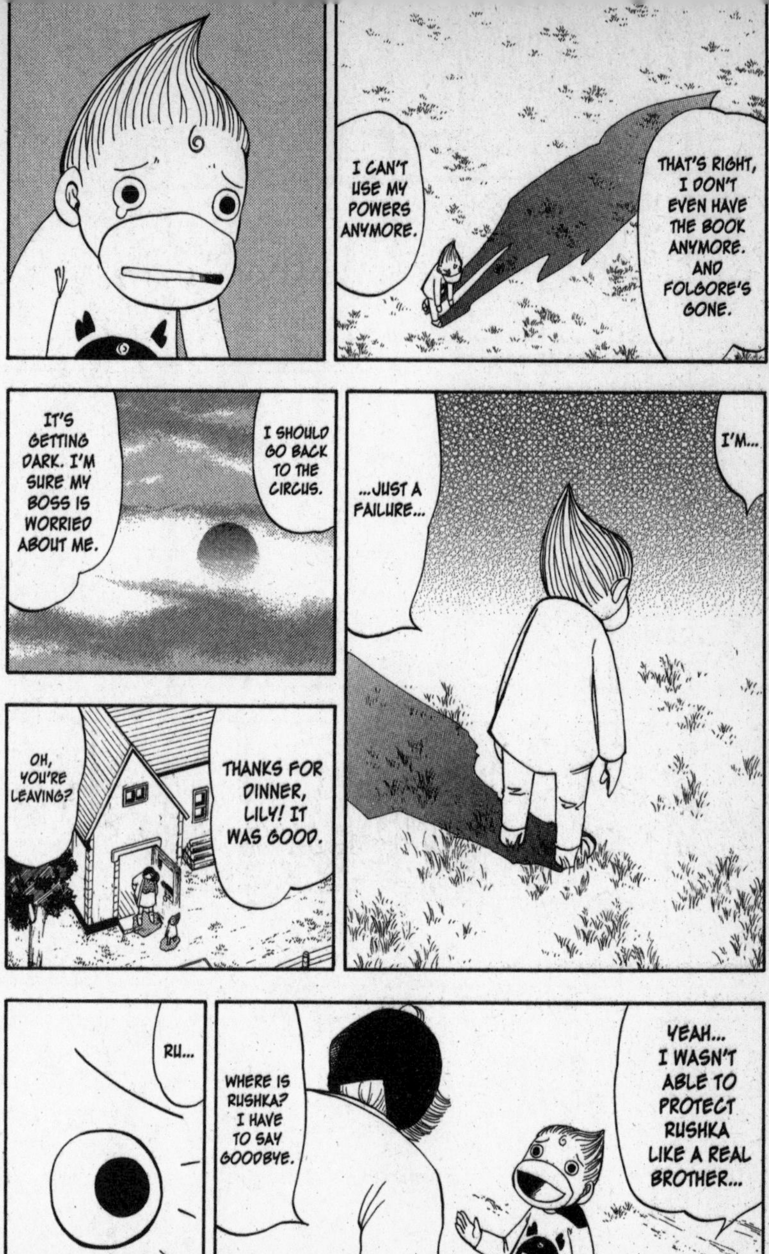
THAT'S RIGHT, I DON'T EVEN HAVE THE BOOK ANYMORE. AND FOLGORE'S GONE.
I CAN'T USE MY POWERS ANYMORE.
I'M...
...JUST A FAILURE...
I SHOULD GO BACK TO THE CIRCUS.
IT'S GETTING DARK. I'M SURE MY BOSS IS WORRIED ABOUT ME.
THANKS FOR DINNER, LILY! IT WAS GOOD.
OH, YOU'RE LEAVING?
YEAH... I WASN'T ABLE TO PROTECT RUSHKA LIKE A REAL BROTHER...
WHERE IS RUSHKA? I HAVE TO SAY GOODBYE.
RU...

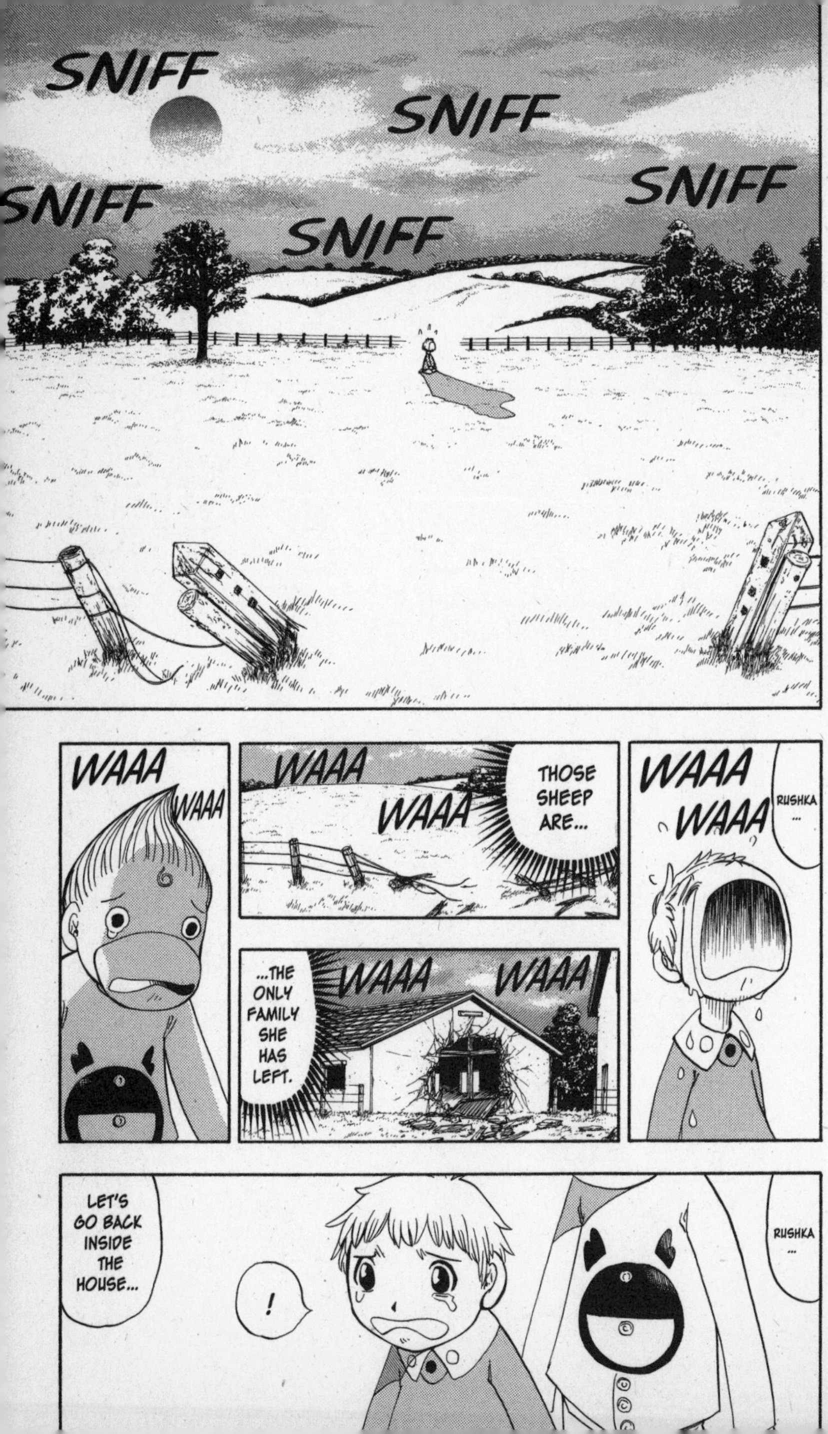
SNIFF
SNIFF
SNIFF
SNIFF
SNIFF
WAAA
WAAA
RUSHKA...
THOSE SHEEP ARE...
WAAA
WAAA
...THE ONLY FAMILY SHE HAS LEFT.
WAAA
WAAA
WAAA
WAAA
RUSHKA...
!
LET'S GO BACK INSIDE THE HOUSE...

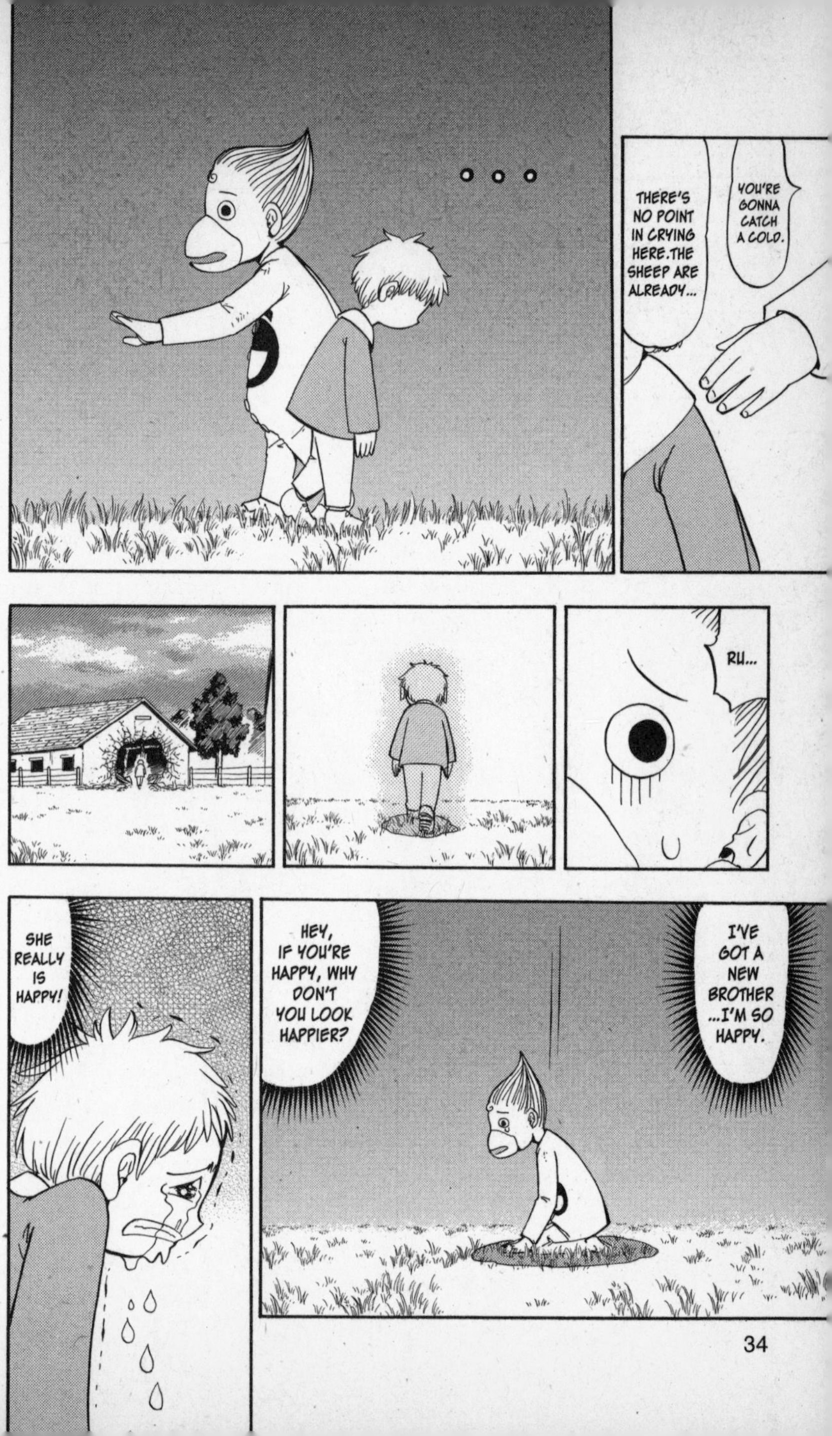
YOU'RE GONNA CATCH A COLD.
THERE'S NO POINT IN CRYING HERE. THE SHEEP ARE ALREADY...
...
RU...
I'VE GOT A NEW BROTHER ...I'M SO HAPPY.
HEY, IF YOU'RE HAPPY, WHY DON'T YOU LOOK HAPPIER?
SHE REALLY IS HAPPY!

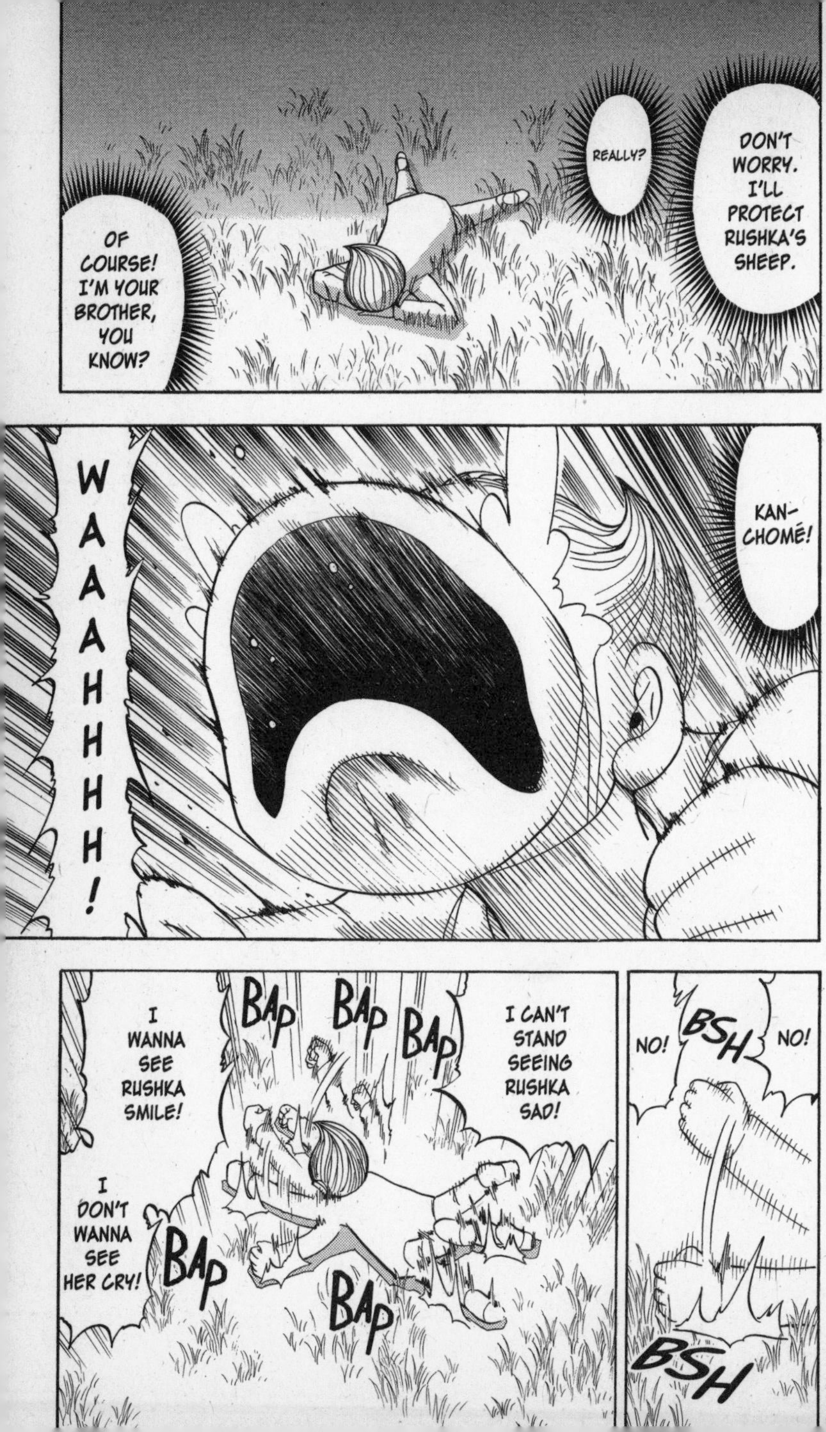
DON'T WORRY. I'LL PROTECT RUSHKA'S SHEEP.
REALLY?
OF COURSE! I'M YOUR BROTHER, YOU KNOW?
KAN-CHOMÉ!
WAAAHHHH!
NO!
BSH
NO!
BSH
I CAN'T STAND SEEING RUSHKA SAD!
BAP
BAP
BAP
I WANNA SEE RUSHKA SMILE!
I DON'T WANNA SEE HER CRY!
BAP
BAP

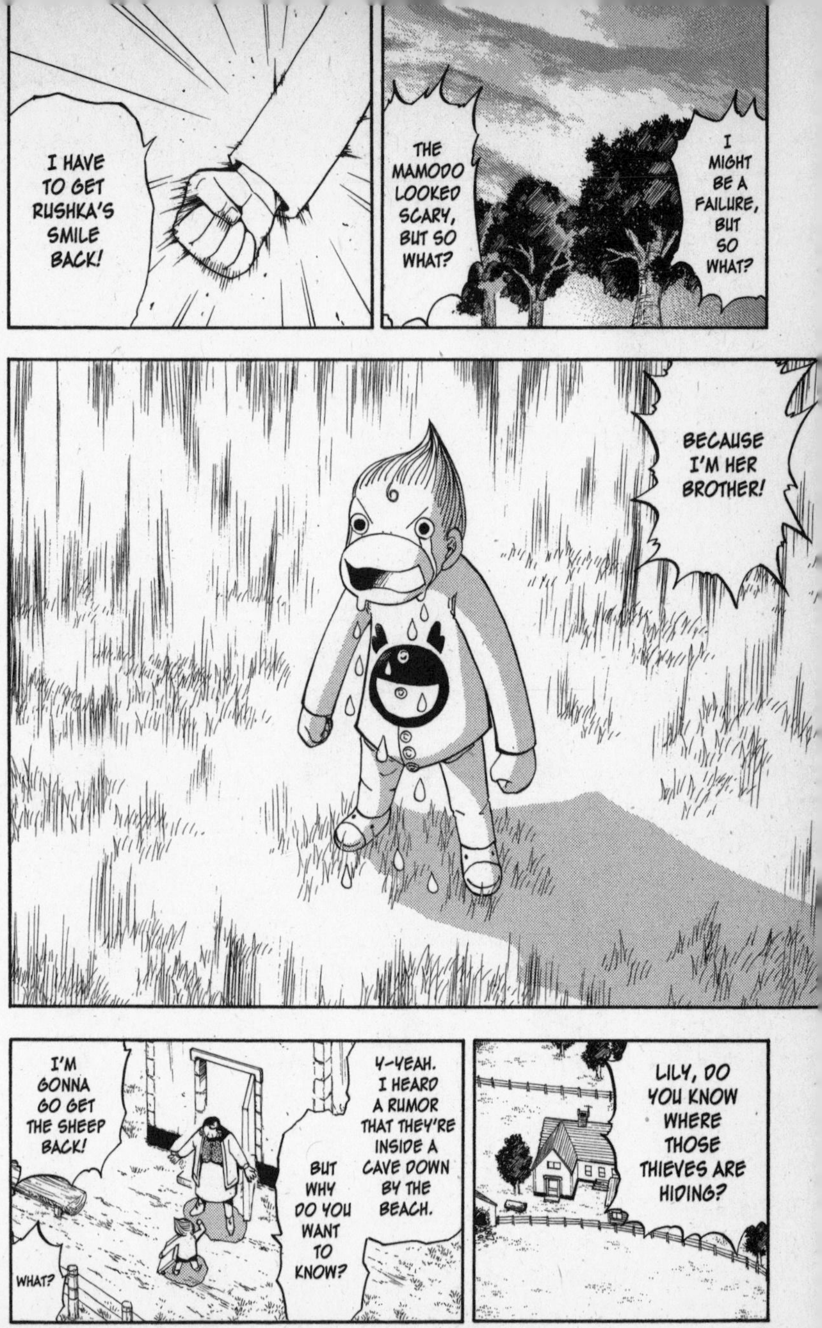
I MIGHT BE A FAILURE, BUT SO WHAT?
THE MAMODO LOOKED SCARY, BUT SO WHAT?
I HAVE TO GET RUSHKA'S SMILE BACK!
BECAUSE I'M HER BROTHER!
LILY, DO YOU KNOW WHERE THOSE THIEVES ARE HIDING?
Y-YEAH. I HEARD A RUMOR THAT THEY'RE INSIDE A CAVE DOWN BY THE BEACH.
BUT WHY DO YOU WANT TO KNOW?
I'M GONNA GO GET THE SHEEP BACK!
WHAT?

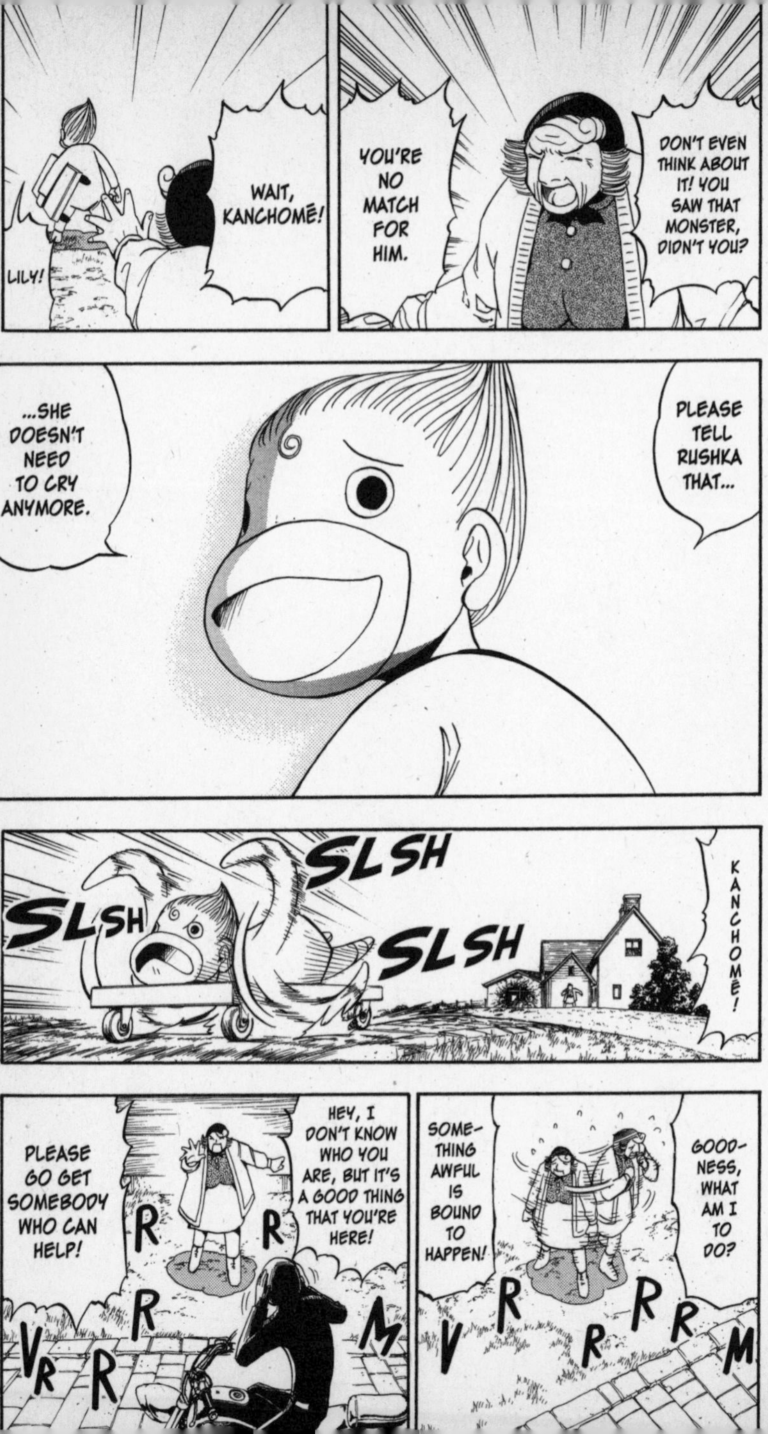
DON'T EVEN THINK ABOUT IT! YOU SAW THAT MONSTER, DIDN'T YOU?
YOU'RE NO MATCH FOR HIM.
WAIT, KANCHOMĒ!
LILY!
PLEASE TELL RUSHKA THAT...
...SHE DOESN'T NEED TO CRY ANYMORE.
KANCHOMĒ!
SLSH
SLSH
SLSH
GOOD-NESS, WHAT AM I TO DO?
SOME-THING AWFUL IS BOUND TO HAPPEN!
VRRRRRM
HEY, I DON'T KNOW WHO YOU ARE, BUT IT'S A GOOD THING THAT YOU'RE HERE!
PLEASE GO GET SOMEBODY WHO CAN HELP!
VRRRRRM

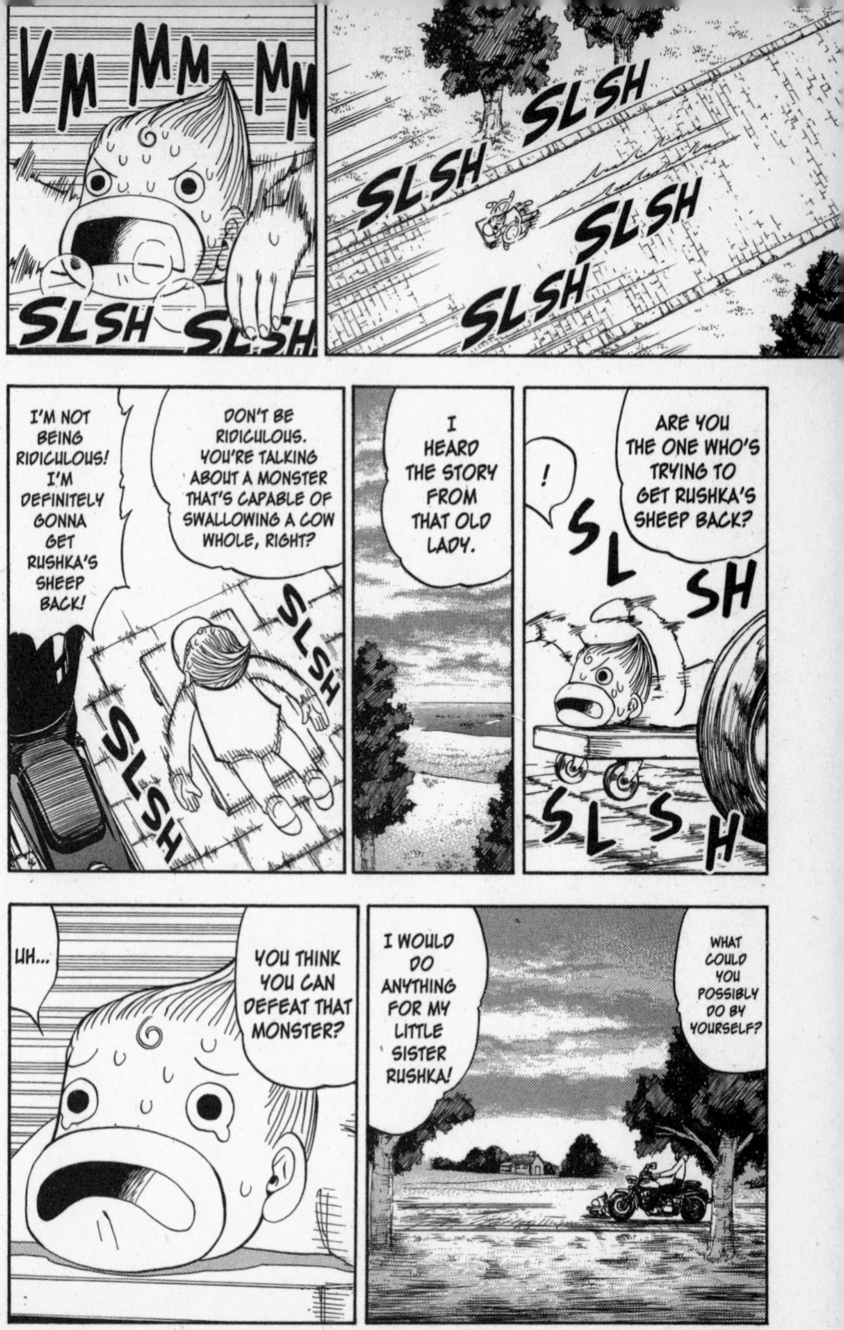
SLSH
SLSH
SLSH
SLSH
VMMMMMM
SLSH
SLSH
ARE YOU THE ONE WHO'S TRYING TO GET RUSHKA'S SHEEP BACK?
!
SLSH
SLSH
I HEARD THE STORY FROM THAT OLD LADY.
DON'T BE RIDICULOUS. YOU'RE TALKING ABOUT A MONSTER THAT'S CAPABLE OF SWALLOWING A COW WHOLE, RIGHT?
I'M NOT BEING RIDICULOUS! I'M DEFINITELY GONNA GET RUSHKA'S SHEEP BACK!
SLSH
SLSH
WHAT COULD YOU POSSIBLY DO BY YOURSELF?
I WOULD DO ANYTHING FOR MY LITTLE SISTER RUSHKA!
YOU THINK YOU CAN DEFEAT THAT MONSTER?
UH...

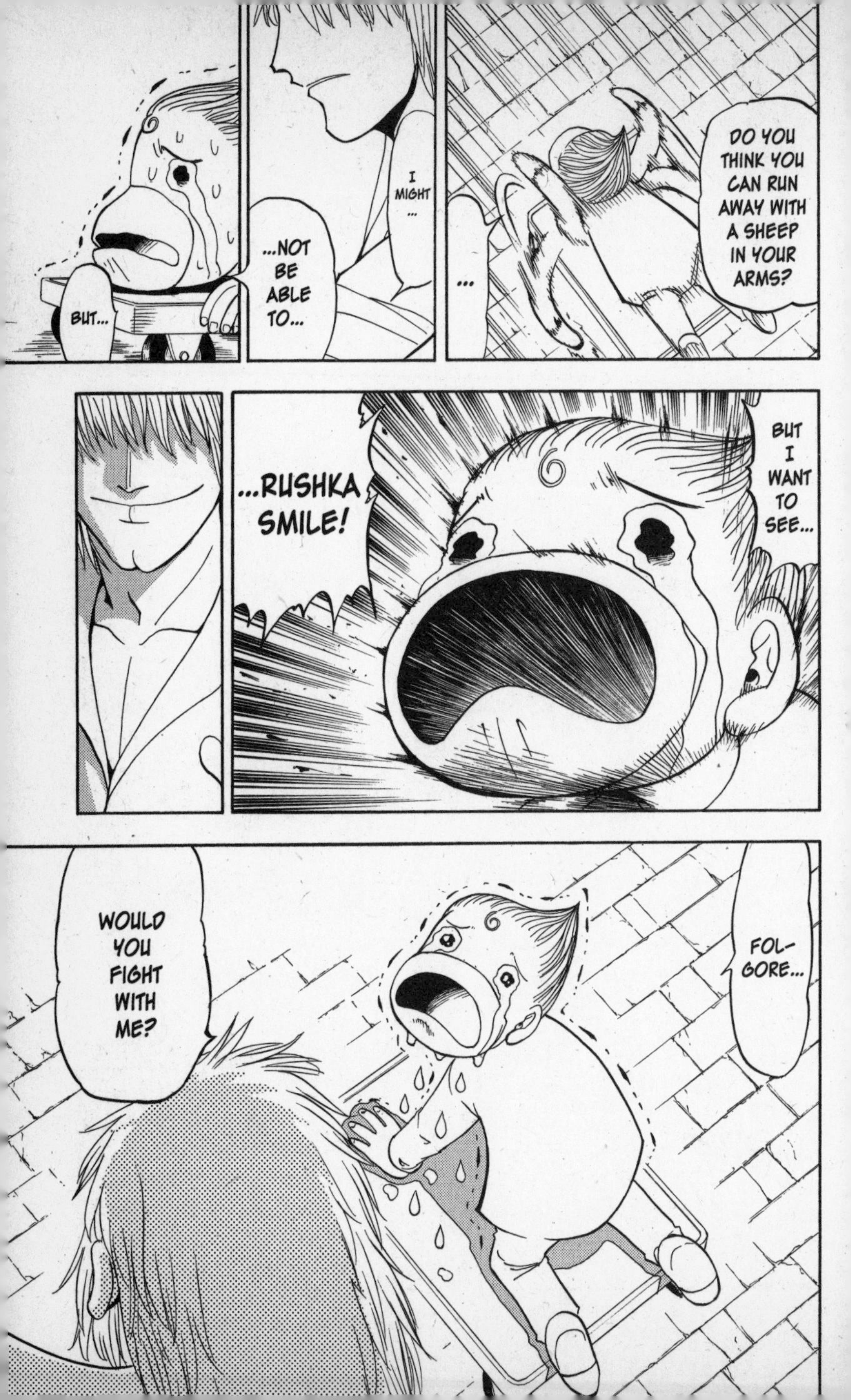
DO YOU THINK YOU CAN RUN AWAY WITH A SHEEP IN YOUR ARMS?
...
I MIGHT ...
...NOT BE ABLE TO...
BUT...
BUT I WANT TO SEE...
...RUSHKA SMILE!
FOL-GORE...
WOULD YOU FIGHT WITH ME?

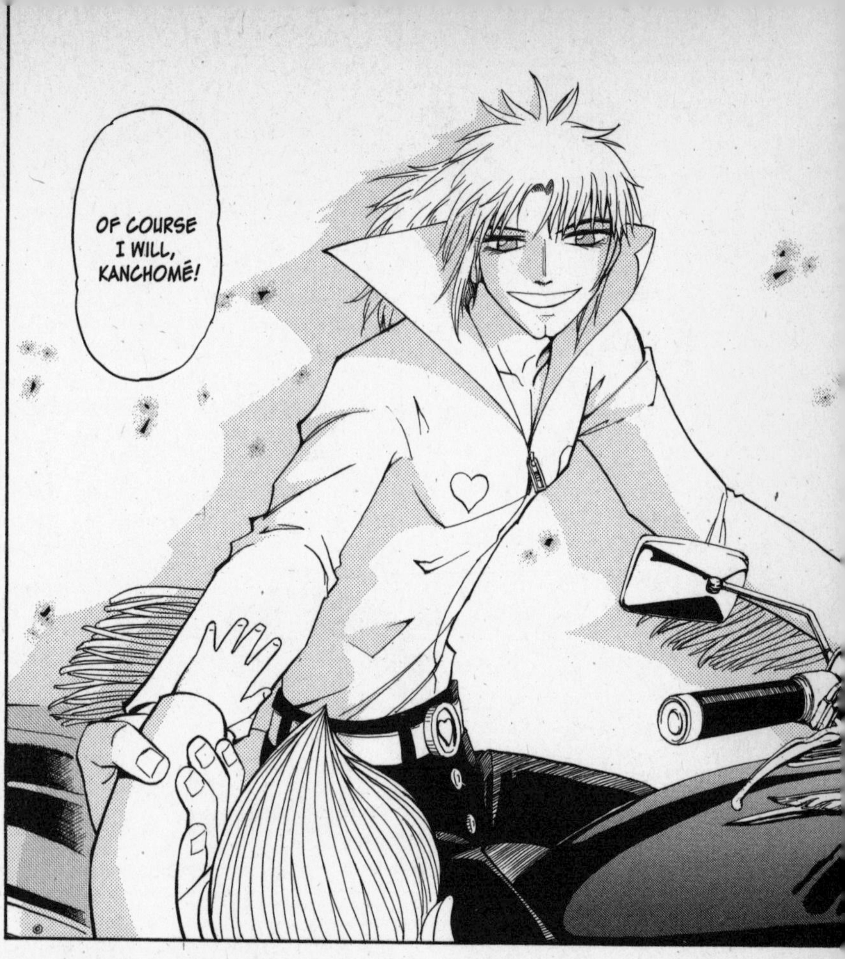
OF COURSE I WILL, KANCHOMÉ!
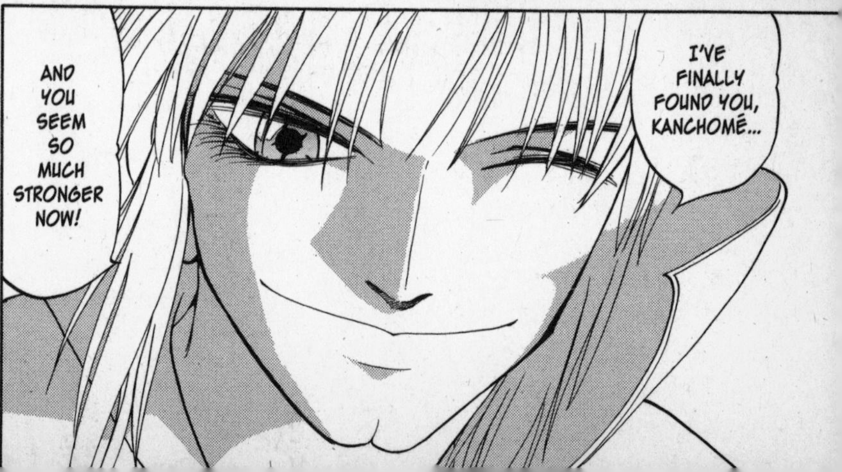
I'VE FINALLY FOUND YOU, KANCHOMÉ...
AND YOU SEEM SO MUCH STRONGER NOW!

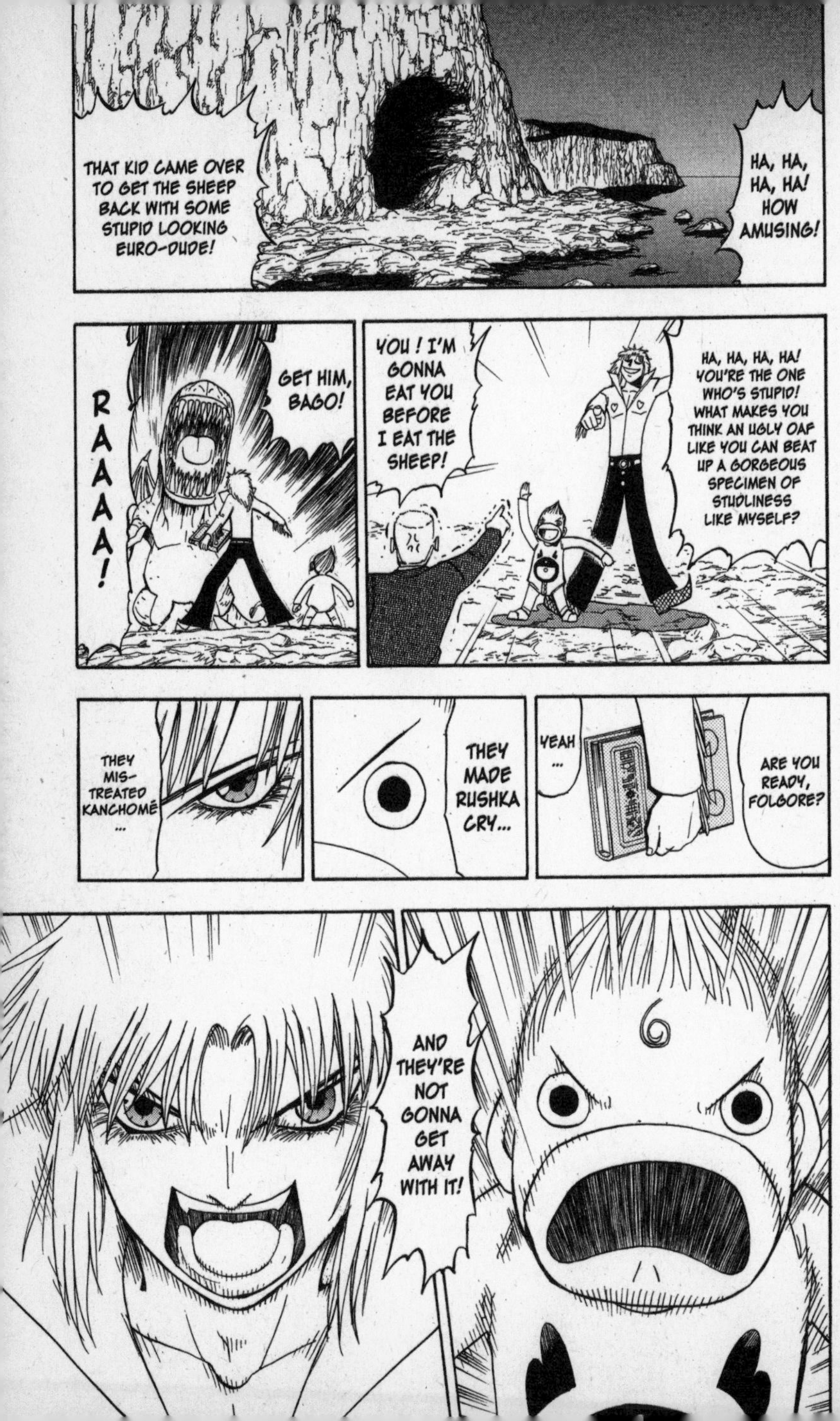
HA, HA, HA, HA! HOW AMUSING!
THAT KID CAME OVER TO GET THE SHEEP BACK WITH SOME STUPID LOOKING EURO-DUDE!
HA, HA, HA, HA! YOU'RE THE ONE WHO'S STUPID! WHAT MAKES YOU THINK AN UGLY OAF LIKE YOU CAN BEAT UP A GORGEOUS SPECIMEN OF STUDLINESS LIKE MYSELF?
YOU! I'M GONNA EAT YOU BEFORE I EAT THE SHEEP!
GET HIM, BAGO!
RAAAAA!
ARE YOU READY, FOLGORE?
YEAH ...
THEY MADE RUSHKA CRY...
THEY MIS-TREATED KANCHOMÉ ...
AND THEY'RE NOT GONNA GET AWAY WITH IT!

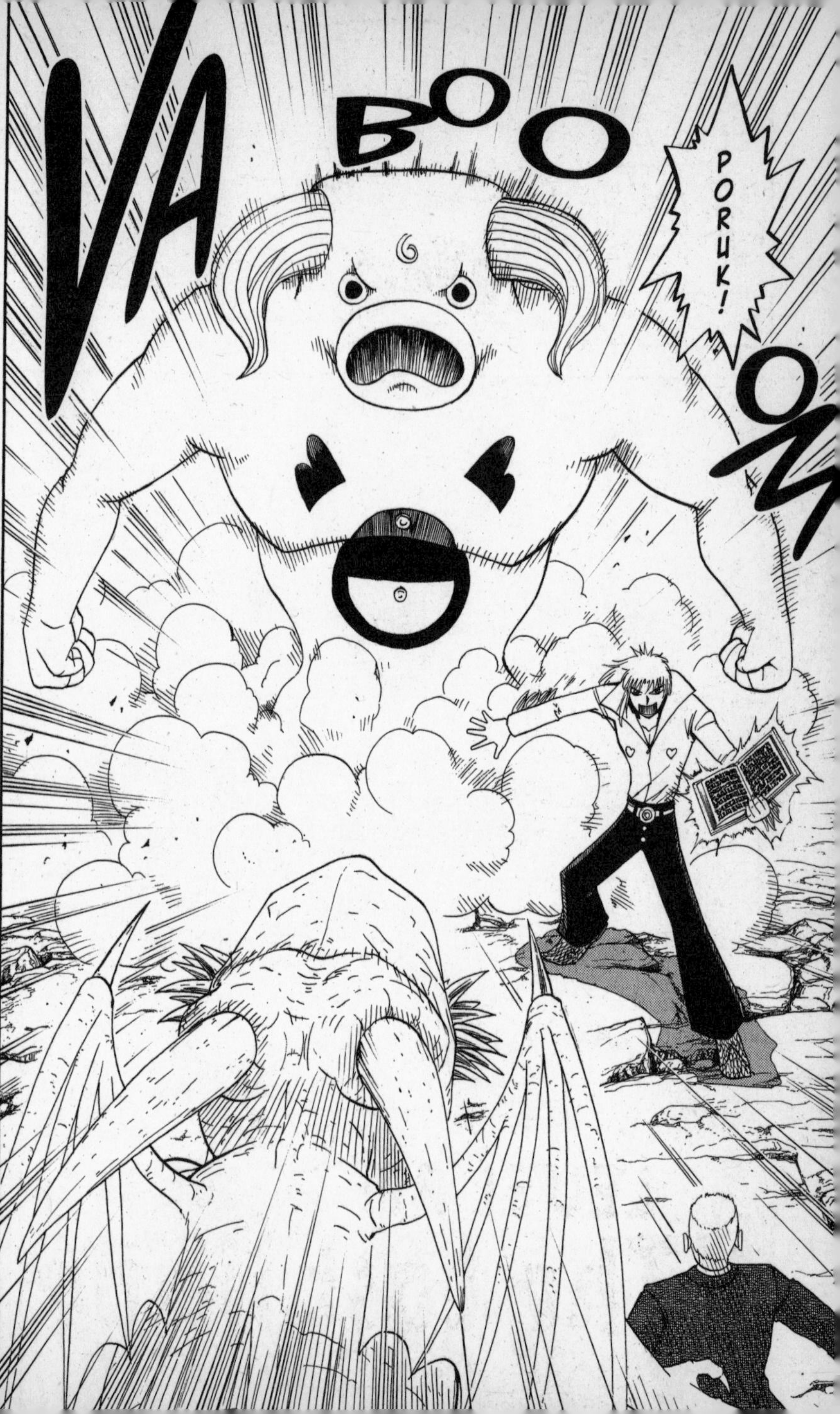
VA BOO OM
PORUK!

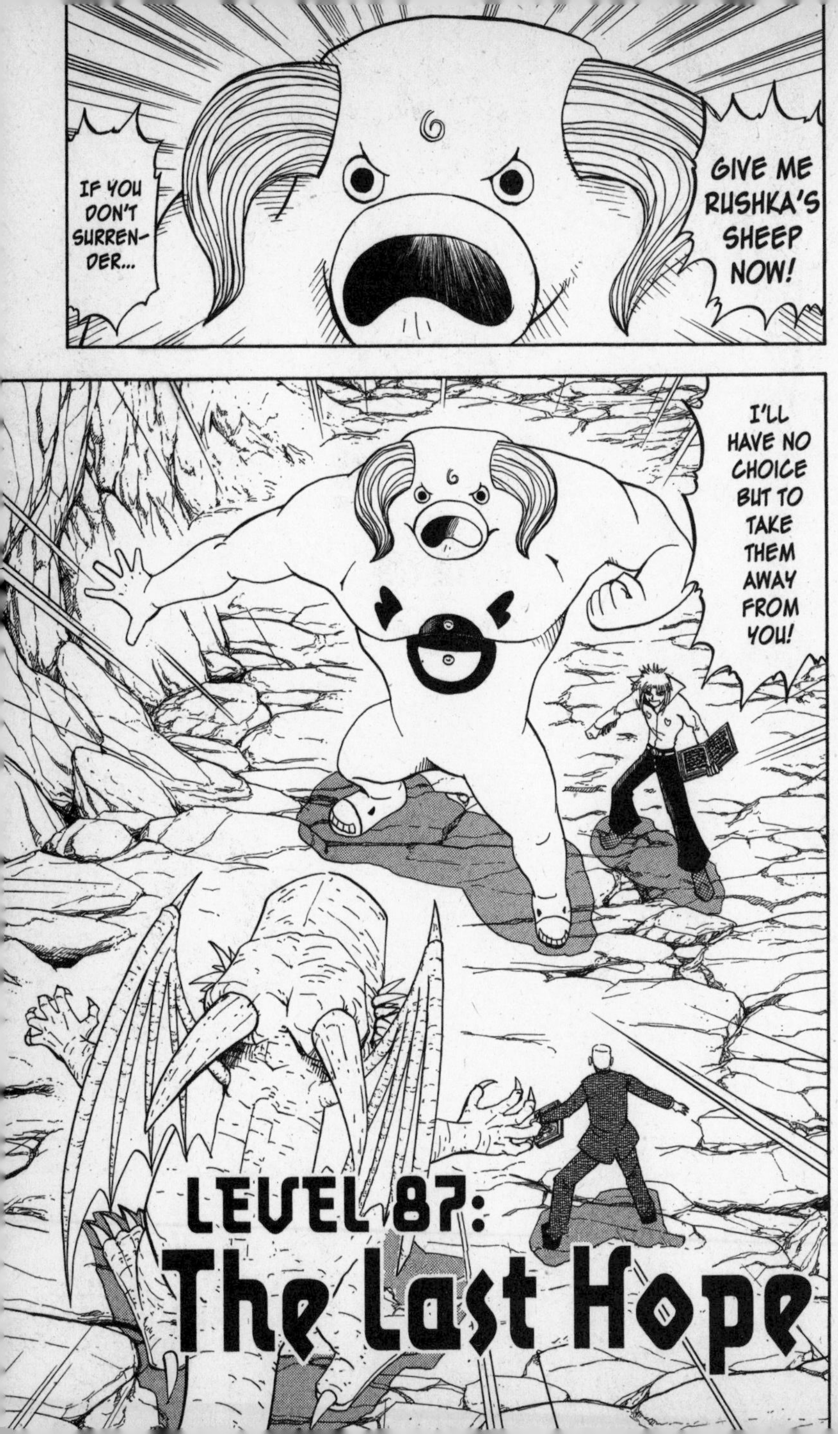
GIVE ME RUSHKA'S SHEEP NOW!
IF YOU DON'T SURREN-DER...
I'LL HAVE NO CHOICE BUT TO TAKE THEM AWAY FROM YOU!
LEVEL 87:
The Last Hope

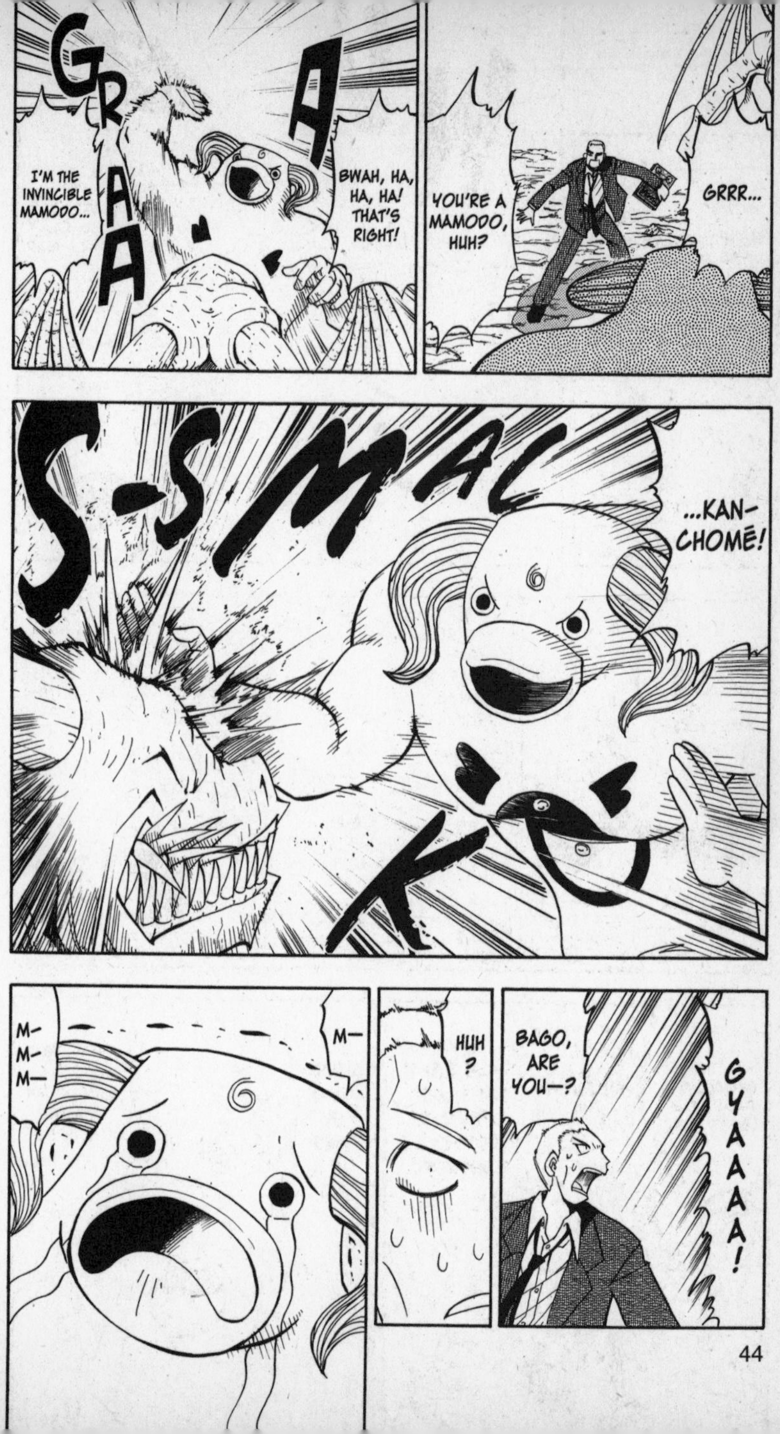
GRRR...
YOU'RE A MAMODO, HUH?
BWAH, HA, HA, HA! THAT'S RIGHT!
I'M THE INVINCIBLE MAMODO...
GRAAAA
...KAN-CHOMĒ!
S-SMACK
GYAAAAA!
BAGO, ARE YOU—?
HUH?
M—
M-M-M—

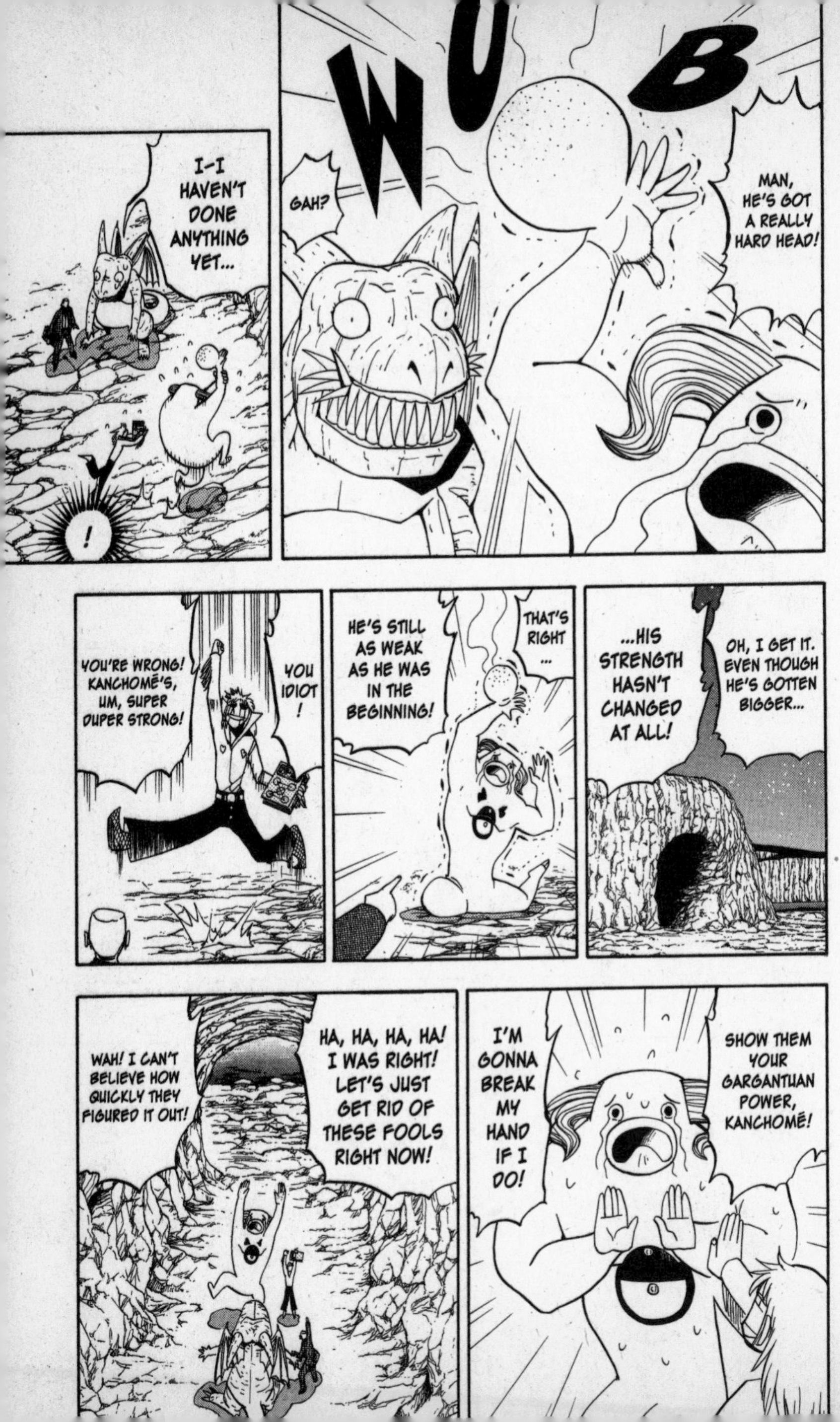
WUB
MAN, HE'S GOT A REALLY HARD HEAD!
GAH?
I-I HAVEN'T DONE ANYTHING YET...
!
OH, I GET IT. EVEN THOUGH HE'S GOTTEN BIGGER...
...HIS STRENGTH HASN'T CHANGED AT ALL!
THAT'S RIGHT ...
HE'S STILL AS WEAK AS HE WAS IN THE BEGINNING!
YOU IDIOT!
YOU'RE WRONG! KANCHOMÉ'S, UM, SUPER DUPER STRONG!
SHOW THEM YOUR GARGANTUAN POWER, KANCHOMÉ!
I'M GONNA BREAK MY HAND IF I DO!
HA, HA, HA, HA! I WAS RIGHT! LET'S JUST GET RID OF THESE FOOLS RIGHT NOW!
WAH! I CAN'T BELIEVE HOW QUICKLY THEY FIGURED IT OUT!

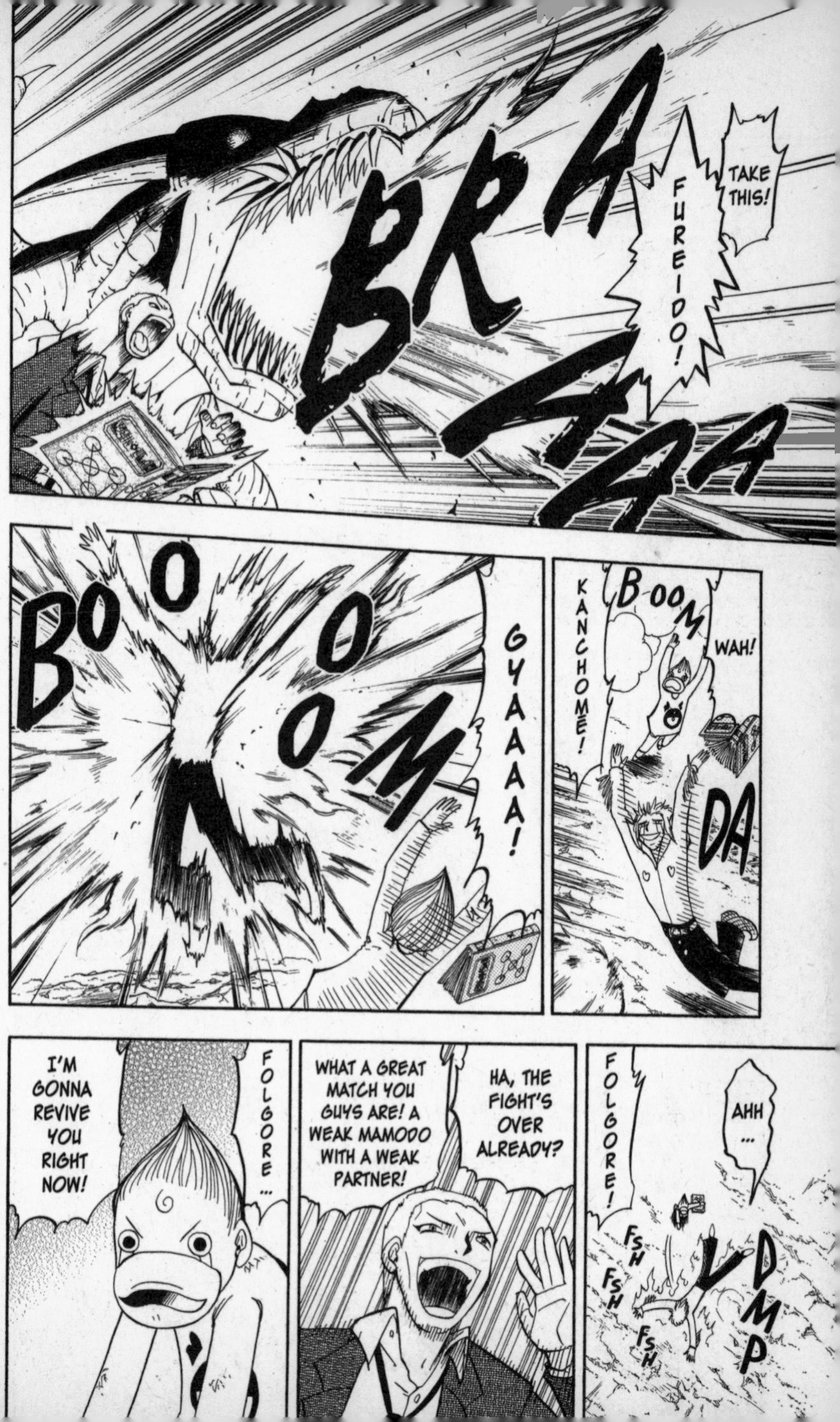
TAKE THIS!
FUREIDO!
BRAAAAA
KANCHOME!
BOOM
WAH!
DA
GYAAAAA!
BOOOOOM
AHH ...
FOLGORE!
FSH
FSH
FSH
DMP
HA, THE FIGHT'S OVER ALREADY?
WHAT A GREAT MATCH YOU GUYS ARE! A WEAK MAMODO WITH A WEAK PARTNER!
FOLGORE ...
I'M GONNA REVIVE YOU RIGHT NOW!

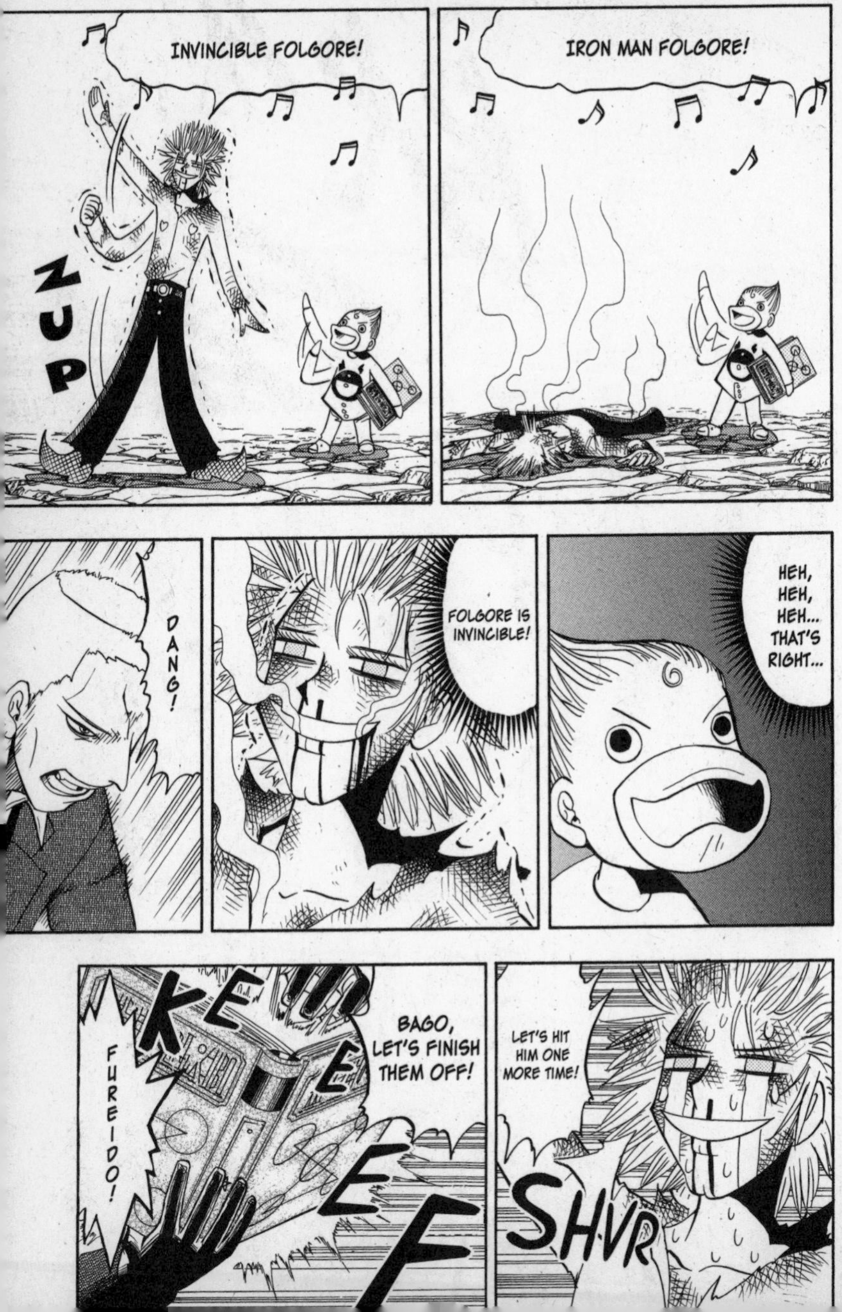
IRON MAN FOLGORE!
INVINCIBLE FOLGORE!
ZUP
HEH, HEH, HEH... THAT'S RIGHT...
FOLGORE IS INVINCIBLE!
DANG!
LET'S HIT HIM ONE MORE TIME!
SHVR
BAGO, LET'S FINISH THEM OFF!
FUREIDO!
KEEEF

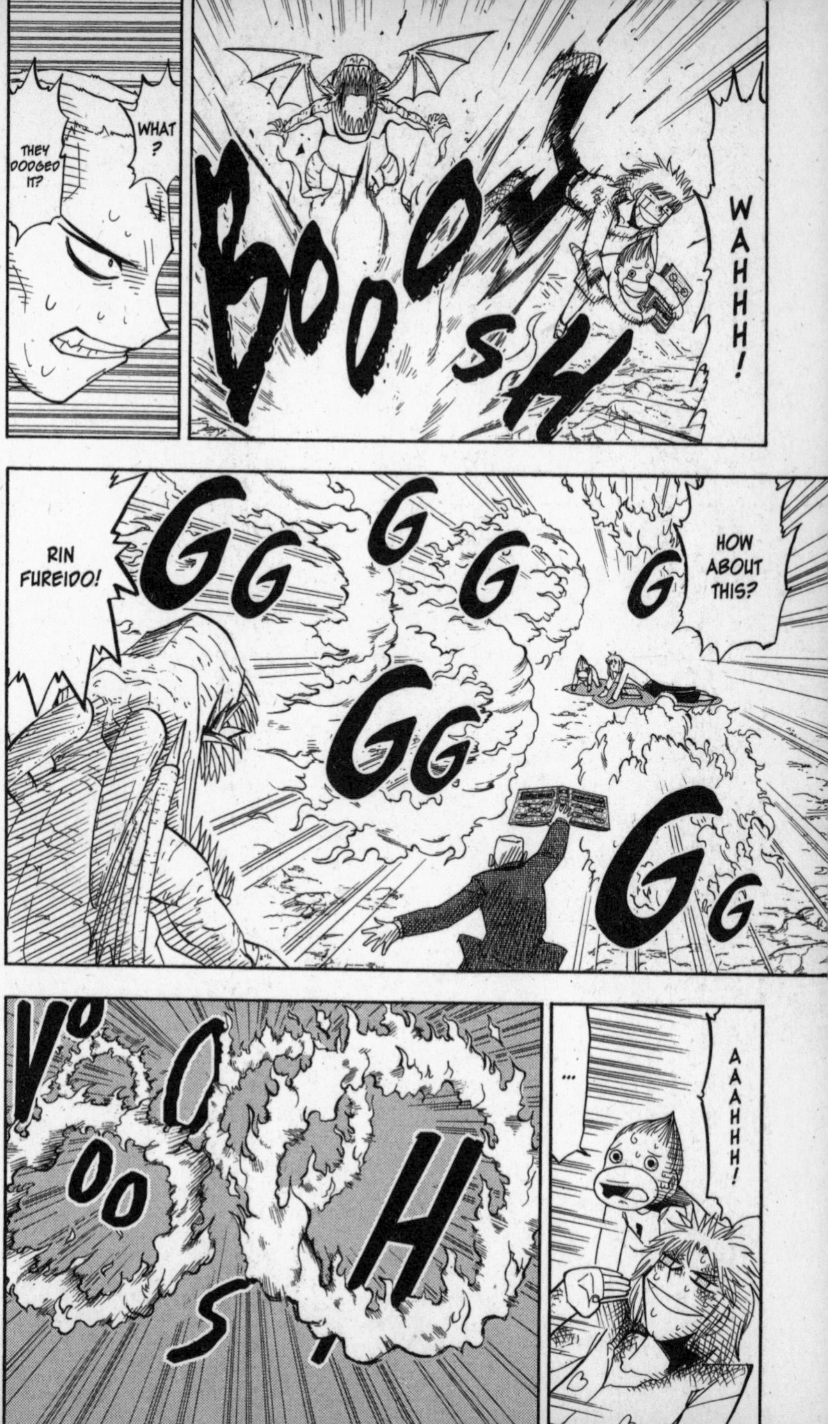
WAHHH!
BOOOOSH
WHAT?
THEY DODGED IT?
HOW ABOUT THIS?
RIN FUREIDO!
GGGGGGGGGG
AAAHHH!
...
VOOOOSH

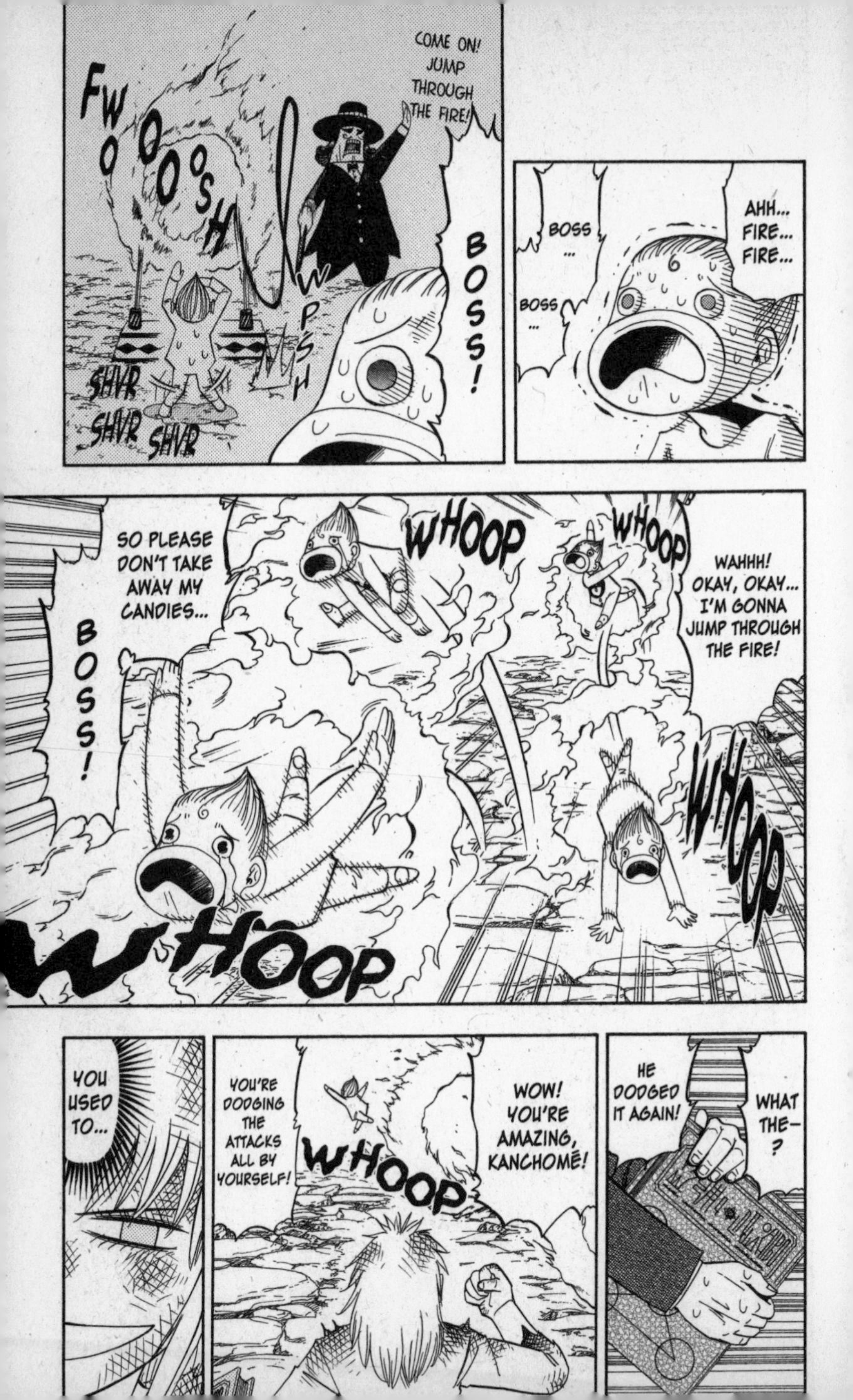
AHH... FIRE... FIRE...
BOSS ...
BOSS ...
COME ON! JUMP THROUGH THE FIRE!
BOSS!
FWOOOOSH
WPSH
SHVR
SHVR SHVR
WAHHH! OKAY, OKAY... I'M GONNA JUMP THROUGH THE FIRE!
WHOOP
WHOOP
SO PLEASE DON'T TAKE AWAY MY CANDIES...
BOSS!
WHOOP
WHOOP
WHAT THE—?
HE DODGED IT AGAIN!
WOW! YOU'RE AMAZING, KANCHOMÉ!
YOU'RE DODGING THE ATTACKS ALL BY YOURSELF!
WHOOP
YOU USED TO...

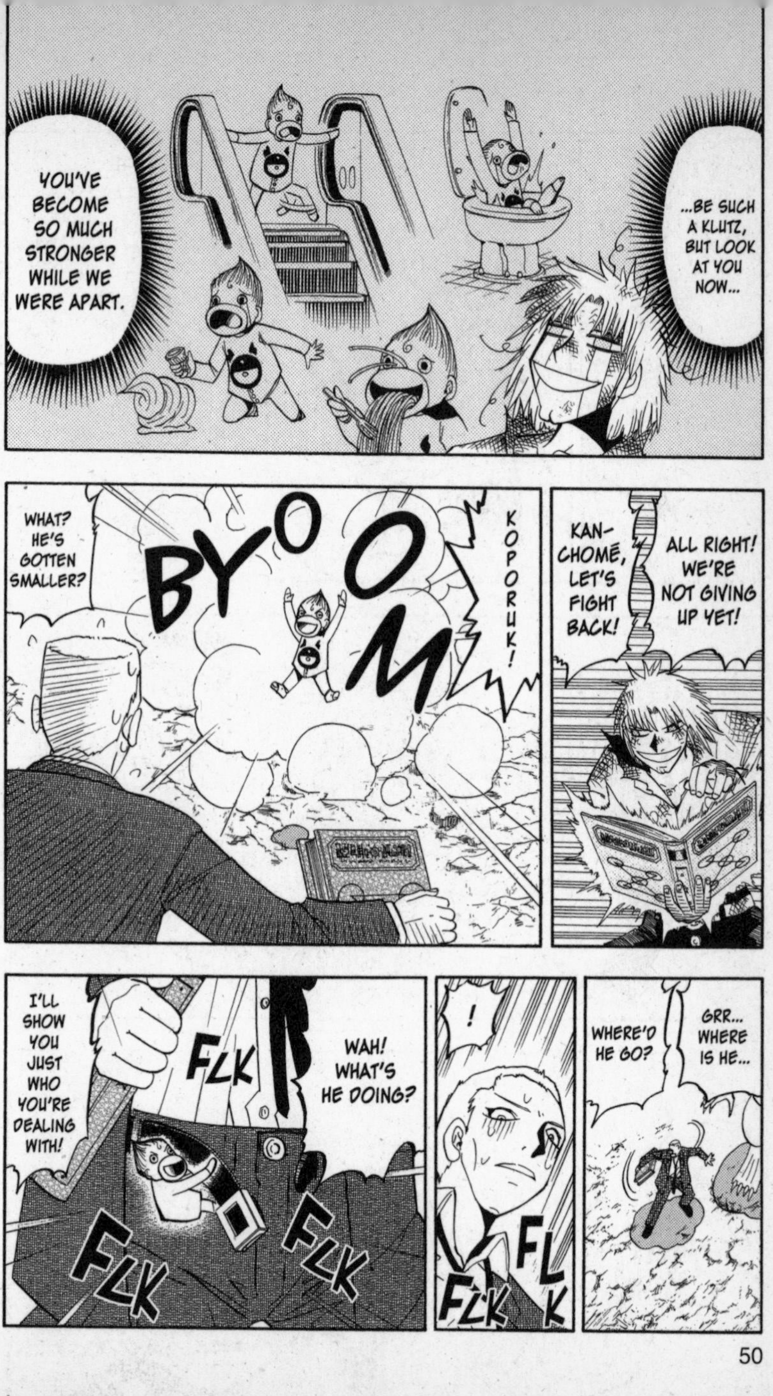
...BE SUCH A KLUTZ, BUT LOOK AT YOU NOW...
YOU'VE BECOME SO MUCH STRONGER WHILE WE WERE APART.
ALL RIGHT! WE'RE NOT GIVING UP YET!
KAN-CHOME, LET'S FIGHT BACK!
KOPORUK!
BYOOM
WHAT? HE'S GOTTEN SMALLER?
GRR... WHERE IS HE...
WHERE'D HE GO?
!
FLK
FLK
WAH! WHAT'S HE DOING?
I'LL SHOW YOU JUST WHO YOU'RE DEALING WITH!
FLK
FLK
FLK

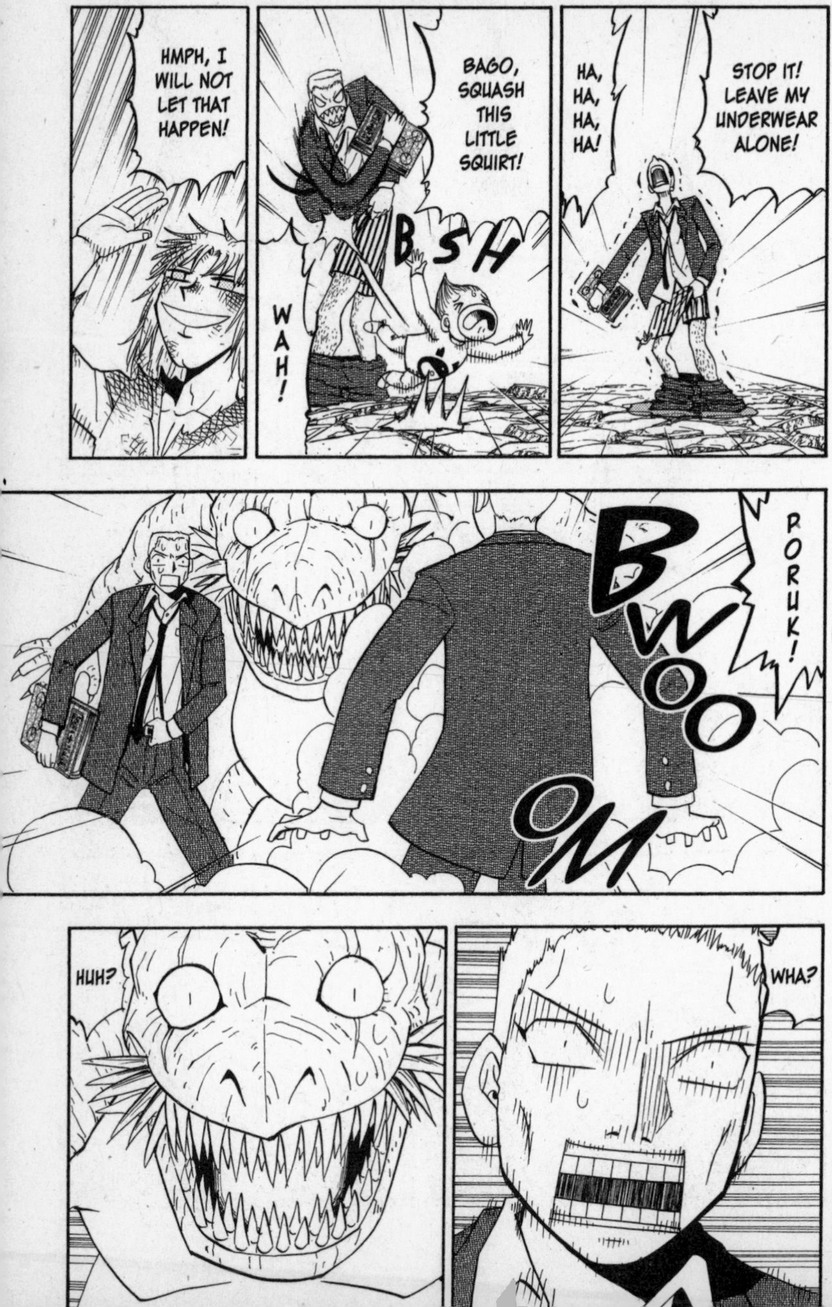
STOP IT! LEAVE MY UNDERWEAR ALONE!
HA, HA, HA, HA!
BAGO, SQUASH THIS LITTLE SQUIRT!
BSH
WAH!
HMPH, I WILL NOT LET THAT HAPPEN!
PORUK!
BWOOOM
WHA?
HUH?

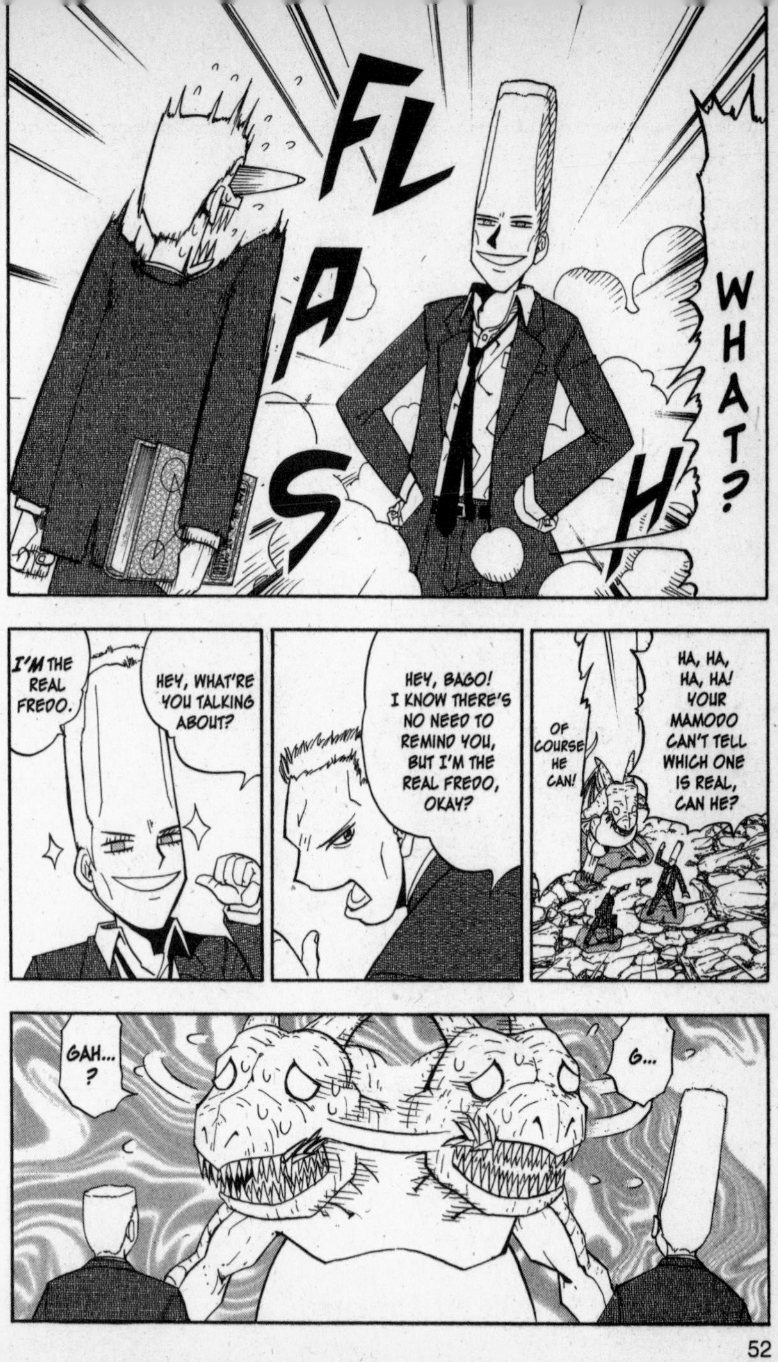
WHAT?
FLASH
HA, HA, HA, HA! YOUR MAMODO CAN'T TELL WHICH ONE IS REAL, CAN HE?
OF COURSE HE CAN!
HEY, BAGO! I KNOW THERE'S NO NEED TO REMIND YOU, BUT I'M THE REAL FREDO, OKAY?
HEY, WHAT'RE YOU TALKING ABOUT?
I'M THE REAL FREDO.
G...
GAH... ?

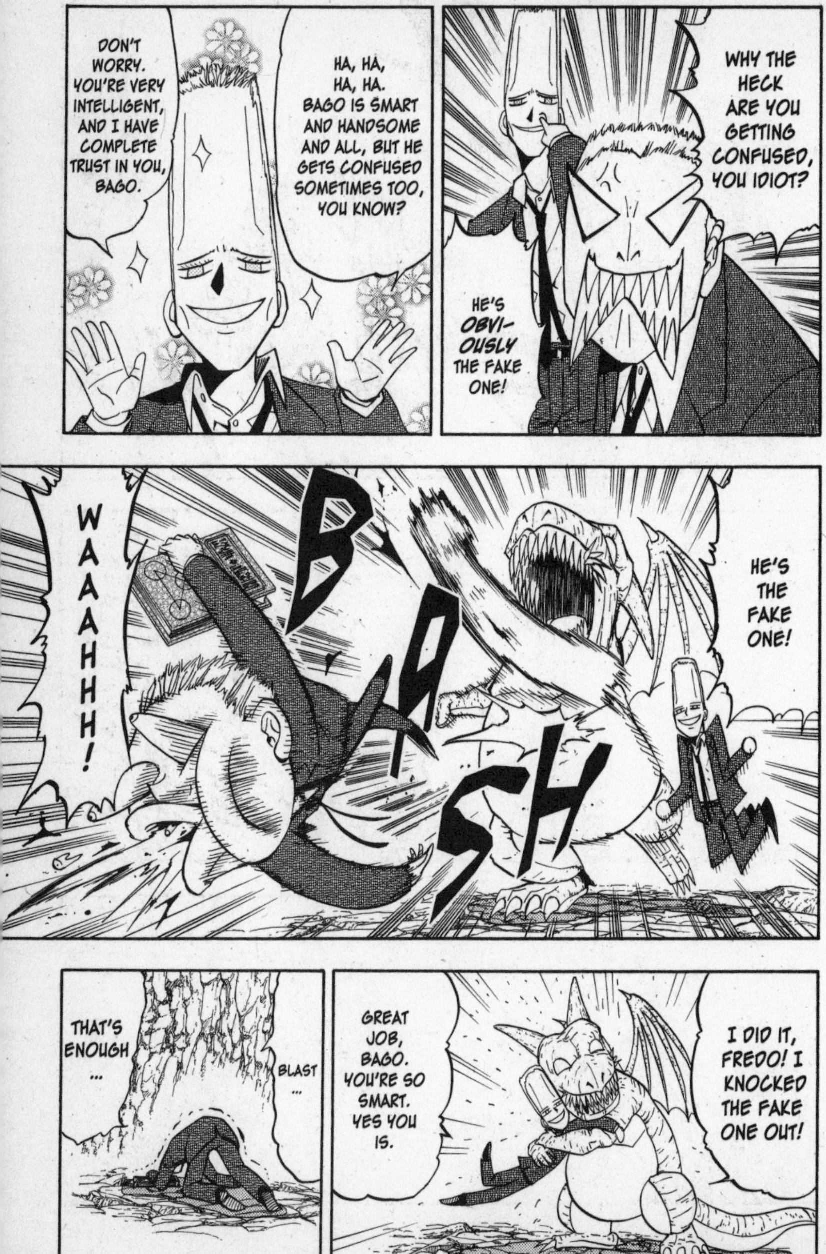
WHY THE HECK ARE YOU GETTING CONFUSED, YOU IDIOT?
HE'S OBVIOUSLY THE FAKE ONE!
HA, HA, HA, HA. BAGO IS SMART AND HANDSOME AND ALL, BUT HE GETS CONFUSED SOMETIMES TOO, YOU KNOW?
DON'T WORRY. YOU'RE VERY INTELLIGENT, AND I HAVE COMPLETE TRUST IN YOU, BAGO.
HE'S THE FAKE ONE!
BASH
WAAAAHHH!
I DID IT, FREDO! I KNOCKED THE FAKE ONE OUT!
GREAT JOB, BAGO. YOU'RE SO SMART. YES YOU IS.
BLAST ...
THAT'S ENOUGH ...

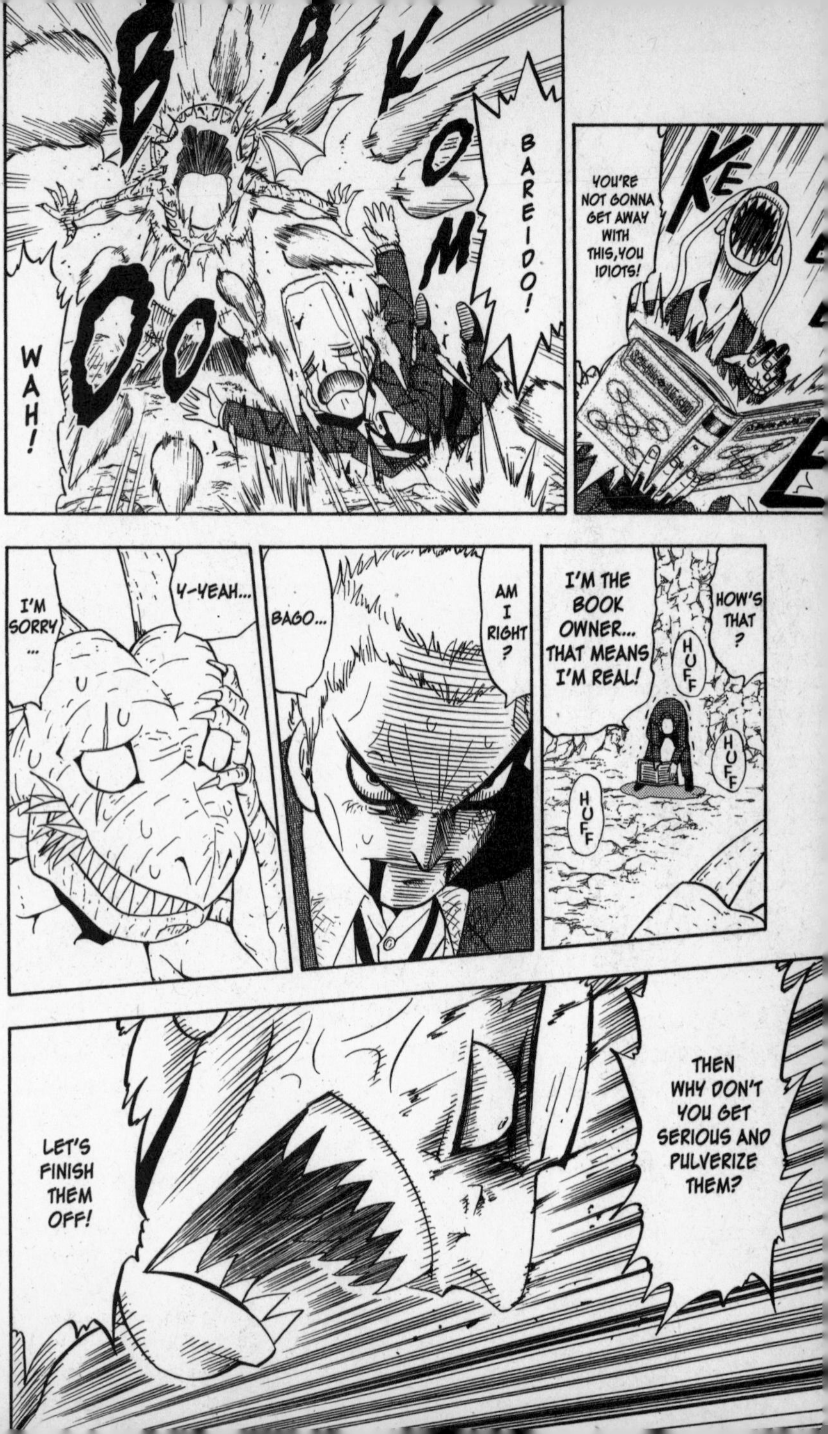
KE
YOU'RE NOT GONNA GET AWAY WITH THIS, YOU IDIOTS!
BAKOM
BAREIDO!
DOOO
WAH!
HOW'S THAT?
I'M THE BOOK OWNER... THAT MEANS I'M REAL!
HUFF
HUFF
HUFF
AM I RIGHT?
BAGO...
Y-YEAH...
I'M SORRY...
THEN WHY DON'T YOU GET SERIOUS AND PULVERIZE THEM?
LET'S FINISH THEM OFF!

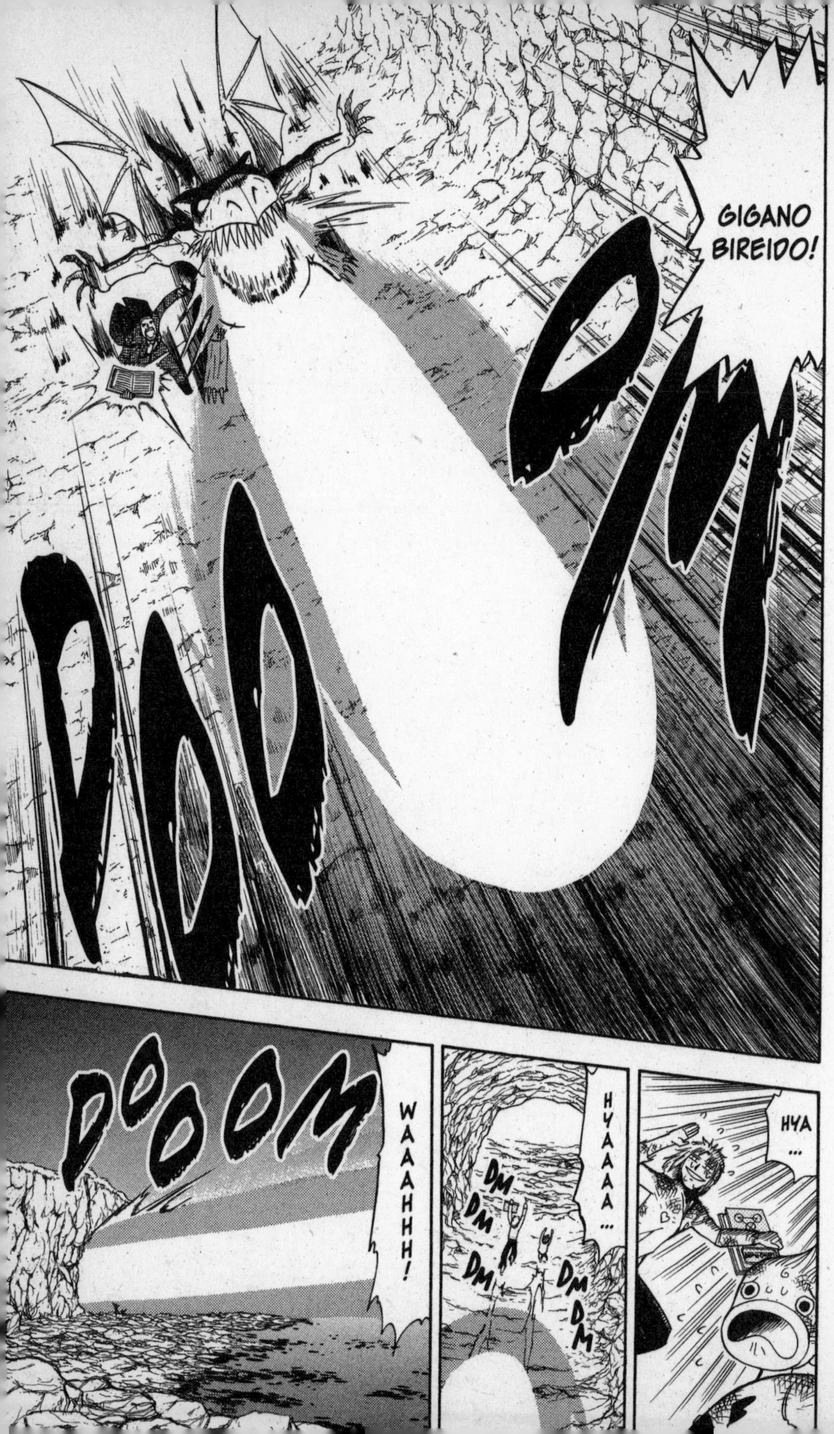
GIGANO BIREIDO!
HYA ...
HYAAAA...
DM DM DM
DM DM DM
WAAAHHH!
DOOOM

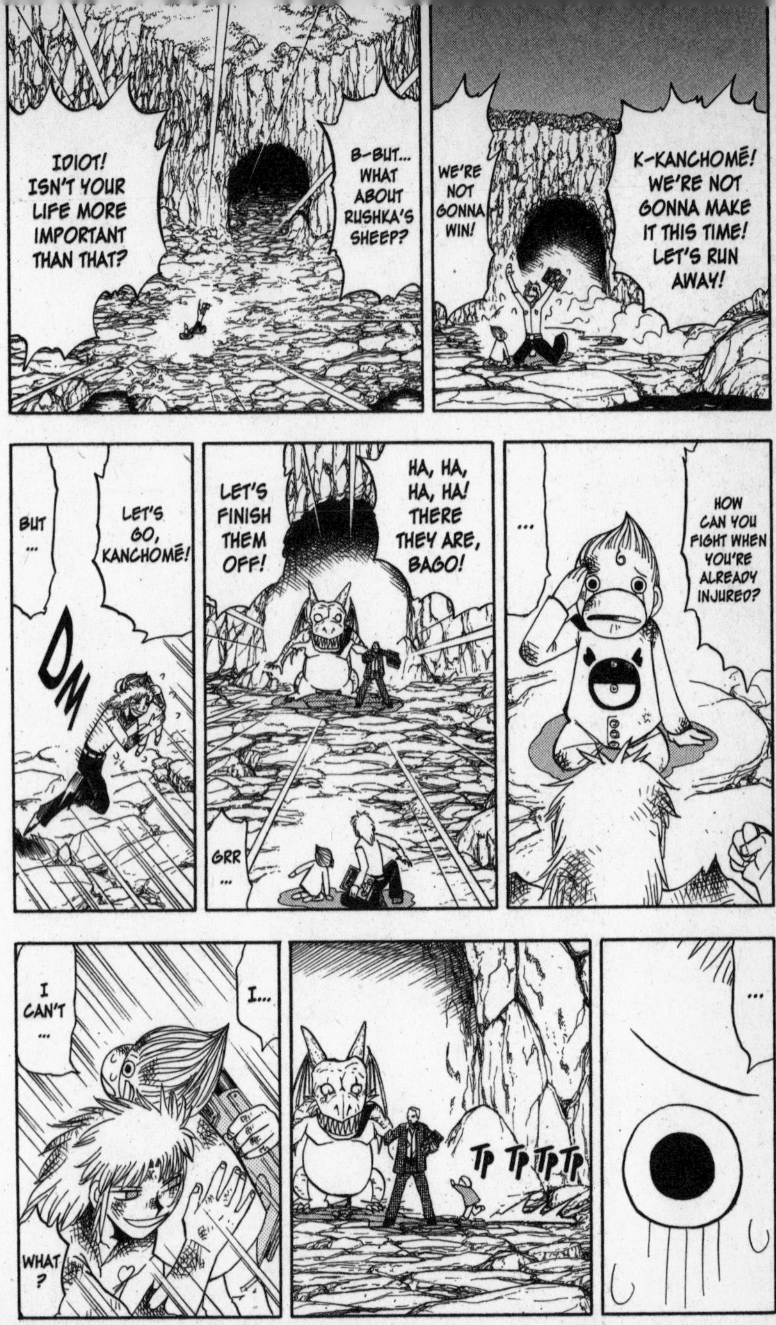
K-KANCHOMÉ! WE'RE NOT GONNA MAKE IT THIS TIME! LET'S RUN AWAY!
WE'RE NOT GONNA WIN!
B-BUT... WHAT ABOUT RUSHKA'S SHEEP?
IDIOT! ISN'T YOUR LIFE MORE IMPORTANT THAN THAT?
HOW CAN YOU FIGHT WHEN YOU'RE ALREADY INJURED?
...
HA, HA, HA, HA! THERE THEY ARE, BAGO!
LET'S FINISH THEM OFF!
GRR ...
LET'S GO, KANCHOMÉ!
BUT ...
DM
...
TP TP TP TP
I...
I CAN'T ...
WHAT ?

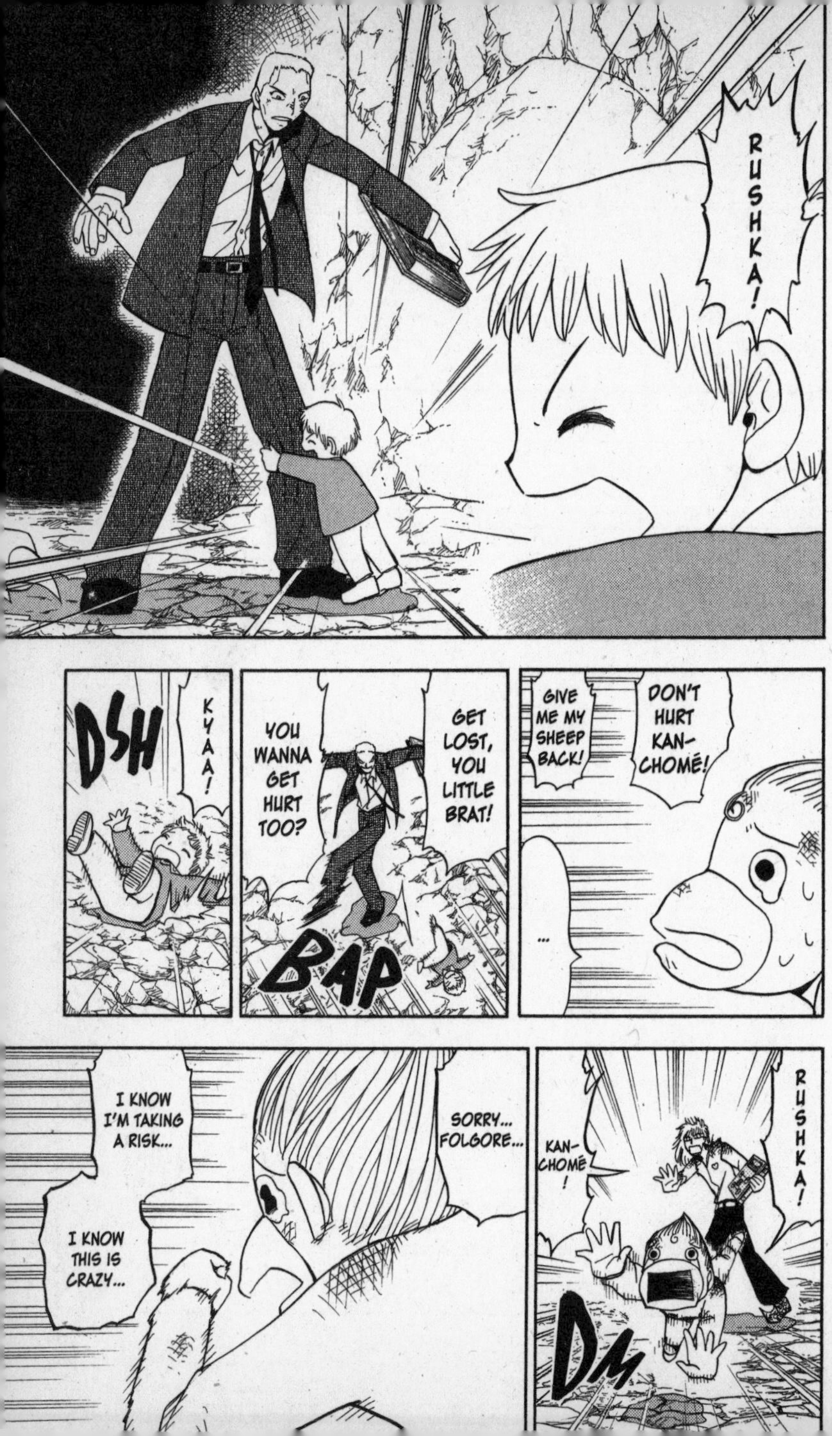
RUSHKA!
DON'T HURT KANCHOMÉ!
GIVE ME MY SHEEP BACK!
...
GET LOST, YOU LITTLE BRAT!
YOU WANNA GET HURT TOO?
BAP
KYAAA!
DSH
RUSHKA!
KANCHOMÉ!
DM
SORRY... FOLGORE...
I KNOW I'M TAKING A RISK...
I KNOW THIS IS CRAZY...

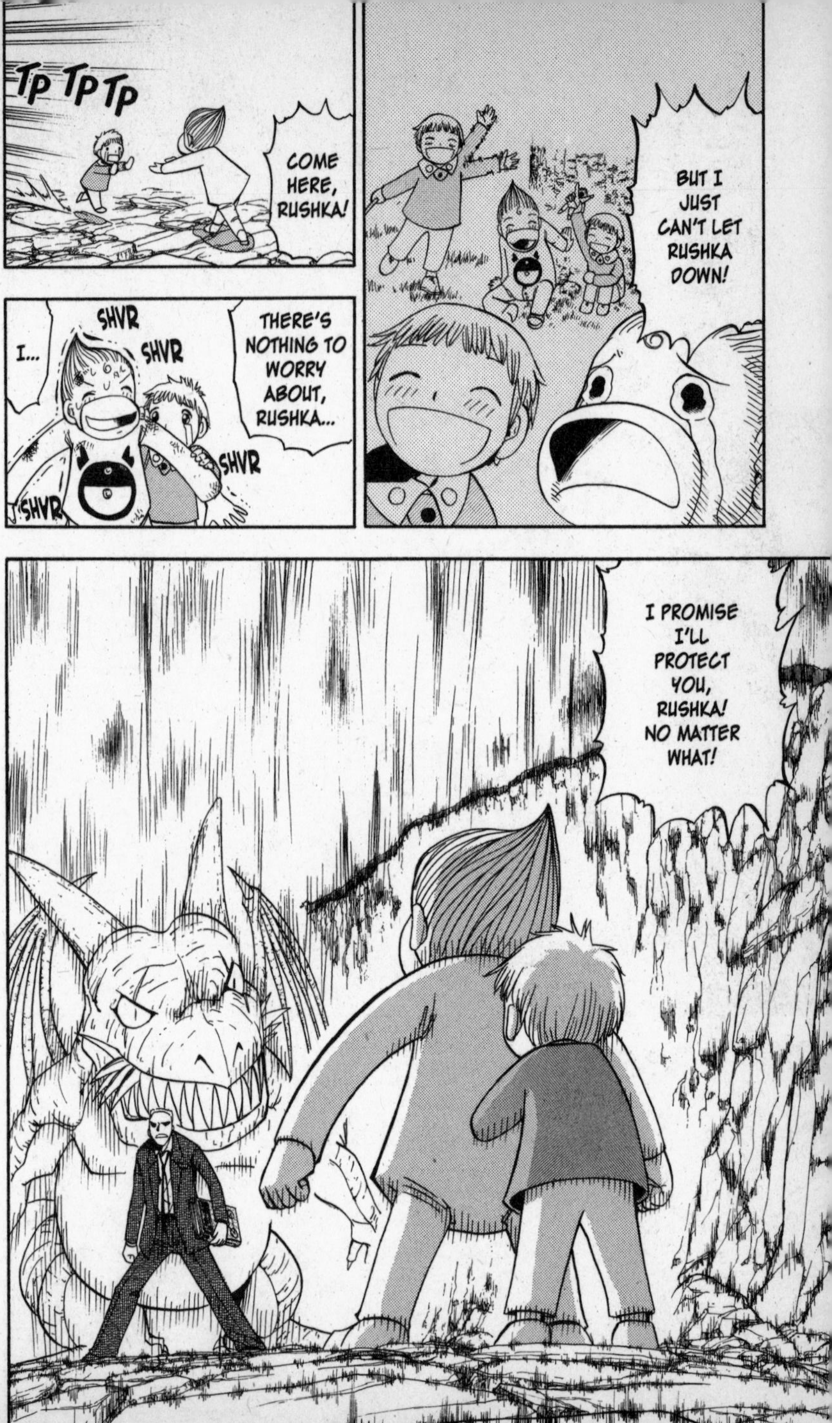
BUT I JUST CAN'T LET RUSHKA DOWN!
COME HERE, RUSHKA!
Tp Tp Tp
THERE'S NOTHING TO WORRY ABOUT, RUSHKA...
SHVR
SHVR
I...
SHVR
SHVR
I PROMISE I'LL PROTECT YOU, RUSHKA! NO MATTER WHAT!

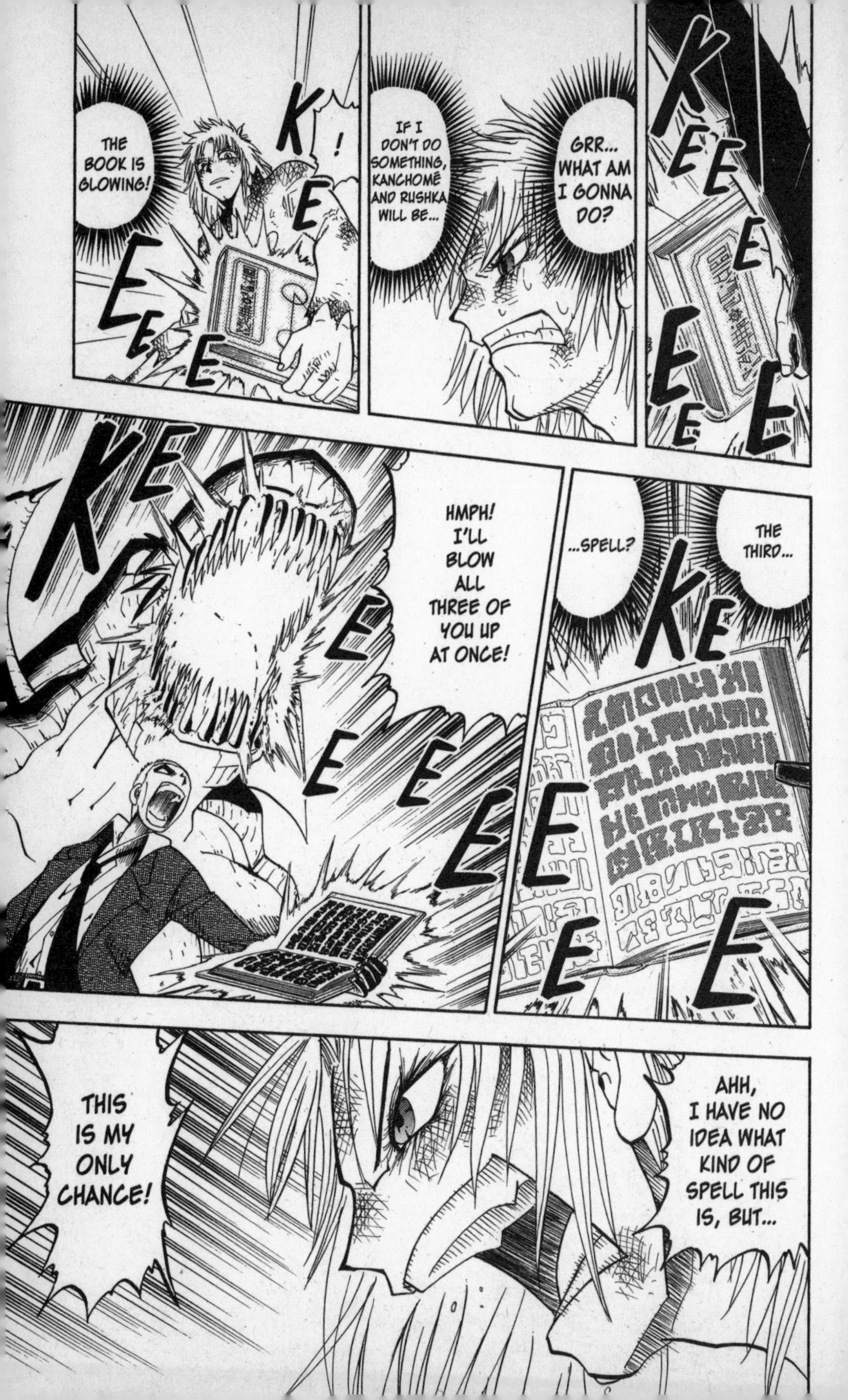
KEEEEEEE
GRR... WHAT AM I GONNA DO?
IF I DON'T DO SOMETHING, KANCHOMÉ AND RUSHKA WILL BE...
THE BOOK IS GLOWING!
KE!
EEEE
THE THIRD...
...SPELL?
KEEEEEE
HMPH! I'LL BLOW ALL THREE OF YOU UP AT ONCE!
KEEEEEE
AHH, I HAVE NO IDEA WHAT KIND OF SPELL THIS IS, BUT...
THIS IS MY ONLY CHANCE!

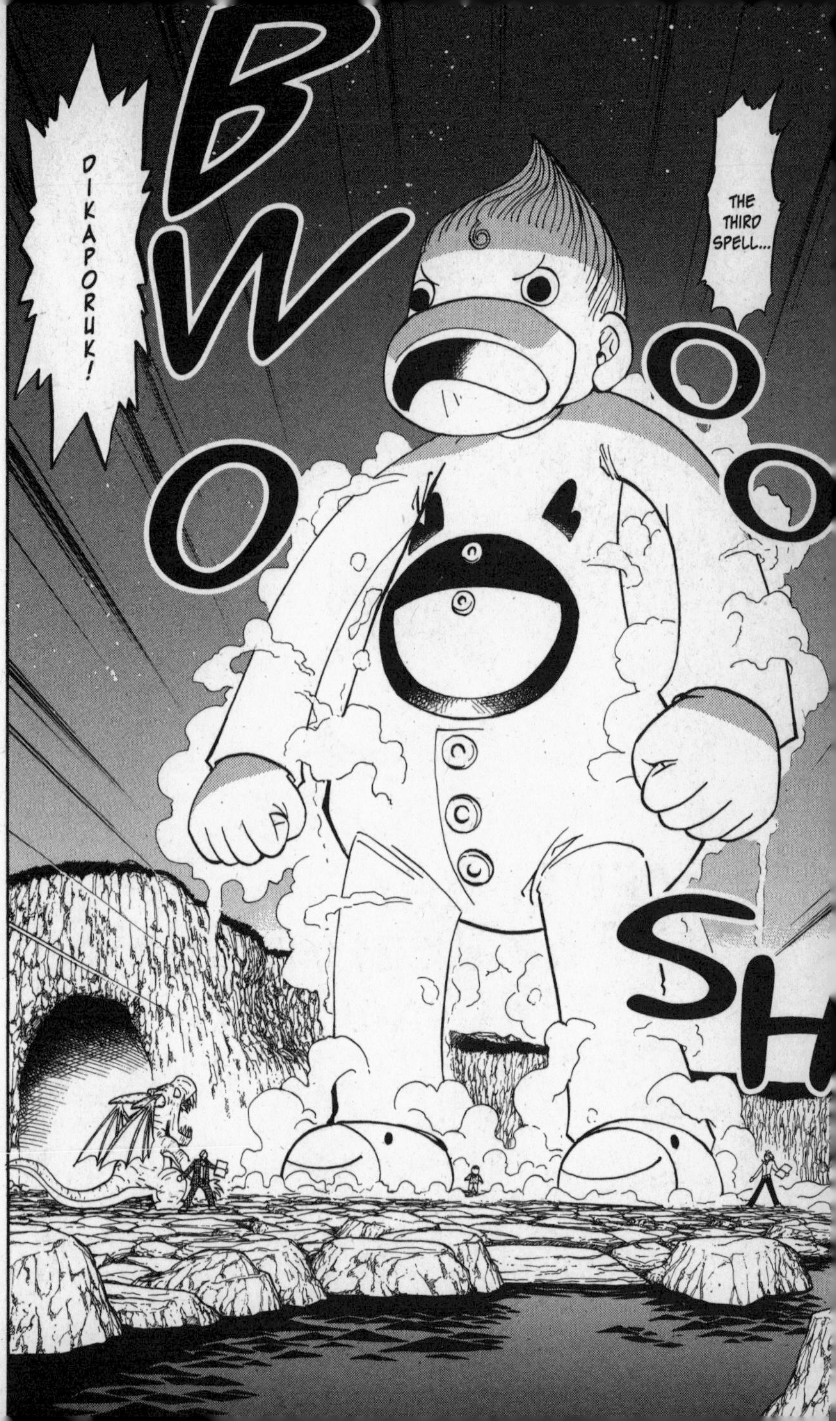
THE THIRD SPELL...
DIKAPORUK!
BWOOOOSH

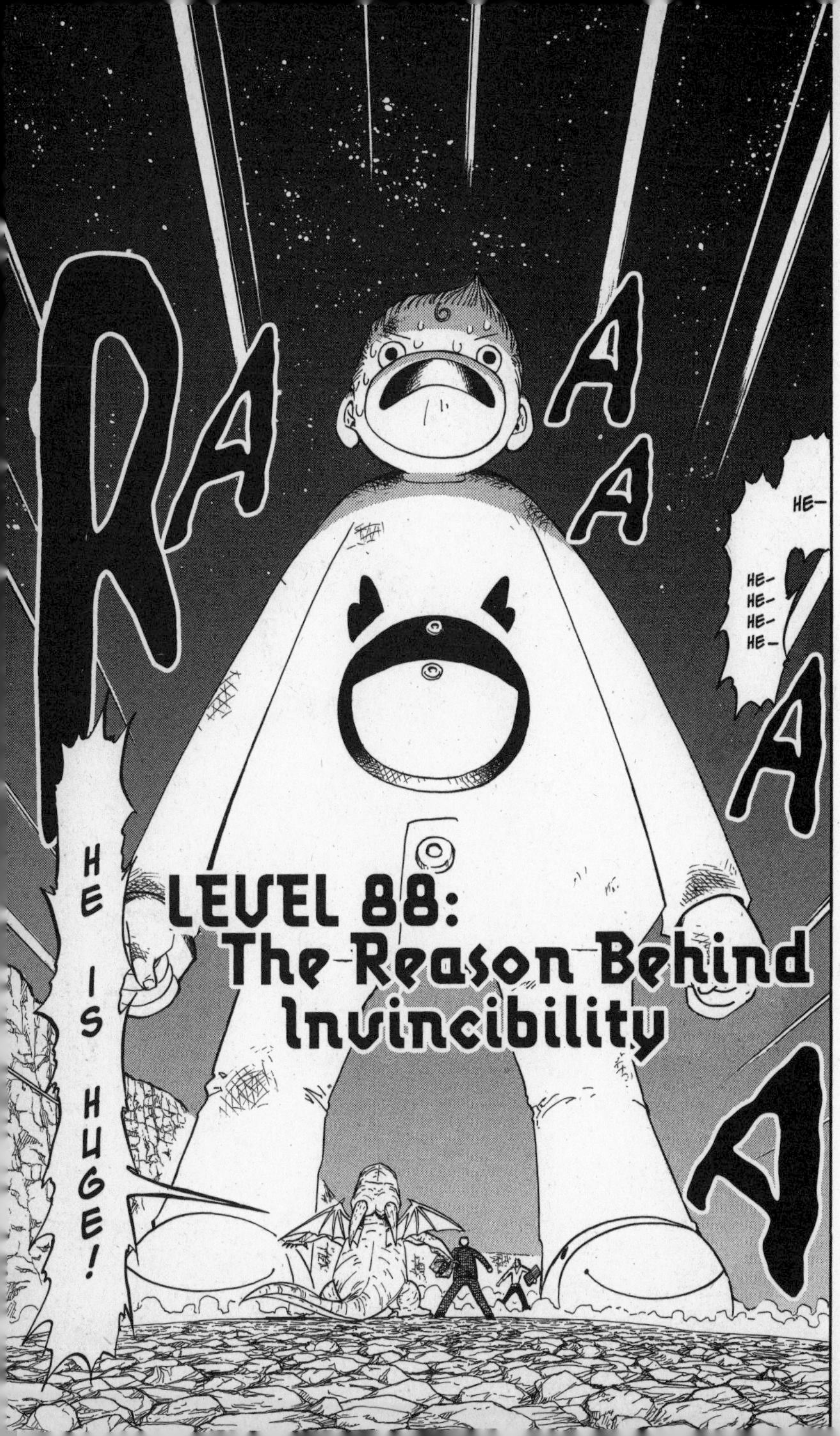
RAAAAA
HE— HE— HE— HE— HE—
HE IS HUGE!
LEVEL 88: The Reason Behind Invincibility

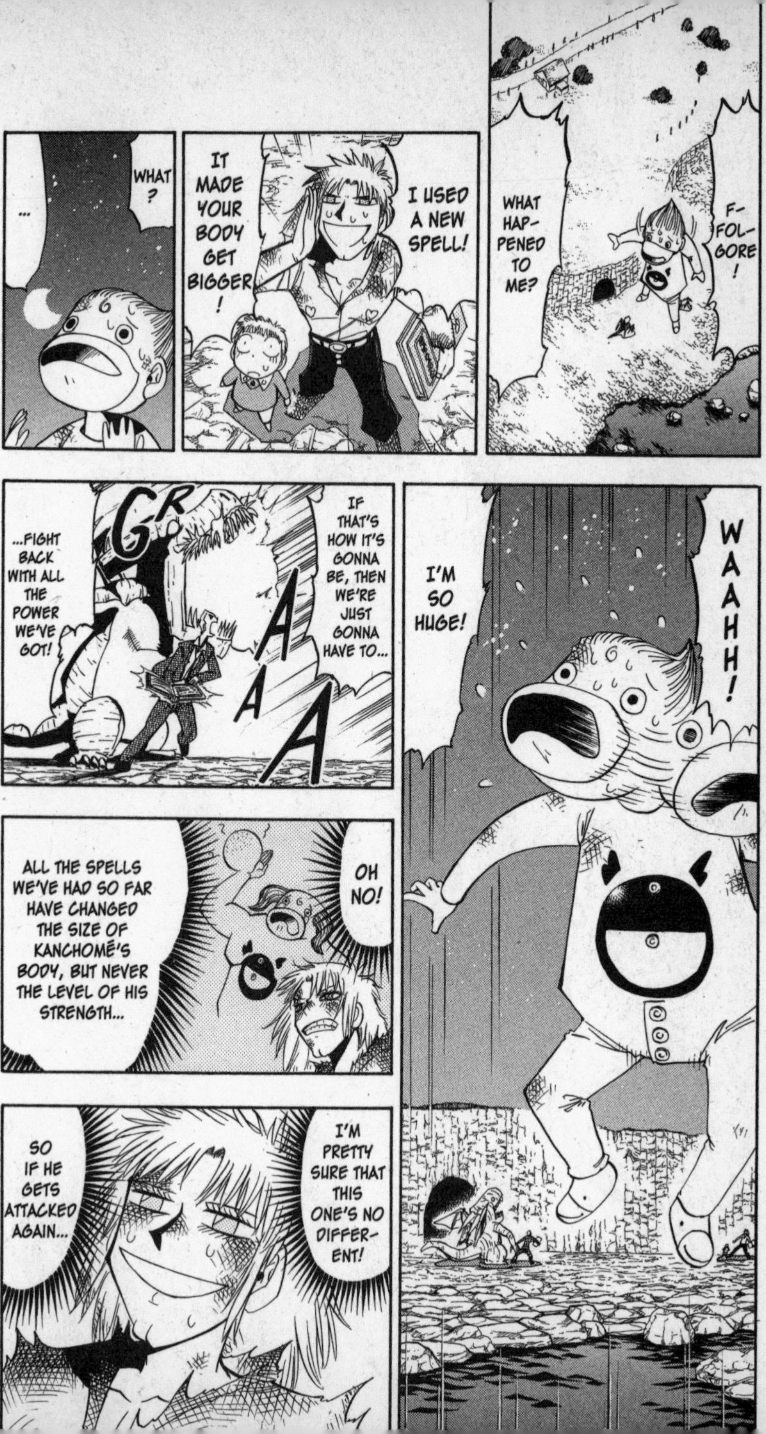
F-FOLGORE!
WHAT HAPPENED TO ME?
I USED A NEW SPELL!
IT MADE YOUR BODY GET BIGGER!
WHAT?
...
WAAHH!
I'M SO HUGE!
IF THAT'S HOW IT'S GONNA BE, THEN WE'RE JUST GONNA HAVE TO...
...FIGHT BACK WITH ALL THE POWER WE'VE GOT!
GRAAAA
OH NO!
ALL THE SPELLS WE'VE HAD SO FAR HAVE CHANGED THE SIZE OF KANCHOMÉ'S BODY, BUT NEVER THE LEVEL OF HIS STRENGTH...
I'M PRETTY SURE THAT THIS ONE'S NO DIFFERENT!
SO IF HE GETS ATTACKED AGAIN...

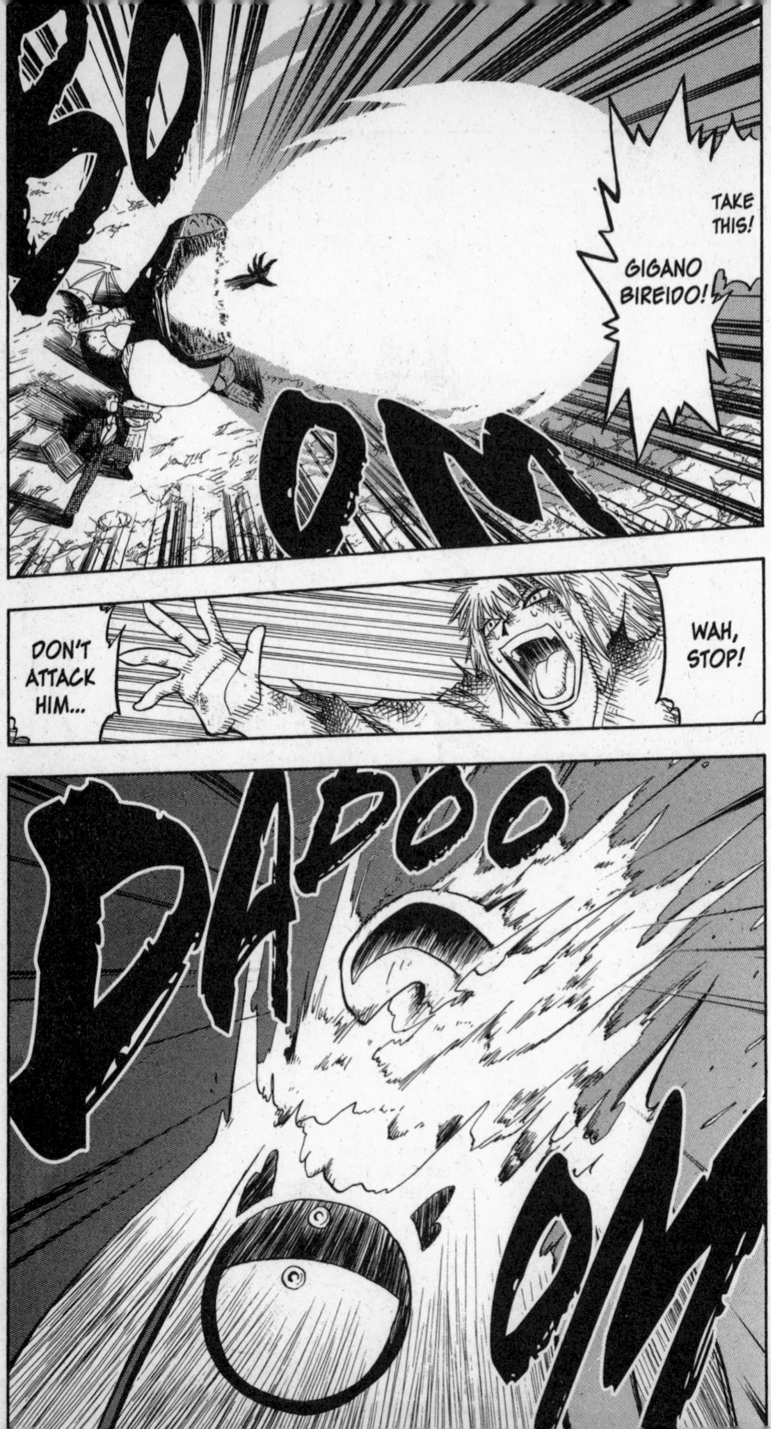
TAKE THIS!
GIGANO BIREIDO!
WAH, STOP!
DON’T ATTACK HIM...

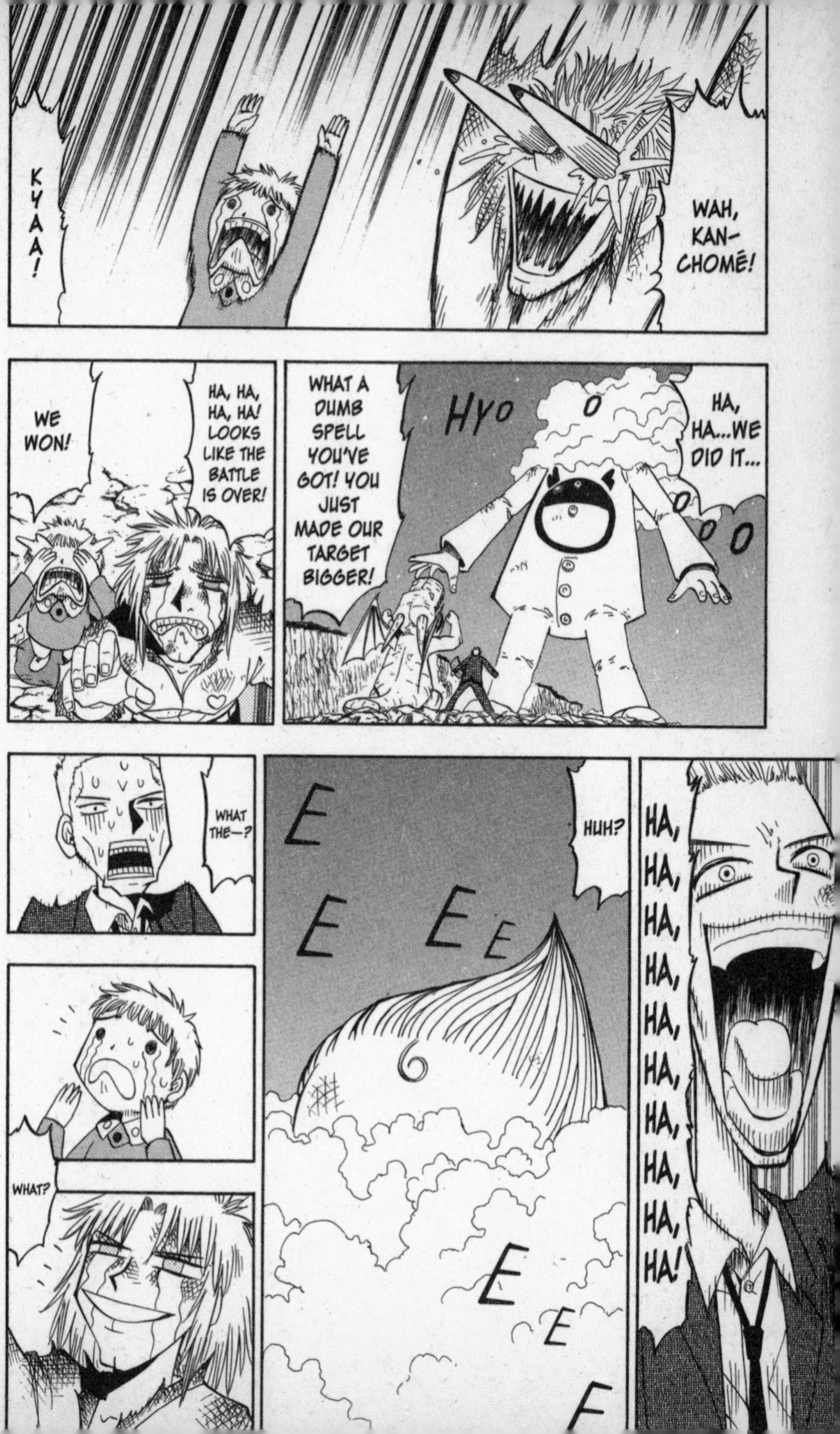
WAH, KAN-CHOMÉ!
KYAAA!
HA, HA...WE DID IT...
Hyo o o o o
WHAT A DUMB SPELL YOU'VE GOT! YOU JUST MADE OUR TARGET BIGGER!
HA, HA, HA, HA! LOOKS LIKE THE BATTLE IS OVER!
WE WON!
HA, HA, HA, HA, HA, HA, HA, HA, HA, HA!
HUH?
E E E E E E E F
WHAT THE—?
WHAT?

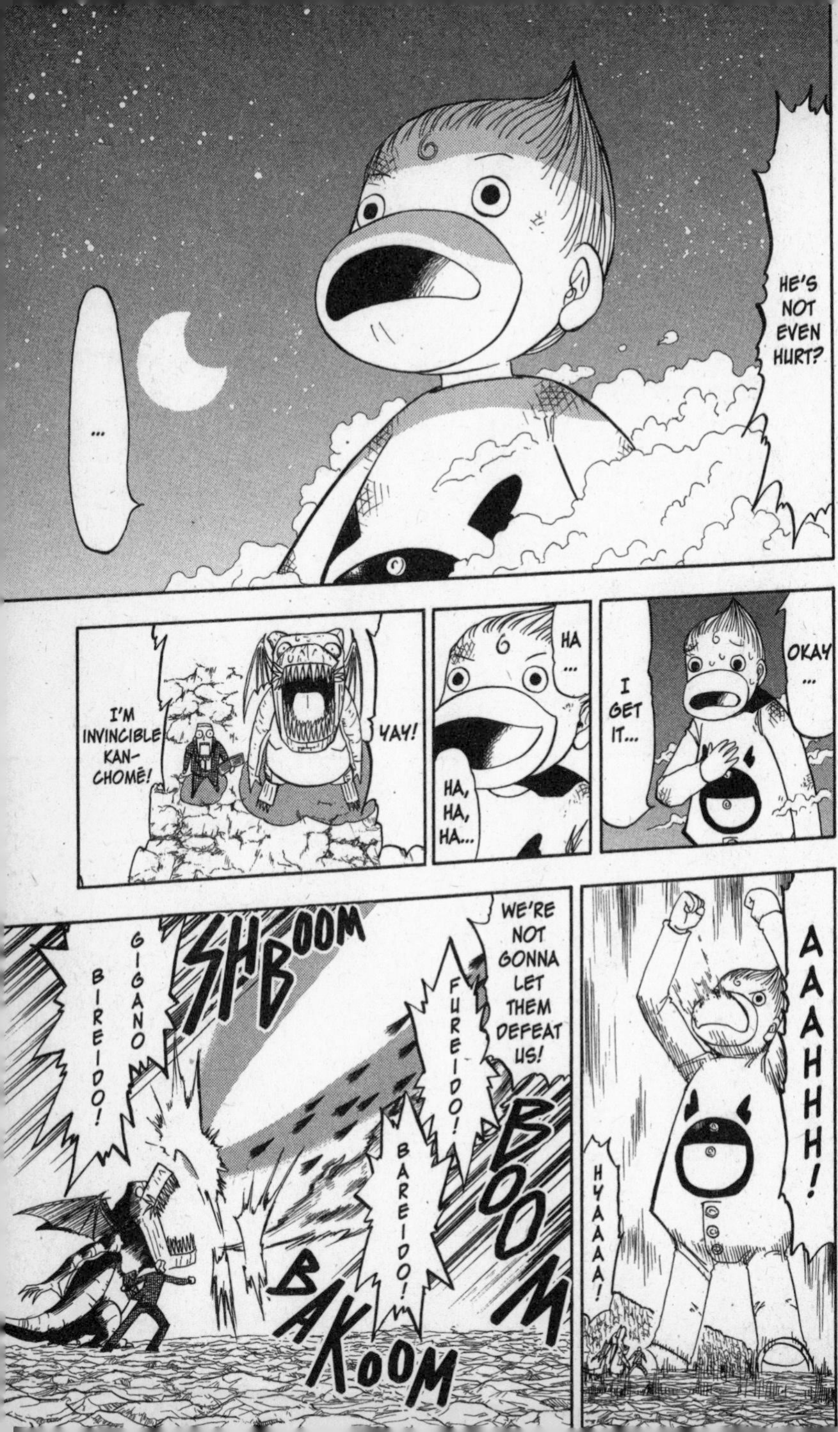
HE'S NOT EVEN HURT?
...
OKAY ...
I GET IT...
HA ...
HA, HA, HA...
YAY!
I'M INVINCIBLE KANCHOMÉ!
AAAHHHH!
HYAAAAA!
WE'RE NOT GONNA LET THEM DEFEAT US!
SHBOOM
GIGANO BIREIDO!
FUREIDO!
BOOM
BAREIDO!
BAKOOM

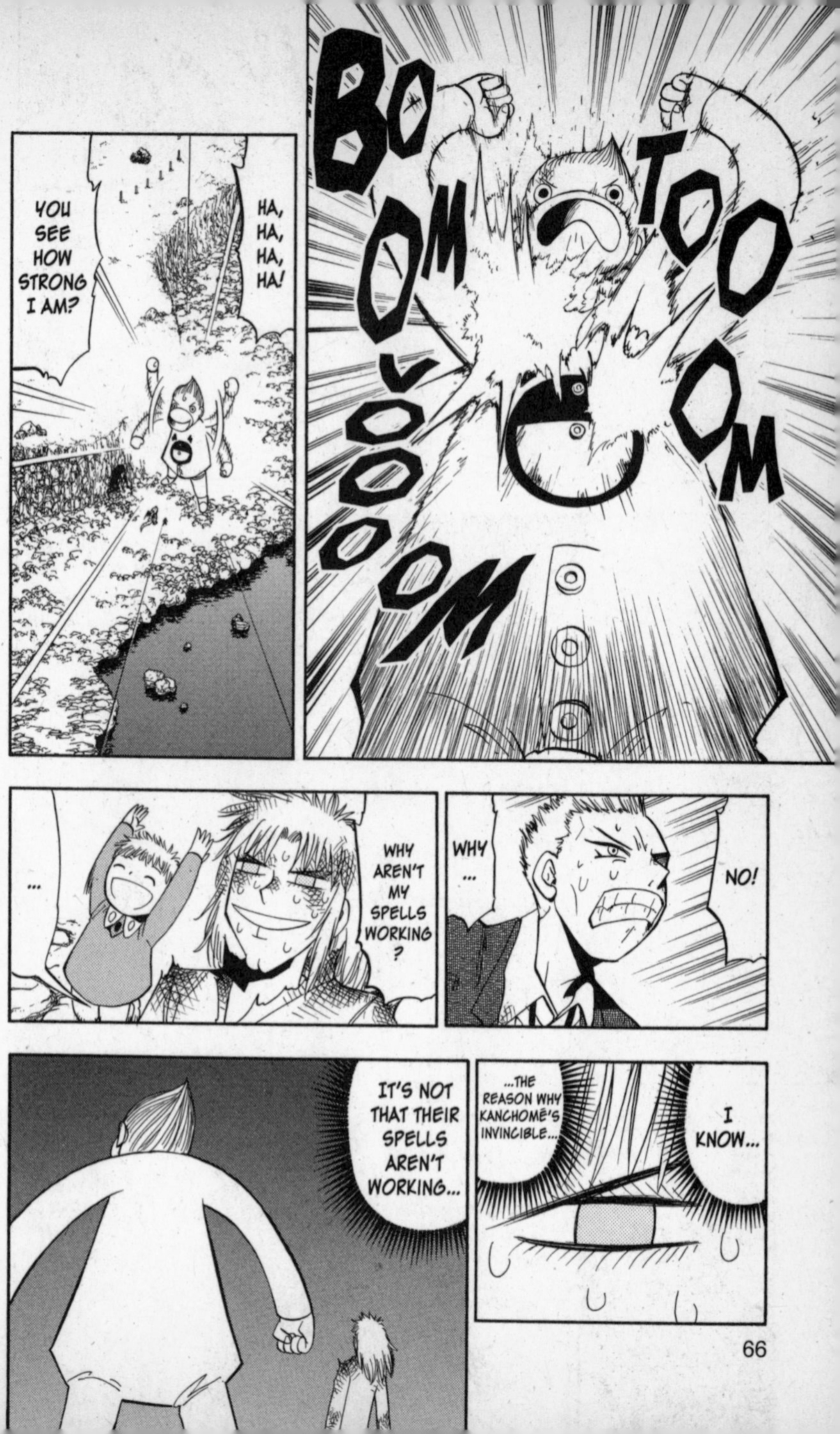
BOOM
TOOOOM
HA, HA, HA, HA!
YOU SEE HOW STRONG I AM?
NO!
WHY ...
WHY AREN'T MY SPELLS WORKING ?
...
I KNOW...
...THE REASON WHY KANCHOMÉ'S INVINCIBLE...
IT'S NOT THAT THEIR SPELLS AREN'T WORKING...

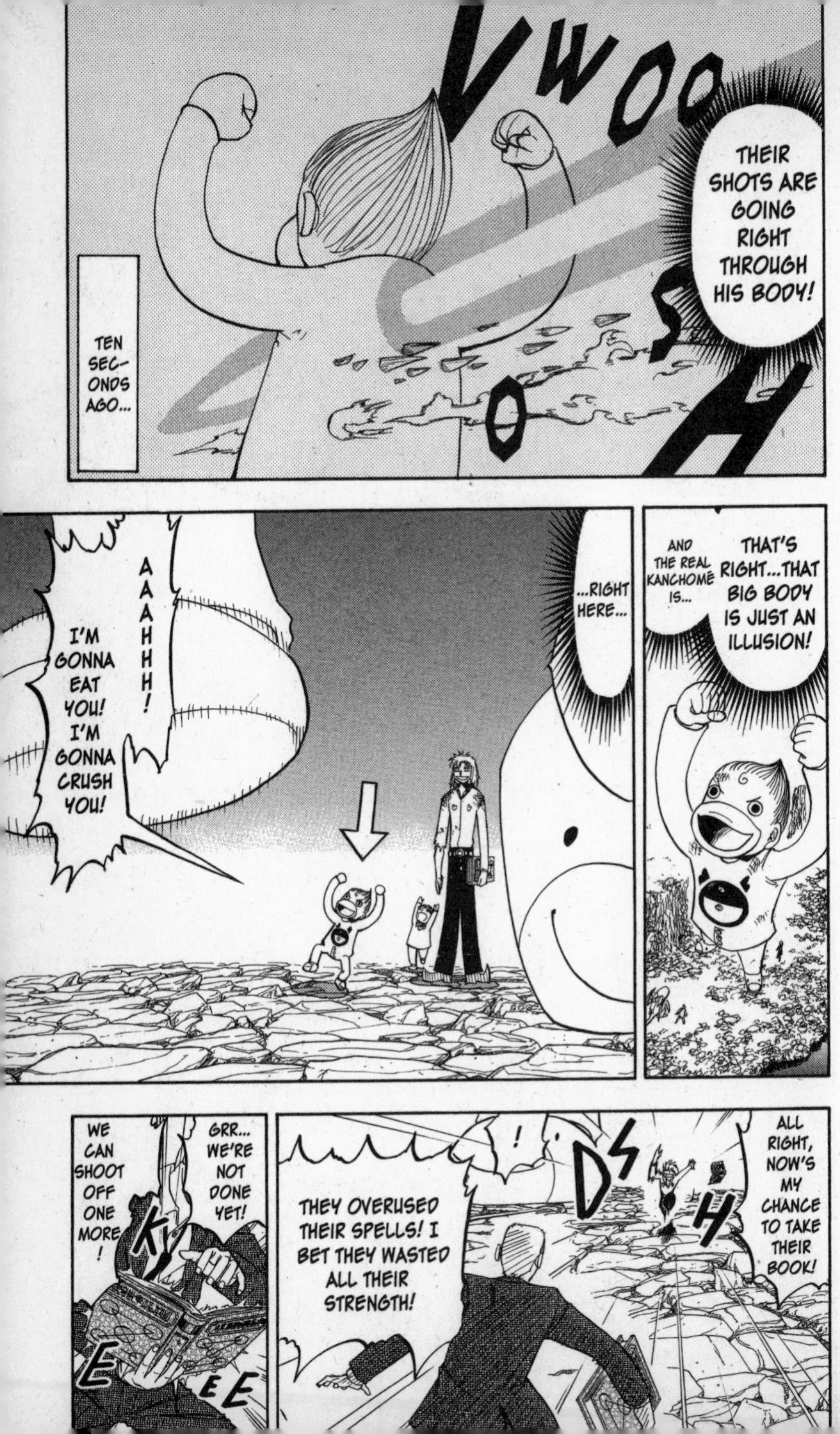
VWOOOSH
THEIR SHOTS ARE GOING RIGHT THROUGH HIS BODY!
TEN SEC-ONDS AGO...
THAT'S RIGHT...THAT BIG BODY IS JUST AN ILLUSION!
AND THE REAL KANCHOMÉ IS...
...RIGHT HERE...
AAAAHHH!
I'M GONNA EAT YOU! I'M GONNA CRUSH YOU!
ALL RIGHT, NOW'S MY CHANCE TO TAKE THEIR BOOK!
DSH
!
THEY OVERUSED THEIR SPELLS! I BET THEY WASTED ALL THEIR STRENGTH!
GRR... WE'RE NOT DONE YET!
WE CAN SHOOT OFF ONE MORE!
KEEE

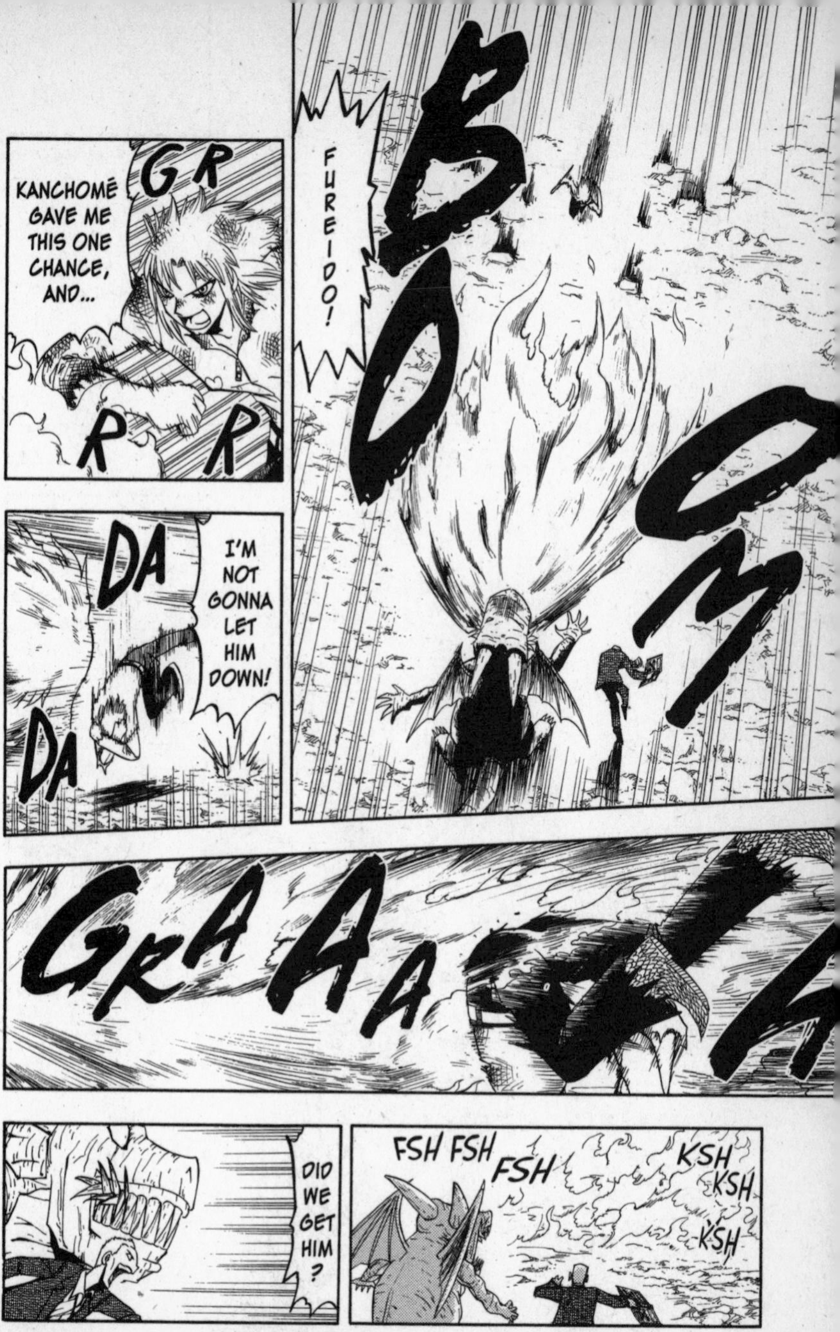
BOOM
FUREIDO!
GRRR
KANCHOMÉ GAVE ME THIS ONE CHANCE, AND...
DA DA
I'M NOT GONNA LET HIM DOWN!
GRAAAA
FSH FSH FSH
KSH KSH KSH
DID WE GET HIM?

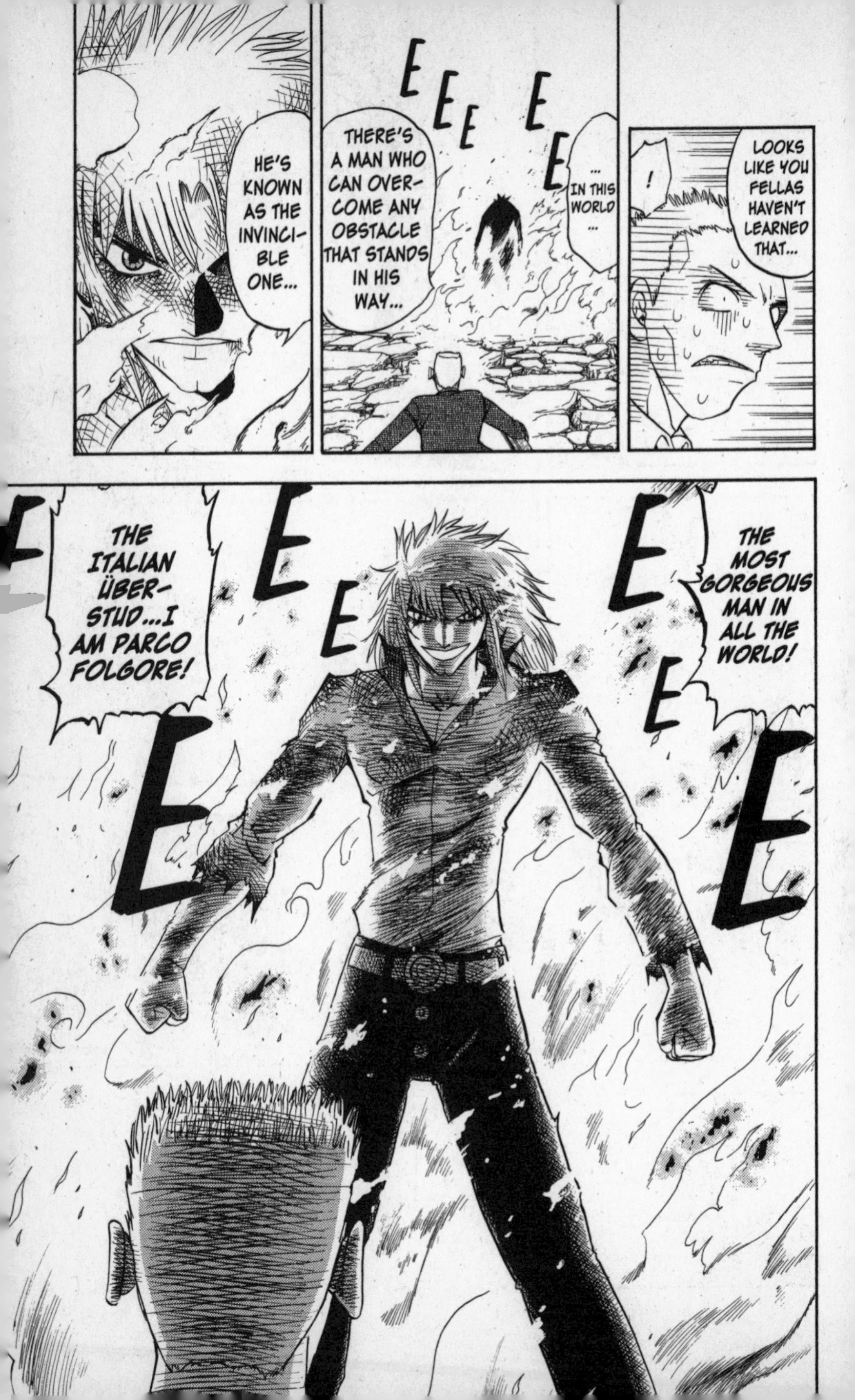
!
LOOKS LIKE YOU FELLAS HAVEN'T LEARNED THAT...
... IN THIS WORLD ...
EEEE
THERE'S A MAN WHO CAN OVER-COME ANY OBSTACLE THAT STANDS IN HIS WAY...
HE'S KNOWN AS THE INVINCI-BLE ONE...
THE MOST GORGEOUS MAN IN ALL THE WORLD!
EEEE
THE ITALIAN ÜBER-STUD...I AM PARCO FOLGORE!
EEE

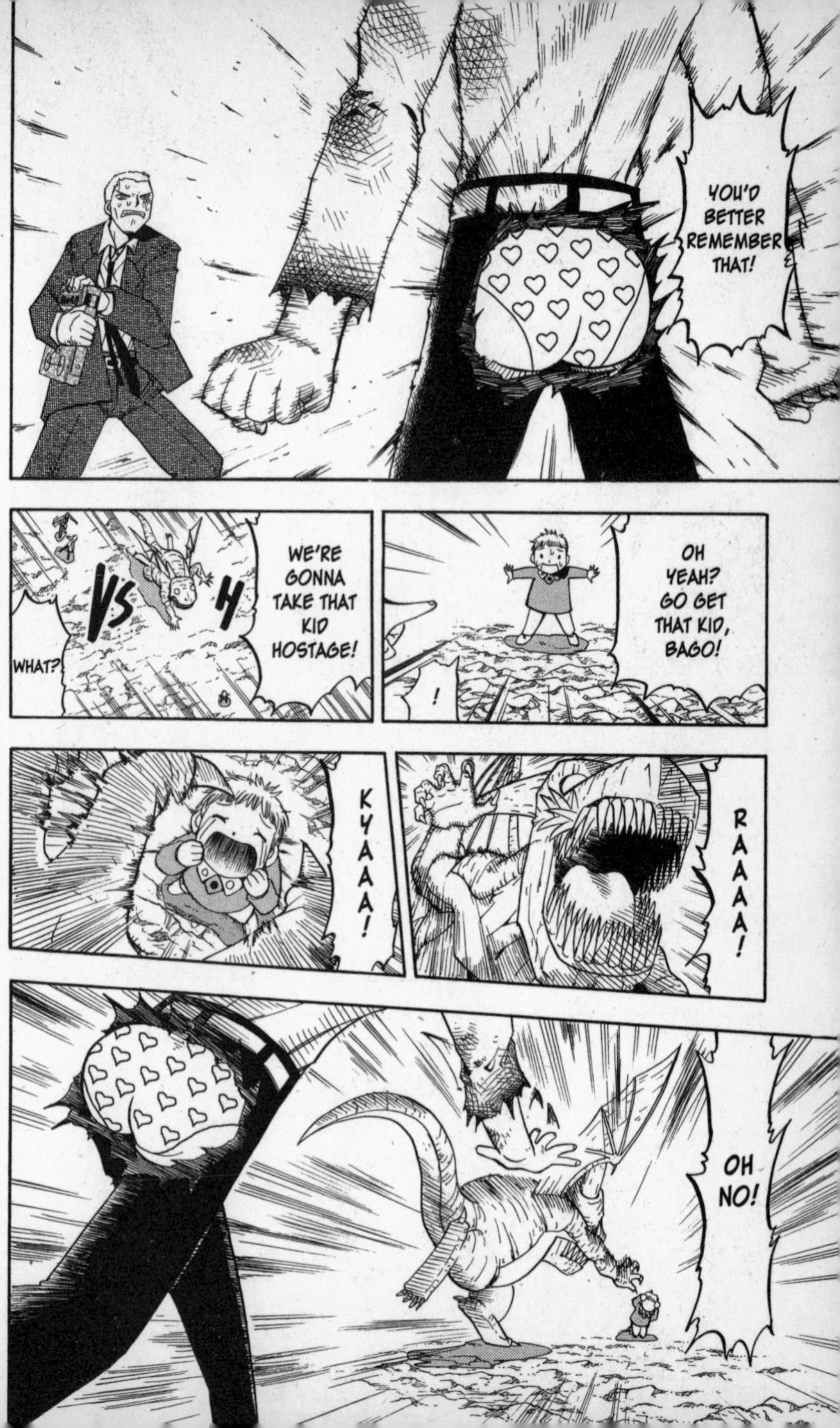
YOU'D BETTER REMEMBER THAT!
OH YEAH? GO GET THAT KID, BAGO!
!
WE'RE GONNA TAKE THAT KID HOSTAGE!
WHAT?
RAAAAA!
KYAAAA!
OH NO!

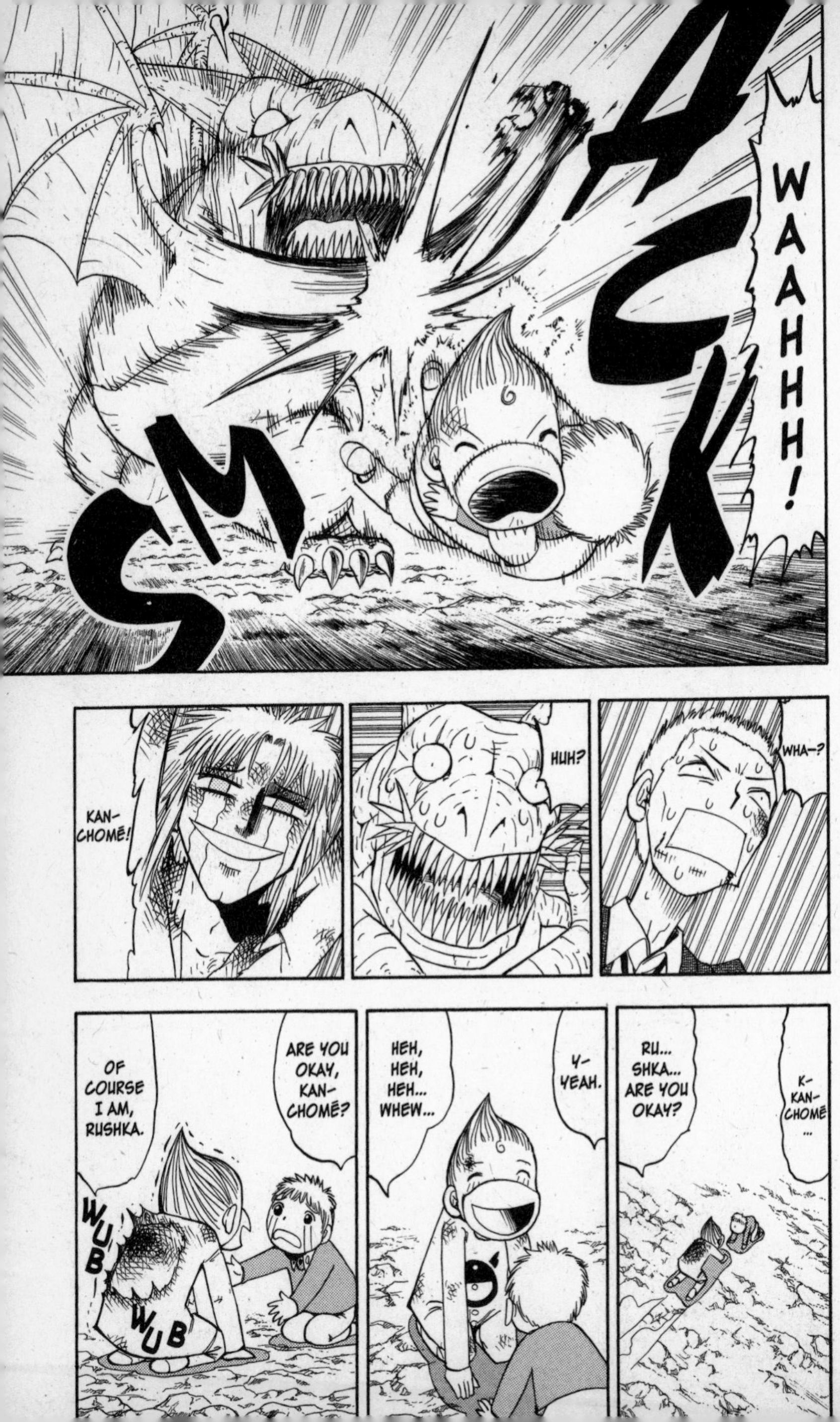
WAAHHH!
SMACK
WHA-?
HUH?
KAN-CHOMÉ!
K-KAN-CHOMÉ...
RU... SHKA... ARE YOU OKAY?
Y-YEAH.
HEH, HEH, HEH... WHEW...
ARE YOU OKAY, KAN-CHOMÉ?
OF COURSE I AM, RUSHKA.
WUB
WUB

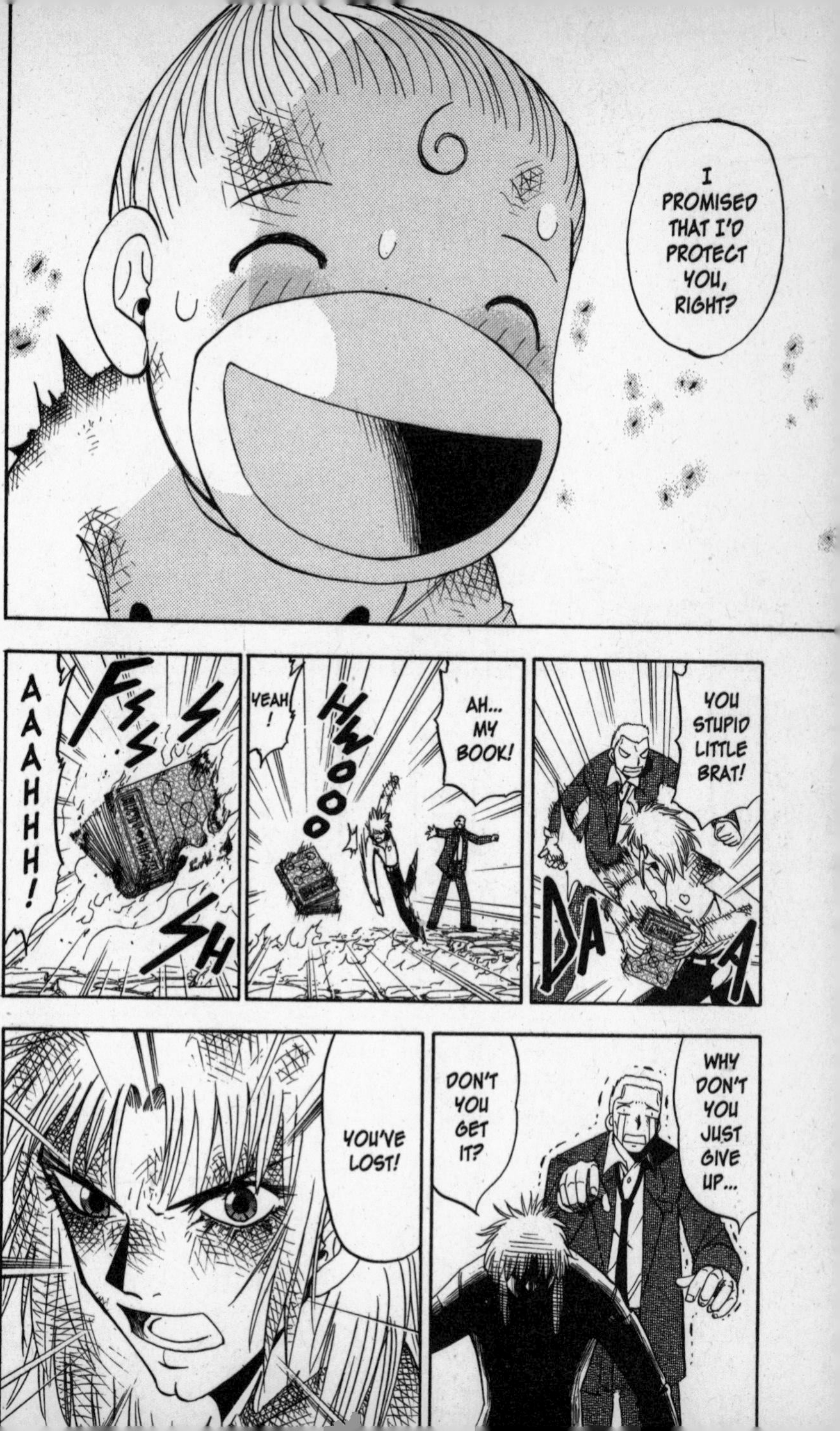
I PROMISED THAT I'D PROTECT YOU, RIGHT?
YOU STUPID LITTLE BRAT!
DAA
AH... MY BOOK!
HWOOOO
YEAH!
FSSSH
AAAAHHHH!
WHY DON'T YOU JUST GIVE UP...
DON'T YOU GET IT?
YOU'VE LOST!

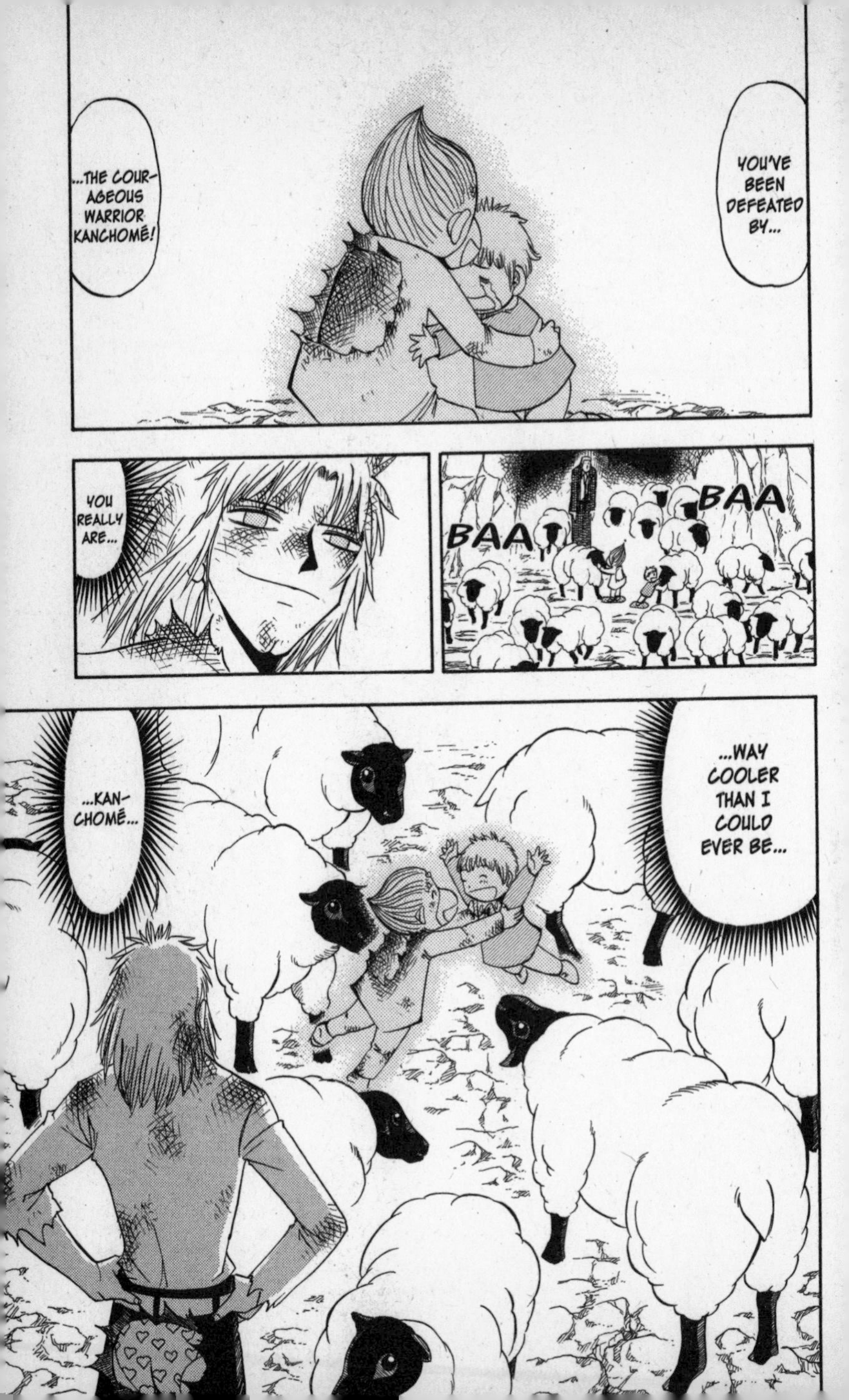
YOU'VE BEEN DEFEATED BY...
...THE COURAGEOUS WARRIOR KANCHOMÉ!
BAA
BAA
YOU REALLY ARE...
...WAY COOLER THAN I COULD EVER BE...
...KANCHOMÉ...

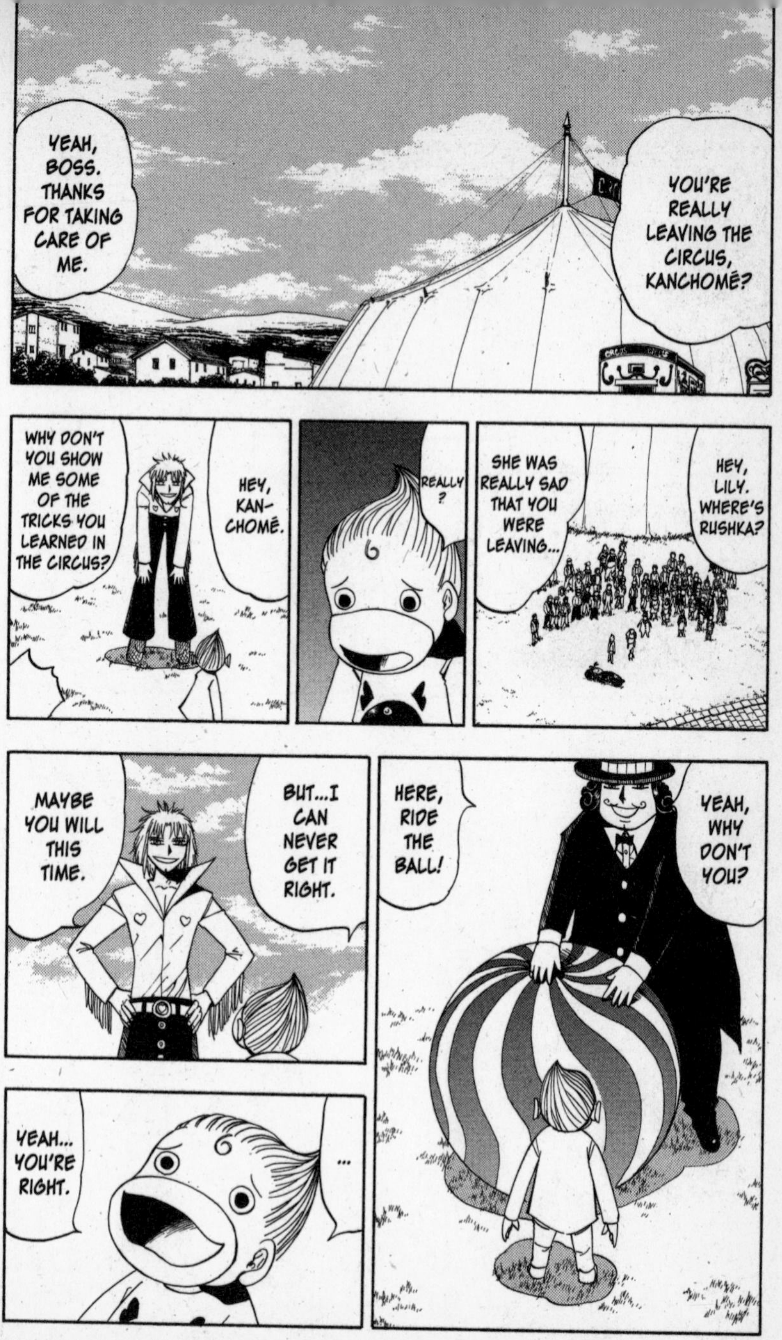
YOU'RE REALLY LEAVING THE CIRCUS, KANCHOMÉ?
YEAH, BOSS. THANKS FOR TAKING CARE OF ME.
HEY, LILY. WHERE'S RUSHKA?
SHE WAS REALLY SAD THAT YOU WERE LEAVING...
REALLY?
HEY, KAN-CHOMÉ.
WHY DON'T YOU SHOW ME SOME OF THE TRICKS YOU LEARNED IN THE CIRCUS?
YEAH, WHY DON'T YOU?
HERE, RIDE THE BALL!
BUT...I CAN NEVER GET IT RIGHT.
MAYBE YOU WILL THIS TIME.
...
YEAH... YOU'RE RIGHT.

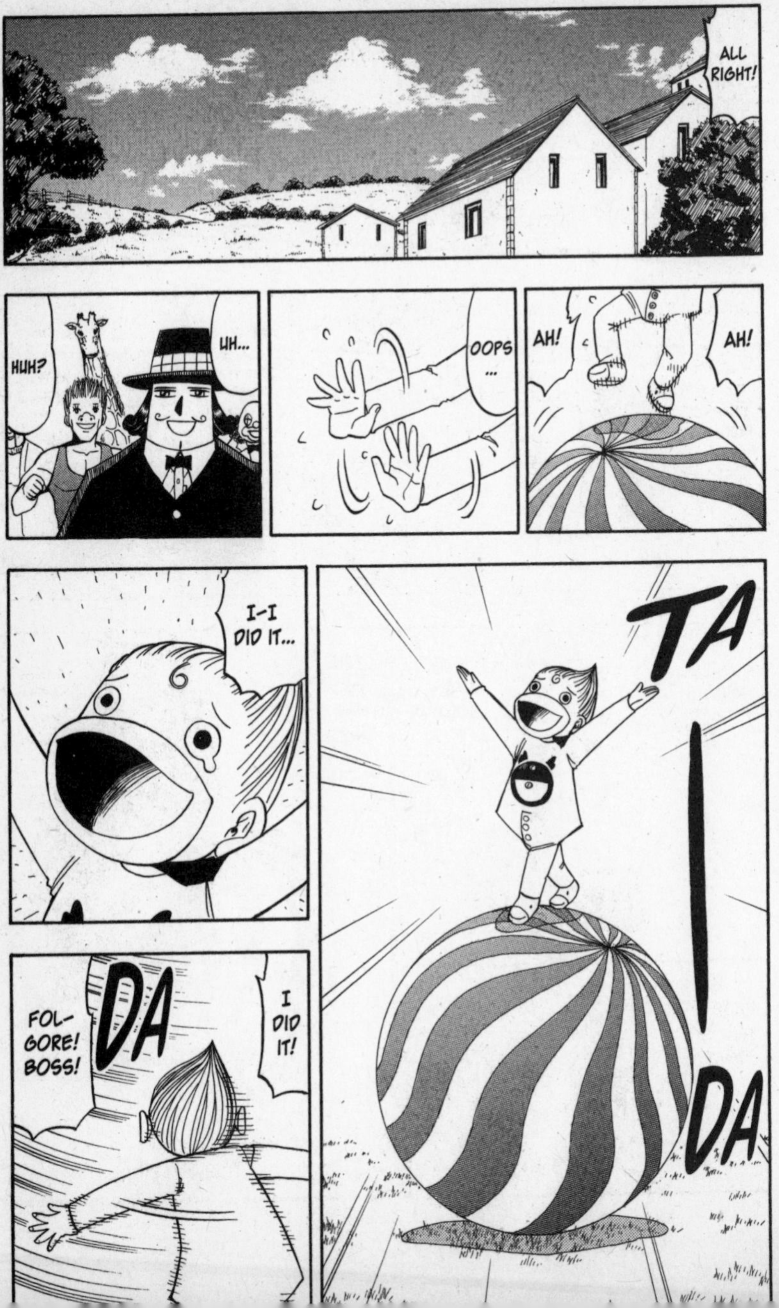

ALL RIGHT!
AH!
AH!
OOPS ...
UH...
HUH?
TA—DA
I-I DID IT...
I DID IT!
DA
FOL-GORE! BOSS!

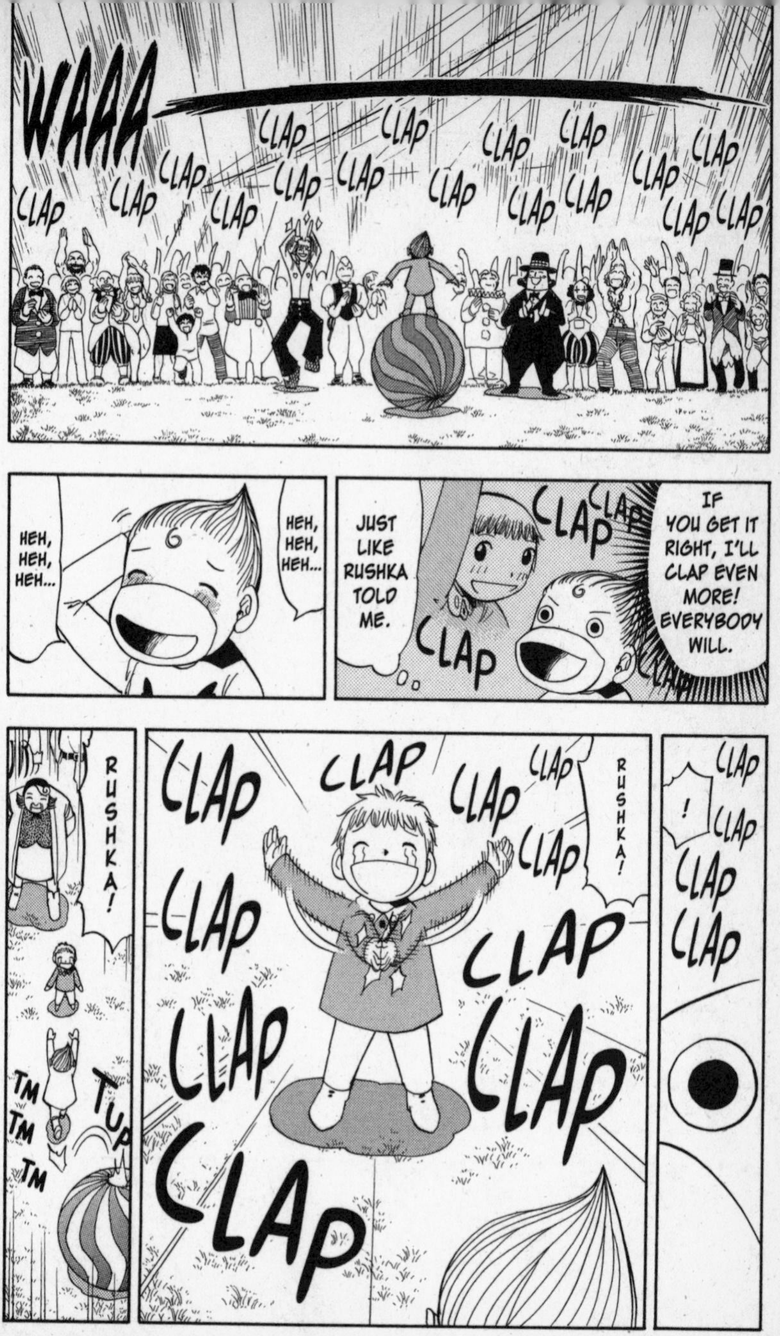
WAAA
CLAP CLAP CLAP CLAP CLAP CLAP CLAP CLAP CLAP CLAP CLAP CLAP CLAP CLAP CLAP CLAP CLAP
IF YOU GET IT RIGHT, I'LL CLAP EVEN MORE! EVERYBODY WILL.
CLAP CLAP
JUST LIKE RUSHKA TOLD ME.
CLAP
HEH, HEH, HEH...
HEH, HEH, HEH...
!
CLAP CLAP CLAP CLAP
RUSHKA!
CLAP CLAP CLAP CLAP CLAP CLAP CLAP CLAP CLAP CLAP
RUSHKA!
TUP
TM TM TM

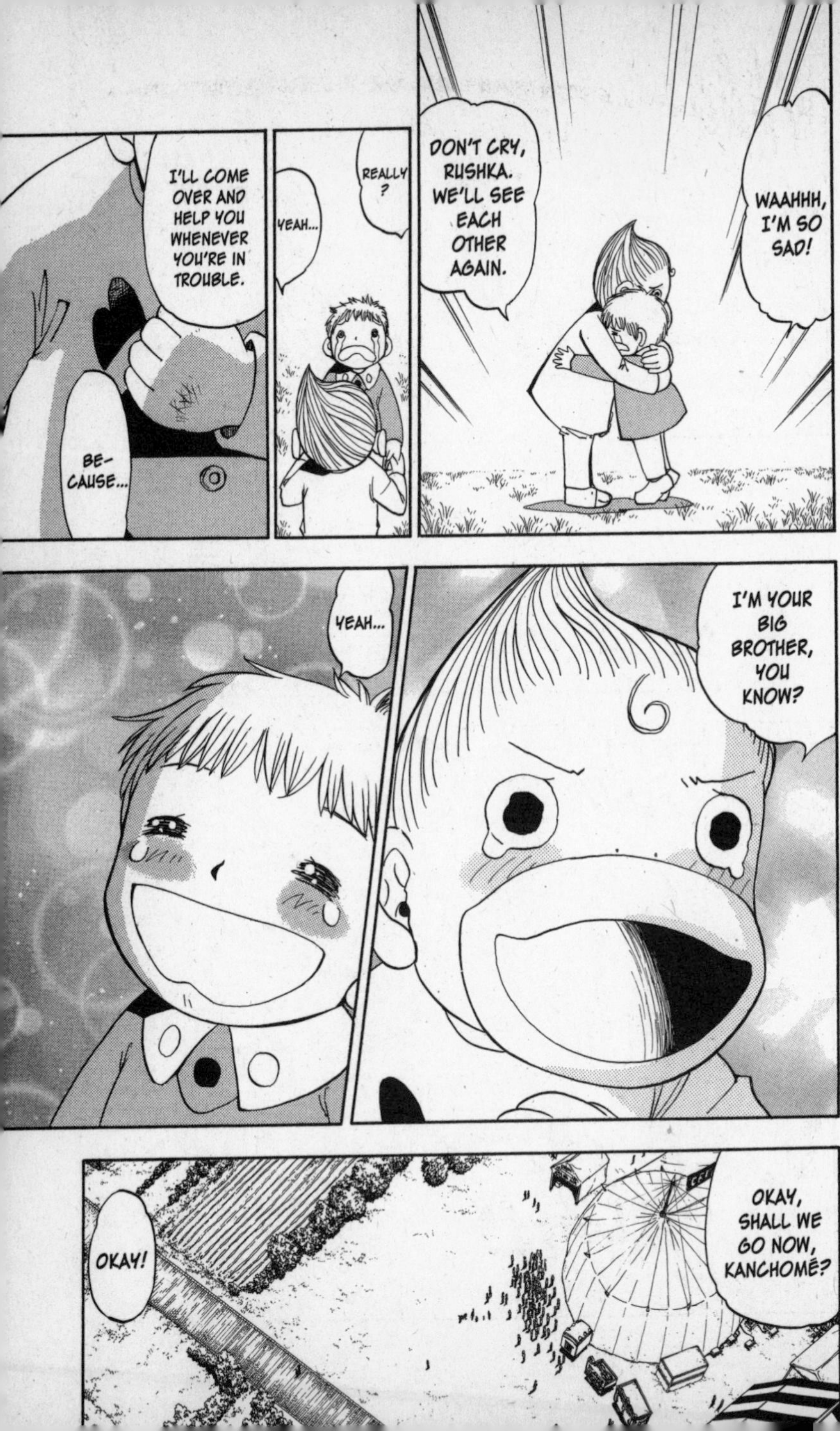
WAAHHH, I'M SO SAD!
DON'T CRY, RUSHKA. WE'LL SEE EACH OTHER AGAIN.
REALLY?
YEAH...
I'LL COME OVER AND HELP YOU WHENEVER YOU'RE IN TROUBLE.
BE-CAUSE...
I'M YOUR BIG BROTHER, YOU KNOW?
YEAH...
OKAY, SHALL WE GO NOW, KANCHOMÉ?
OKAY!

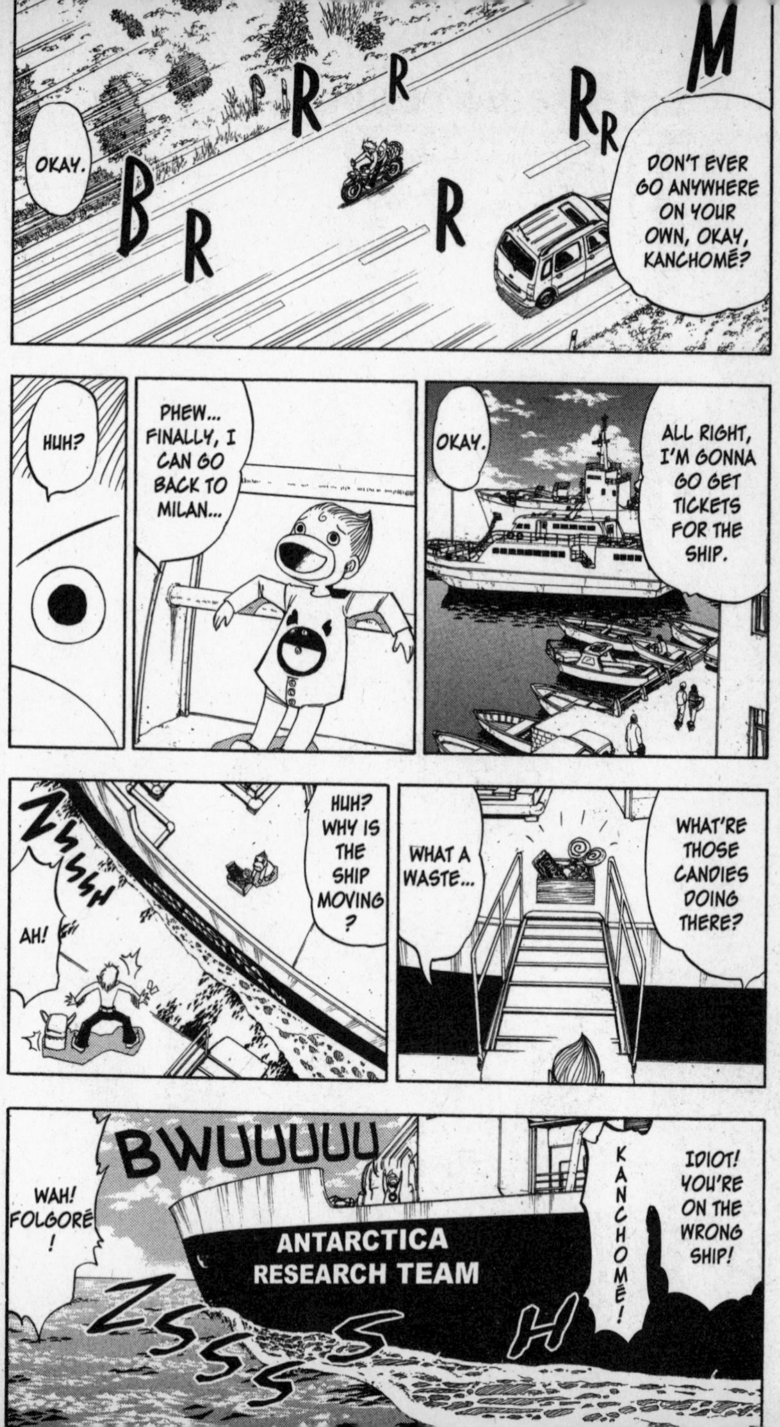
DON'T EVER GO ANYWHERE ON YOUR OWN, OKAY, KANCHOMÉ?
BRRRRRRRM
OKAY.
ALL RIGHT, I'M GONNA GO GET TICKETS FOR THE SHIP.
OKAY.
PHEW... FINALLY, I CAN GO BACK TO MILAN...
HUH?
WHAT'RE THOSE CANDIES DOING THERE?
WHAT A WASTE...
HUH? WHY IS THE SHIP MOVING?
ZSSSHH
AH!
IDIOT! YOU'RE ON THE WRONG SHIP!
KANCHOMÉ!
BWUUUUUU
ANTARCTICA RESEARCH TEAM
WAH! FOLGORÉ!
ZSSSSH

# LEVEL 89: Facing Forward

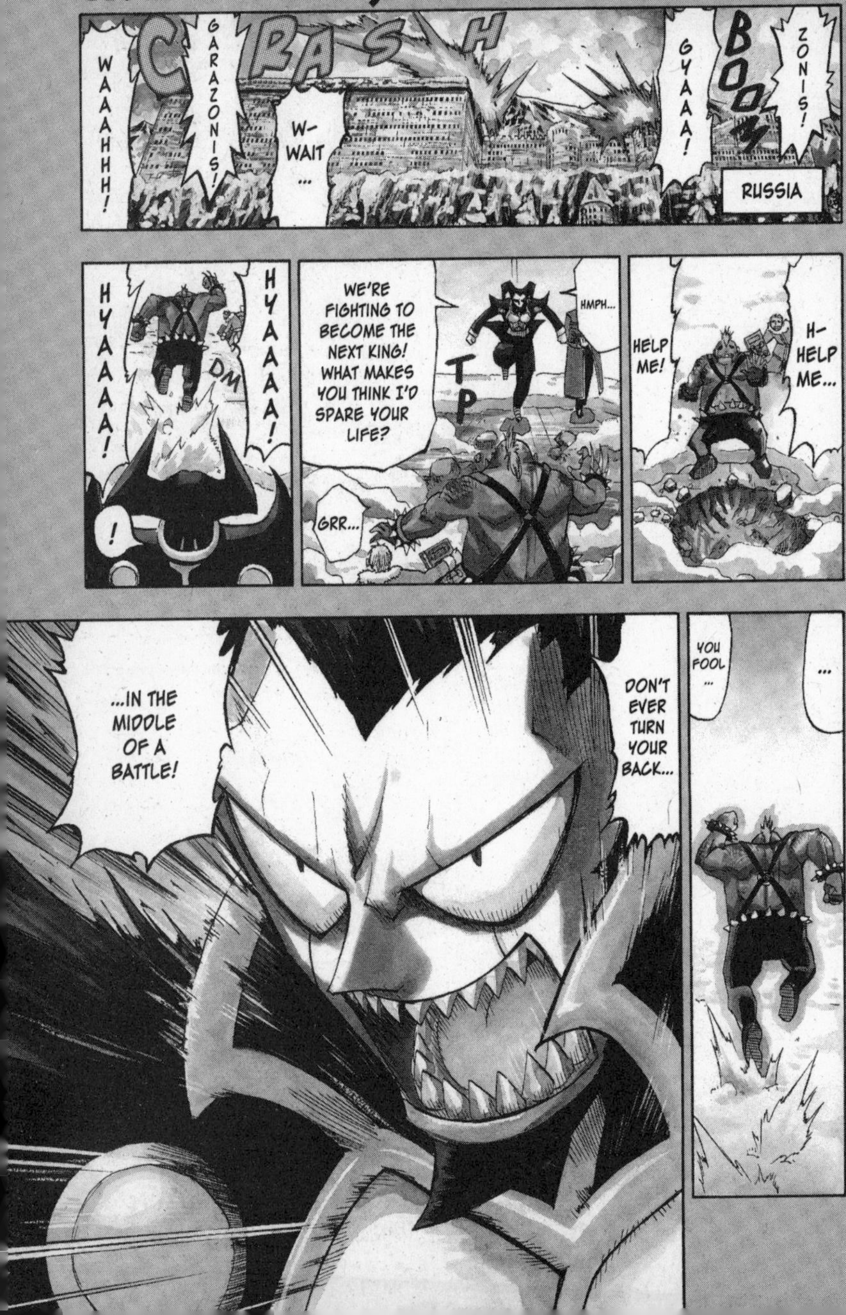

ZONIS!
BOOM
GYAAA!
RUSSIA
W-WAIT...
GARAZONIS!
CRASH
WAAAAHHH!
H-HELP ME...
HELP ME!
HMPH...
WE'RE FIGHTING TO BECOME THE NEXT KING! WHAT MAKES YOU THINK I'D SPARE YOUR LIFE?
TP
GRR...
HYAAAAA!
DM
HYAAAAA!
!
...
YOU FOOL...
DON'T EVER TURN YOUR BACK...
...IN THE MIDDLE OF A BATTLE!

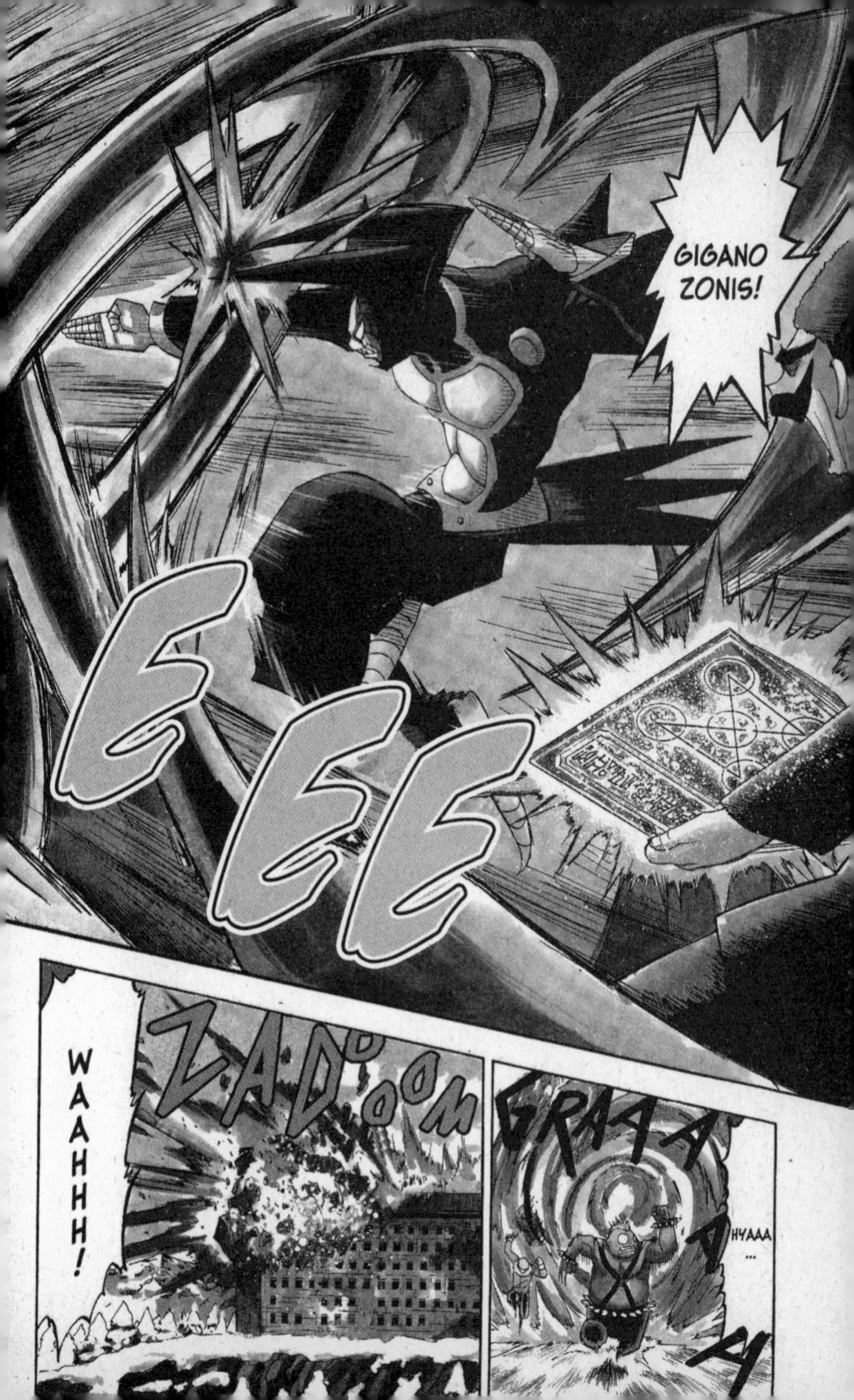
GIGANO ZONIS!
EEE
ZADOOOM
GRAAAAAA
HYAAA...
WAAHHHH!

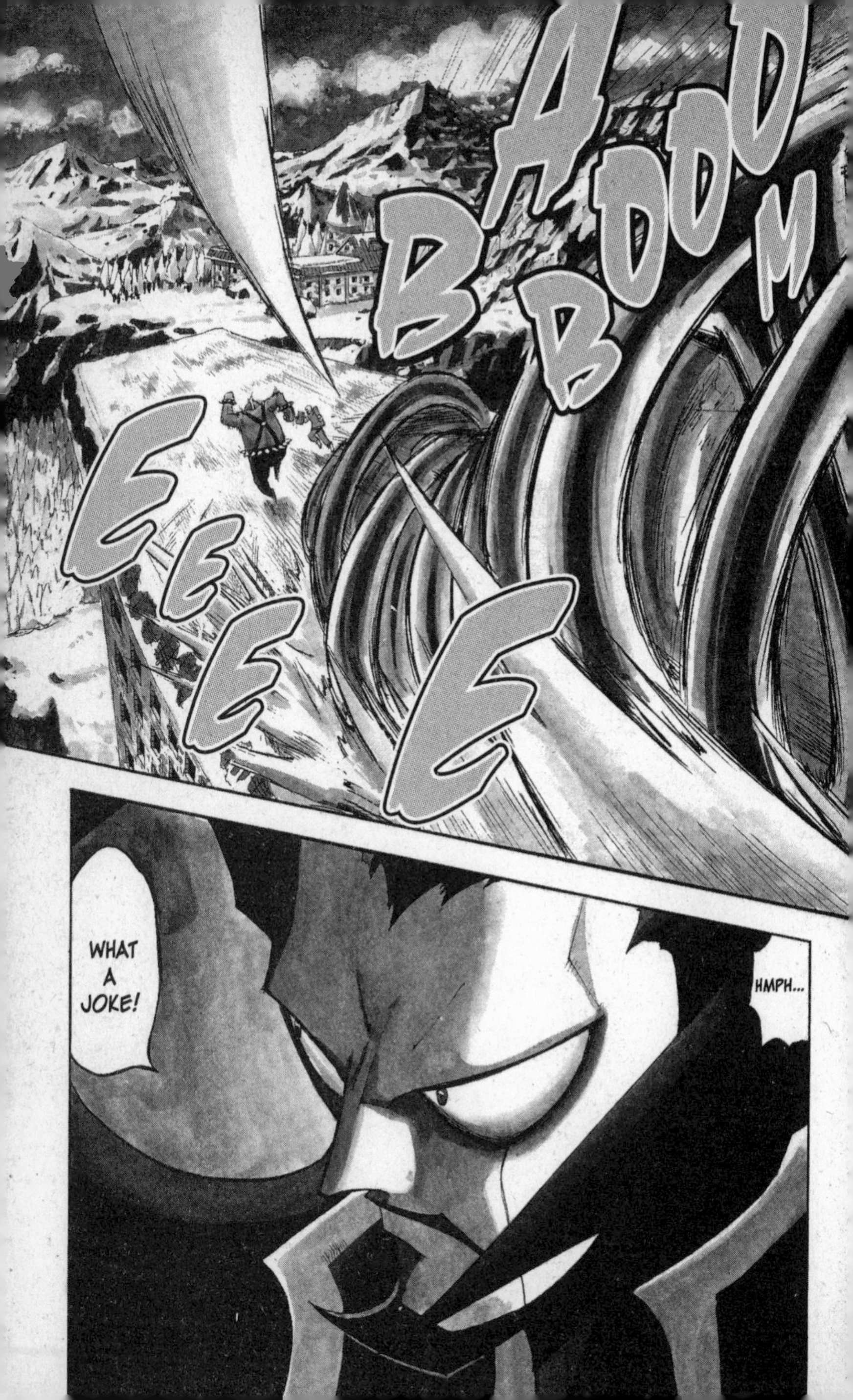
EEEE
HMPH...
WHAT A JOKE!

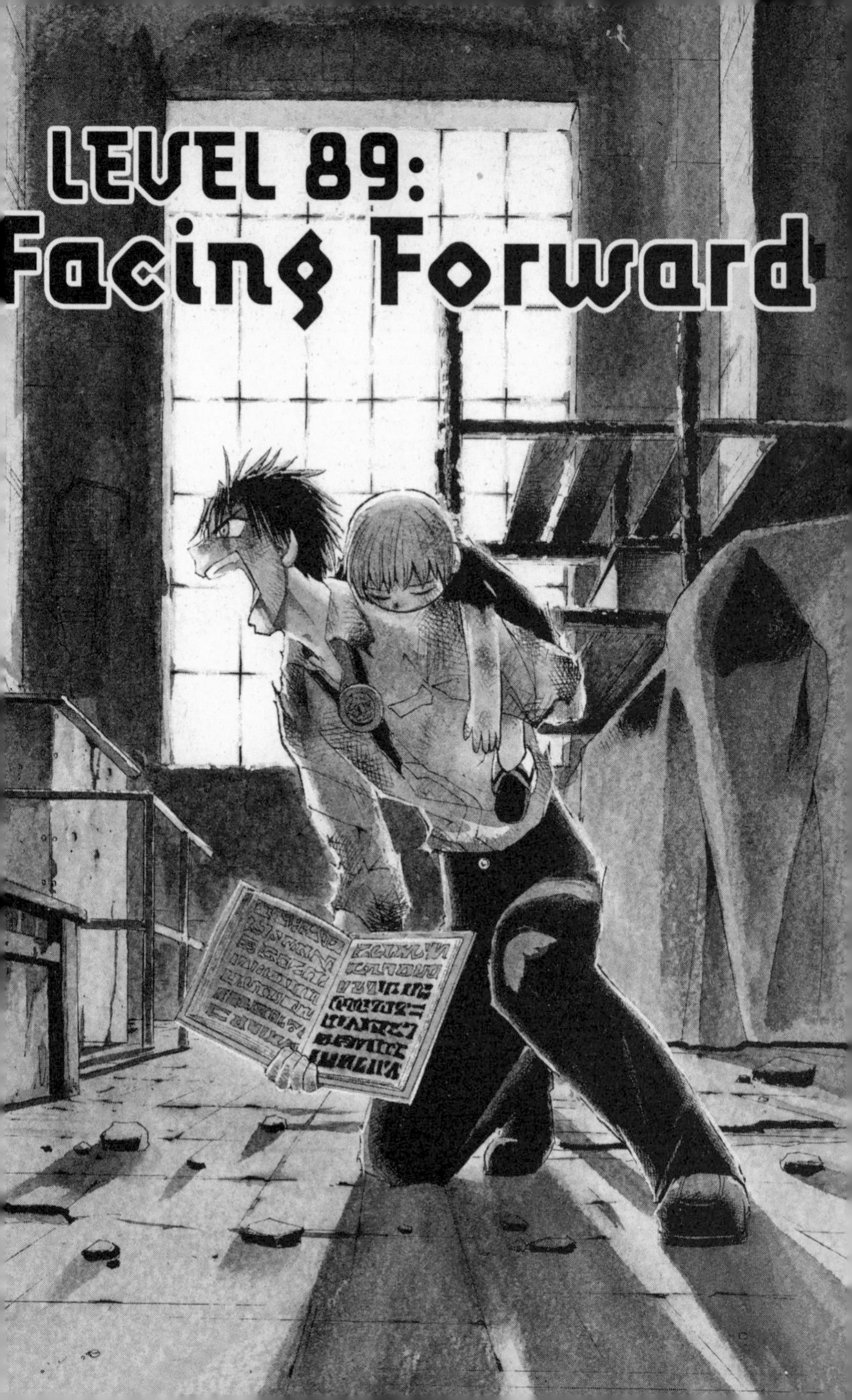
LEVEL 89:
Facing Forward

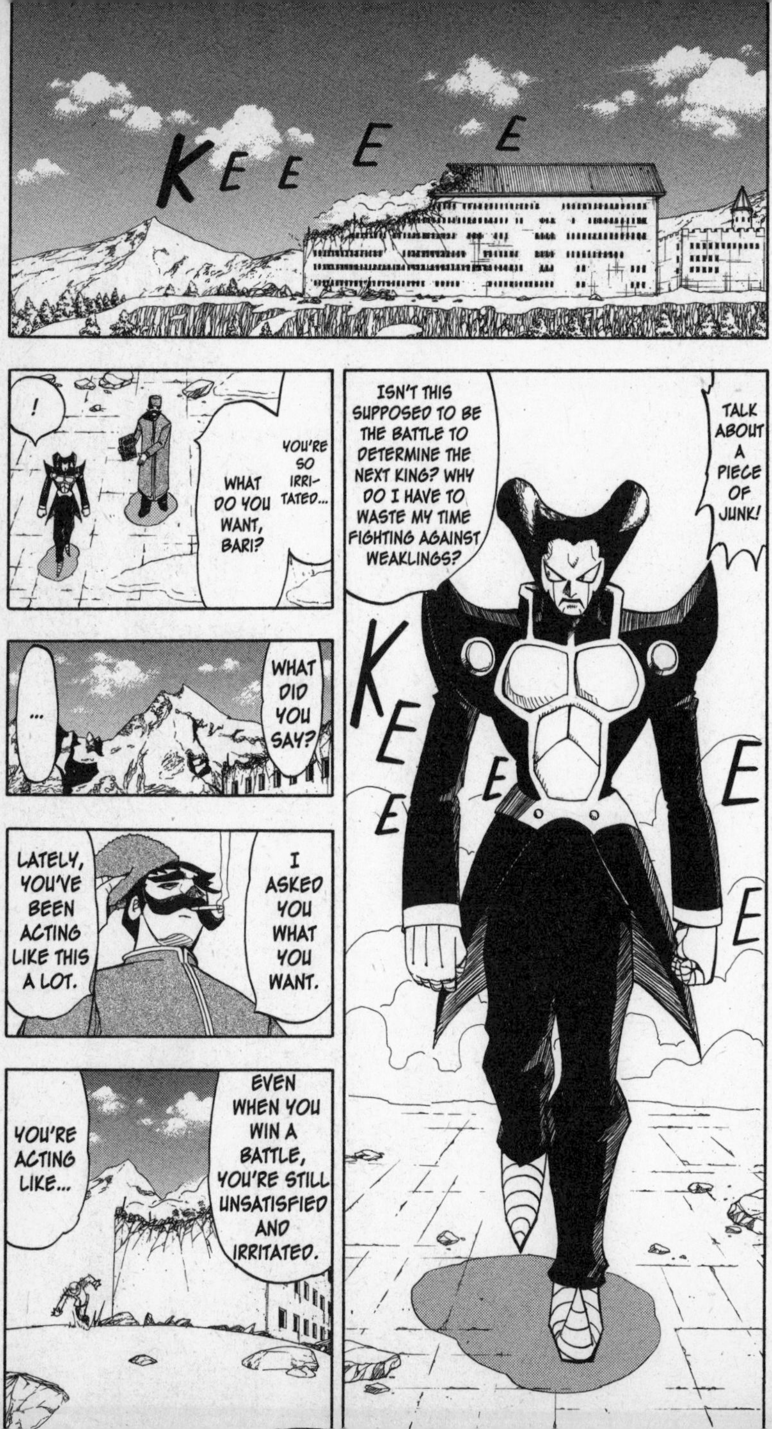
KEEEE
TALK ABOUT A PIECE OF JUNK!
ISN'T THIS SUPPOSED TO BE THE BATTLE TO DETERMINE THE NEXT KING? WHY DO I HAVE TO WASTE MY TIME FIGHTING AGAINST WEAKLINGS?
KEEEEE
YOU'RE SO IRRITATED...
WHAT DO YOU WANT, BARI?
!
WHAT DID YOU SAY?
...
I ASKED YOU WHAT YOU WANT.
LATELY, YOU'VE BEEN ACTING LIKE THIS A LOT.
EVEN WHEN YOU WIN A BATTLE, YOU'RE STILL UNSATISFIED AND IRRITATED.
YOU'RE ACTING LIKE...

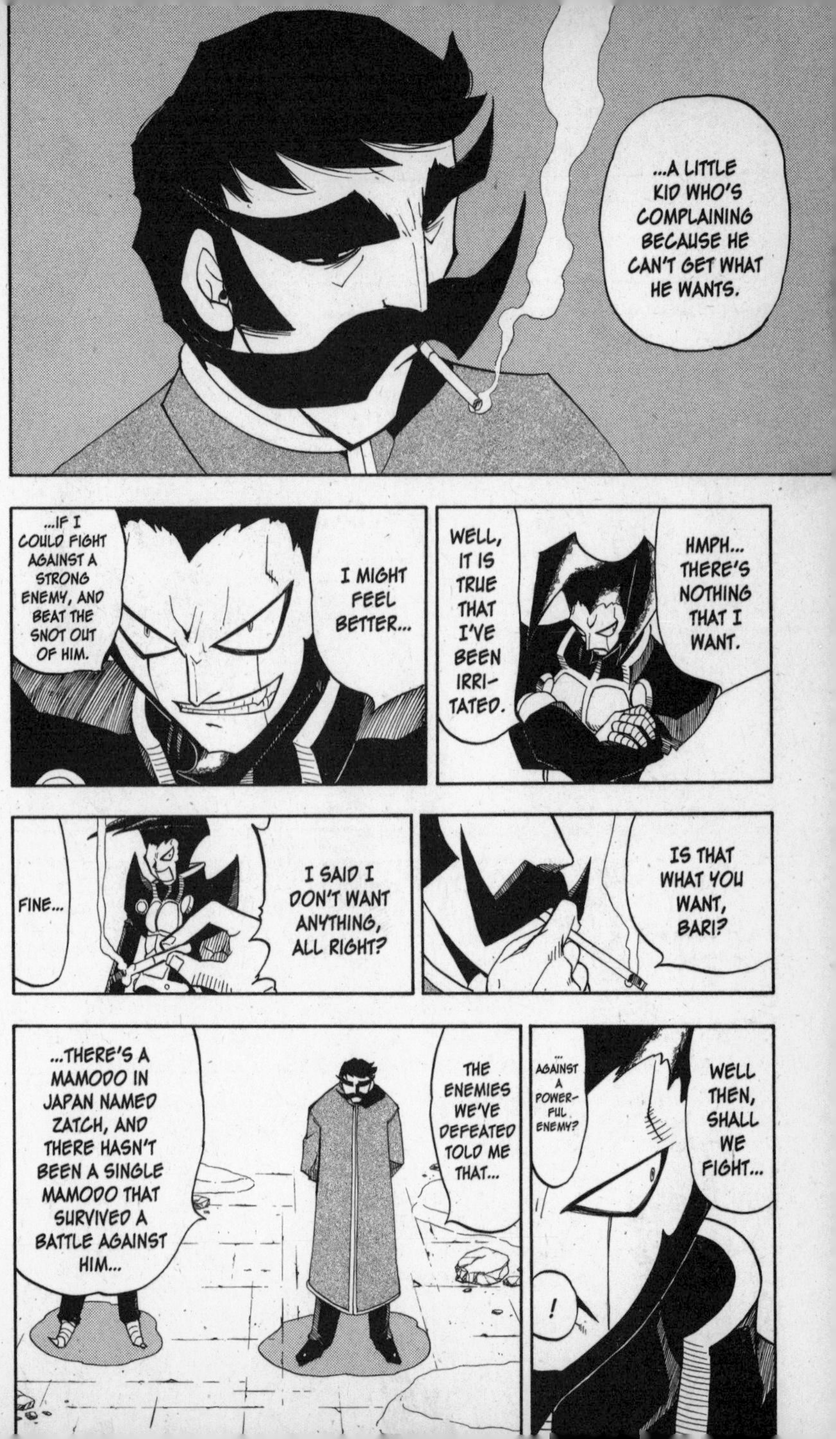
...A LITTLE KID WHO'S COMPLAINING BECAUSE HE CAN'T GET WHAT HE WANTS.
HMPH... THERE'S NOTHING THAT I WANT.
WELL, IT IS TRUE THAT I'VE BEEN IRRI-TATED.
I MIGHT FEEL BETTER...
...IF I COULD FIGHT AGAINST A STRONG ENEMY, AND BEAT THE SNOT OUT OF HIM.
IS THAT WHAT YOU WANT, BARI?
I SAID I DON'T WANT ANYTHING, ALL RIGHT?
FINE...
WELL THEN, SHALL WE FIGHT...
...AGAINST A POWER-FUL ENEMY?
!
THE ENEMIES WE'VE DEFEATED TOLD ME THAT...
...THERE'S A MAMODO IN JAPAN NAMED ZATCH, AND THERE HASN'T BEEN A SINGLE MAMODO THAT SURVIVED A BATTLE AGAINST HIM...

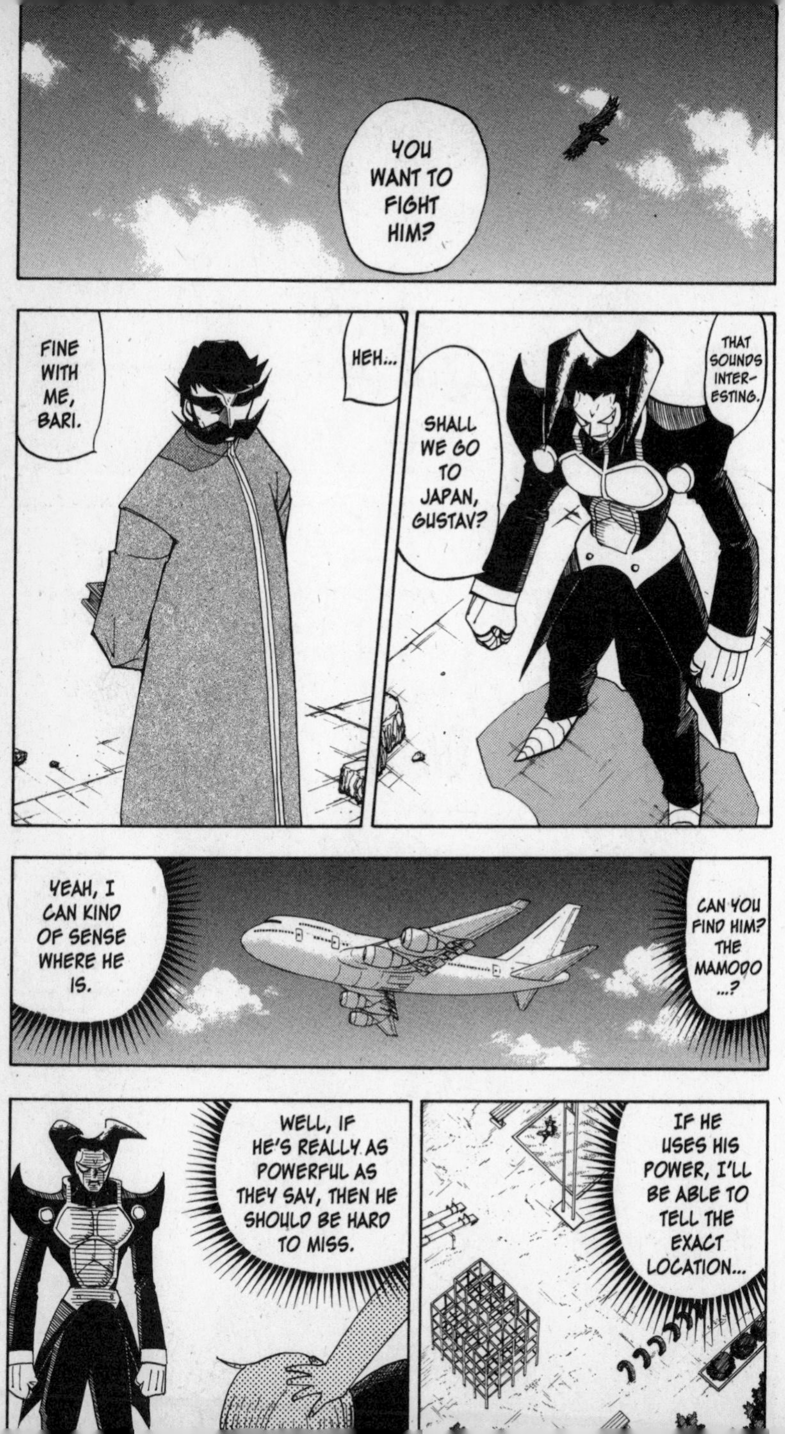
YOU WANT TO FIGHT HIM?
THAT SOUNDS INTER-ESTING.
SHALL WE GO TO JAPAN, GUSTAV?
HEH...
FINE WITH ME, BARI.
CAN YOU FIND HIM? THE MAMODO ...?
YEAH, I CAN KIND OF SENSE WHERE HE IS.
IF HE USES HIS POWER, I'LL BE ABLE TO TELL THE EXACT LOCATION...
WELL, IF HE'S REALLY AS POWERFUL AS THEY SAY, THEN HE SHOULD BE HARD TO MISS.

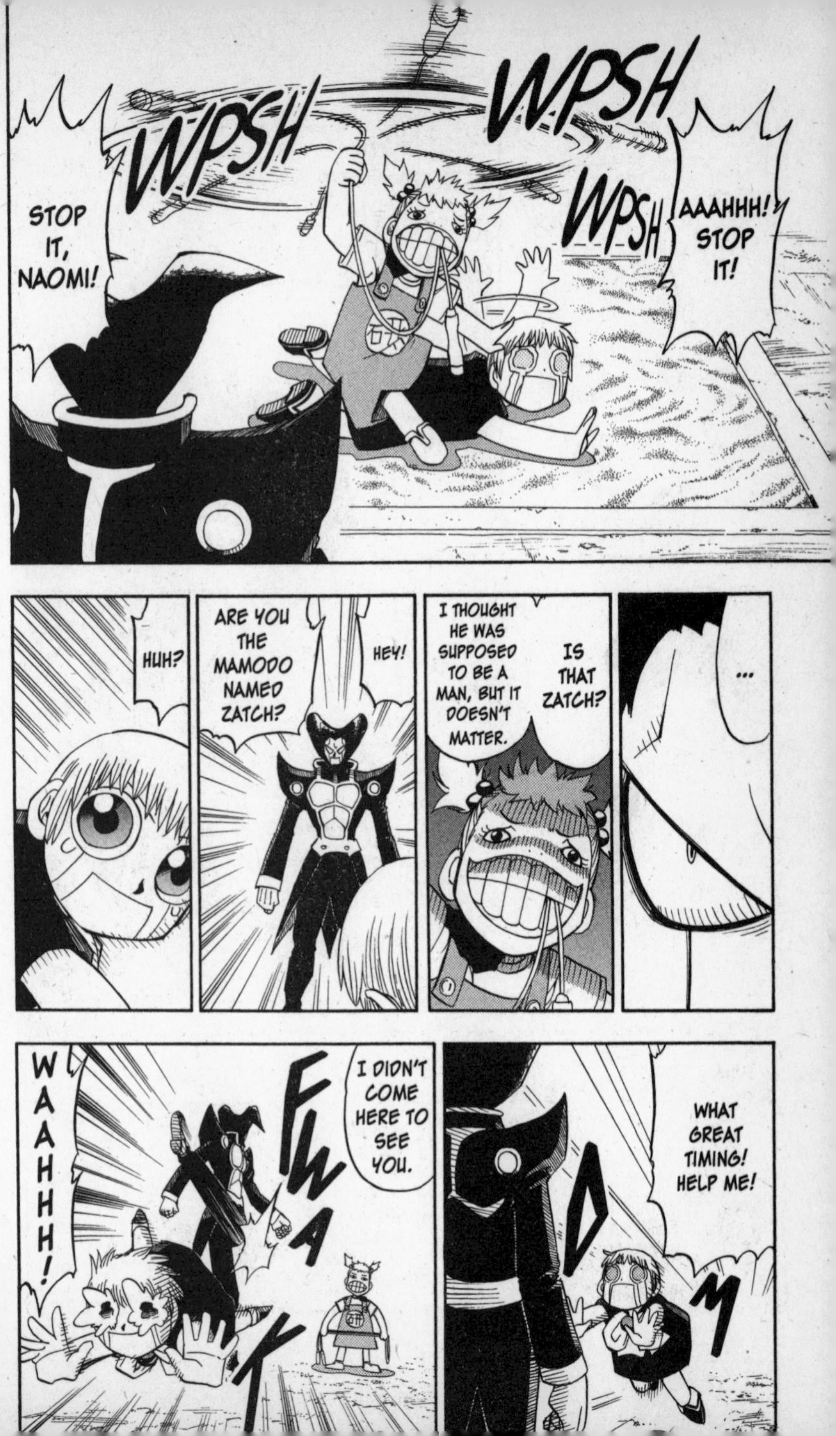
WPSH
AAAHHH! STOP IT!
WPSH
WPSH
STOP IT, NAOMI!
...
IS THAT ZATCH?
I THOUGHT HE WAS SUPPOSED TO BE A MAN, BUT IT DOESN'T MATTER.
HEY!
ARE YOU THE MAMODO NAMED ZATCH?
HUH?
WHAT GREAT TIMING! HELP ME!
DM
I DIDN'T COME HERE TO SEE YOU.
FWAK
WAAHHH!

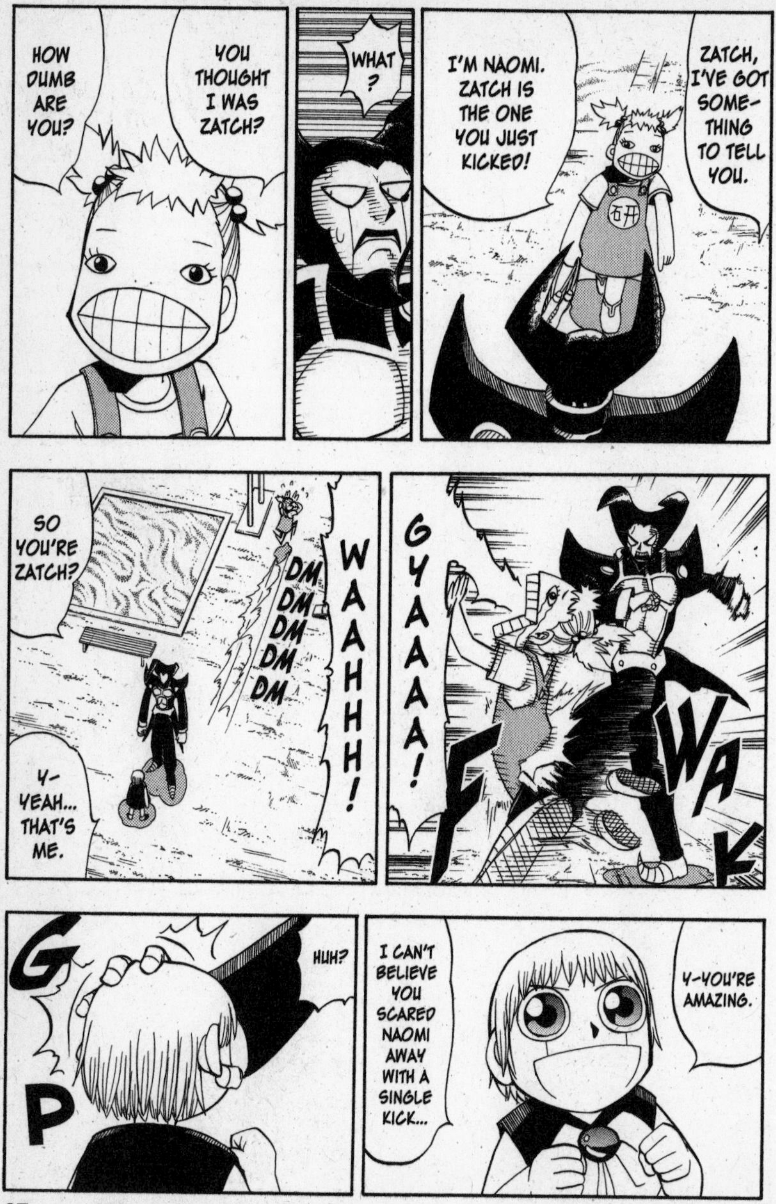
ZATCH, I'VE GOT SOME-THING TO TELL YOU.
I'M NAOMI. ZATCH IS THE ONE YOU JUST KICKED!
WHAT?
YOU THOUGHT I WAS ZATCH?
HOW DUMB ARE YOU?
GYAAAAA!
WAK
WAAAHHH!
DM DM DM DM DM
SO YOU'RE ZATCH?
Y-YEAH... THAT'S ME.
Y-YOU'RE AMAZING.
I CAN'T BELIEVE YOU SCARED NAOMI AWAY WITH A SINGLE KICK...
HUH?
GP

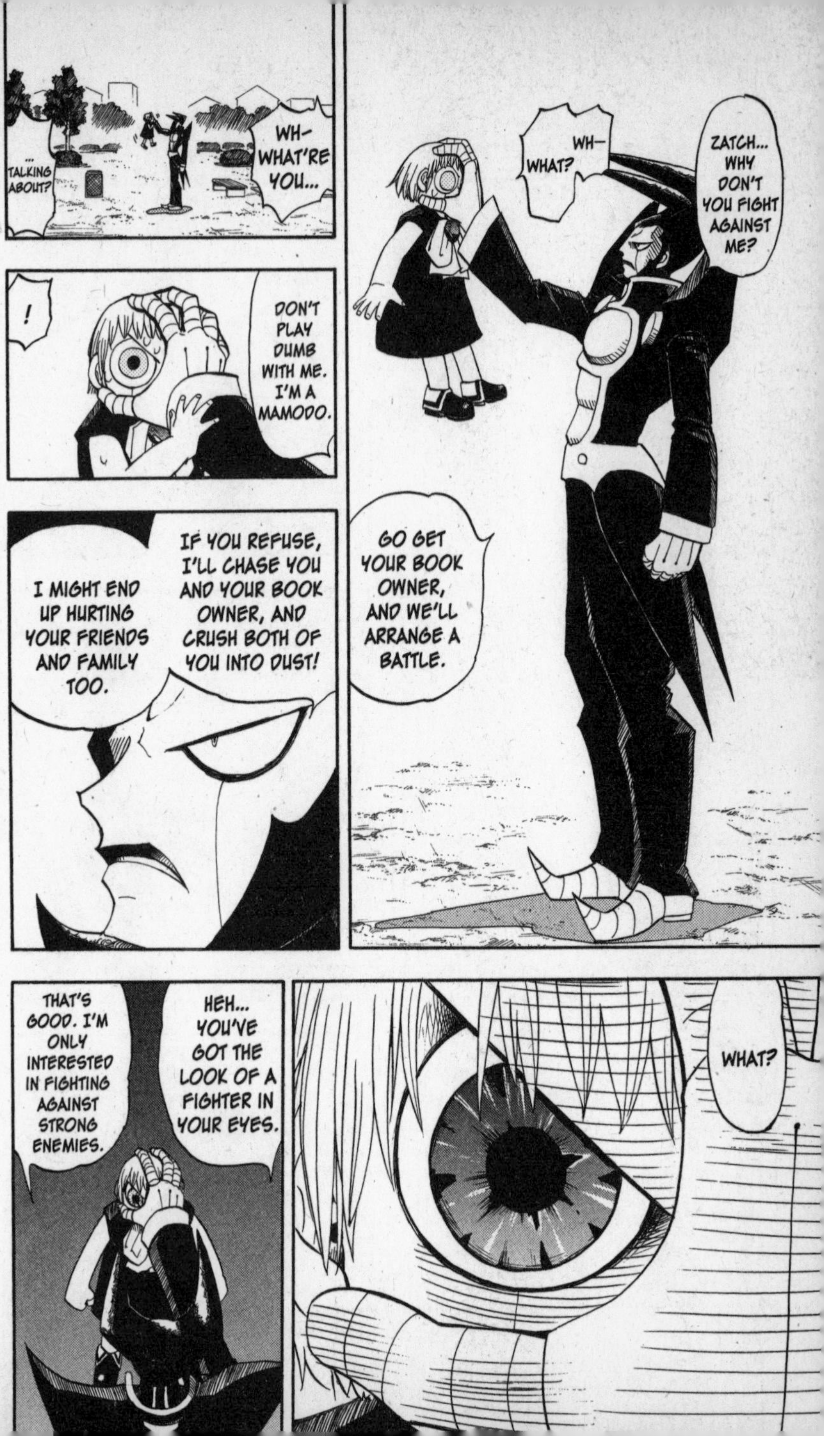
ZATCH... WHY DON'T YOU FIGHT AGAINST ME?
WH- WHAT?
GO GET YOUR BOOK OWNER, AND WE'LL ARRANGE A BATTLE.
WH- WHAT'RE YOU...
... TALKING ABOUT?
DON'T PLAY DUMB WITH ME. I'M A MAMODO.
!
IF YOU REFUSE, I'LL CHASE YOU AND YOUR BOOK OWNER, AND CRUSH BOTH OF YOU INTO DUST!
I MIGHT END UP HURTING YOUR FRIENDS AND FAMILY TOO.
WHAT?
HEH... YOU'VE GOT THE LOOK OF A FIGHTER IN YOUR EYES.
THAT'S GOOD. I'M ONLY INTERESTED IN FIGHTING AGAINST STRONG ENEMIES.

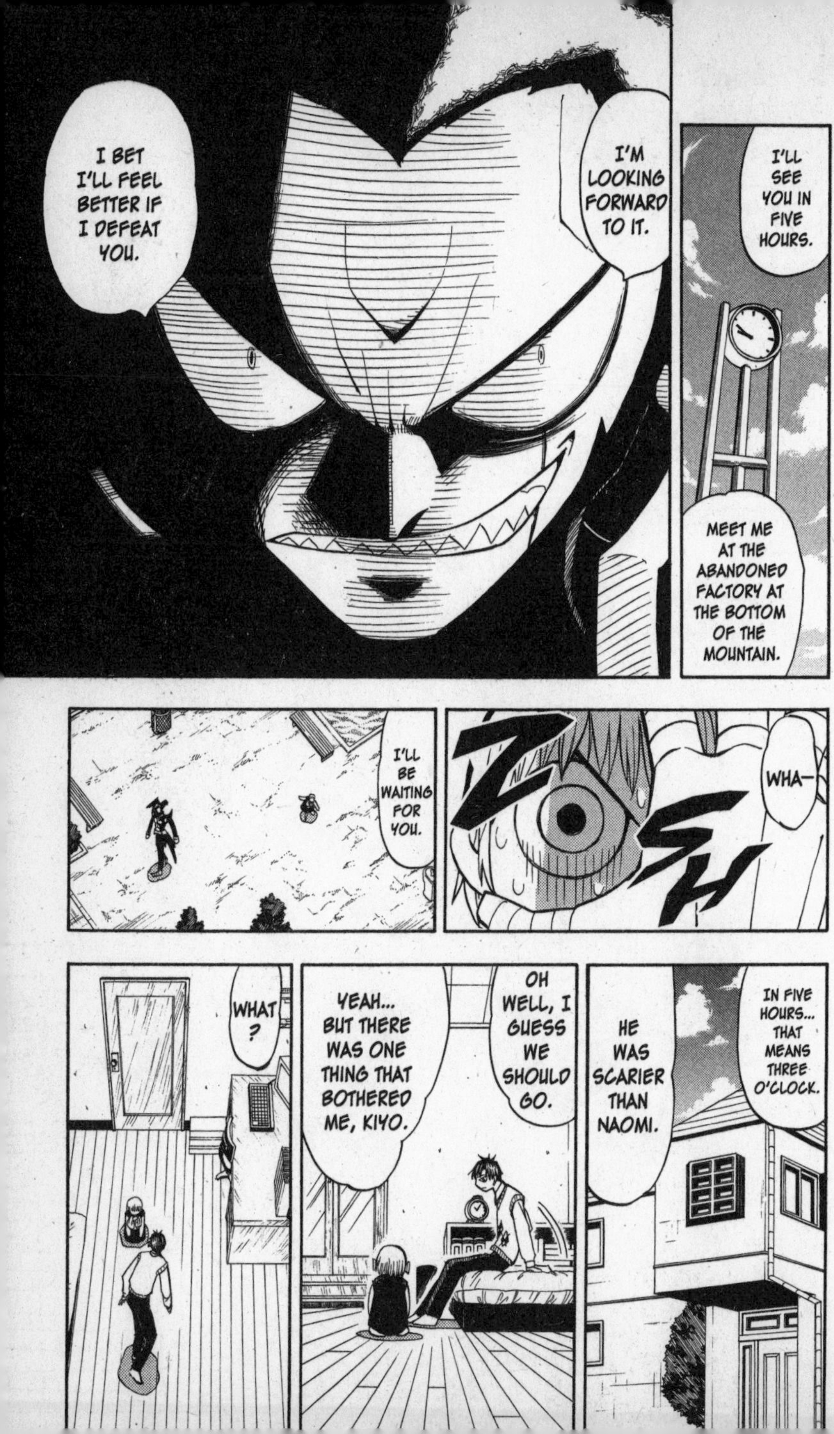
I'LL SEE YOU IN FIVE HOURS.
MEET ME AT THE ABANDONED FACTORY AT THE BOTTOM OF THE MOUNTAIN.
I'M LOOKING FORWARD TO IT.
I BET I'LL FEEL BETTER IF I DEFEAT YOU.
WHA—
ZSH
I'LL BE WAITING FOR YOU.
IN FIVE HOURS... THAT MEANS THREE O'CLOCK.
HE WAS SCARIER THAN NAOMI.
OH WELL, I GUESS WE SHOULD GO.
YEAH... BUT THERE WAS ONE THING THAT BOTHERED ME, KIYO.
WHAT?

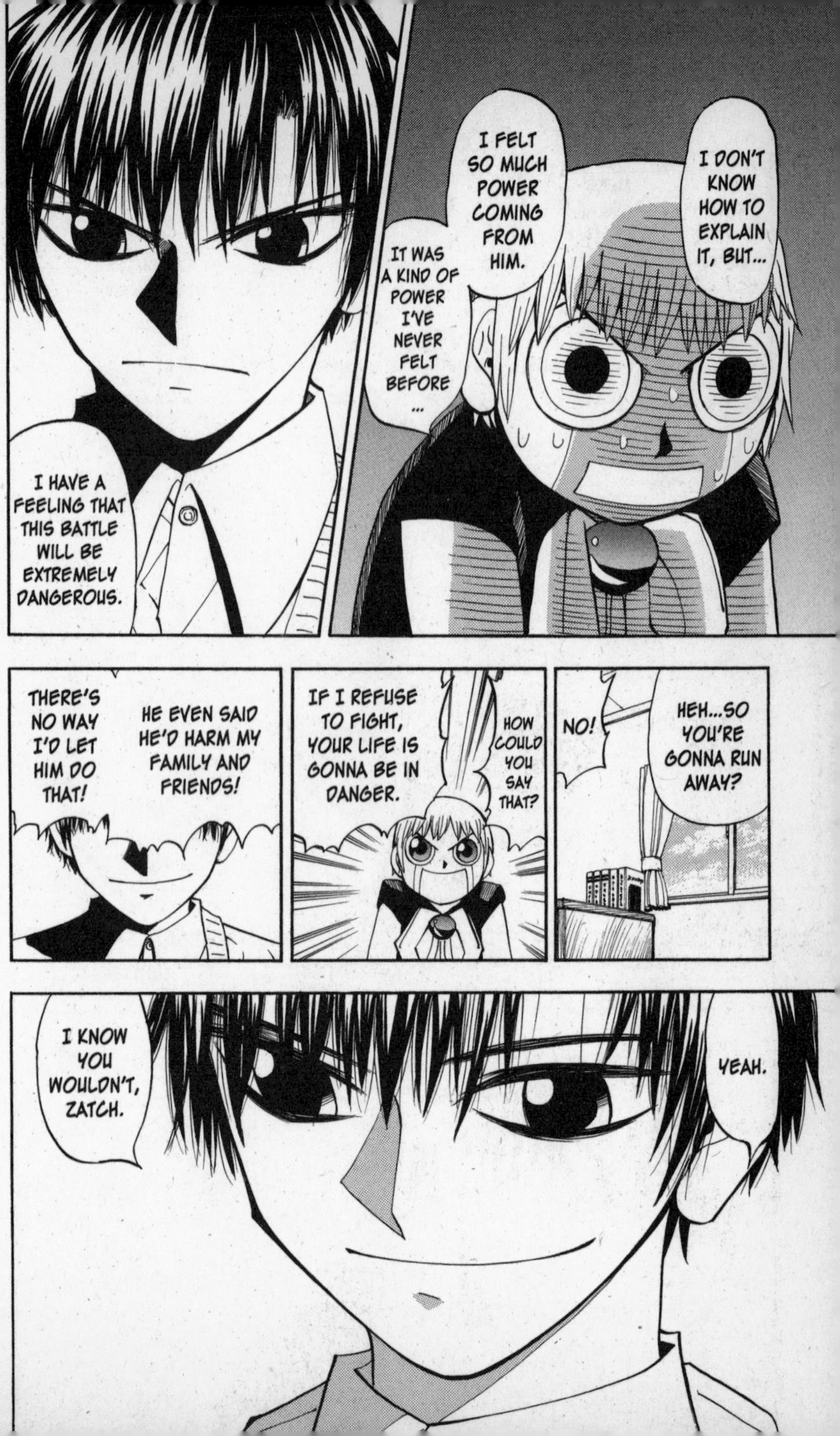
I DON'T KNOW HOW TO EXPLAIN IT, BUT...
I FELT SO MUCH POWER COMING FROM HIM.
IT WAS A KIND OF POWER I'VE NEVER FELT BEFORE...
I HAVE A FEELING THAT THIS BATTLE WILL BE EXTREMELY DANGEROUS.
HEH...SO YOU'RE GONNA RUN AWAY?
NO!
IF I REFUSE TO FIGHT, YOUR LIFE IS GONNA BE IN DANGER.
HOW COULD YOU SAY THAT?
HE EVEN SAID HE'D HARM MY FAMILY AND FRIENDS!
THERE'S NO WAY I'D LET HIM DO THAT!
YEAH.
I KNOW YOU WOULDN'T, ZATCH.

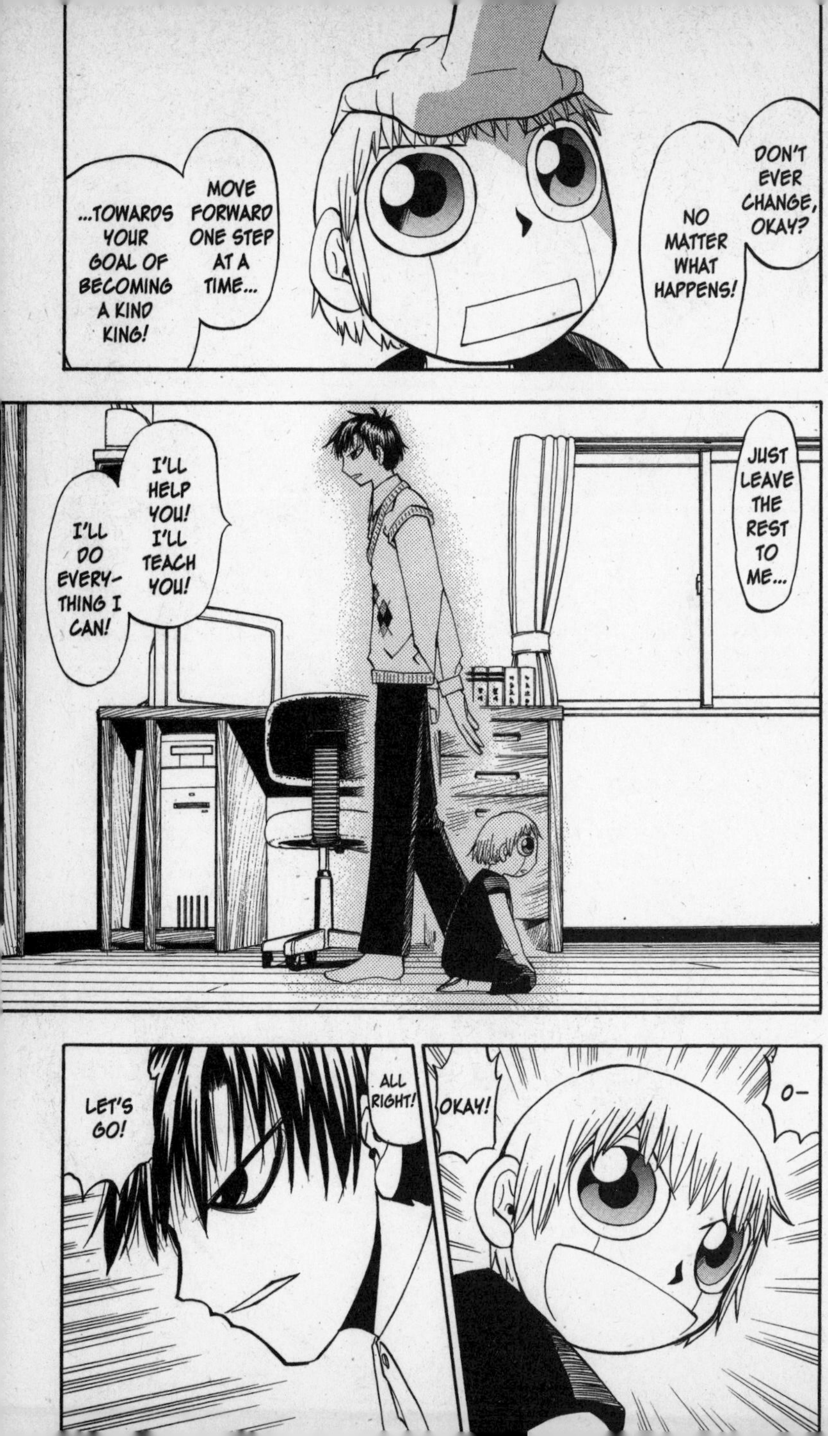
DON'T EVER CHANGE, OKAY?
NO MATTER WHAT HAPPENS!
MOVE FORWARD ONE STEP AT A TIME...
...TOWARDS YOUR GOAL OF BECOMING A KIND KING!
JUST LEAVE THE REST TO ME...
I'LL HELP YOU! I'LL TEACH YOU!
I'LL DO EVERY-THING I CAN!
O-
OKAY!
ALL RIGHT!
LET'S GO!

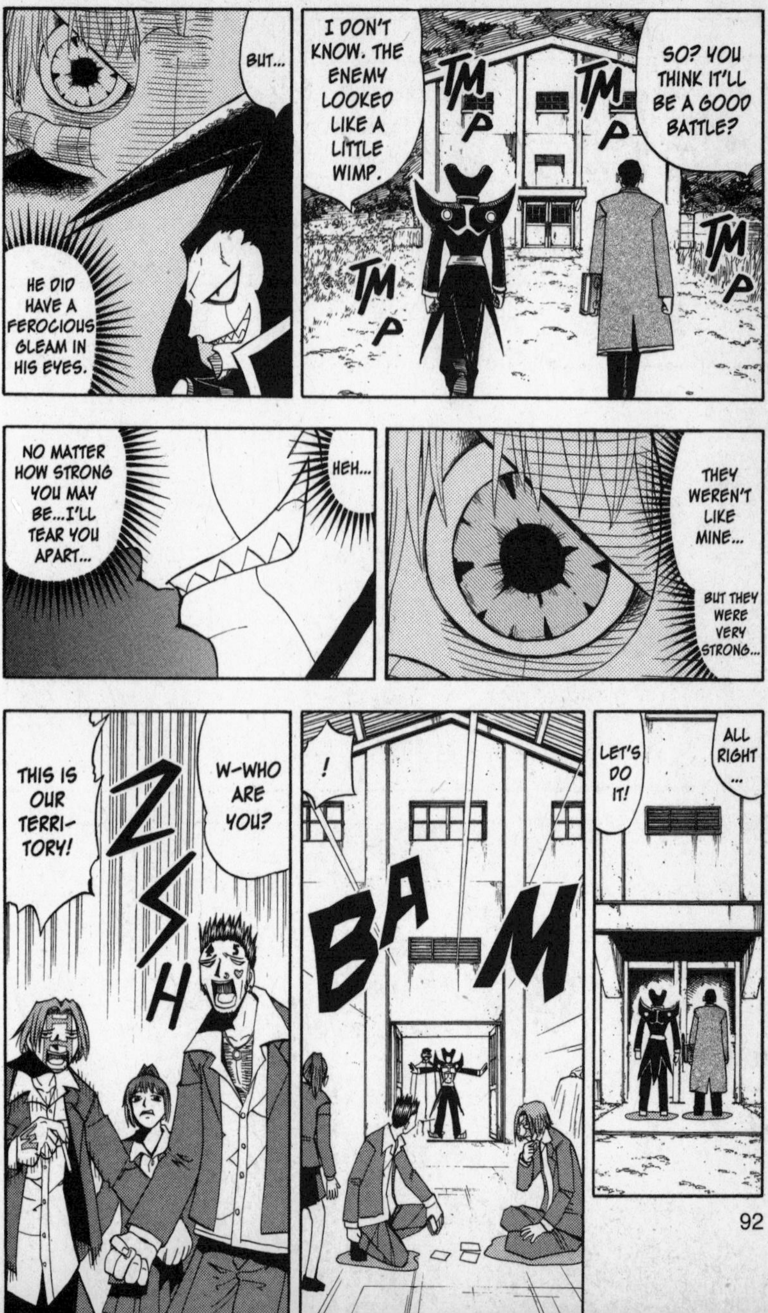
SO? YOU THINK IT'LL BE A GOOD BATTLE?
I DON'T KNOW. THE ENEMY LOOKED LIKE A LITTLE WIMP.
TMP
TMP
TMP
TMP
BUT...
HE DID HAVE A FEROCIOUS GLEAM IN HIS EYES.
THEY WEREN'T LIKE MINE...
BUT THEY WERE VERY STRONG...
HEH...
NO MATTER HOW STRONG YOU MAY BE...I'LL TEAR YOU APART...
ALL RIGHT ...
LET'S DO IT!
!
BAM
W-WHO ARE YOU?
THIS IS OUR TERRITORY!
ZSH

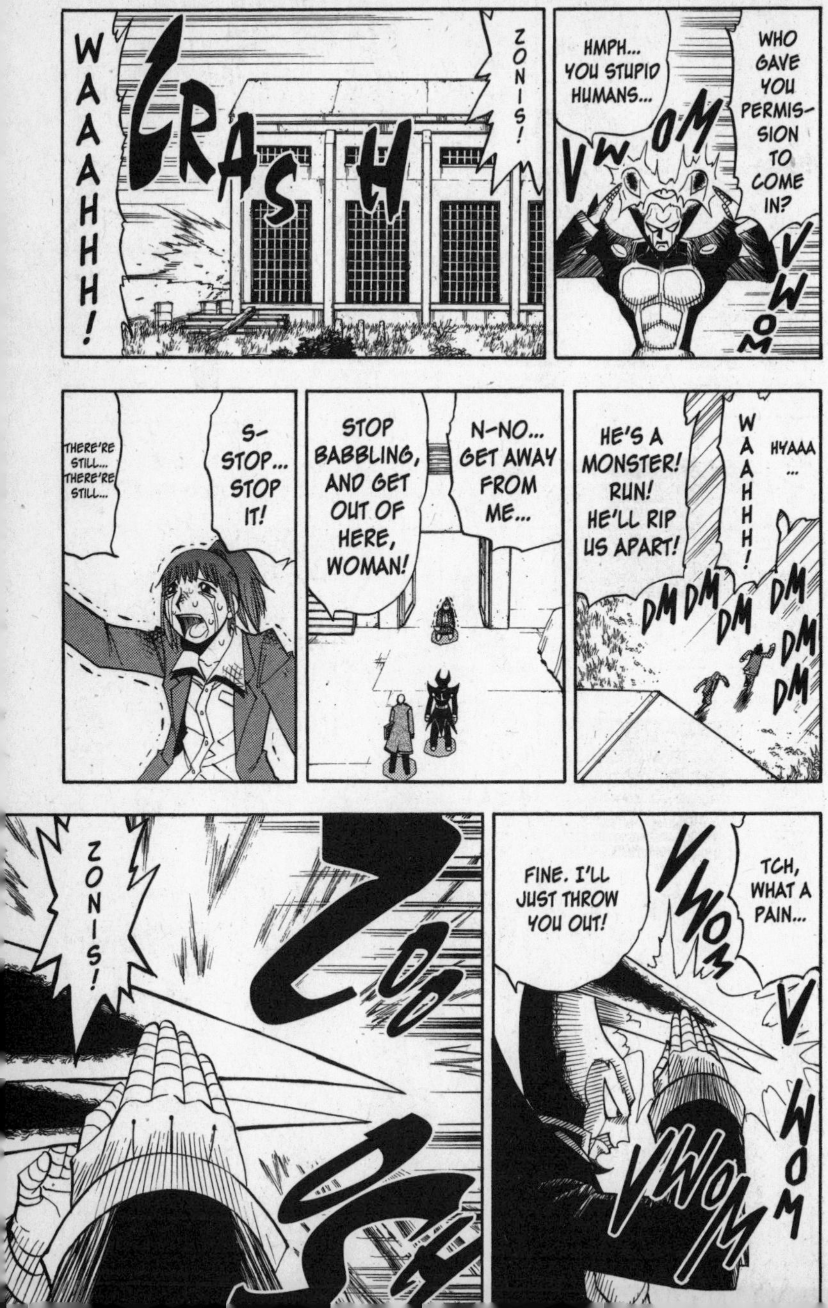
WHO GAVE YOU PERMISSION TO COME IN?
HMPH... YOU STUPID HUMANS...
VWOM
VWOM
ZONIS!
CRASH
WAAAAHHHH!
HYAAA...
WAAHHHH!
HE'S A MONSTER! RUN! HE'LL RIP US APART!
DM DM DM DM DM DM
N-NO... GET AWAY FROM ME...
STOP BABBLING, AND GET OUT OF HERE, WOMAN!
S-STOP... STOP IT!
THERE'RE STILL... THERE'RE STILL...
TCH, WHAT A PAIN...
FINE. I'LL JUST THROW YOU OUT!
VWOM
VWOM
VWOM
ZONIS!

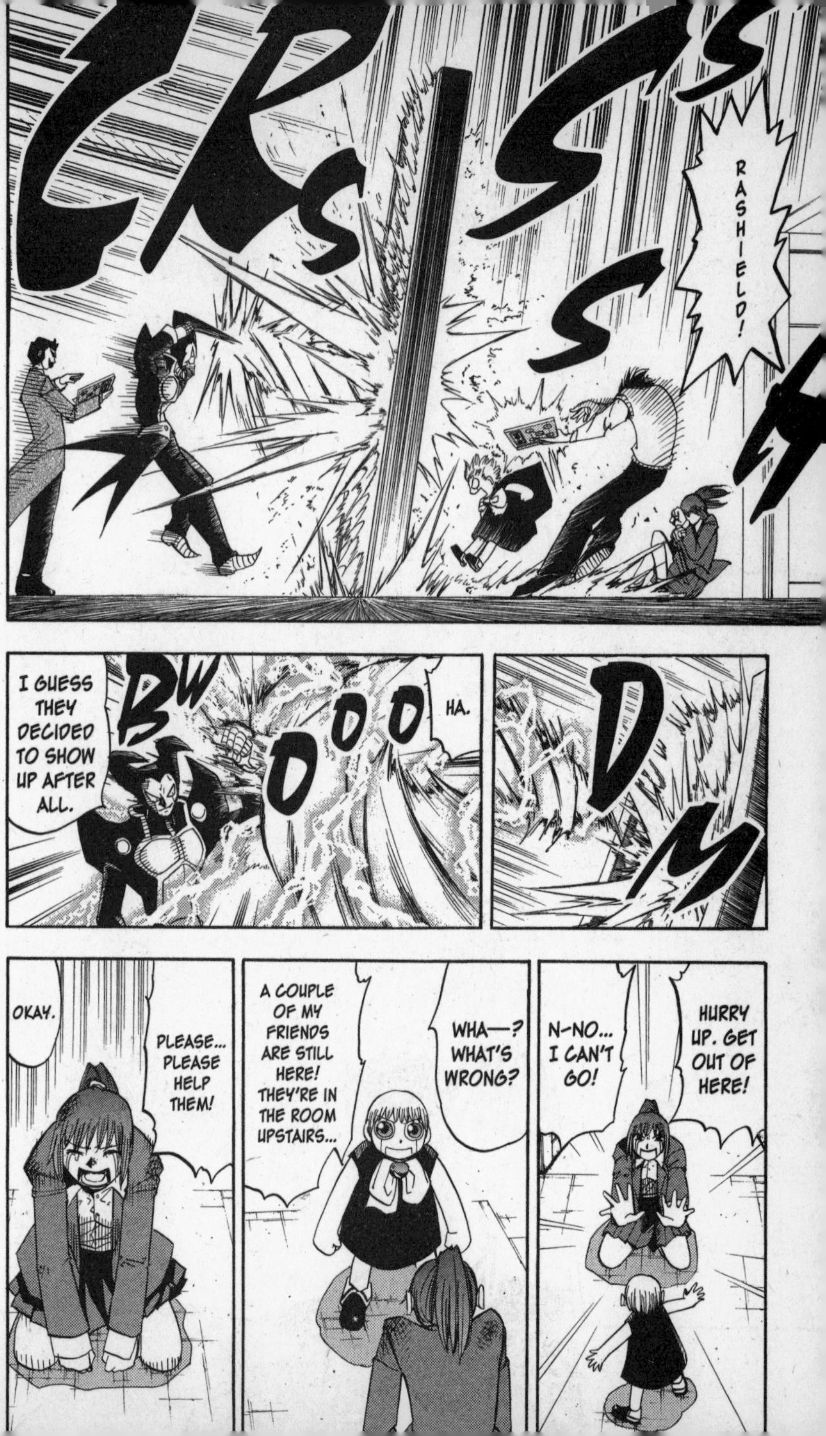
RASHIELD!
HA.
I GUESS THEY DECIDED TO SHOW UP AFTER ALL.
HURRY UP. GET OUT OF HERE!
N-NO... I CAN'T GO!
WHA—? WHAT'S WRONG?
A COUPLE OF MY FRIENDS ARE STILL HERE! THEY'RE IN THE ROOM UPSTAIRS...
PLEASE... PLEASE HELP THEM!
OKAY.

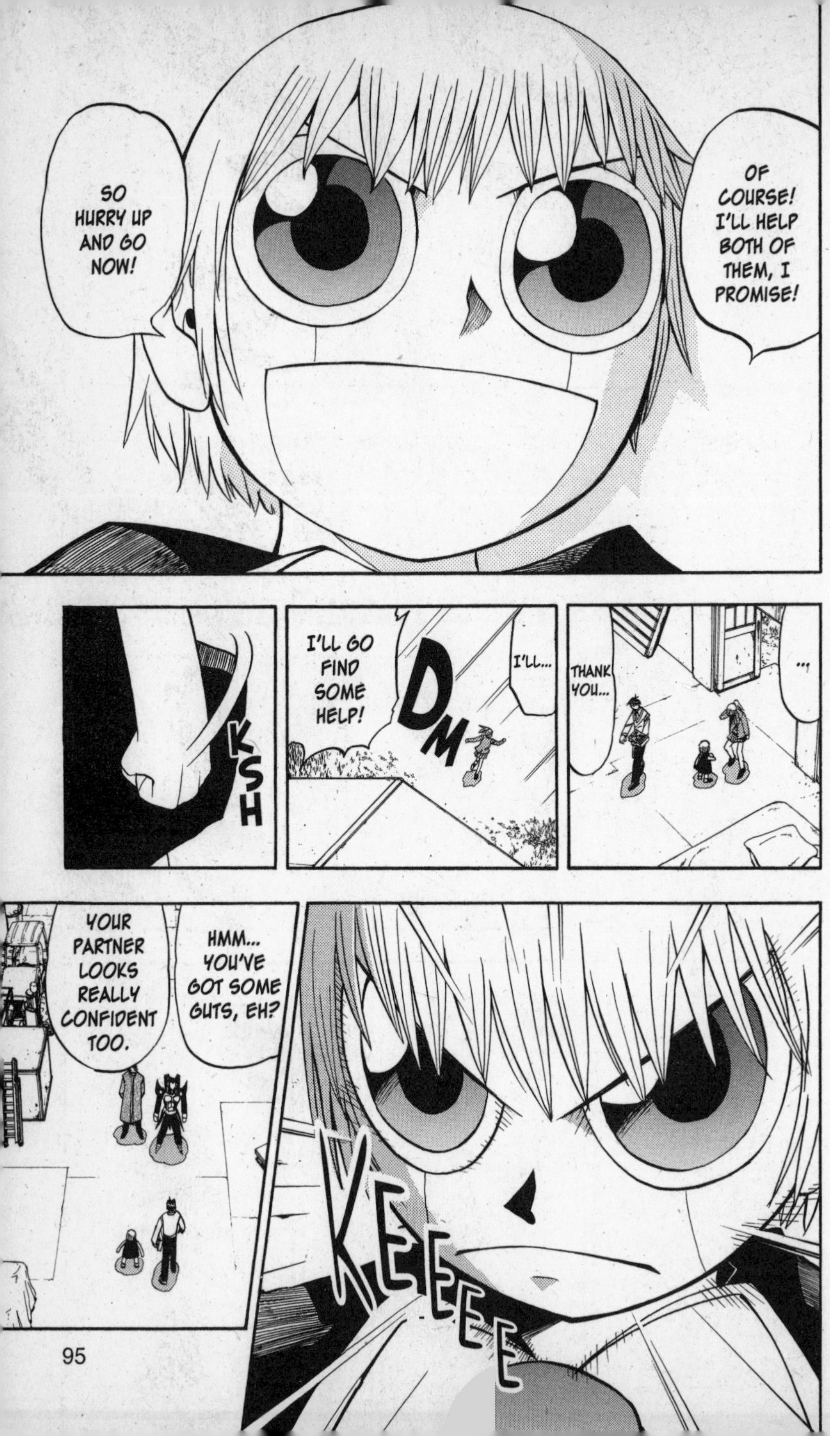
OF COURSE! I'LL HELP BOTH OF THEM, I PROMISE!
SO HURRY UP AND GO NOW!
...
THANK YOU...
I'LL...
DM
I'LL GO FIND SOME HELP!
KSH
KEEEEE
HMM... YOU'VE GOT SOME GUTS, EH?
YOUR PARTNER LOOKS REALLY CONFIDENT TOO.

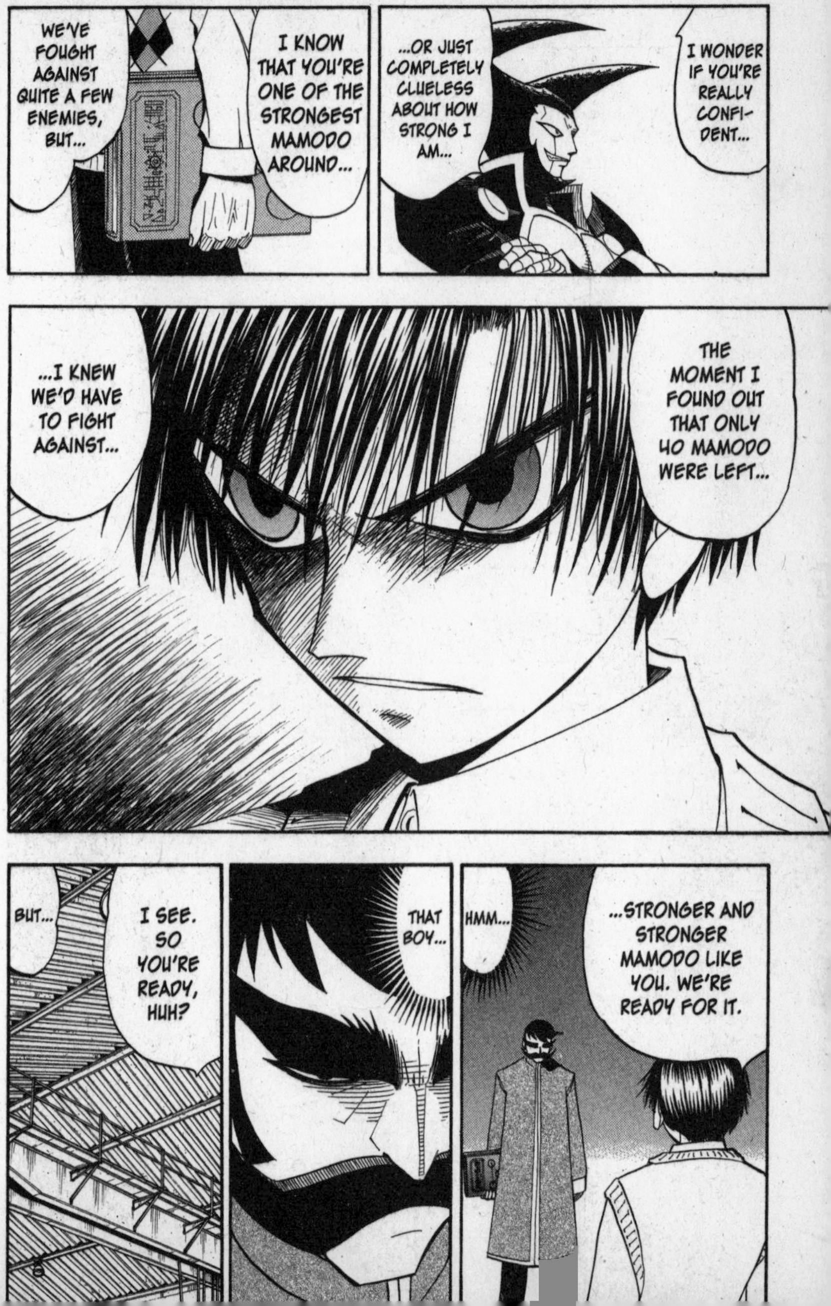
I WONDER IF YOU'RE REALLY CONFI-DENT...
...OR JUST COMPLETELY CLUELESS ABOUT HOW STRONG I AM...
I KNOW THAT YOU'RE ONE OF THE STRONGEST MAMODO AROUND...
WE'VE FOUGHT AGAINST QUITE A FEW ENEMIES, BUT...
THE MOMENT I FOUND OUT THAT ONLY 40 MAMODO WERE LEFT...
...I KNEW WE'D HAVE TO FIGHT AGAINST...
...STRONGER AND STRONGER MAMODO LIKE YOU. WE'RE READY FOR IT.
HMM...
THAT BOY...
I SEE. SO YOU'RE READY, HUH?
BUT...

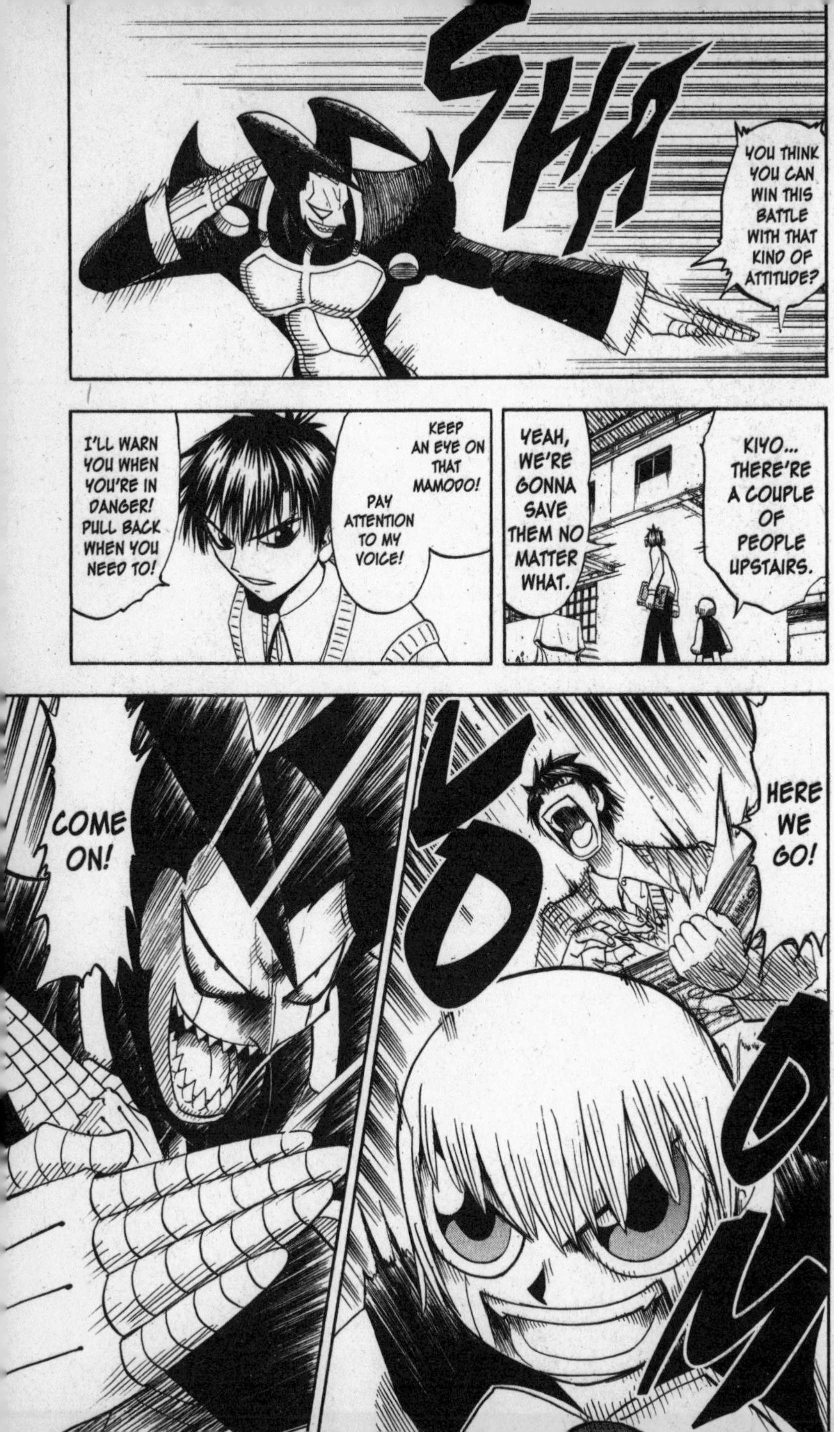
SHA
YOU THINK YOU CAN WIN THIS BATTLE WITH THAT KIND OF ATTITUDE?
KIYO... THERE'RE A COUPLE OF PEOPLE UPSTAIRS.
YEAH, WE'RE GONNA SAVE THEM NO MATTER WHAT.
KEEP AN EYE ON THAT MAMODO!
PAY ATTENTION TO MY VOICE!
I'LL WARN YOU WHEN YOU'RE IN DANGER! PULL BACK WHEN YOU NEED TO!
HERE WE GO!
COME ON!

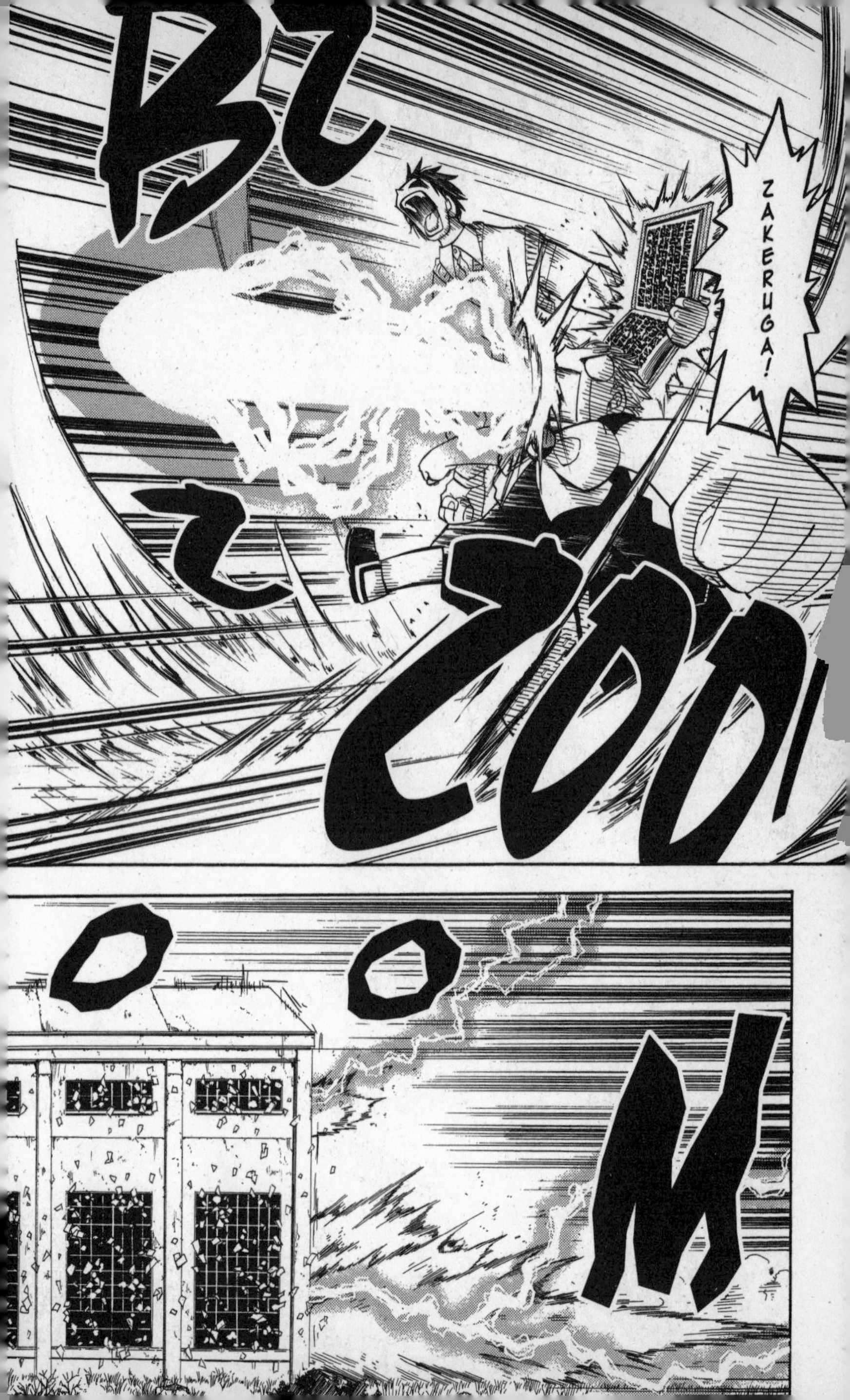
ZAKERUGA!
BZZZOOOOM

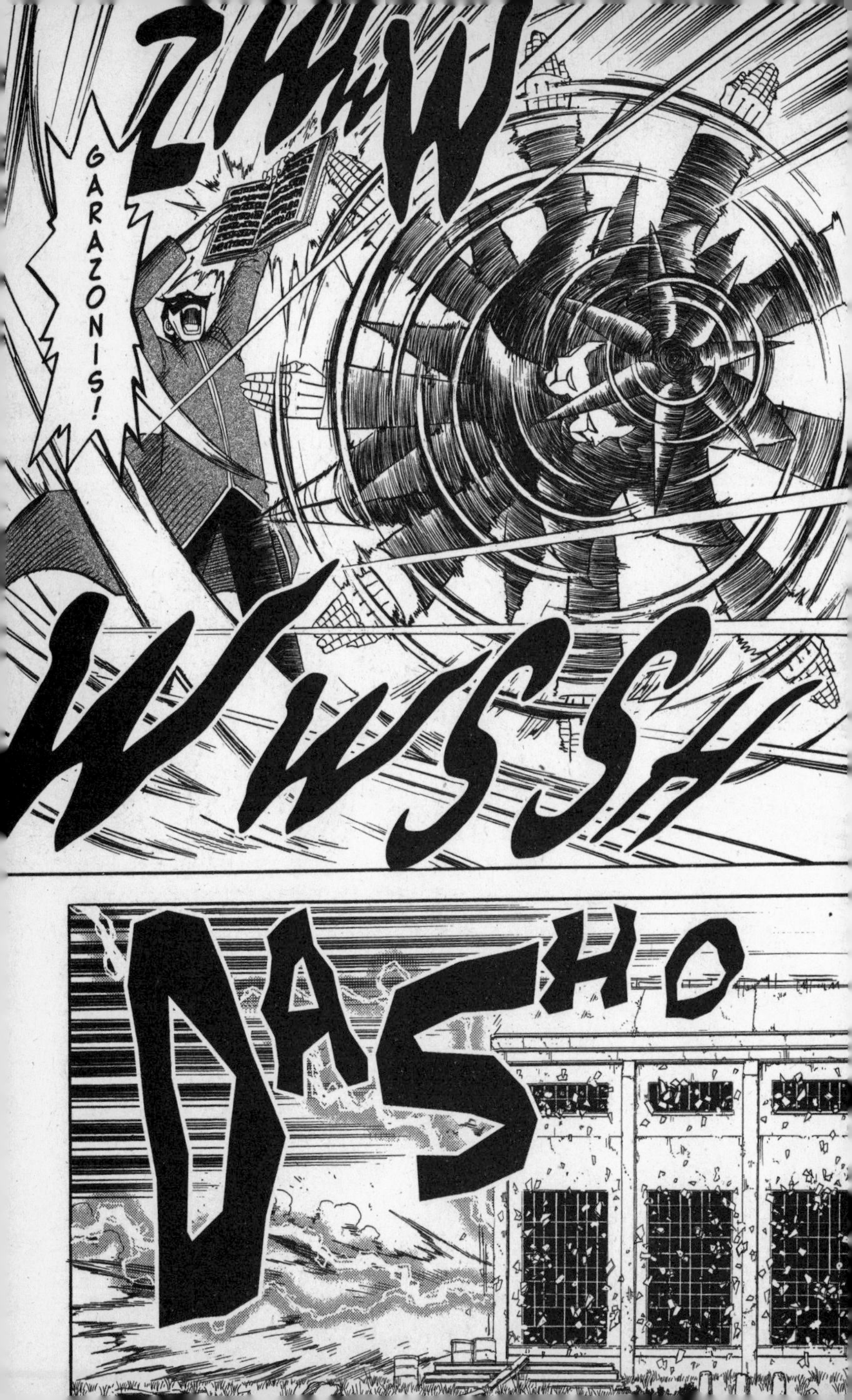
GARAZONIS!
DASHO

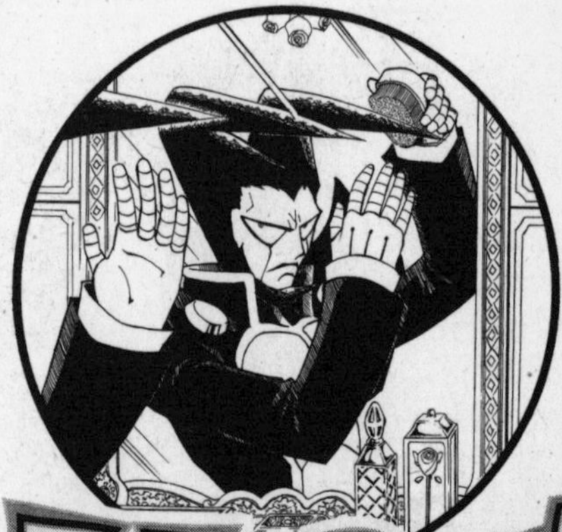

ZATCH BELL!

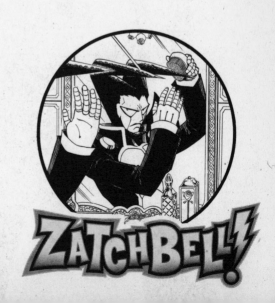

# LEVEL 90:
# Not Strong Enough

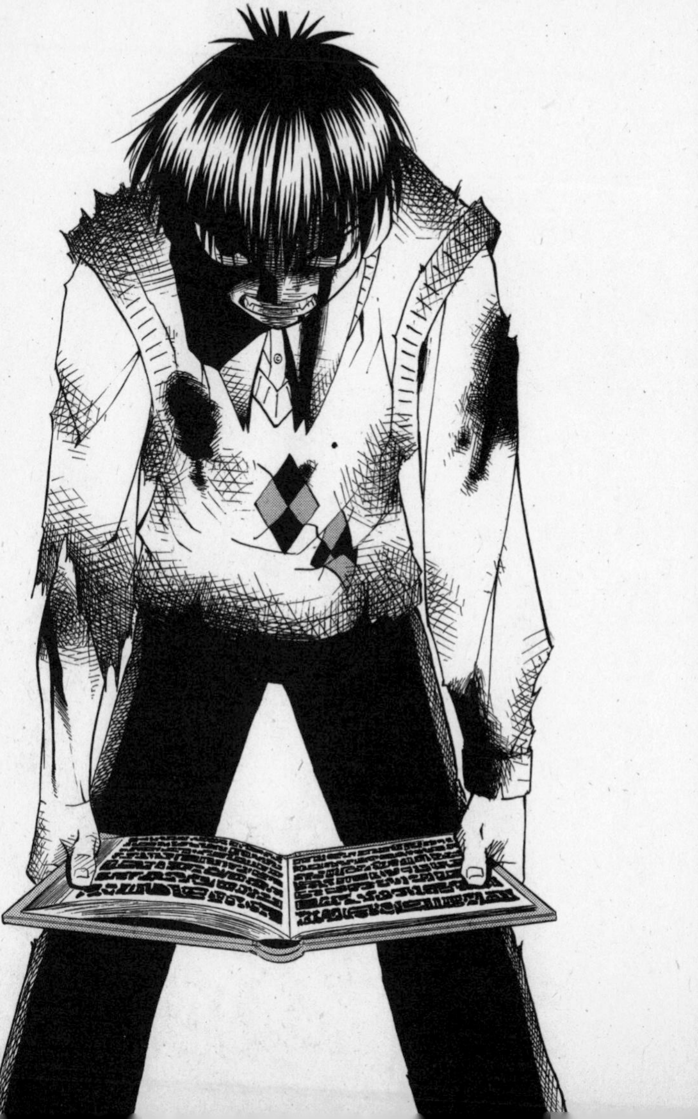

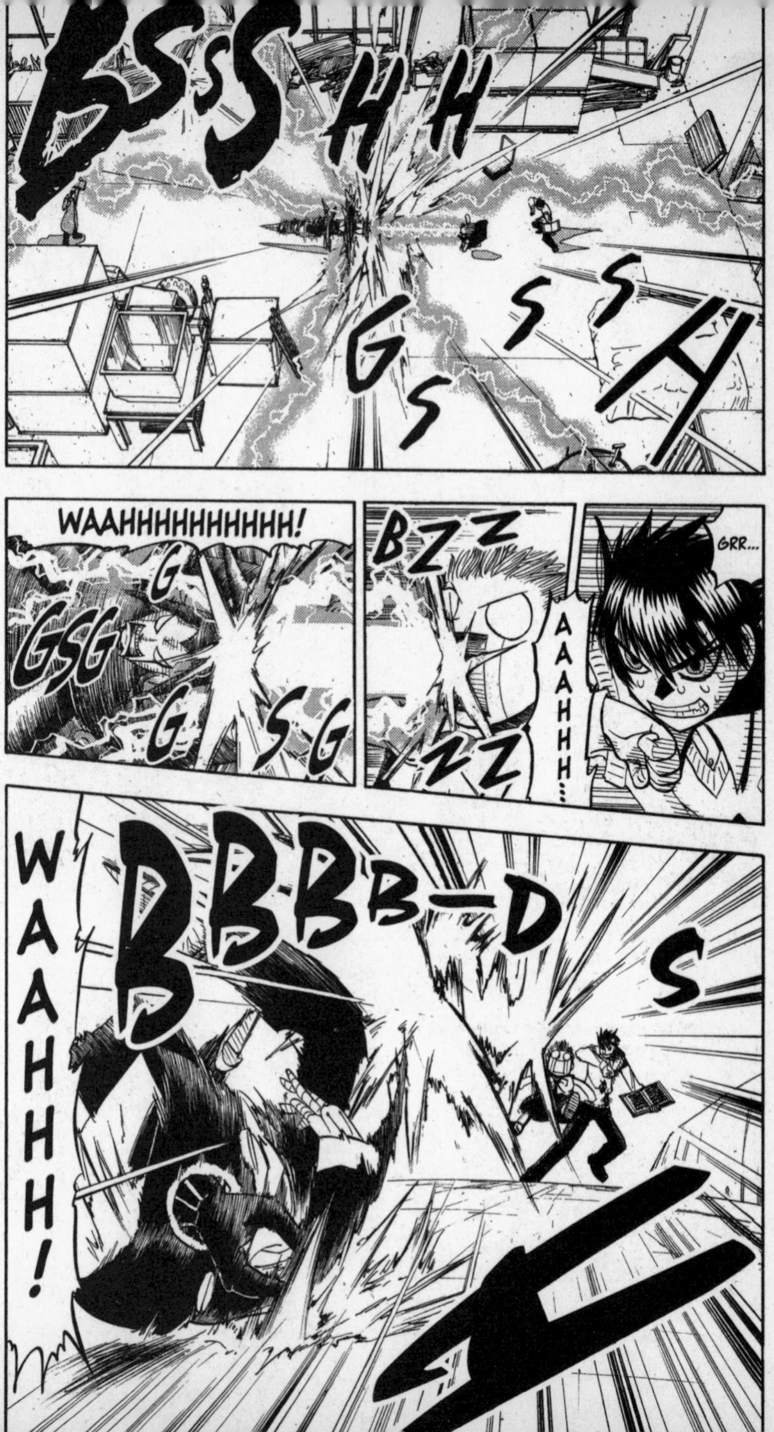
BSSSHH
GSSSH
GRR...
AAAHHH...
BZZZ
ZZZ
WAAHHHHHHHHHH!
GSG
GSG
WAAHHH!
BBBB-D
S

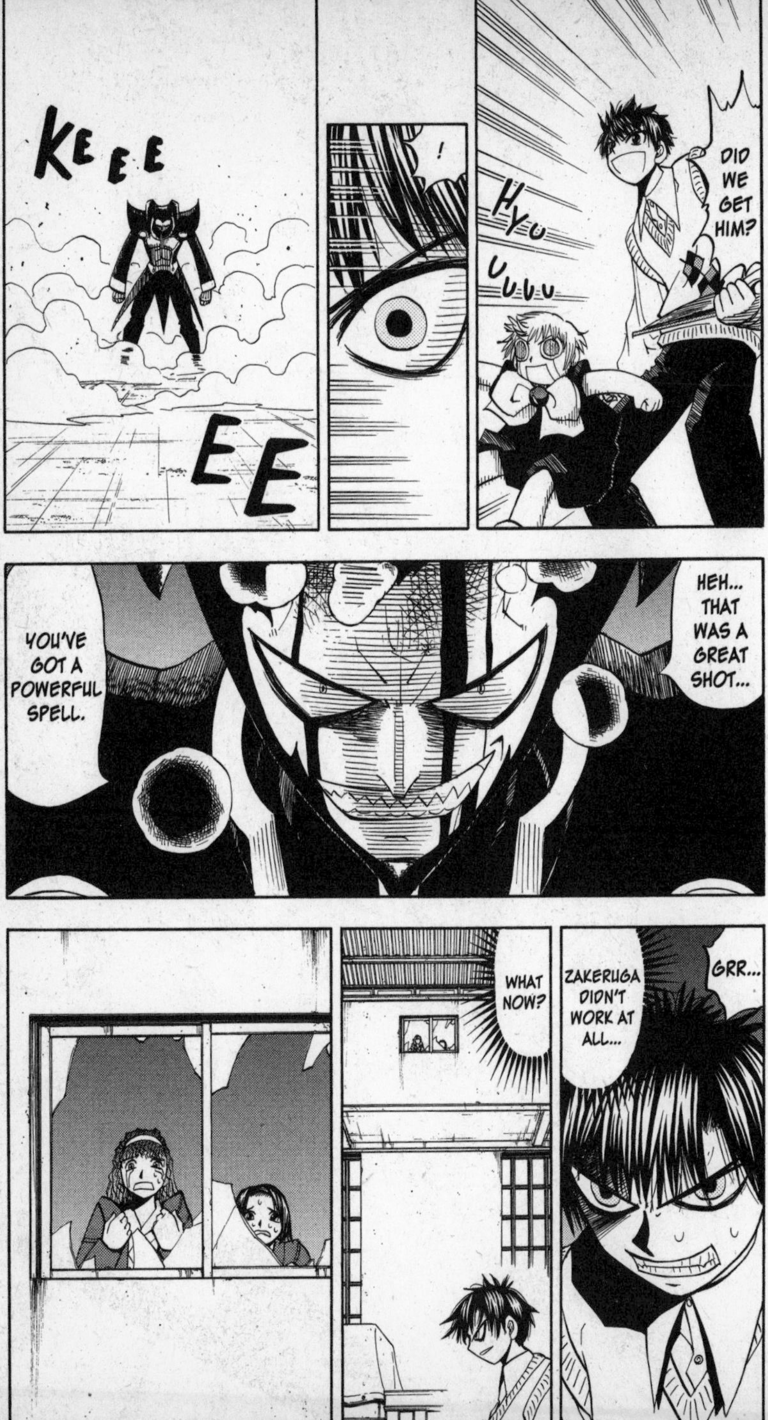
DID WE GET HIM?
HYUUUUU
!
KEEEEE
HEH... THAT WAS A GREAT SHOT...
YOU'VE GOT A POWERFUL SPELL.
GRR...
ZAKERUGA DIDN'T WORK AT ALL...
WHAT NOW?

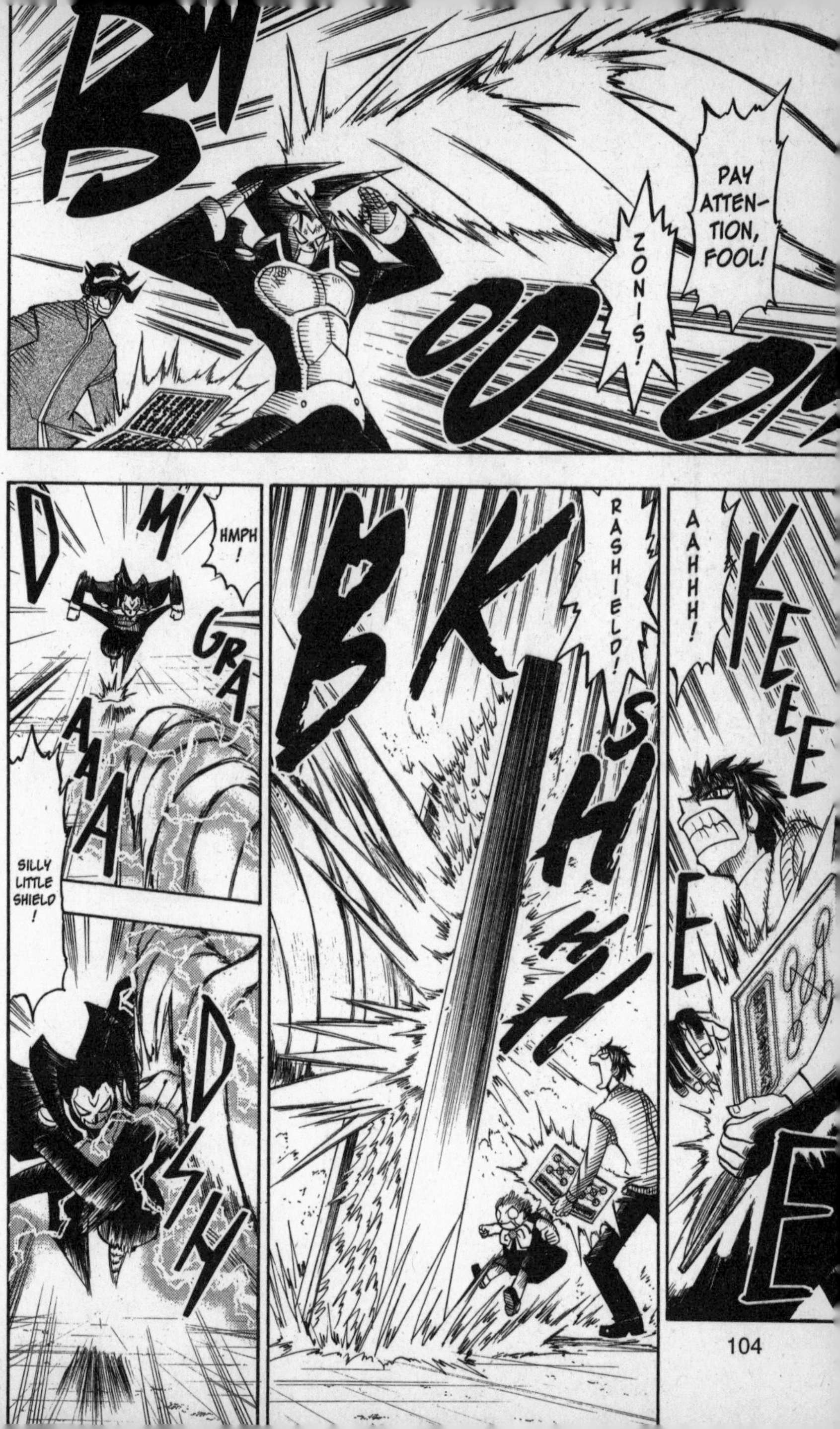
PAY ATTEN- TION, FOOL!
ZONIS!
AAHHH!
RASHIELD!
HMPH!
SILLY LITTLE SHIELD!

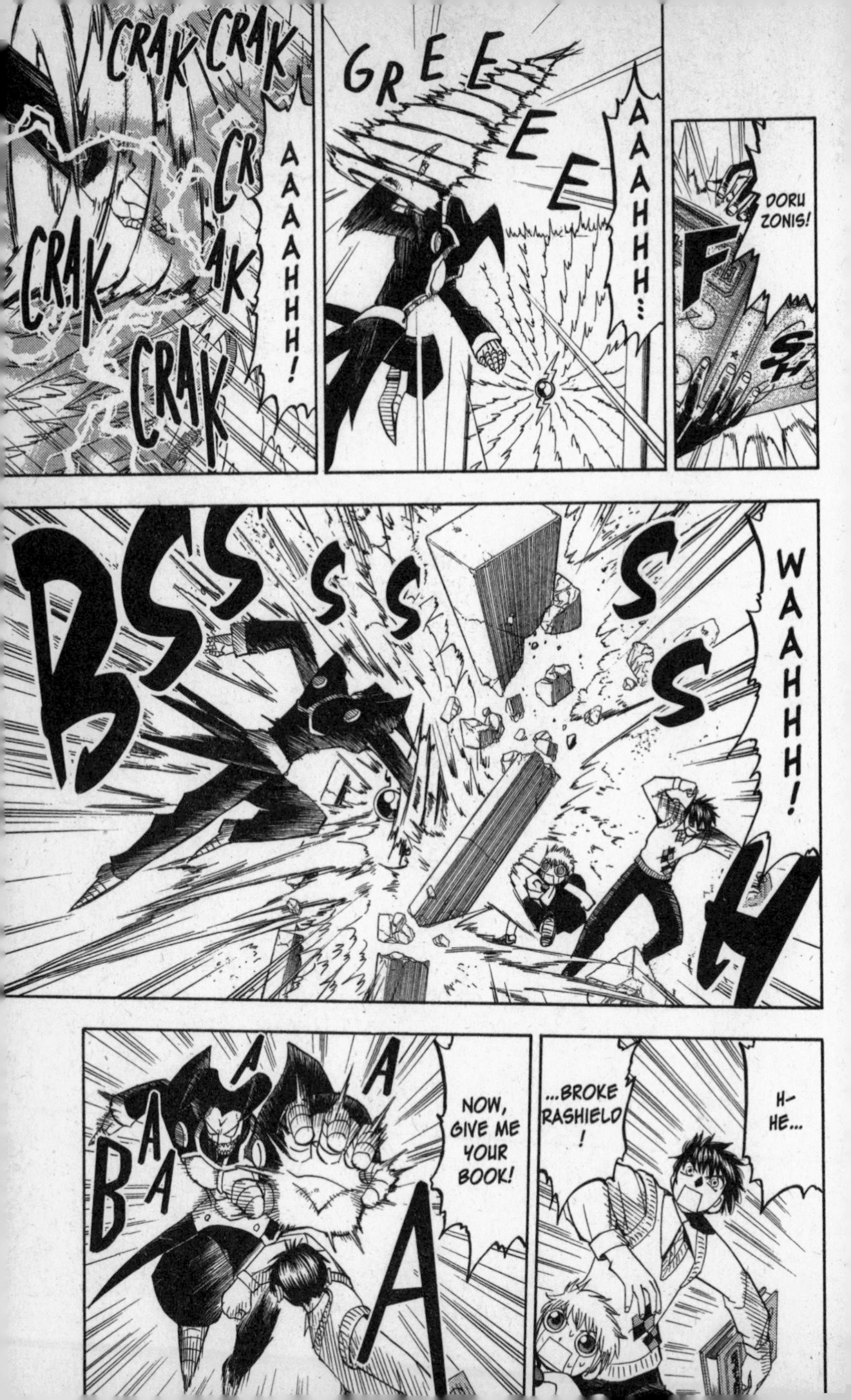
DORU ZONIS!
FSH
AAAHHHH...
GREEEEE
CRAK CRAK
CRAK
CRAK
CRAK
AAAAAHHHH!
WAAHHHH!
BSSSSSSH
H-
HE...
...BROKE RASHIELD!
NOW, GIVE ME YOUR BOOK!

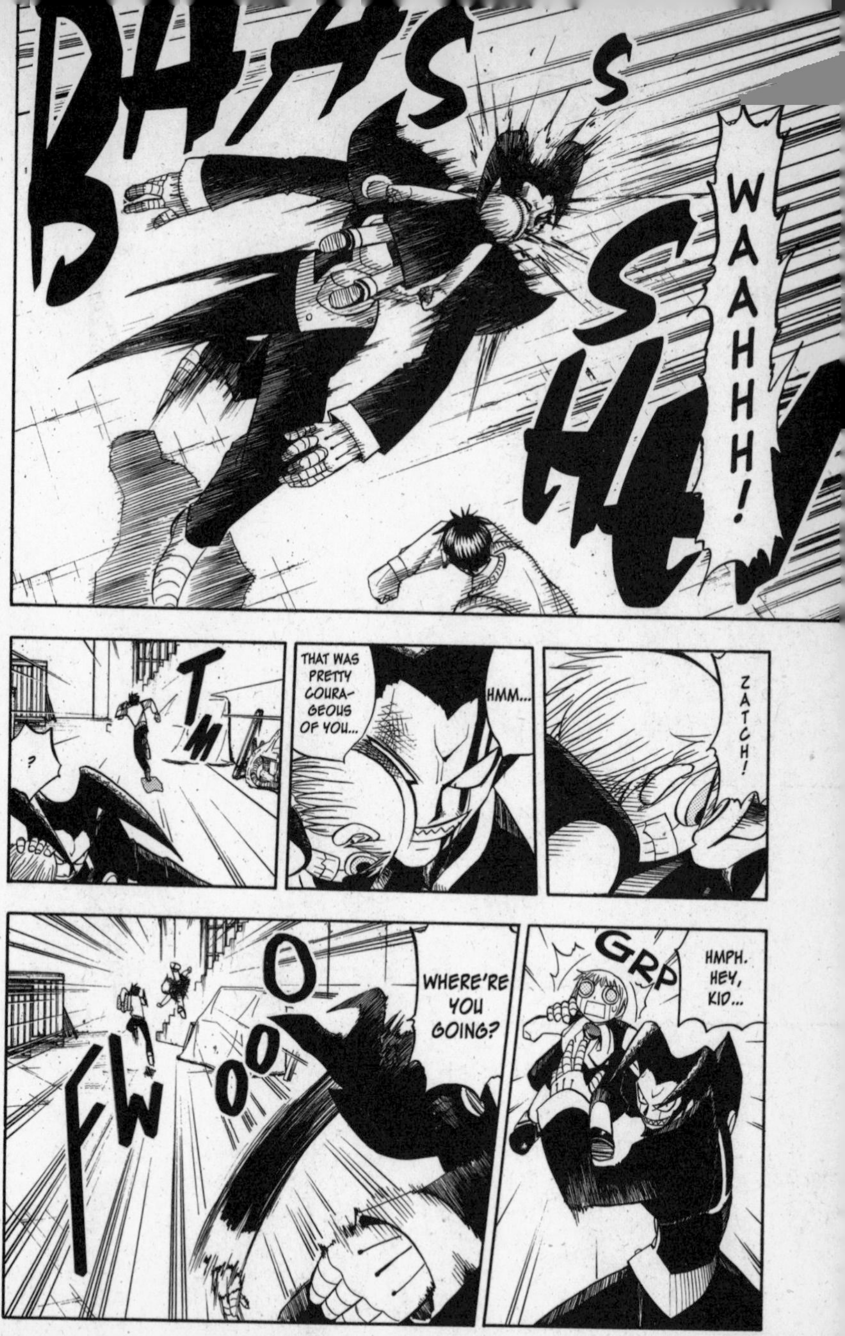
WAAHHH!
ZATCH!
HMM...
THAT WAS PRETTY COURAGEOUS OF YOU...
?
HMPH. HEY, KID...
GRP
WHERE'RE YOU GOING?
FWOOO

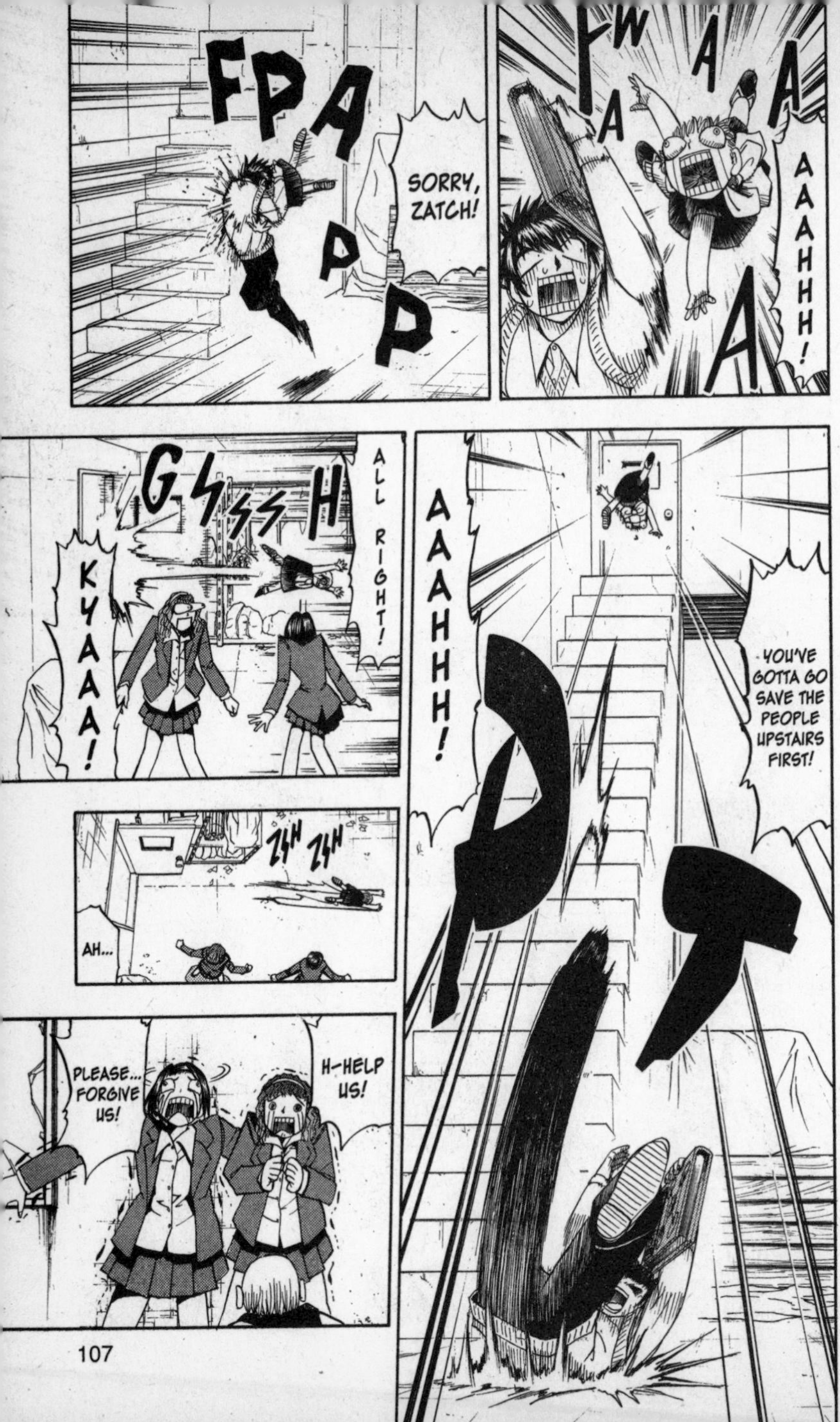
WAAAA
AAAHHH!
FPAPP
SORRY, ZATCH!
AAAAHHH!
YOU'VE GOTTA GO SAVE THE PEOPLE UPSTAIRS FIRST!
ALL RIGHT!
GSSSH
KYAAAA!
ZSH ZSH
AH...
H-HELP US!
PLEASE... FORGIVE US!

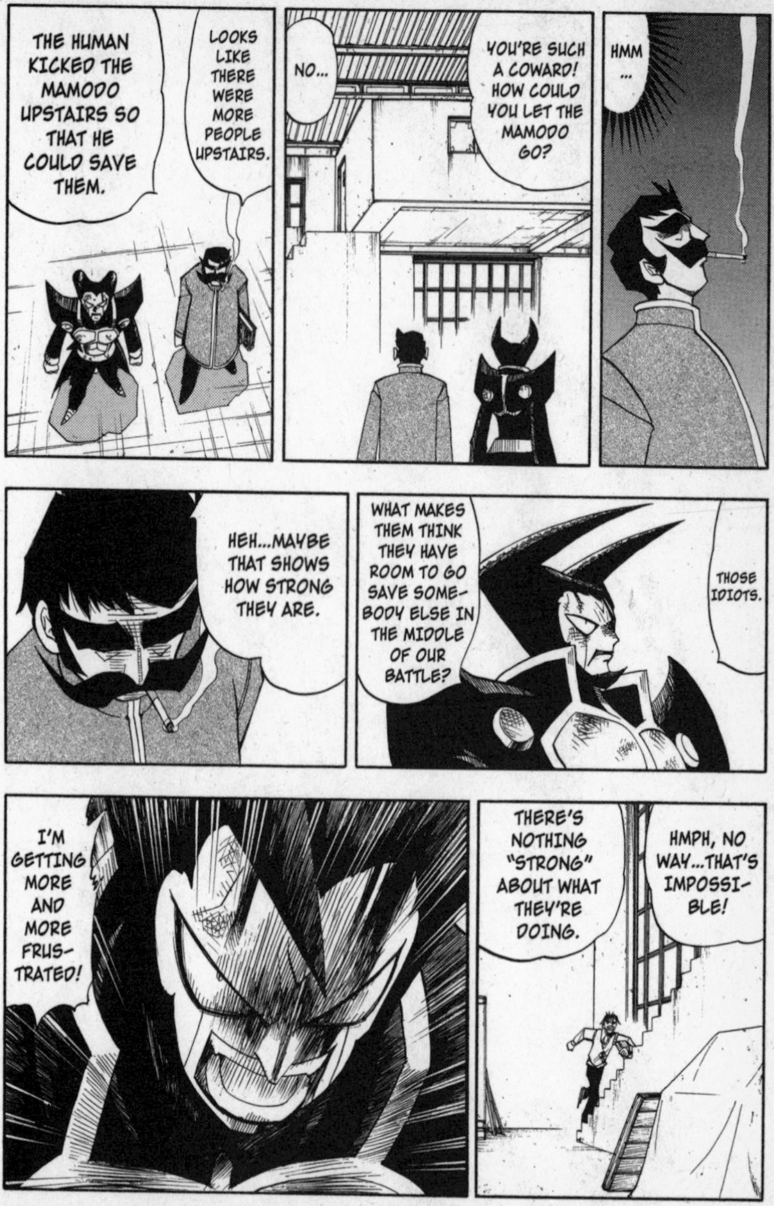
HMM ...
YOU'RE SUCH A COWARD! HOW COULD YOU LET THE MAMODO GO?
NO...
LOOKS LIKE THERE WERE MORE PEOPLE UPSTAIRS.
THE HUMAN KICKED THE MAMODO UPSTAIRS SO THAT HE COULD SAVE THEM.
THOSE IDIOTS.
WHAT MAKES THEM THINK THEY HAVE ROOM TO GO SAVE SOME-BODY ELSE IN THE MIDDLE OF OUR BATTLE?
HEH...MAYBE THAT SHOWS HOW STRONG THEY ARE.
HMPH, NO WAY...THAT'S IMPOSSI-BLE!
THERE'S NOTHING "STRONG" ABOUT WHAT THEY'RE DOING.
I'M GETTING MORE AND MORE FRUS-TRATED!

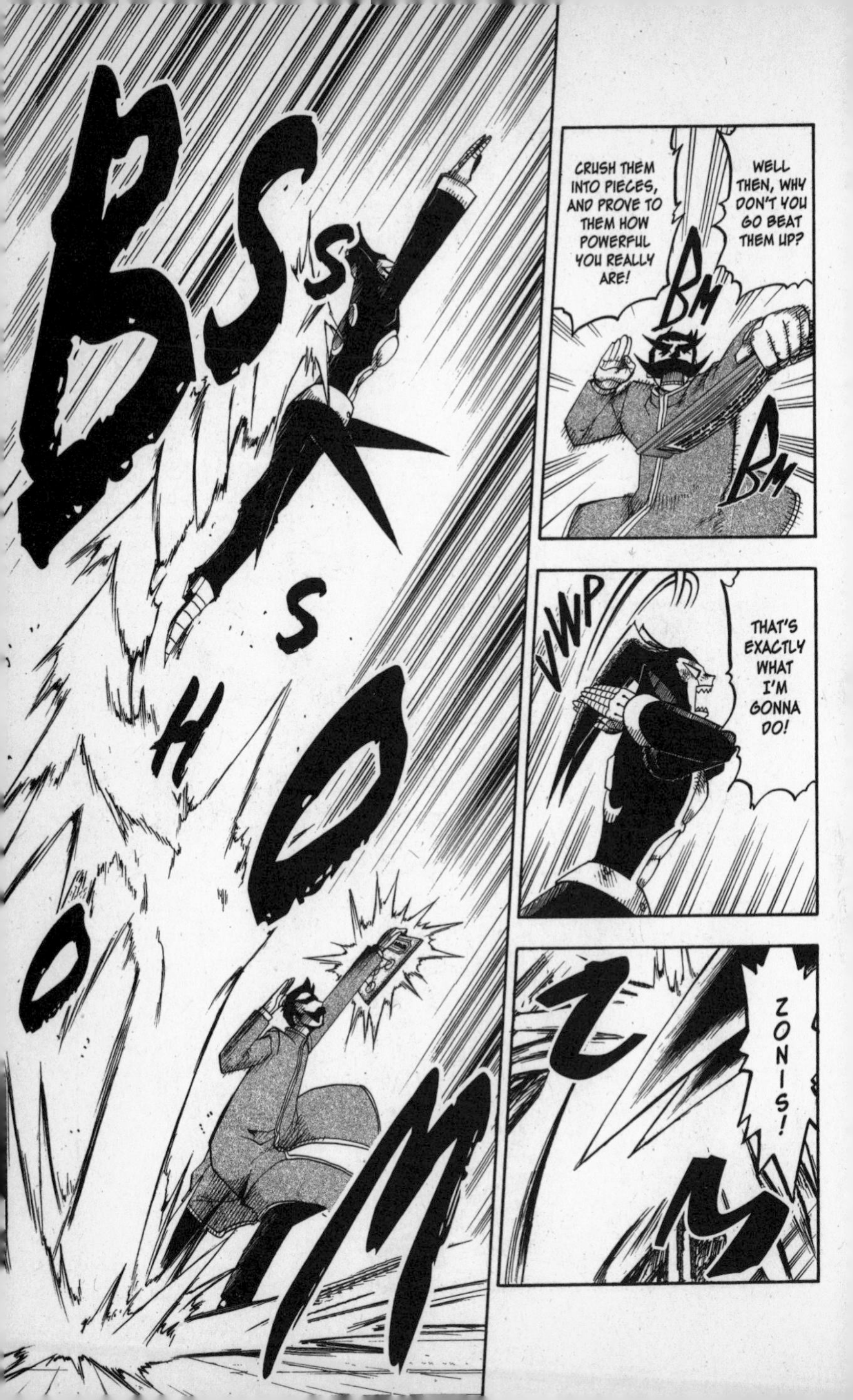
WELL THEN, WHY DON'T YOU GO BEAT THEM UP?
CRUSH THEM INTO PIECES, AND PROVE TO THEM HOW POWERFUL YOU REALLY ARE!
BM
BM
VWP
THAT'S EXACTLY WHAT I'M GONNA DO!
ZONIS!

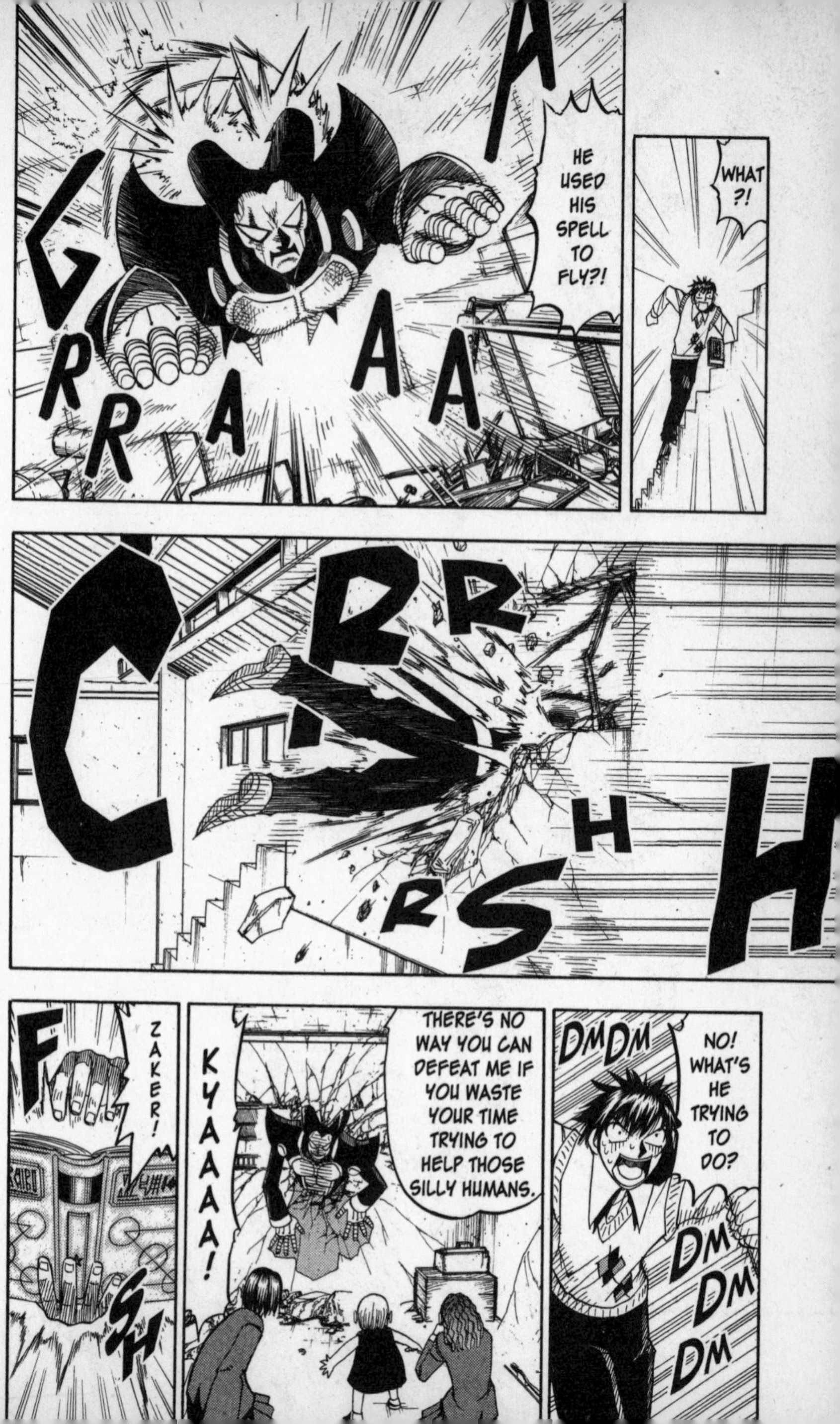
WHAT ?!
HE USED HIS SPELL TO FLY?!
GRRAAAA
CRRRSHH
DMDM
NO! WHAT'S HE TRYING TO DO?
DM DM DM
THERE'S NO WAY YOU CAN DEFEAT ME IF YOU WASTE YOUR TIME TRYING TO HELP THOSE SILLY HUMANS.
KYAAAAA!
ZAKER!
F
SH

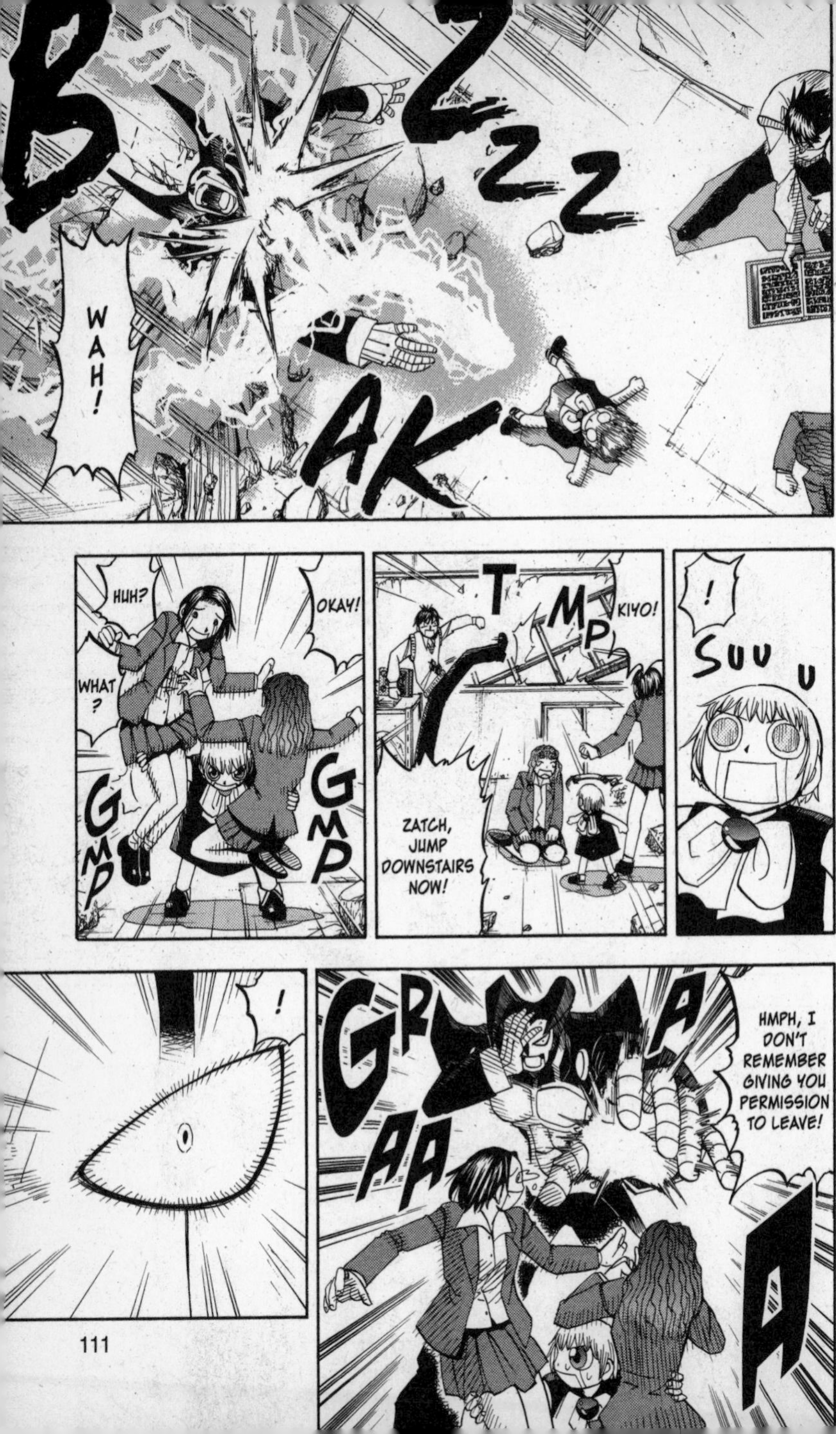
BZZZAK
WAH!
!
SUUU
KIYO!
TMP
ZATCH, JUMP DOWNSTAIRS NOW!
OKAY!
HUH?
WHAT?
GMP
GMP
HMPH, I DON'T REMEMBER GIVING YOU PERMISSION TO LEAVE!
GRAAAA
!

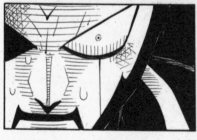

KYAAA!

WAAHHH!

BM

ZATCH!

OKAY!

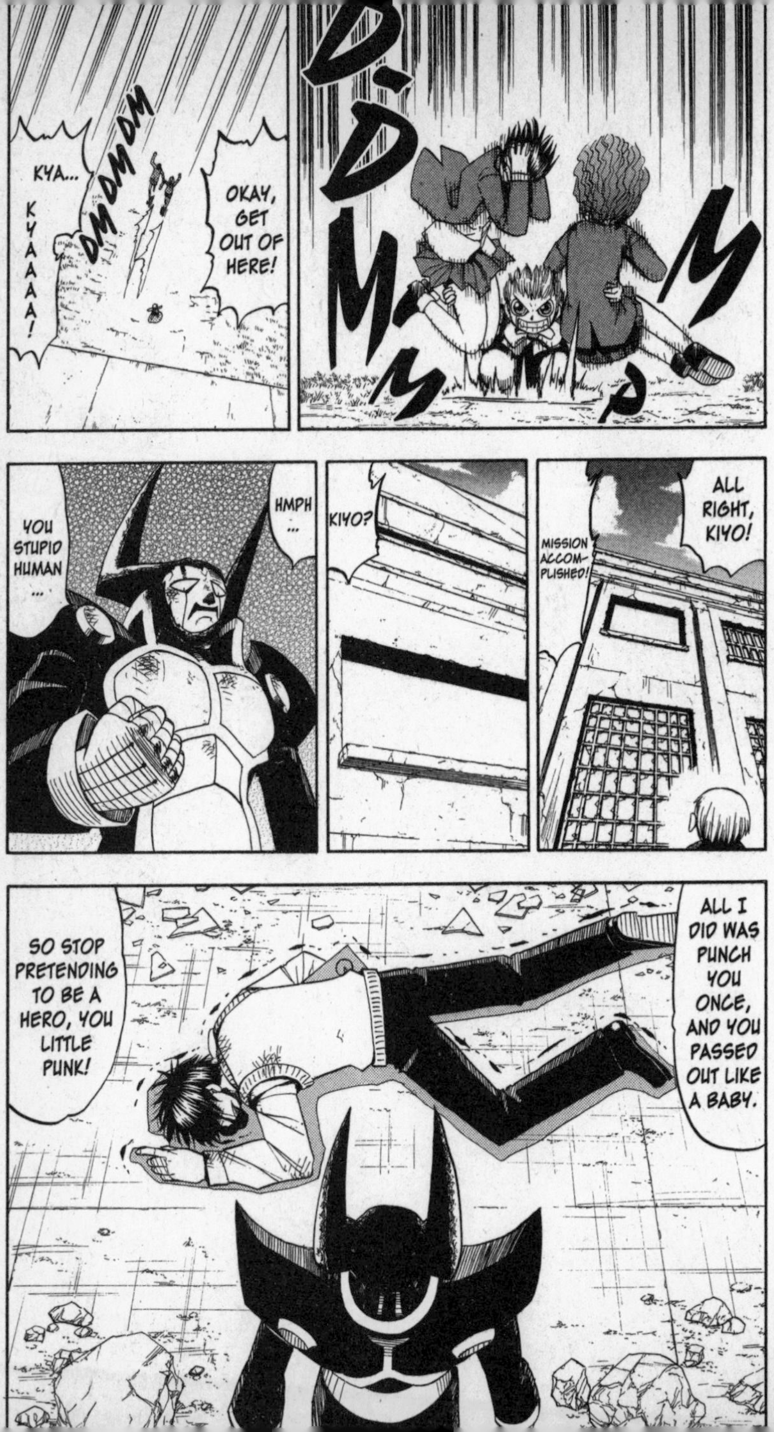
D-DMMMM
OKAY, GET OUT OF HERE!
DM DM DM
KYA...
KYAAAAA!
ALL RIGHT, KIYO!
MISSION ACCOMPLISHED!
KIYO?
HMPH ...
YOU STUPID HUMAN ...
ALL I DID WAS PUNCH YOU ONCE, AND YOU PASSED OUT LIKE A BABY.
SO STOP PRETENDING TO BE A HERO, YOU LITTLE PUNK!

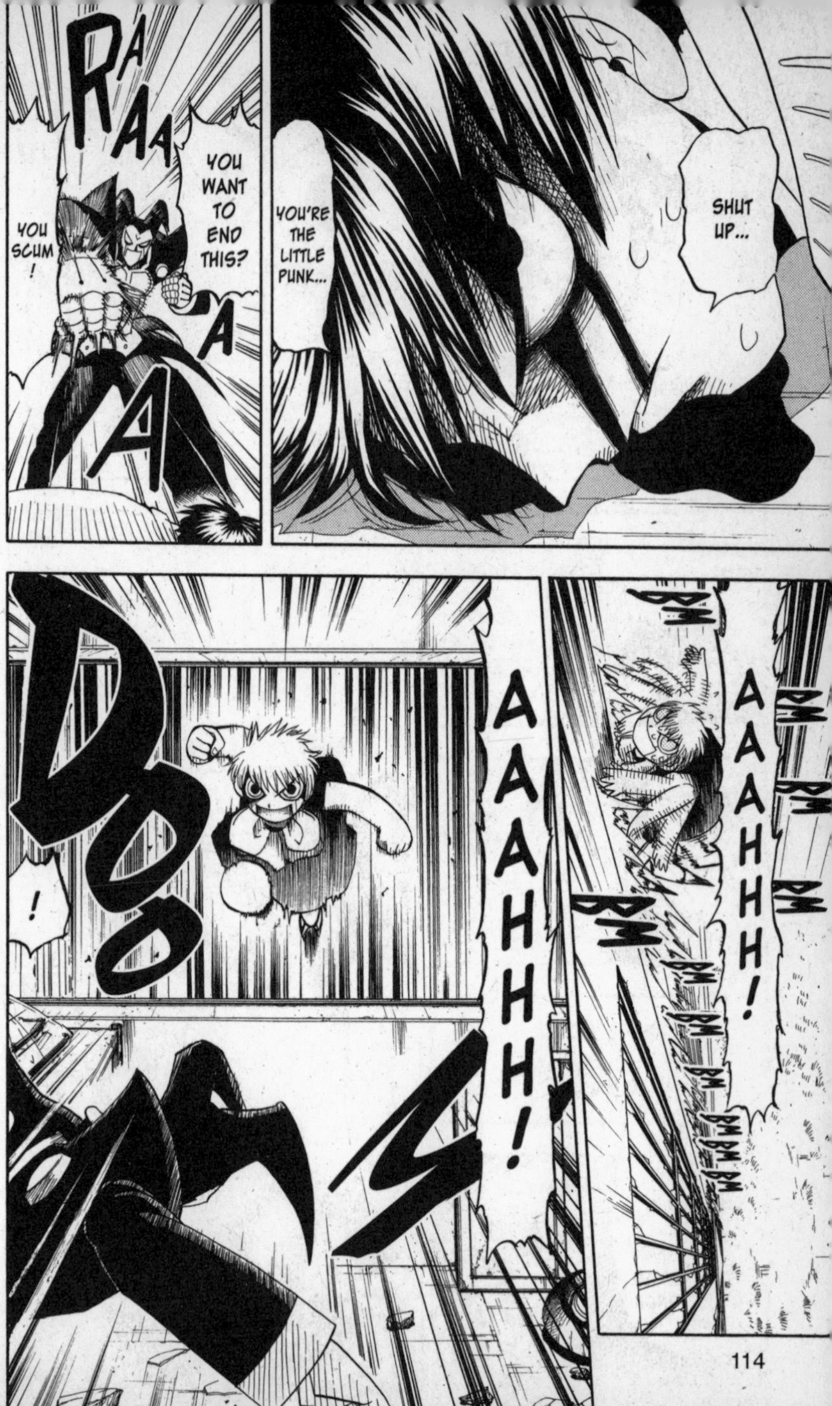
SHUT UP...
YOU'RE THE LITTLE PUNK...
RAAAAA
YOU WANT TO END THIS?
YOU SCUM!
BM BM BM BM BM BM BM BM BM BM BM BM BM
AAAHHH!
AAAHHH!
DOS
!

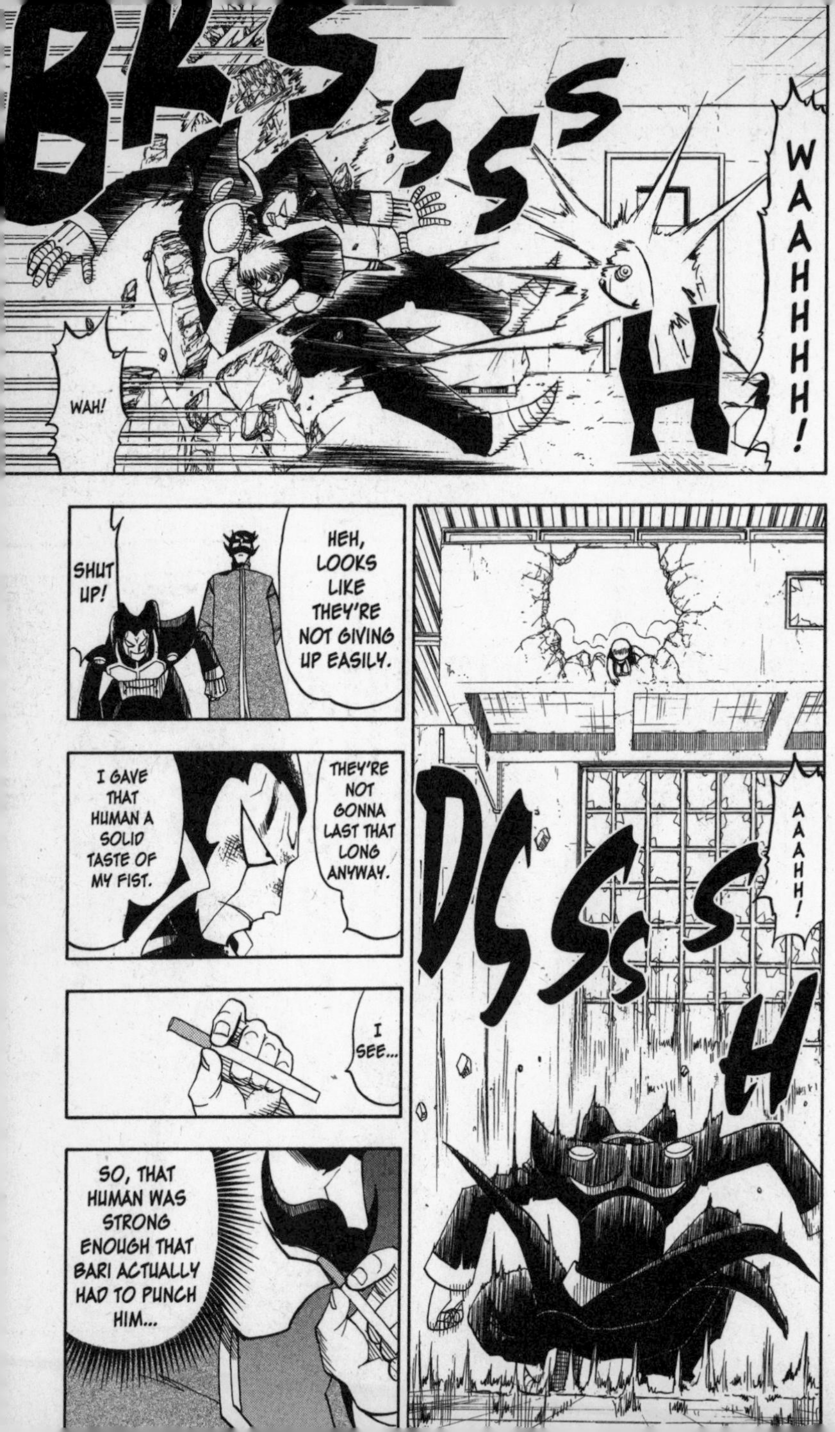
WAAHHHHH!
BKSSSSH
WAH!
AAAHH!
DSSSSH
HEH, LOOKS LIKE THEY'RE NOT GIVING UP EASILY.
SHUT UP!
THEY'RE NOT GONNA LAST THAT LONG ANYWAY.
I GAVE THAT HUMAN A SOLID TASTE OF MY FIST.
I SEE...
SO, THAT HUMAN WAS STRONG ENOUGH THAT BARI ACTUALLY HAD TO PUNCH HIM...

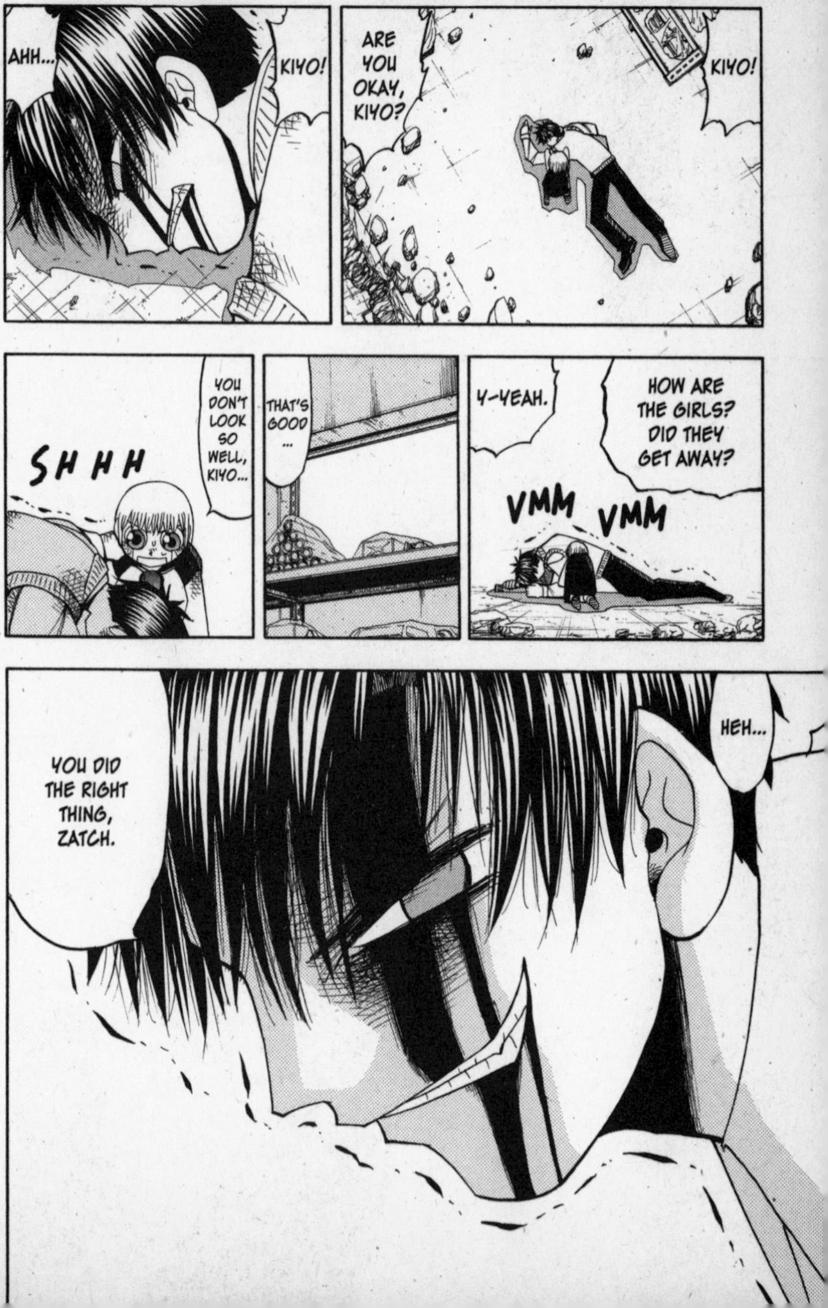
KIYO!
ARE YOU OKAY, KIYO?
KIYO!
AHH...
HOW ARE THE GIRLS? DID THEY GET AWAY?
Y-YEAH.
VMM VMM
THAT'S GOOD ...
YOU DON'T LOOK SO WELL, KIYO...
SHHH
HEH...
YOU DID THE RIGHT THING, ZATCH.

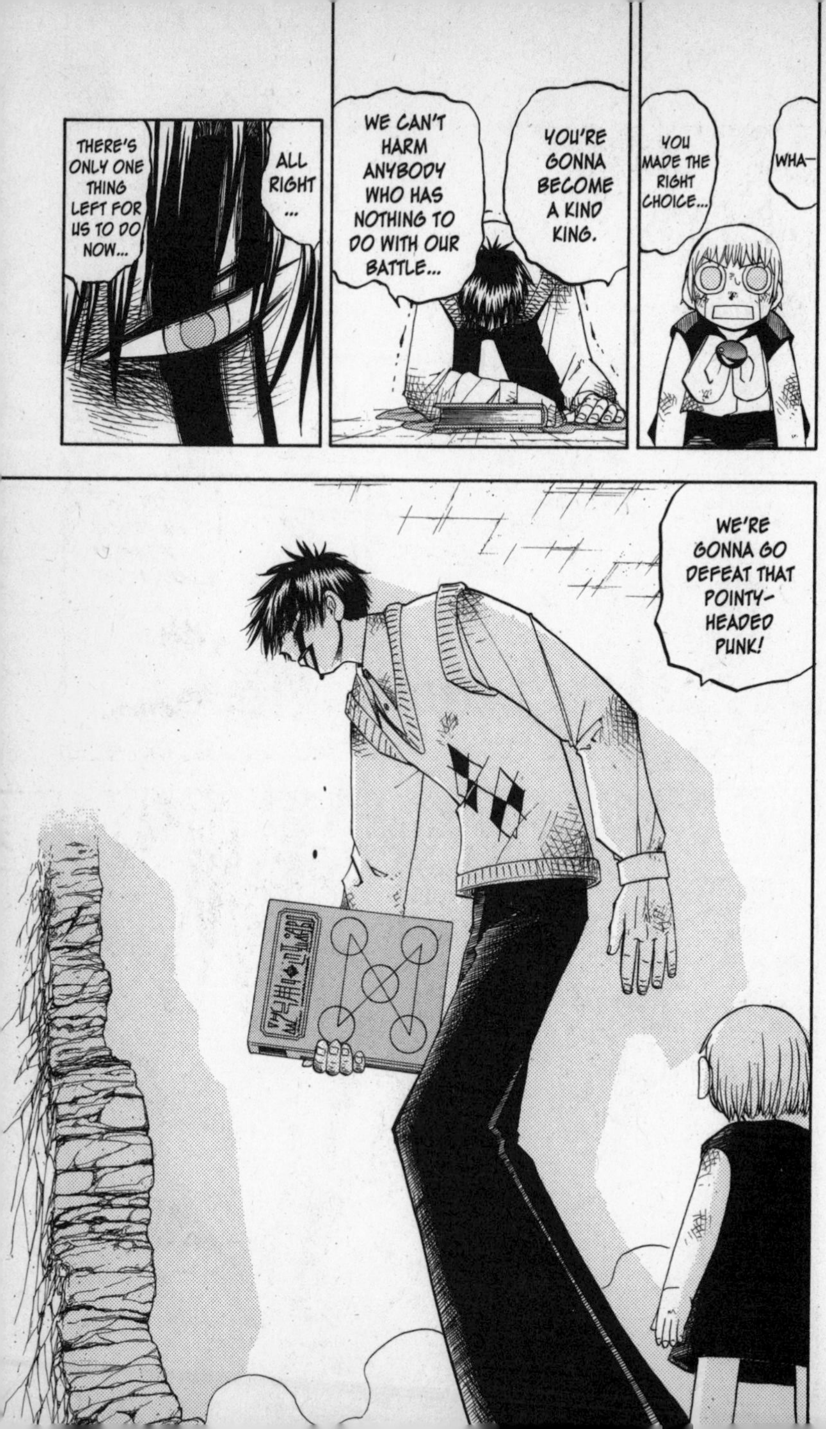
WHA—
YOU MADE THE RIGHT CHOICE...
YOU'RE GONNA BECOME A KIND KING.
WE CAN'T HARM ANYBODY WHO HAS NOTHING TO DO WITH OUR BATTLE...
ALL RIGHT...
THERE'S ONLY ONE THING LEFT FOR US TO DO NOW...
WE'RE GONNA GO DEFEAT THAT POINTY-HEADED PUNK!

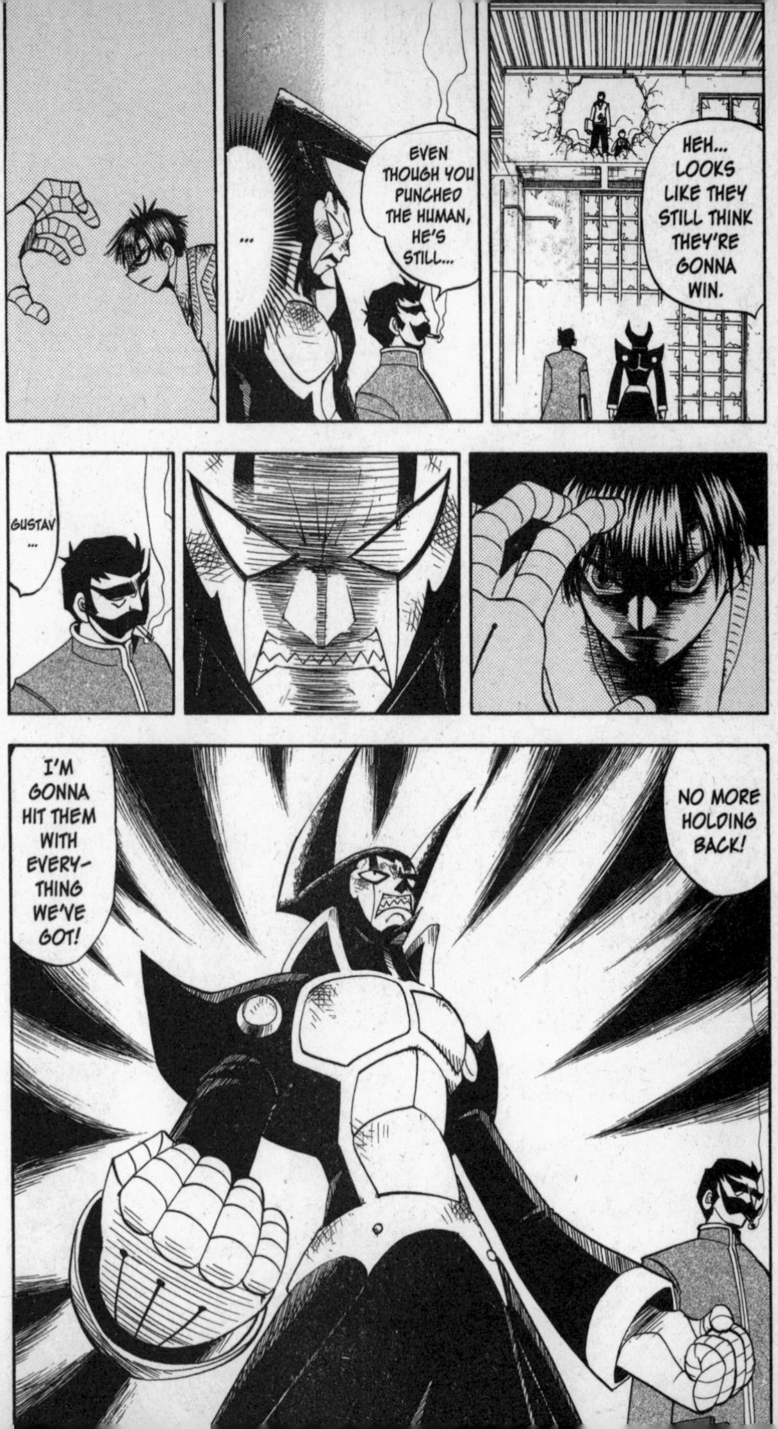
HEH... LOOKS LIKE THEY STILL THINK THEY'RE GONNA WIN.
EVEN THOUGH YOU PUNCHED THE HUMAN, HE'S STILL...
...
GUSTAV...
NO MORE HOLDING BACK!
I'M GONNA HIT THEM WITH EVERY-THING WE'VE GOT!

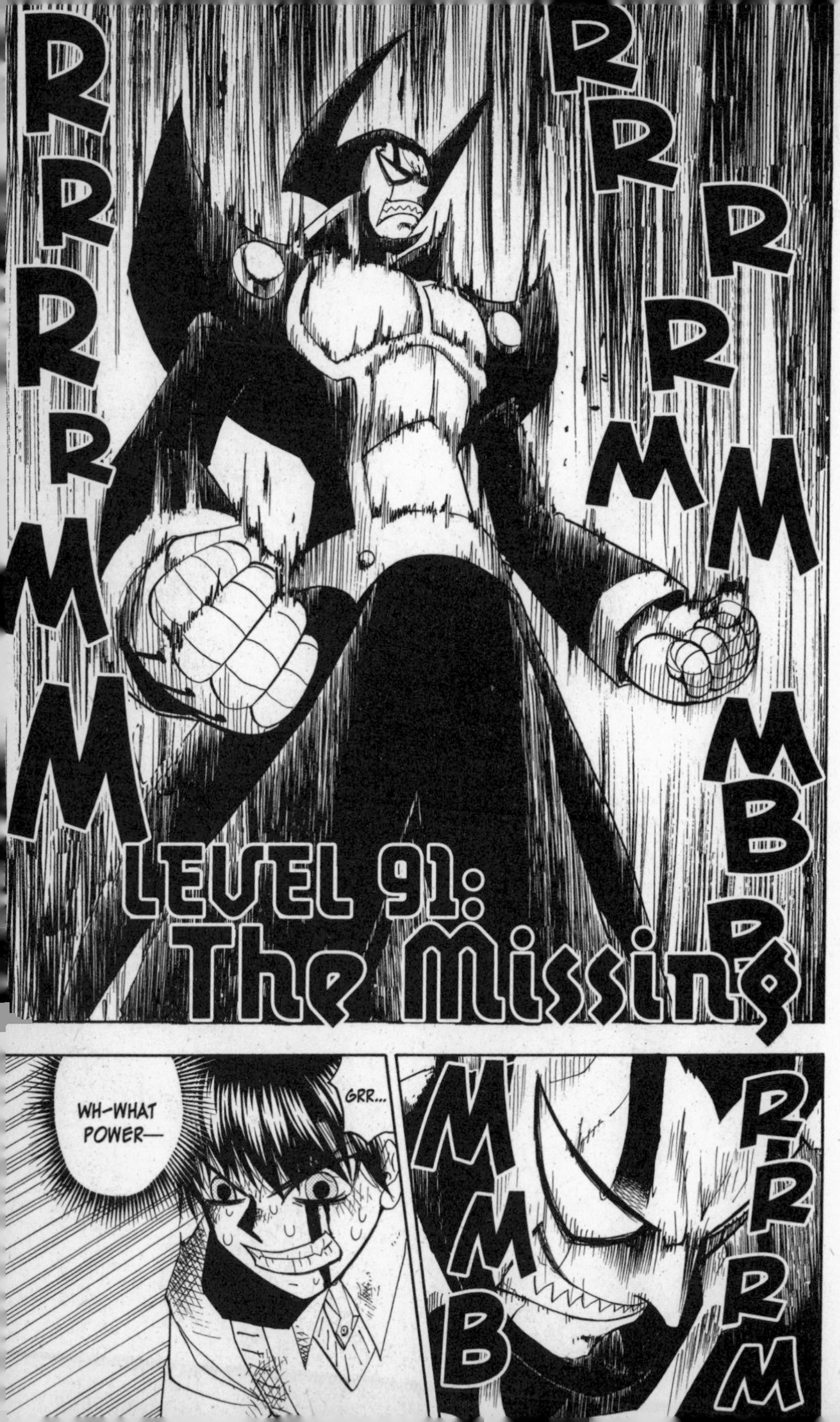
RRRRMM
RRRMMMBB
LEVEL 91:
The Missing
MMMB
RRRRM
GRR...
WH-WHAT POWER—

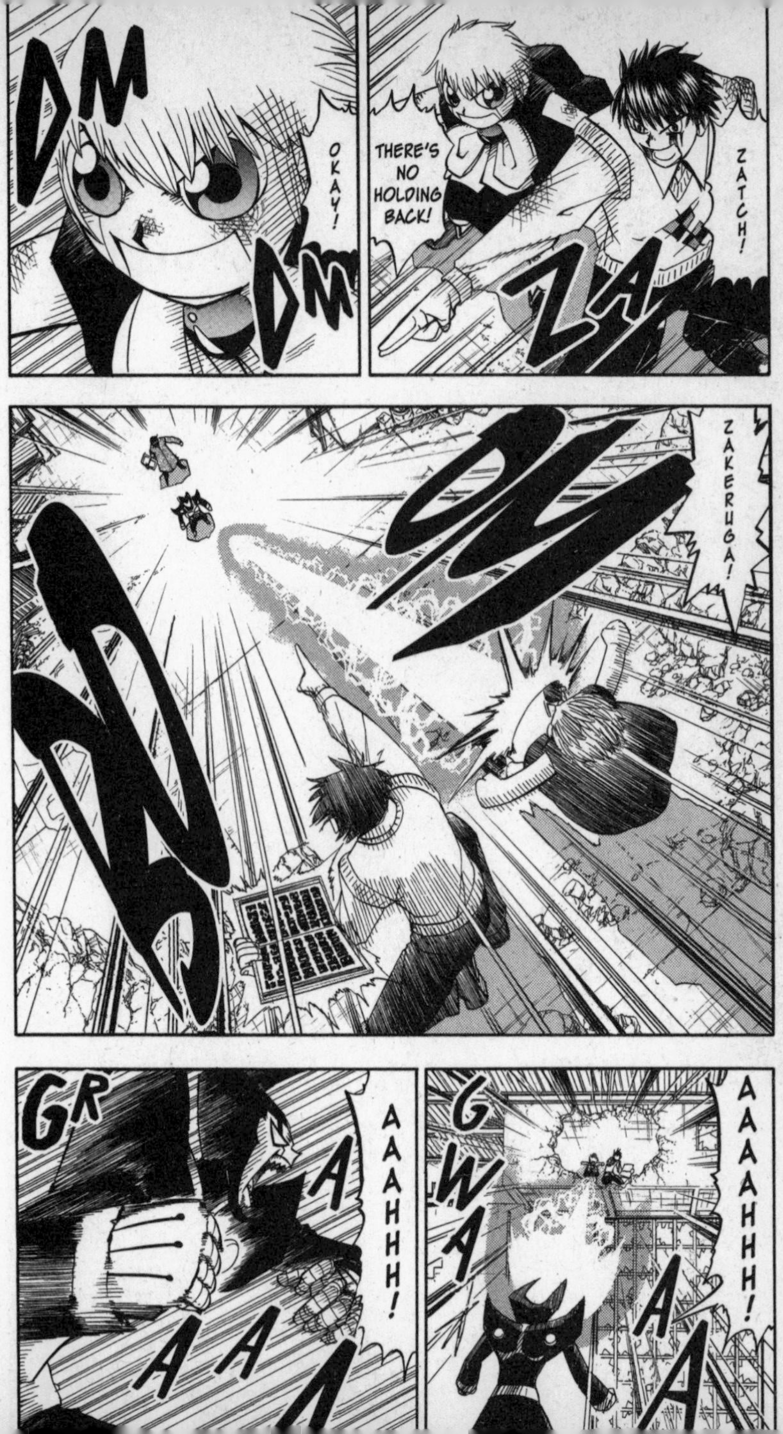
ZATCH!
THERE'S NO HOLDING BACK!
ZA
OKAY!
DM
DM
ZAKERUGA!
AAAAAHHH!
GWA
AAA
AAAHHH!
GR
AAA

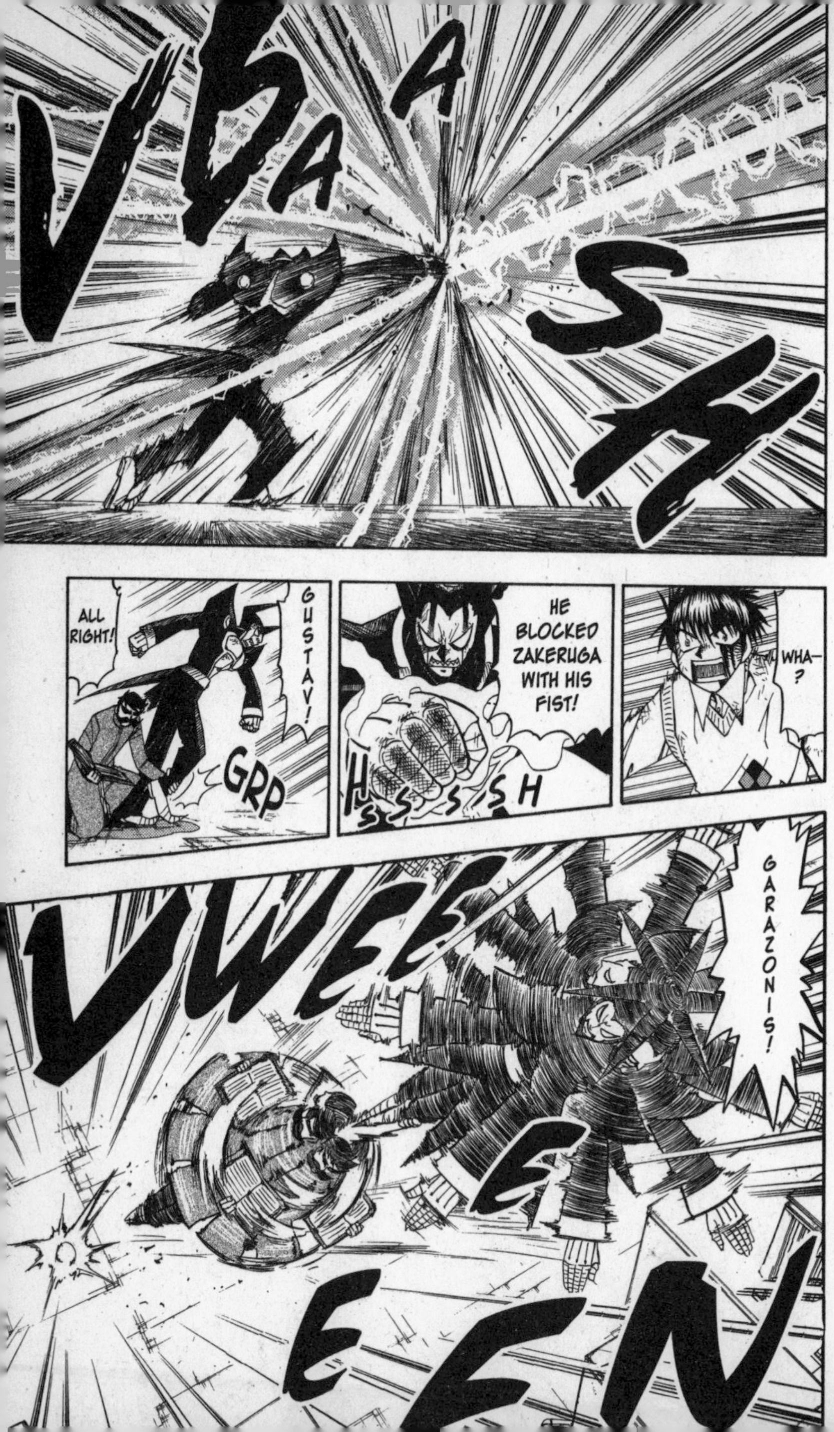
VBAAA
SH
WHA-?
HE BLOCKED ZAKERUGA WITH HIS FIST!
HSSSSH
GUSTAV!
ALL RIGHT!
GRP
GARAZONIS!
VWEEEEEN

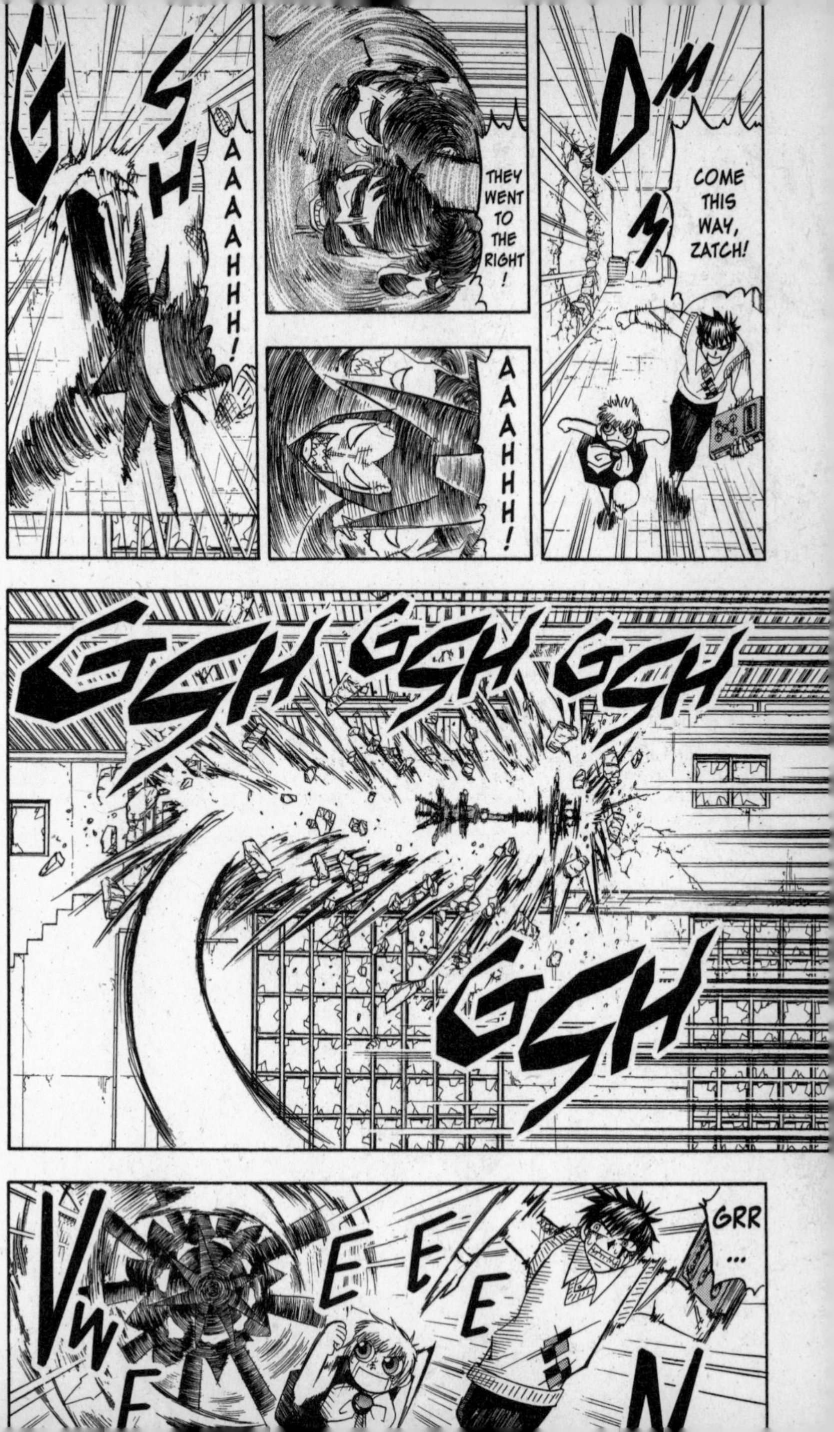
DMMM
COME THIS WAY, ZATCH!
THEY WENT TO THE RIGHT!
AAAHHH!
GSH
AAAAHHH!
GSH GSH GSH
GSH
GRR...
VWFEEEEN

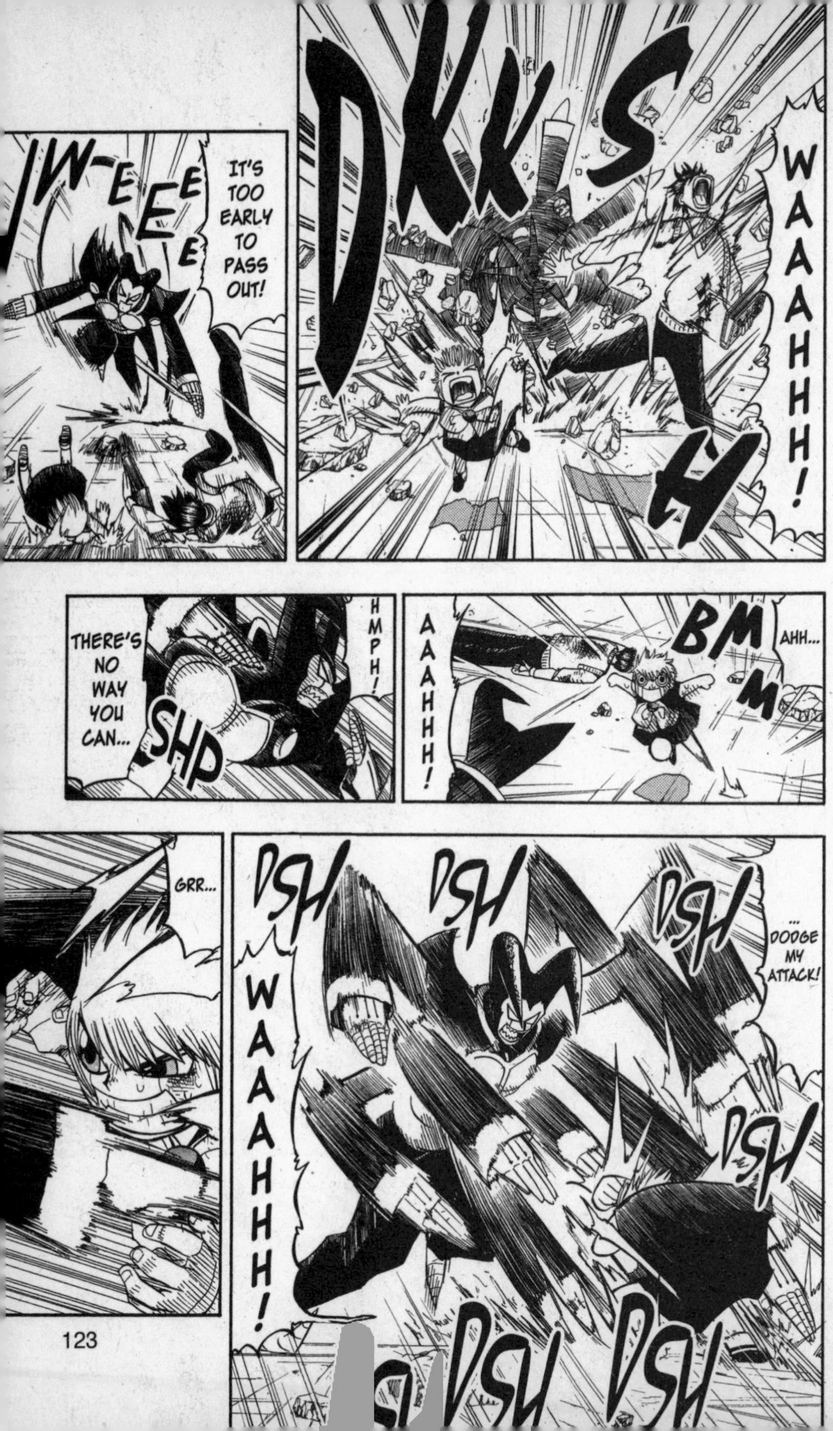
DKKSH
WAAAAHHH!
W-EEEE
IT'S TOO EARLY TO PASS OUT!
BMM
AHH...
AAAHHHH!
HMPH!
THERE'S NO WAY YOU CAN...
SHP
DSH DSH DSH
...DODGE MY ATTACK!
WAAAAHHH!
DSH DSH DSH
GRR...

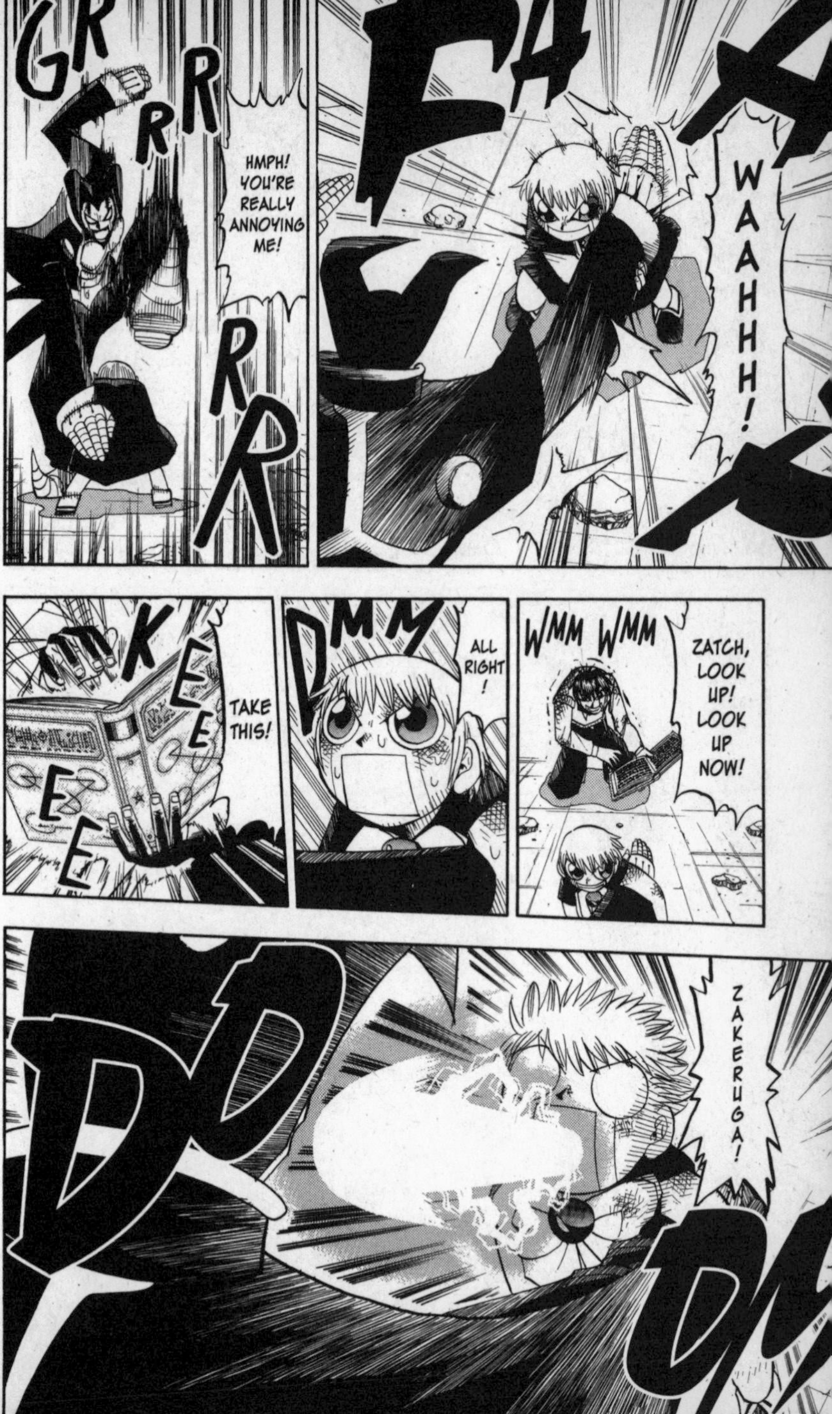
WAAHHHH!
GRRRRR
HMPH! YOU'RE REALLY ANNOYING ME!
WMM WMM
ZATCH, LOOK UP! LOOK UP NOW!
DMM
ALL RIGHT!
TAKE THIS!
ZAKERUGA!

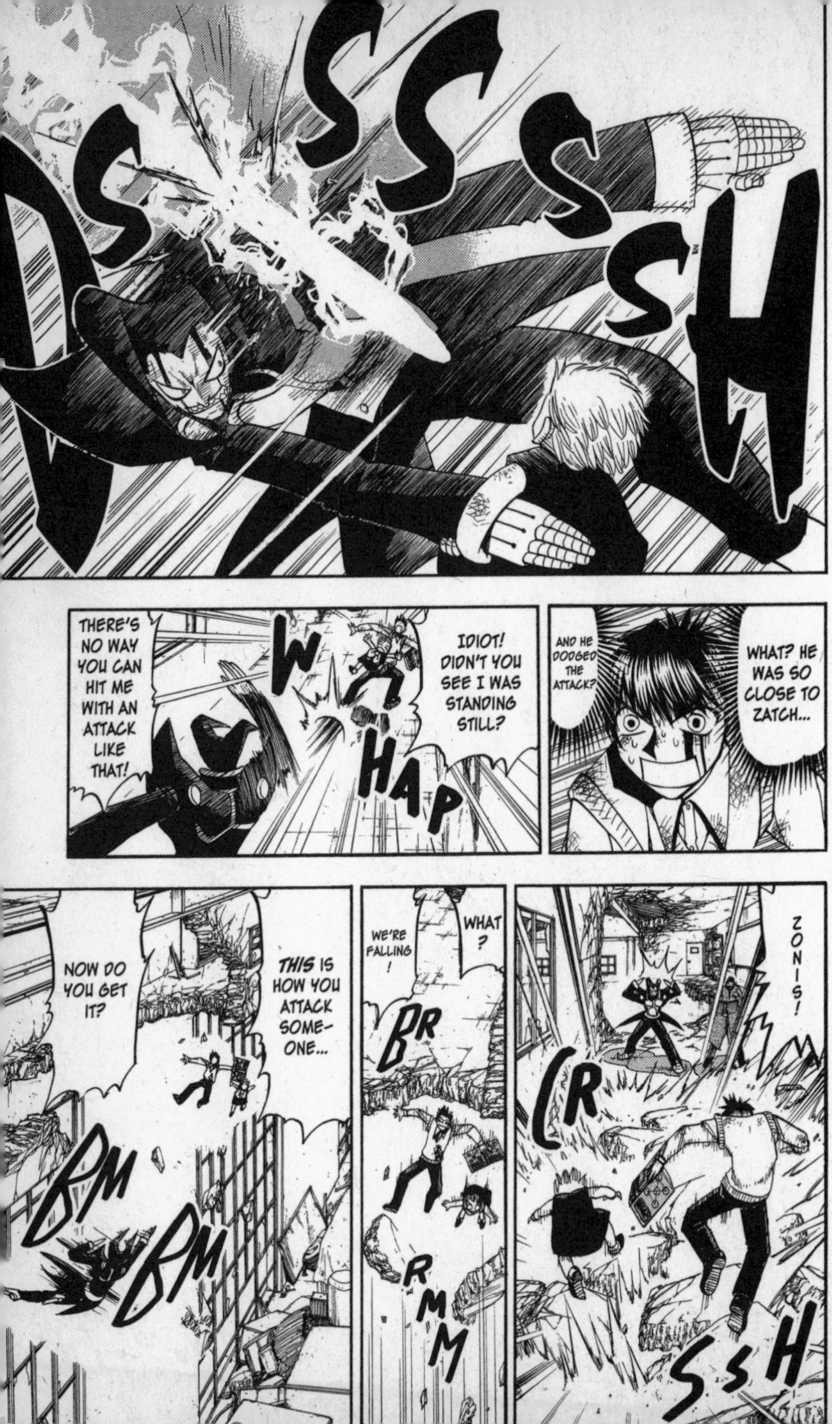
DSSSSSH
WHAT? HE WAS SO CLOSE TO ZATCH...
AND HE DODGED THE ATTACK?
IDIOT! DIDN'T YOU SEE I WAS STANDING STILL?
WHAP
THERE'S NO WAY YOU CAN HIT ME WITH AN ATTACK LIKE THAT!
ZONIS!
CR
SSH
WHAT?
WE'RE FALLING!
BRRMM
*THIS* IS HOW YOU ATTACK SOME-ONE...
NOW DO YOU GET IT?
BM BM

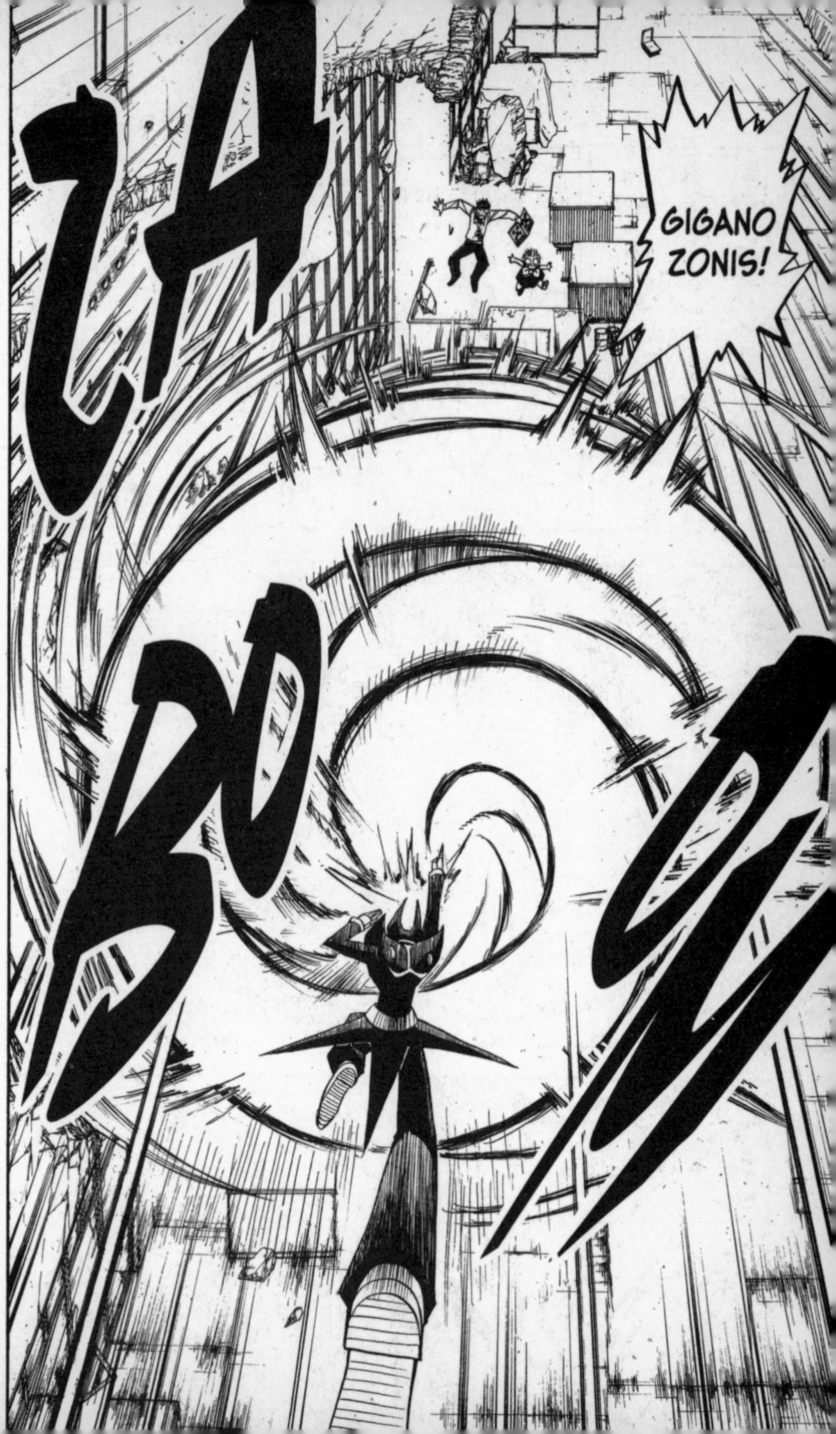
GIGANO ZONIS!

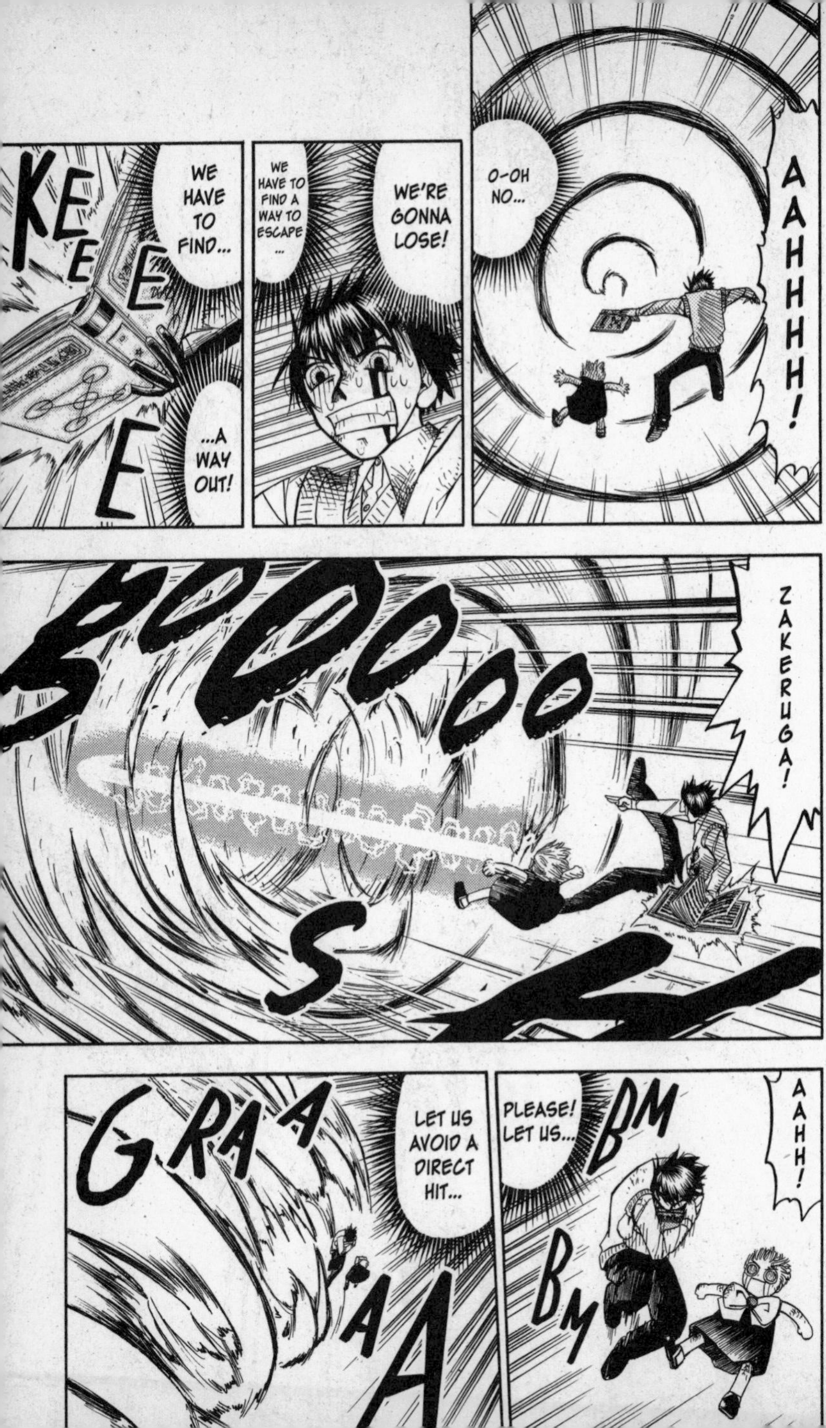
AAHHHHH!
O-OH NO...
WE'RE GONNA LOSE!
WE HAVE TO FIND A WAY TO ESCAPE ...
WE HAVE TO FIND...
...A WAY OUT!
KEEEE
ZAKERUGA!
BOOOOOSH
AAHH!
BM
BM
PLEASE! LET US...
LET US AVOID A DIRECT HIT...
GRAAAA

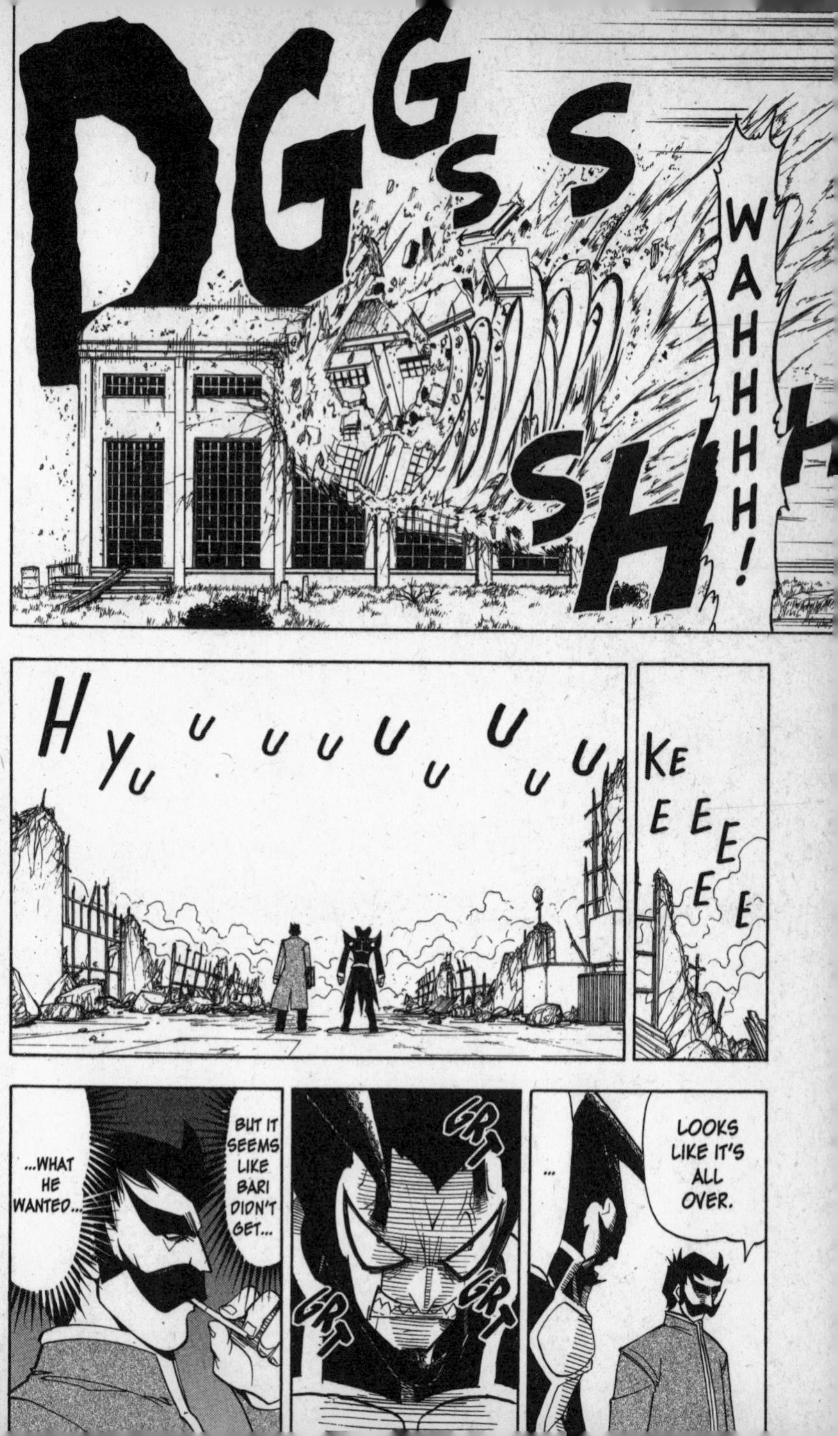
WAHHHH!
DGGSS
SH
KEEEEEE
HYUUUUUUUUUU
LOOKS LIKE IT'S ALL OVER.
...
GRT
GRT
GRT
BUT IT SEEMS LIKE BARI DIDN'T GET...
...WHAT HE WANTED...

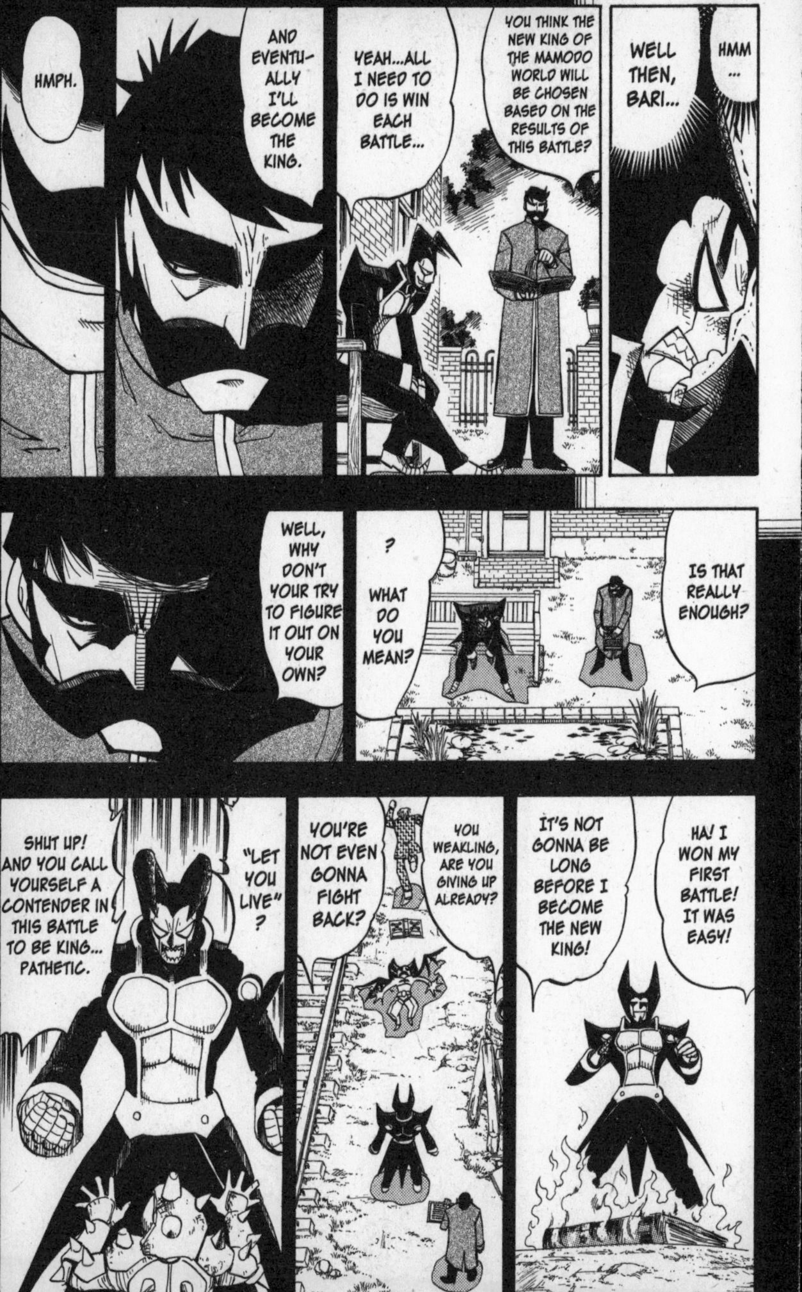
HMM ...
WELL THEN, BARI...
YOU THINK THE NEW KING OF THE MAMODO WORLD WILL BE CHOSEN BASED ON THE RESULTS OF THIS BATTLE?
YEAH...ALL I NEED TO DO IS WIN EACH BATTLE...
AND EVENTU-ALLY I'LL BECOME THE KING.
HMPH.
IS THAT REALLY ENOUGH?
? WHAT DO YOU MEAN?
WELL, WHY DON'T YOUR TRY TO FIGURE IT OUT ON YOUR OWN?
HA! I WON MY FIRST BATTLE! IT WAS EASY!
IT'S NOT GONNA BE LONG BEFORE I BECOME THE NEW KING!
YOU WEAKLING, ARE YOU GIVING UP ALREADY?
YOU'RE NOT EVEN GONNA FIGHT BACK?
"LET YOU LIVE" ?
SHUT UP! AND YOU CALL YOURSELF A CONTENDER IN THIS BATTLE TO BE KING... PATHETIC.

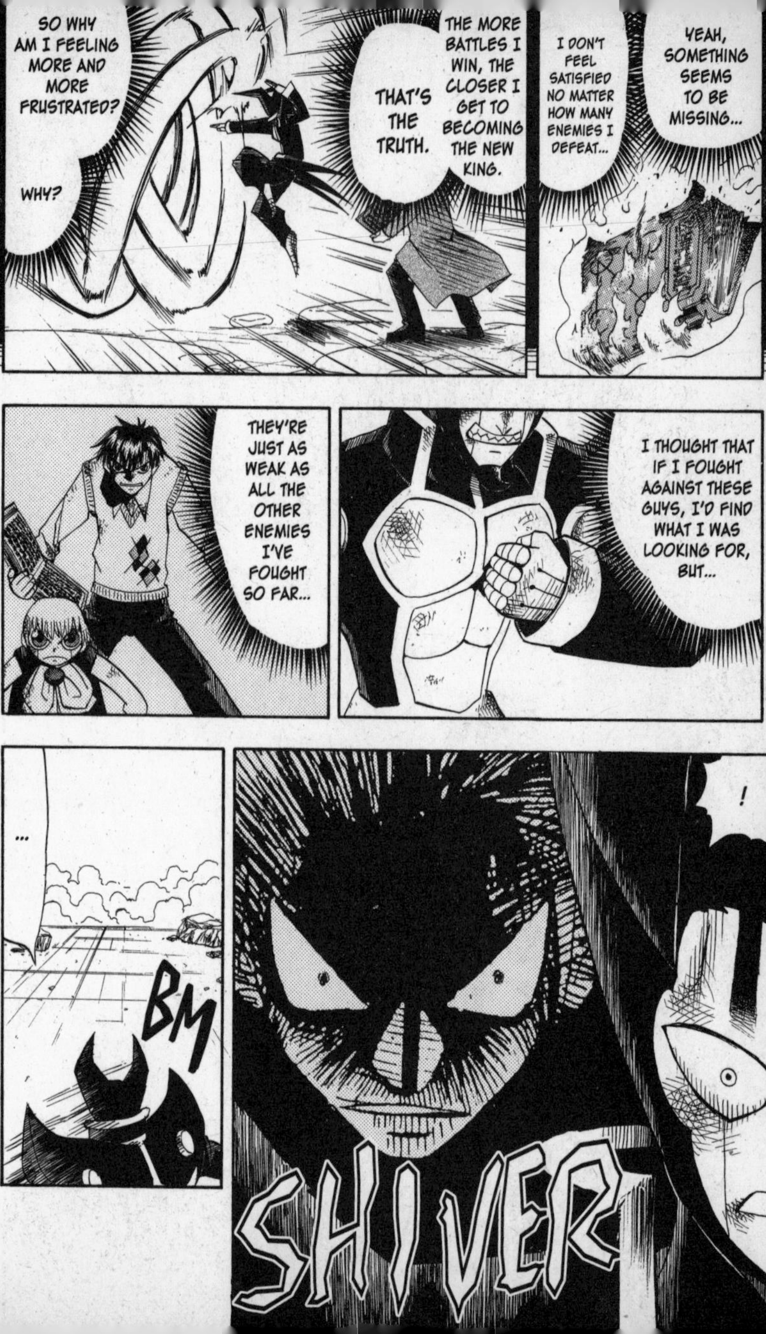
YEAH, SOMETHING SEEMS TO BE MISSING...
I DON'T FEEL SATISFIED NO MATTER HOW MANY ENEMIES I DEFEAT...
THE MORE BATTLES I WIN, THE CLOSER I GET TO BECOMING THE NEW KING.
THAT'S THE TRUTH.
SO WHY AM I FEELING MORE AND MORE FRUSTRATED?
WHY?
I THOUGHT THAT IF I FOUGHT AGAINST THESE GUYS, I'D FIND WHAT I WAS LOOKING FOR, BUT...
THEY'RE JUST AS WEAK AS ALL THE OTHER ENEMIES I'VE FOUGHT SO FAR...
!
SHIVER
...
BM

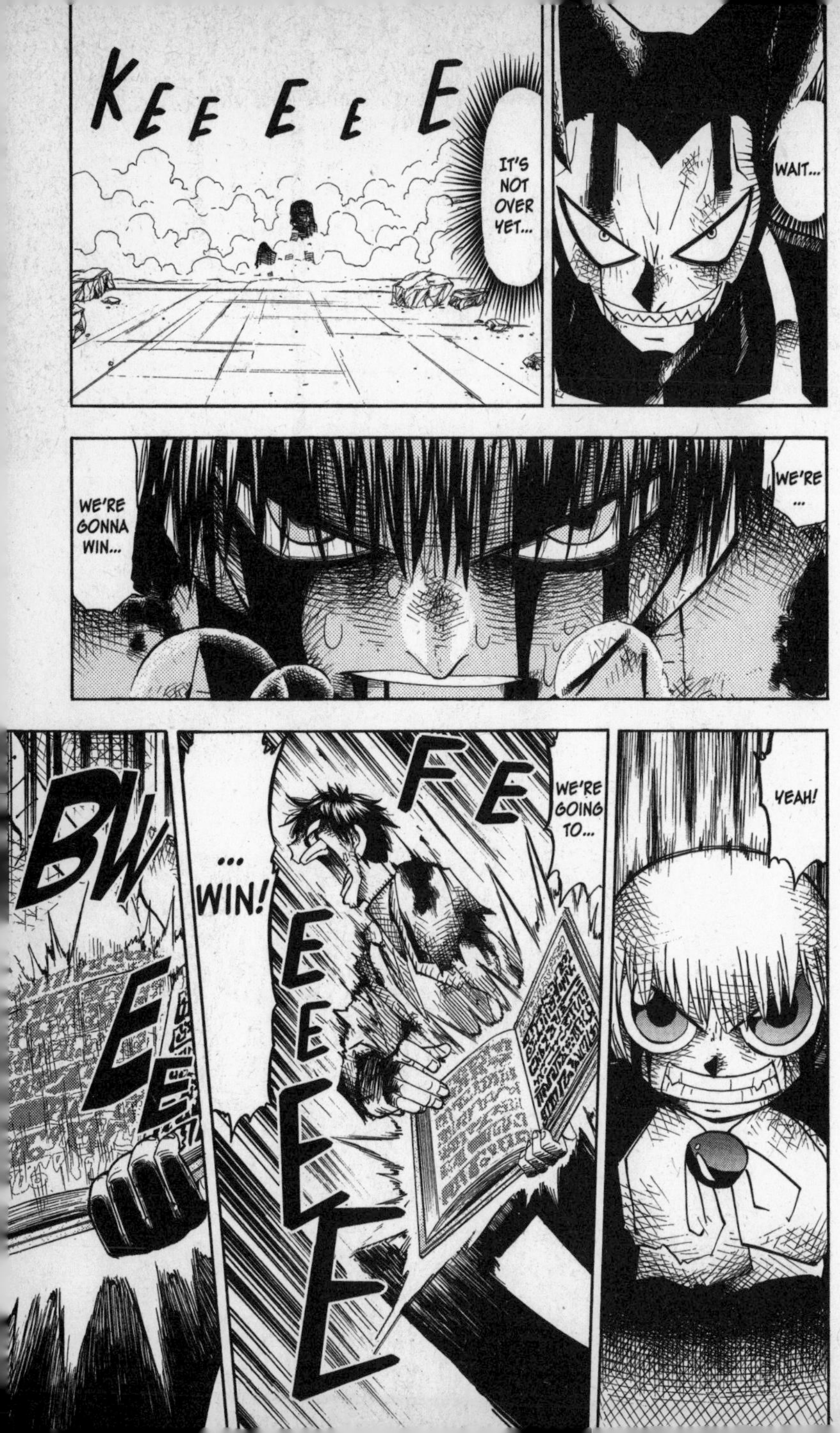
WAIT...
IT'S NOT OVER YET...
KEEEEE
WE'RE ...
WE'RE GONNA WIN...
YEAH!
WE'RE GOING TO...
... WIN!
FEEEEEE
BWEEE

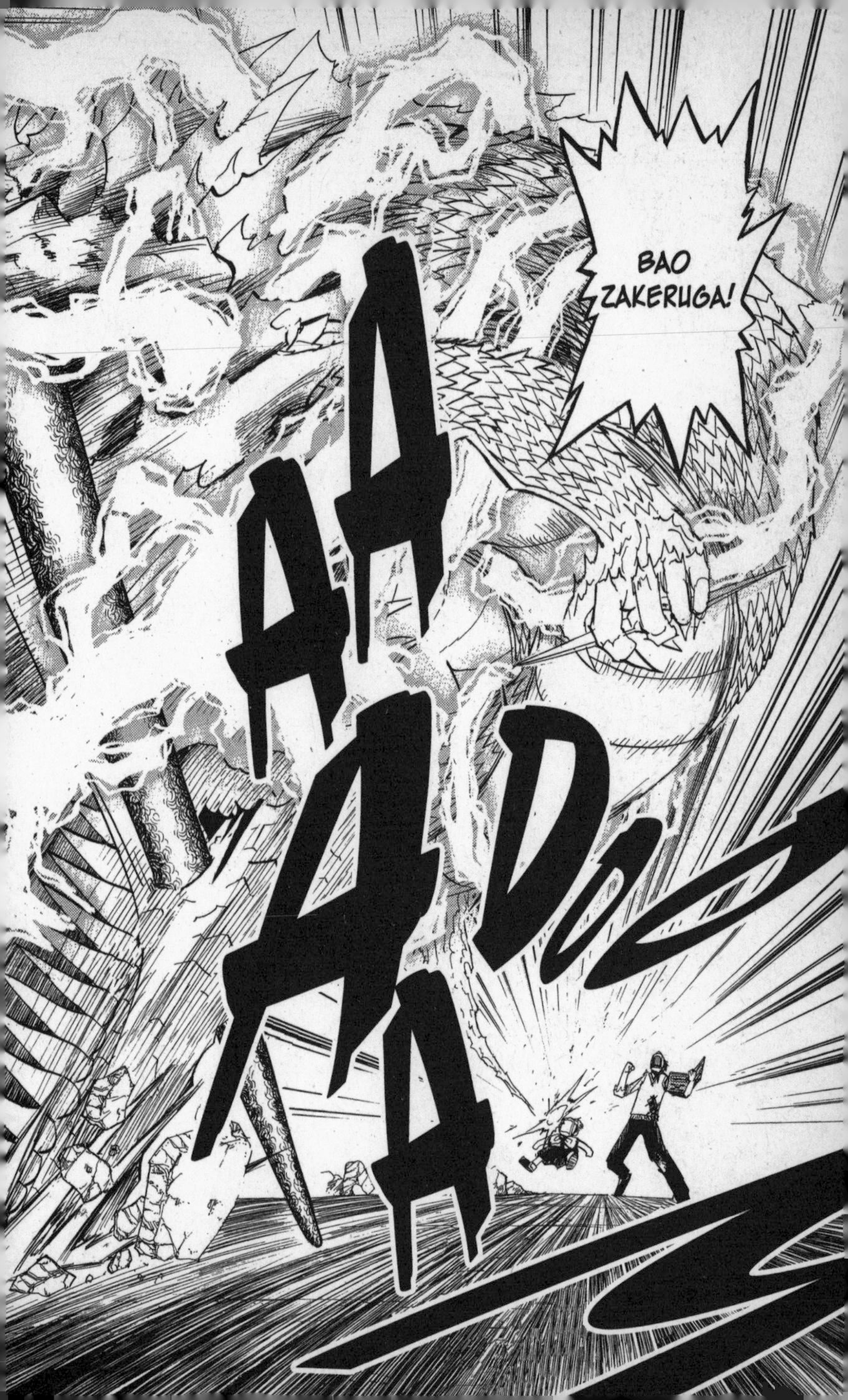
BAO ZAKERUGA!
AAAADo

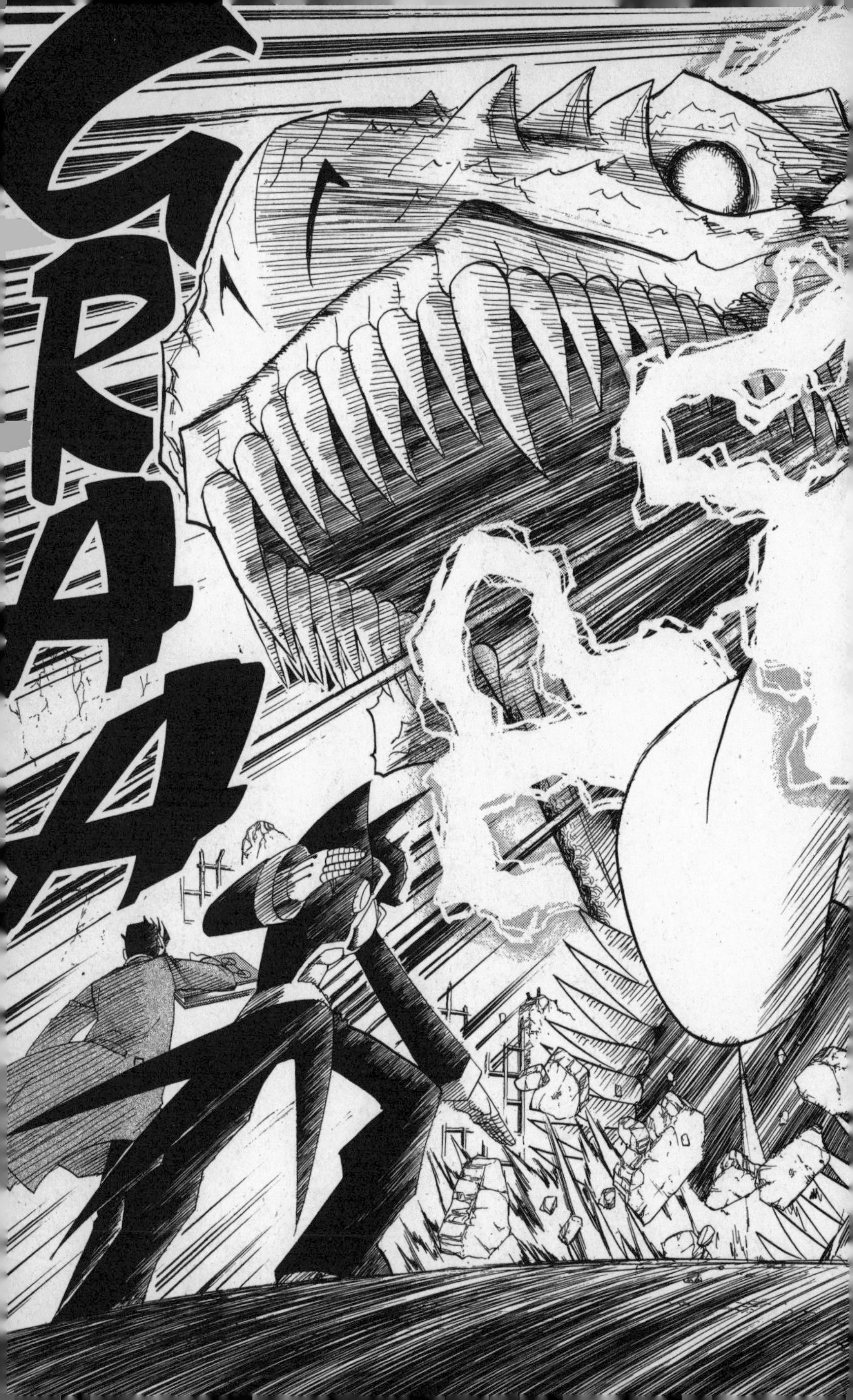
GRAAA

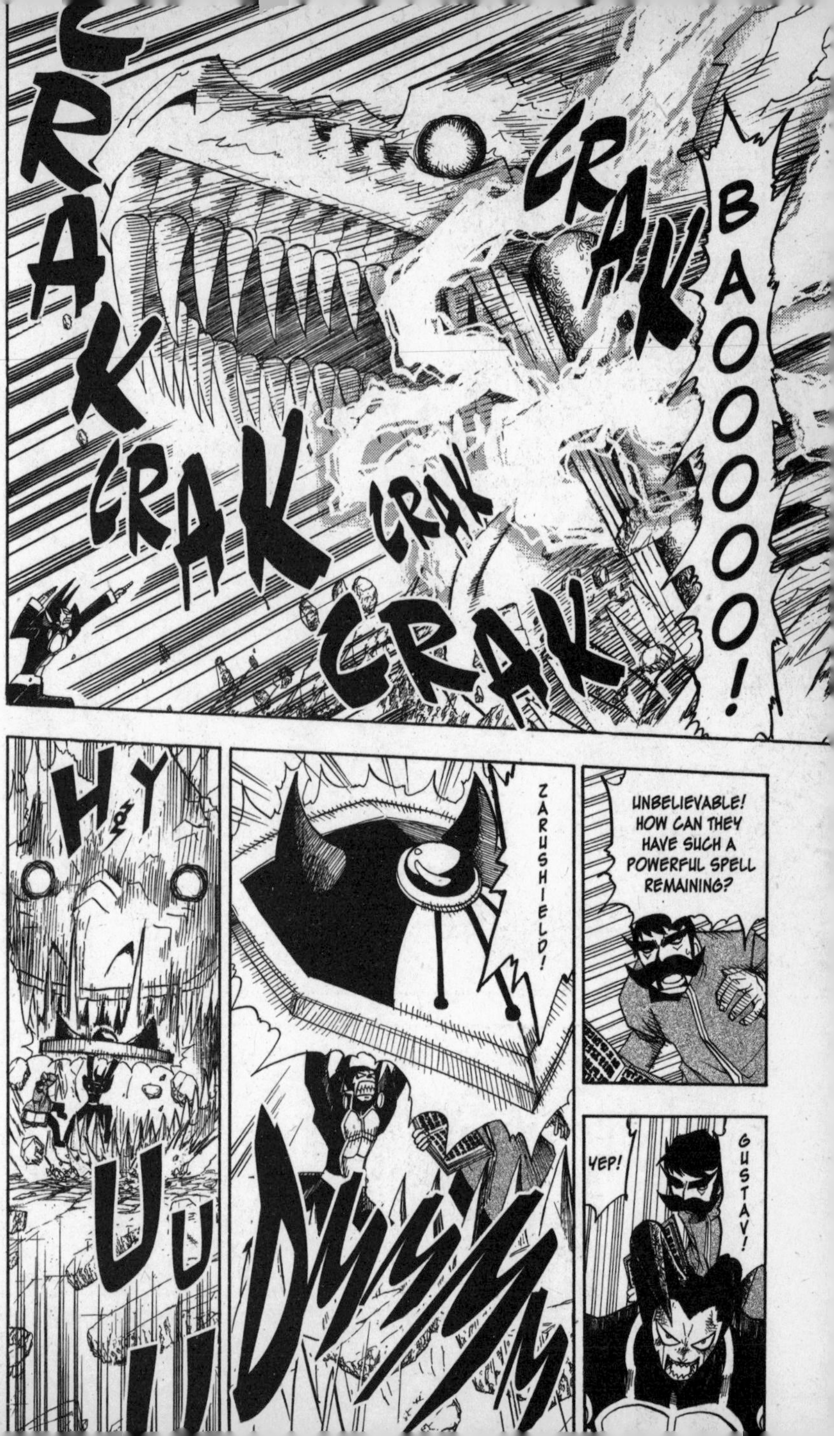
BAOOOOOO!
CRAK
CRAK
CRAK
CRAK
CRAK
UNBELIEVABLE! HOW CAN THEY HAVE SUCH A POWERFUL SPELL REMAINING?
GUSTAV!
YEP!
ZARUSHIELD!
HYUUU

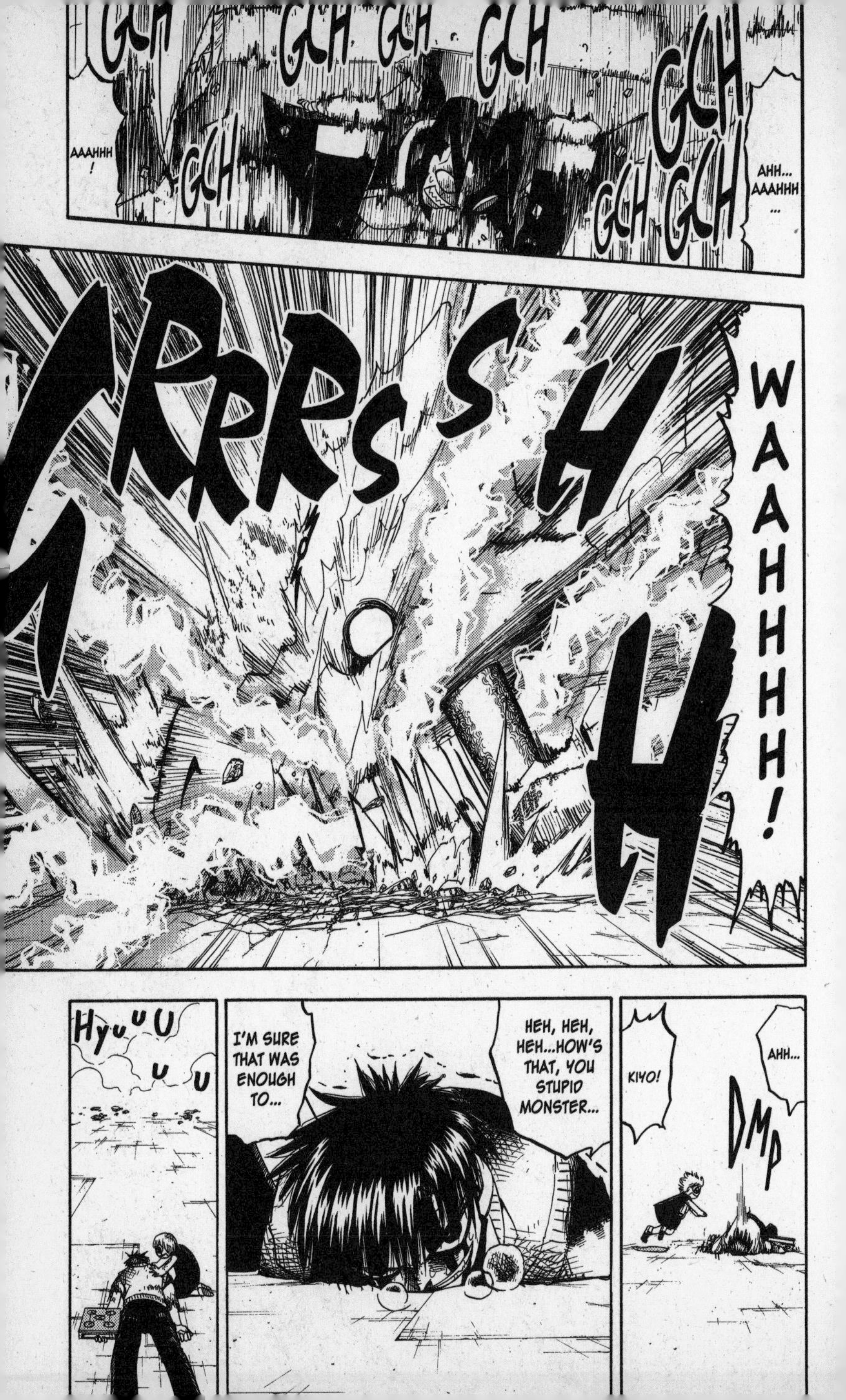
AHH... AAAHHH ...
GCH
GCH GCH
GCH
GCH GCH
GCH
GCH
AAAHHH !
WAAHHHH!
CRRRSSHH
AHH...
KIYO!
DMP
HEH, HEH, HEH...HOW'S THAT, YOU STUPID MONSTER...
I'M SURE THAT WAS ENOUGH TO...
HYUUU UUU

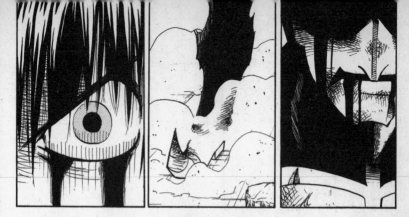

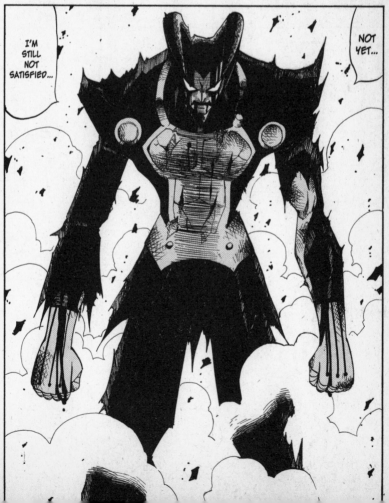

I'M STILL NOT SATISFIED...

NOT YET...

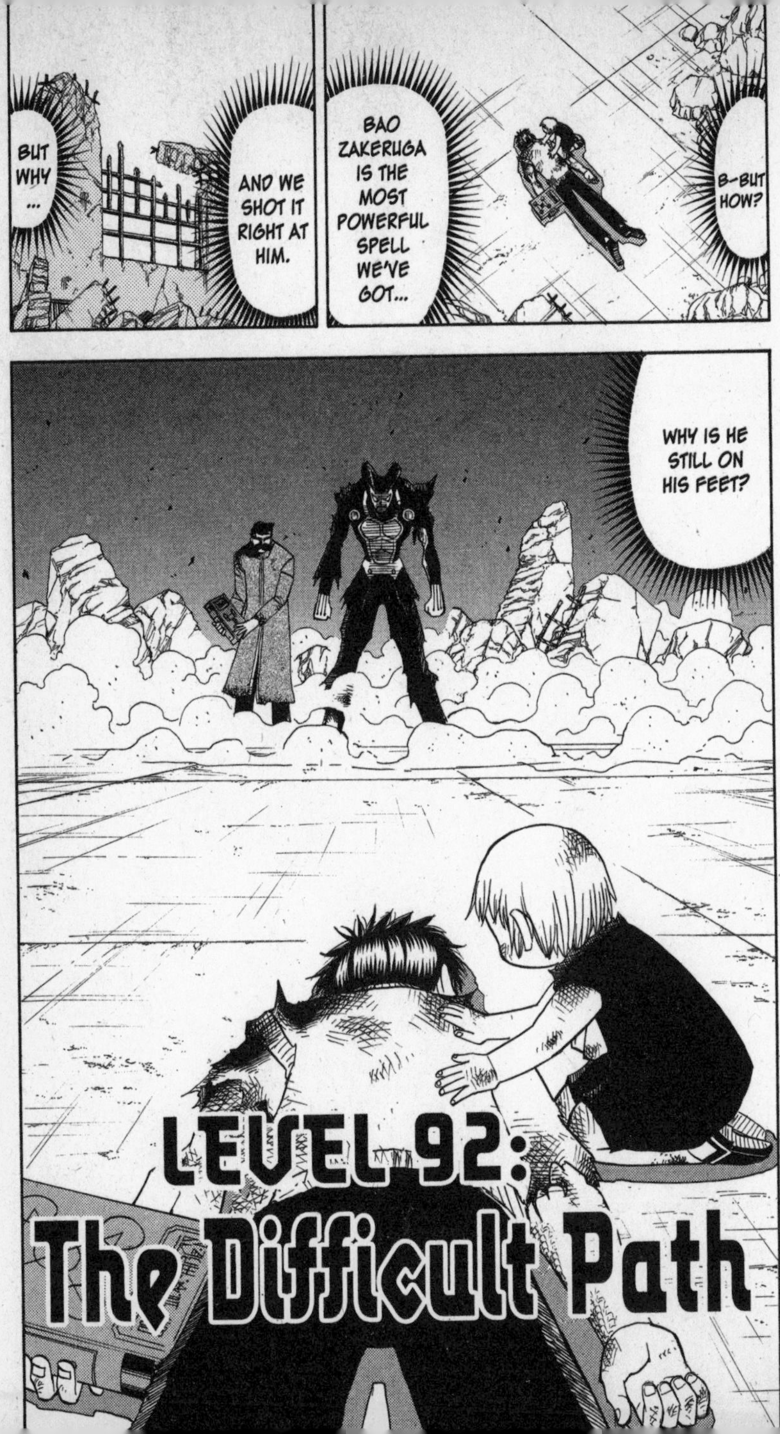
B-BUT HOW?
BAO ZAKERUGA IS THE MOST POWERFUL SPELL WE'VE GOT...
AND WE SHOT IT RIGHT AT HIM.
BUT WHY ...
WHY IS HE STILL ON HIS FEET?
LEVEL 92:
The Difficult Path

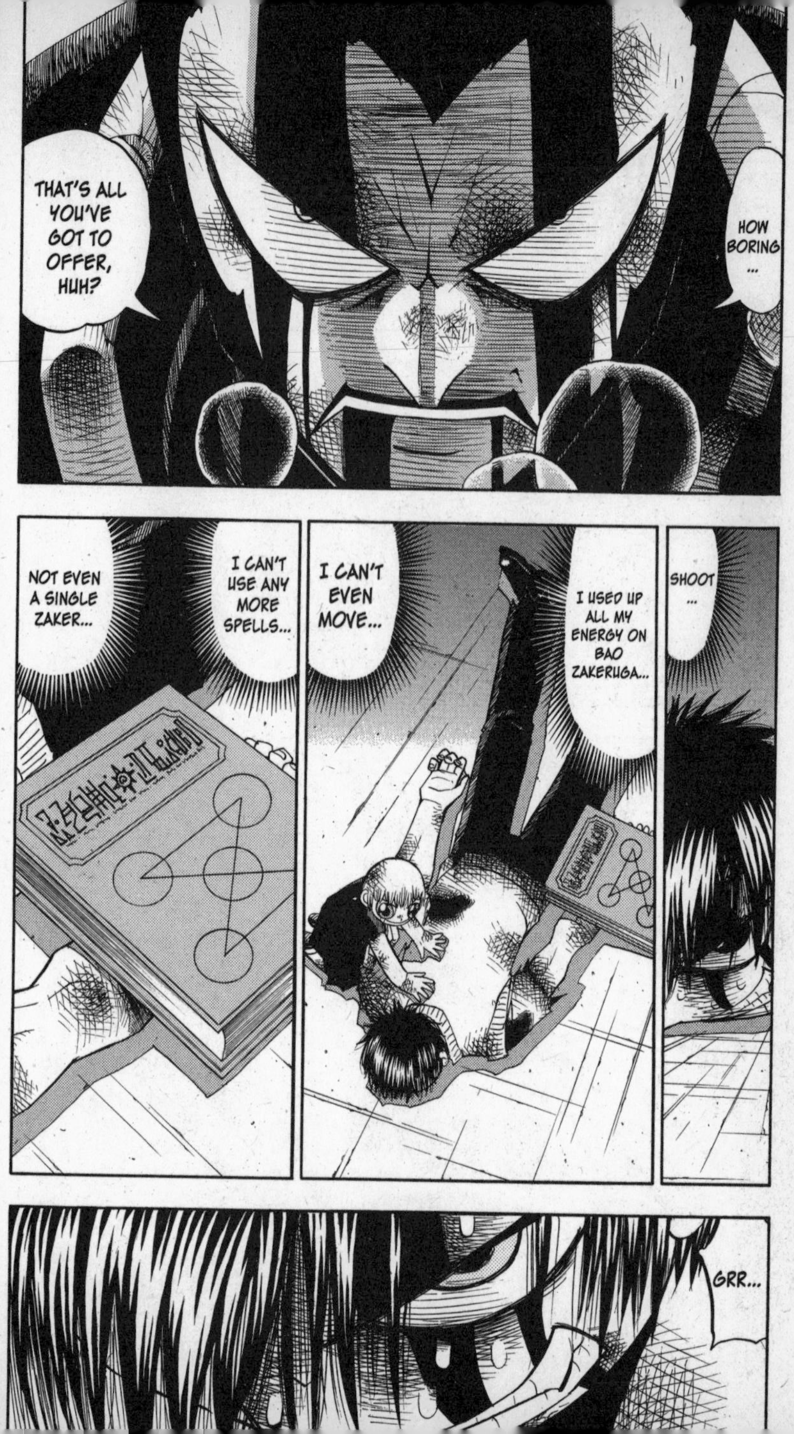
HOW BORING ...
THAT'S ALL YOU'VE GOT TO OFFER, HUH?
SHOOT ...
I USED UP ALL MY ENERGY ON BAO ZAKERUGA...
I CAN'T EVEN MOVE...
I CAN'T USE ANY MORE SPELLS...
NOT EVEN A SINGLE ZAKER...
GRR...

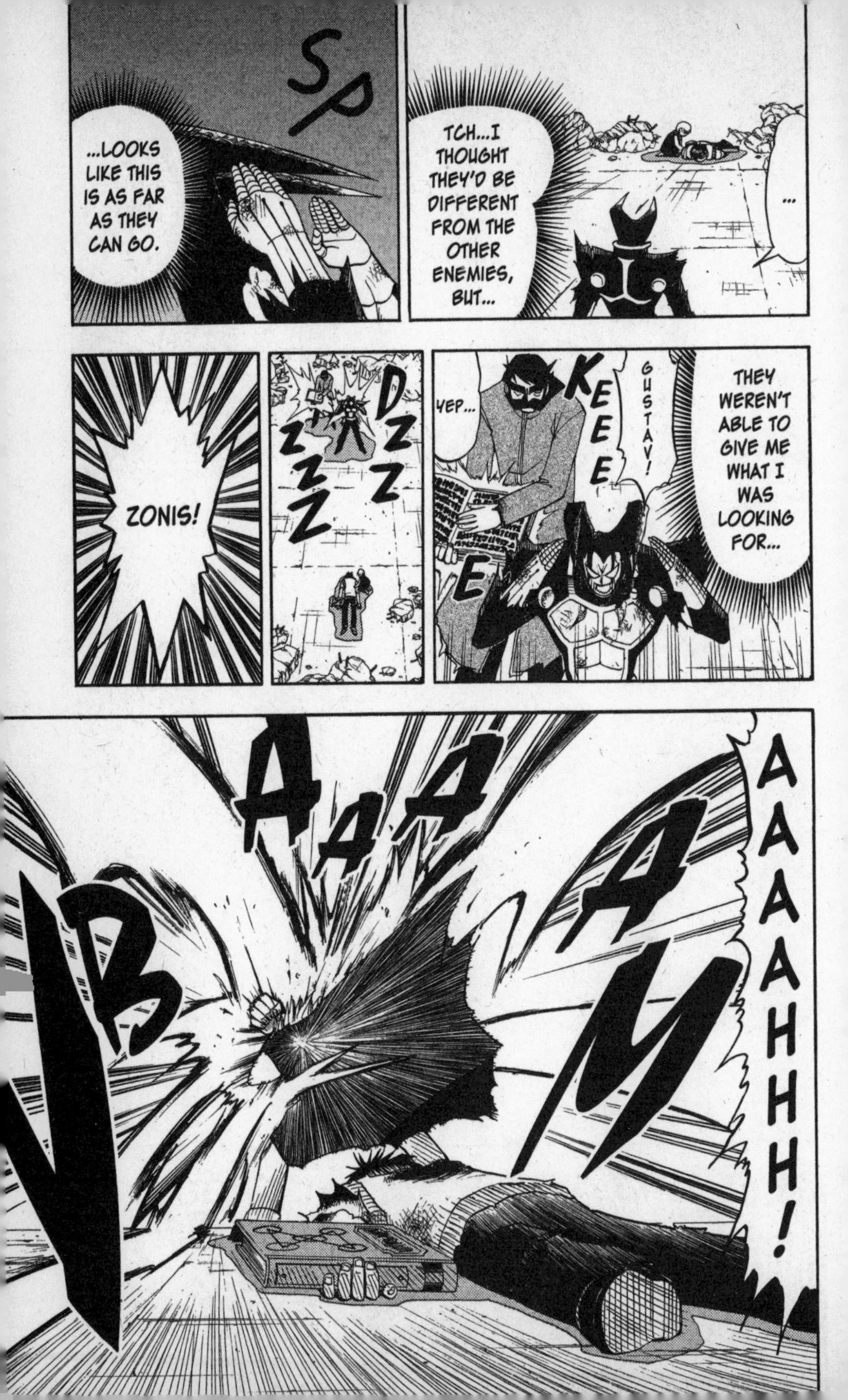
...
TCH...I THOUGHT THEY'D BE DIFFERENT FROM THE OTHER ENEMIES, BUT...
SP
...LOOKS LIKE THIS IS AS FAR AS THEY CAN GO.
THEY WEREN'T ABLE TO GIVE ME WHAT I WAS LOOKING FOR...
GUSTAV!
KEEEE
YEP...
DZZZZZ
ZONIS!
AAAAHHH!
BAAAAM

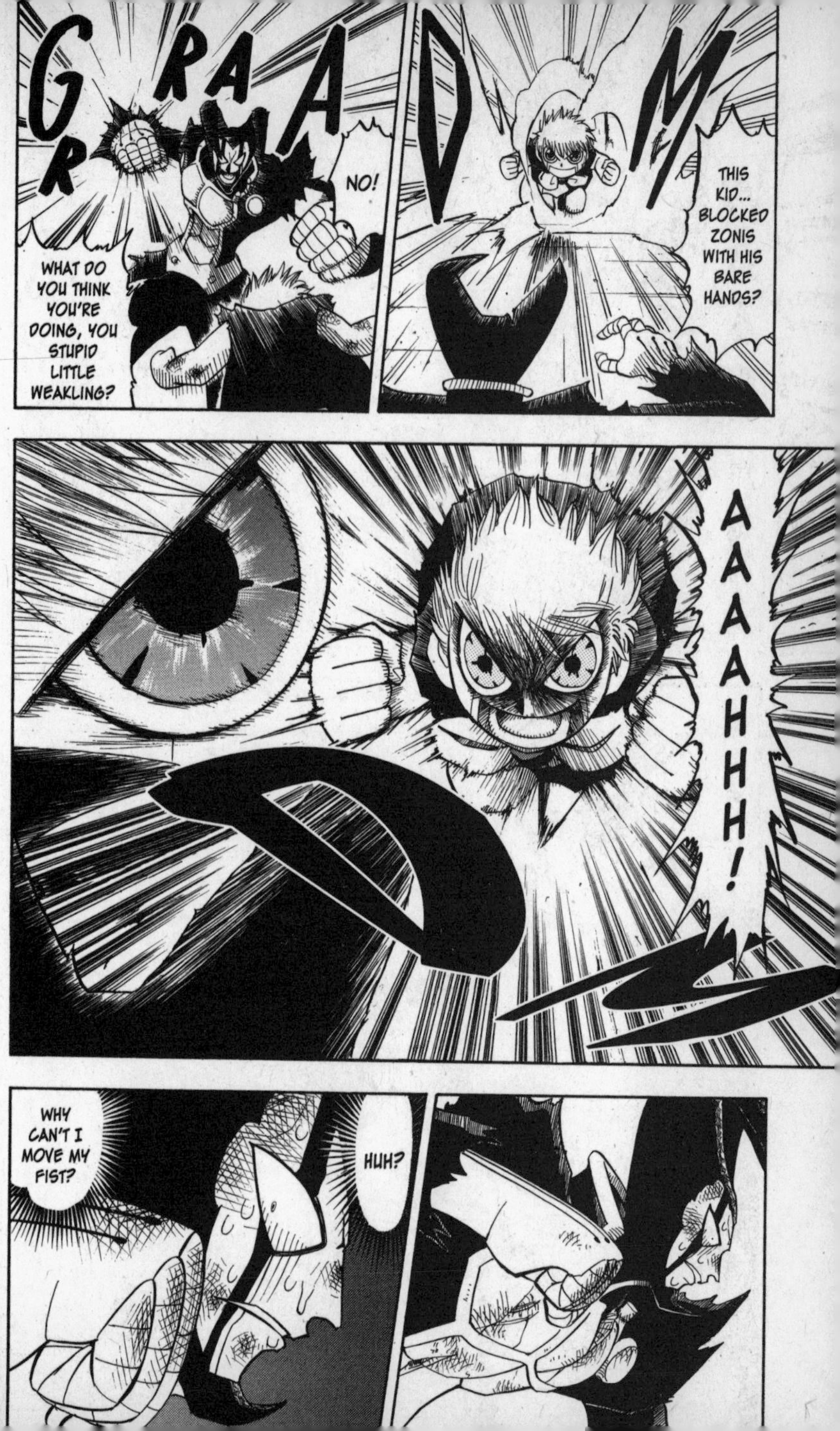
THIS KID... BLOCKED ZONIS WITH HIS BARE HANDS?
GRRAADM
NO!
WHAT DO YOU THINK YOU'RE DOING, YOU STUPID LITTLE WEAKLING?
AAAAHHH!
HUH?
WHY CAN'T I MOVE MY FIST?

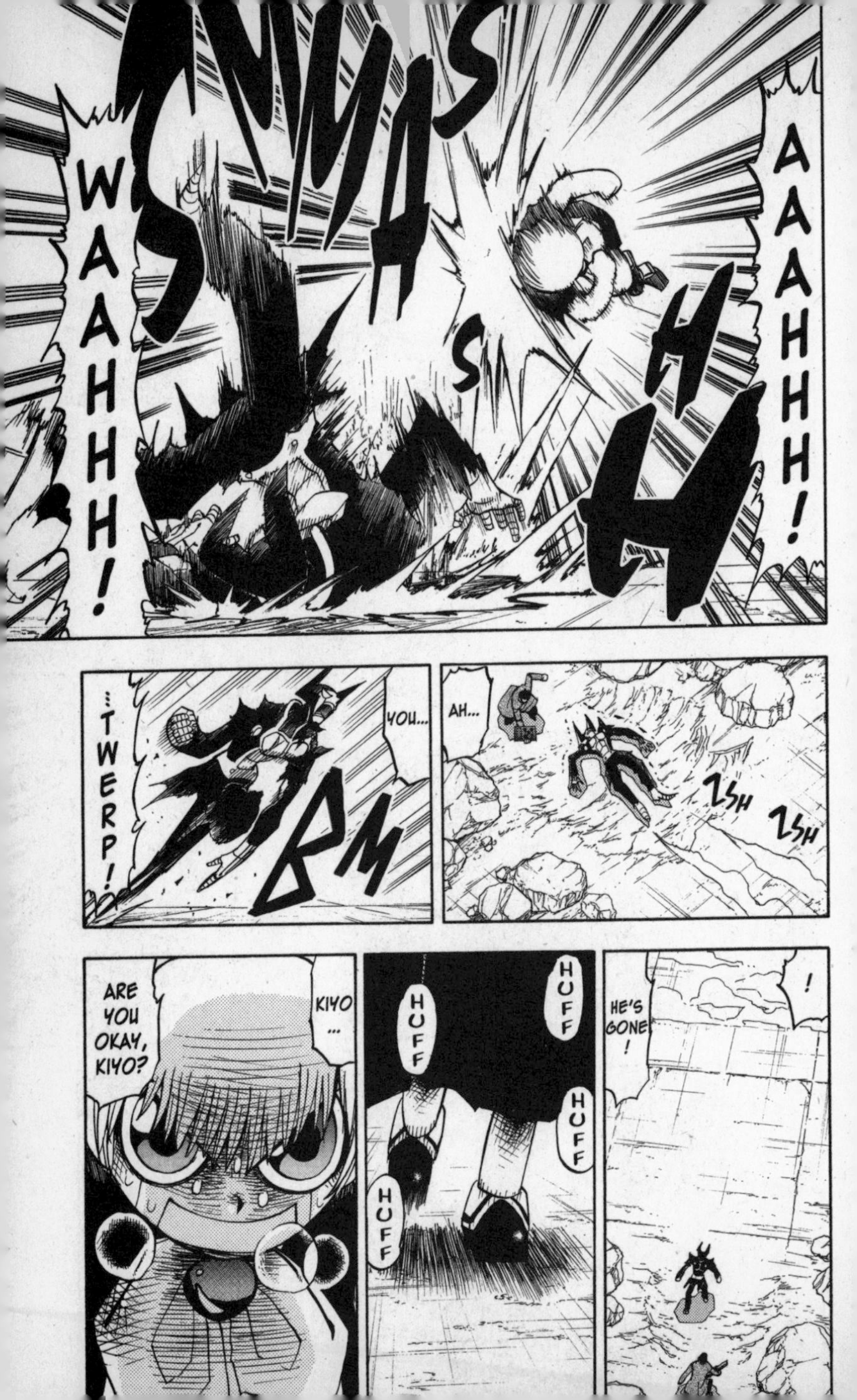
AAAHHH!
WAAHHH!
AH...
ZSH
ZSH
YOU...
...TWERP!
BRM
!
HE'S GONE!
HUFF
HUFF
HUFF
HUFF
KIYO...
ARE YOU OKAY, KIYO?

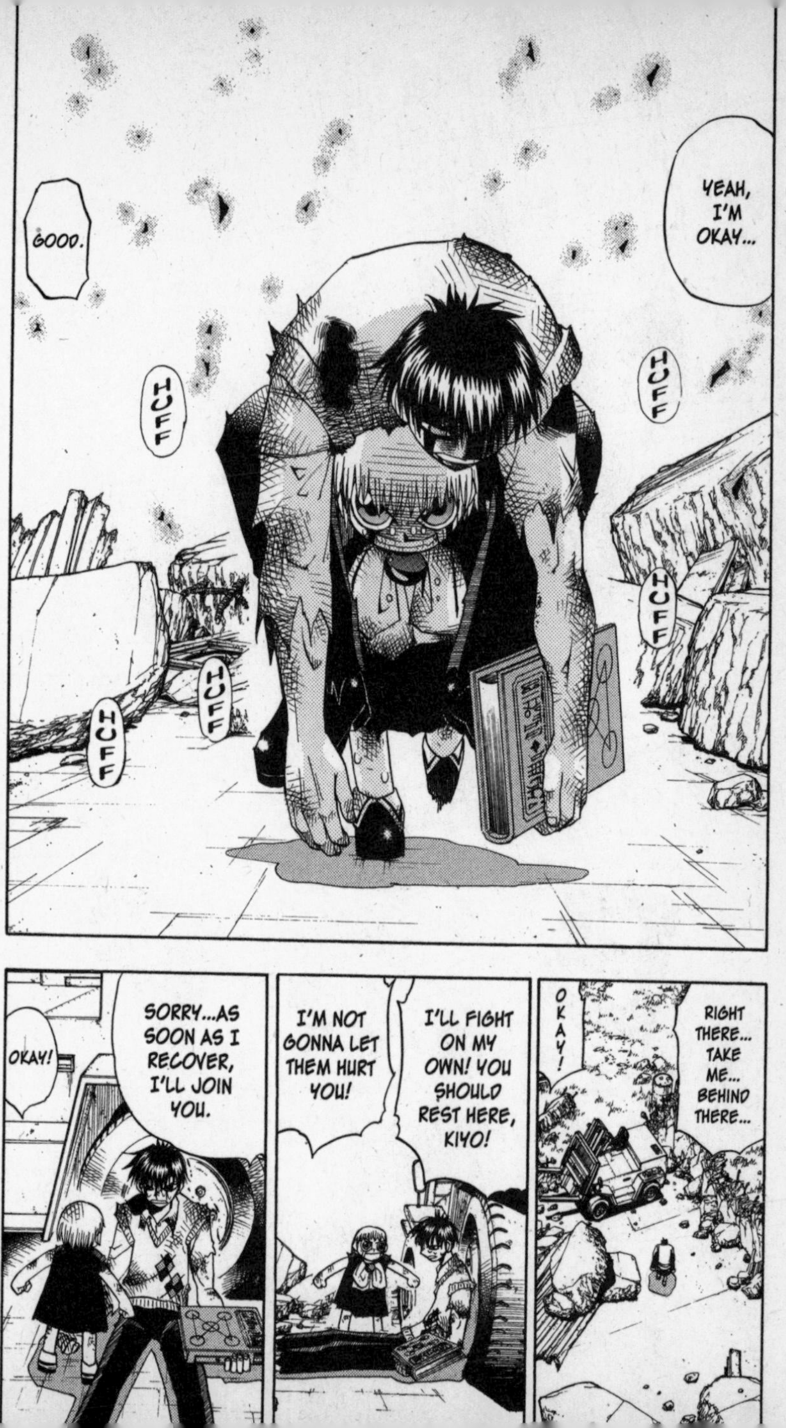
YEAH, I'M OKAY...
GOOD.
HUFF
HUFF
HUFF
HUFF
RIGHT THERE... TAKE ME... BEHIND THERE...
OKAY!
I'LL FIGHT ON MY OWN! YOU SHOULD REST HERE, KIYO!
I'M NOT GONNA LET THEM HURT YOU!
SORRY...AS SOON AS I RECOVER, I'LL JOIN YOU.
OKAY!

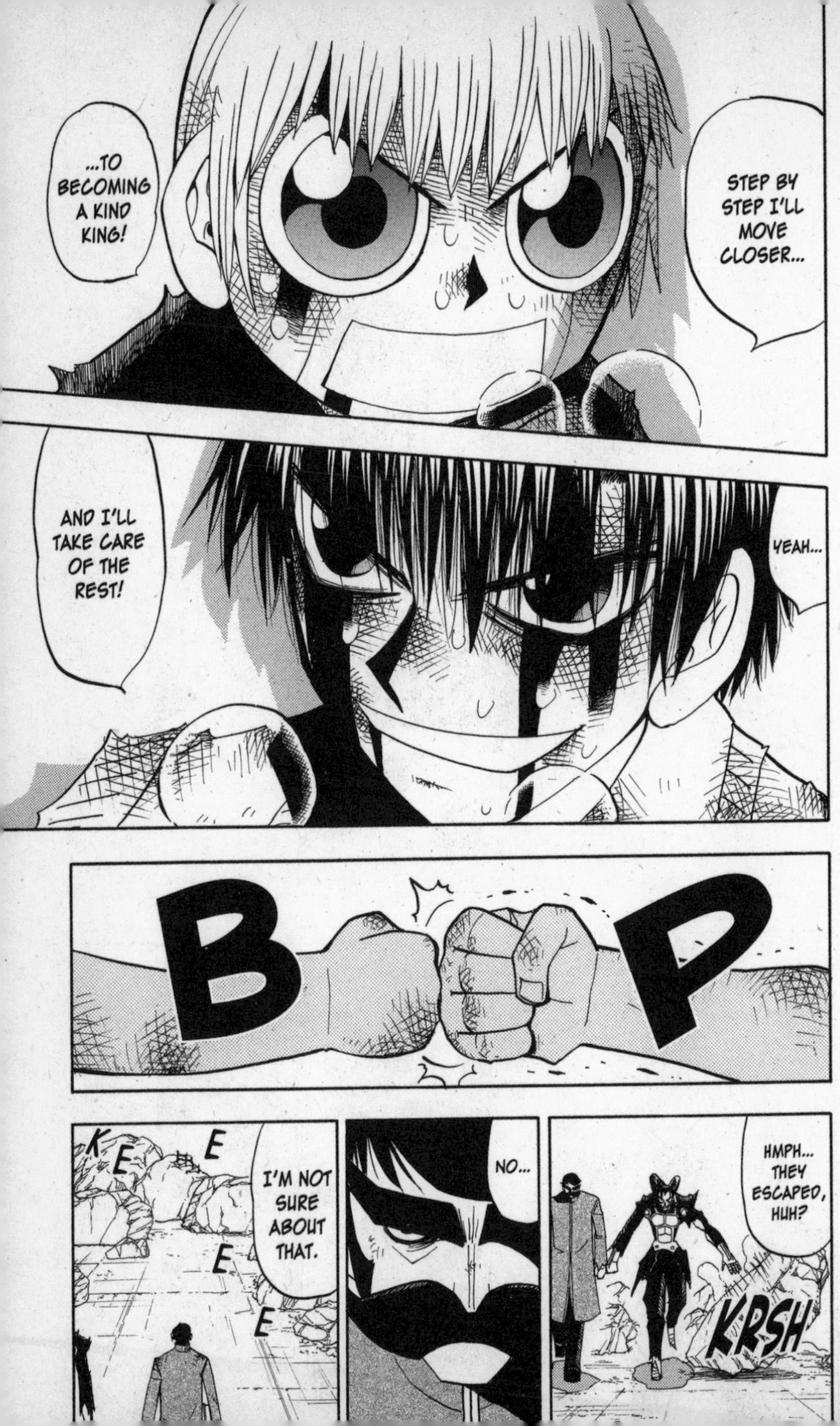
STEP BY STEP I'LL MOVE CLOSER...
...TO BECOMING A KIND KING!
YEAH...
AND I'LL TAKE CARE OF THE REST!
B P
HMPH... THEY ESCAPED, HUH?
KRSH
NO...
I'M NOT SURE ABOUT THAT.
KEEEE

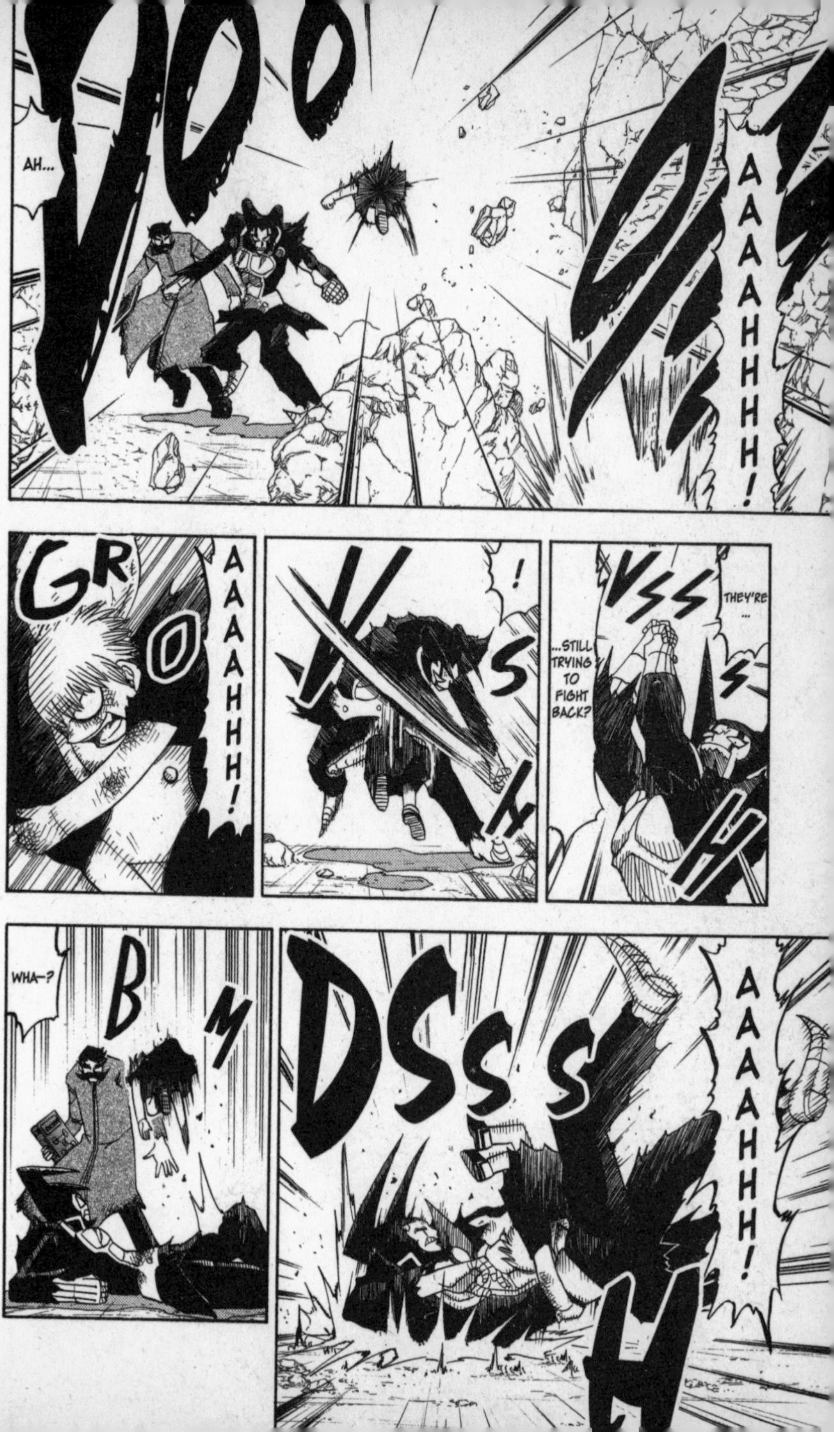
AAAAHHHH!
AH...
THEY'RE ...
...STILL TRYING TO FIGHT BACK?
!
AAAAHHH!
GRO
DSSSH
AAAAHHH!
BM
WHA-?

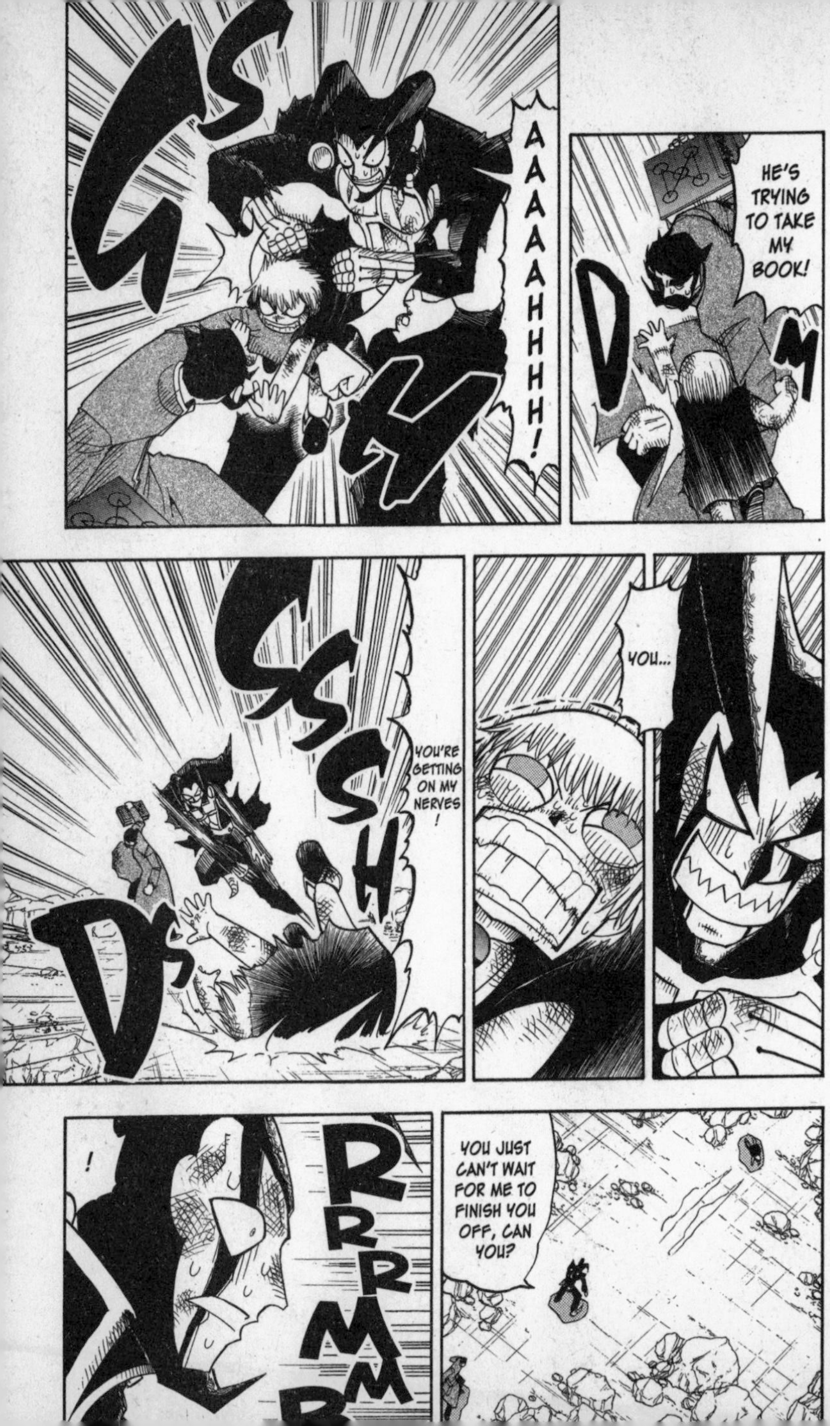

HE'S TRYING TO TAKE MY BOOK!
DM
AAAAAHHHH!
YOU...
YOU'RE GETTING ON MY NERVES!
YOU JUST CAN'T WAIT FOR ME TO FINISH YOU OFF, CAN YOU?
!

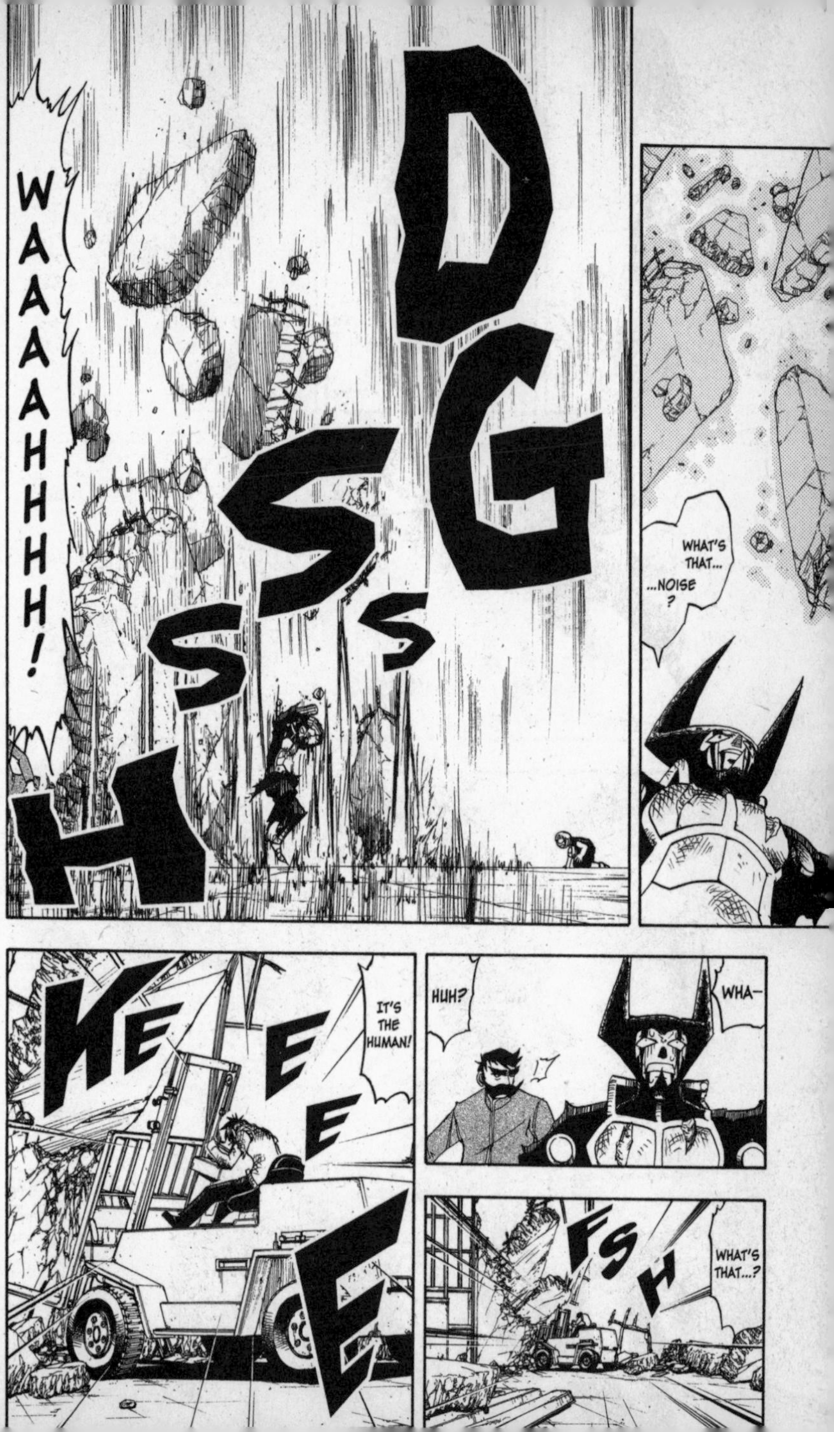
WHAT'S THAT...
...NOISE?
WAAAAHHHHH!
WHA-
HUH?
WHAT'S THAT...?
FSH
IT'S THE HUMAN!

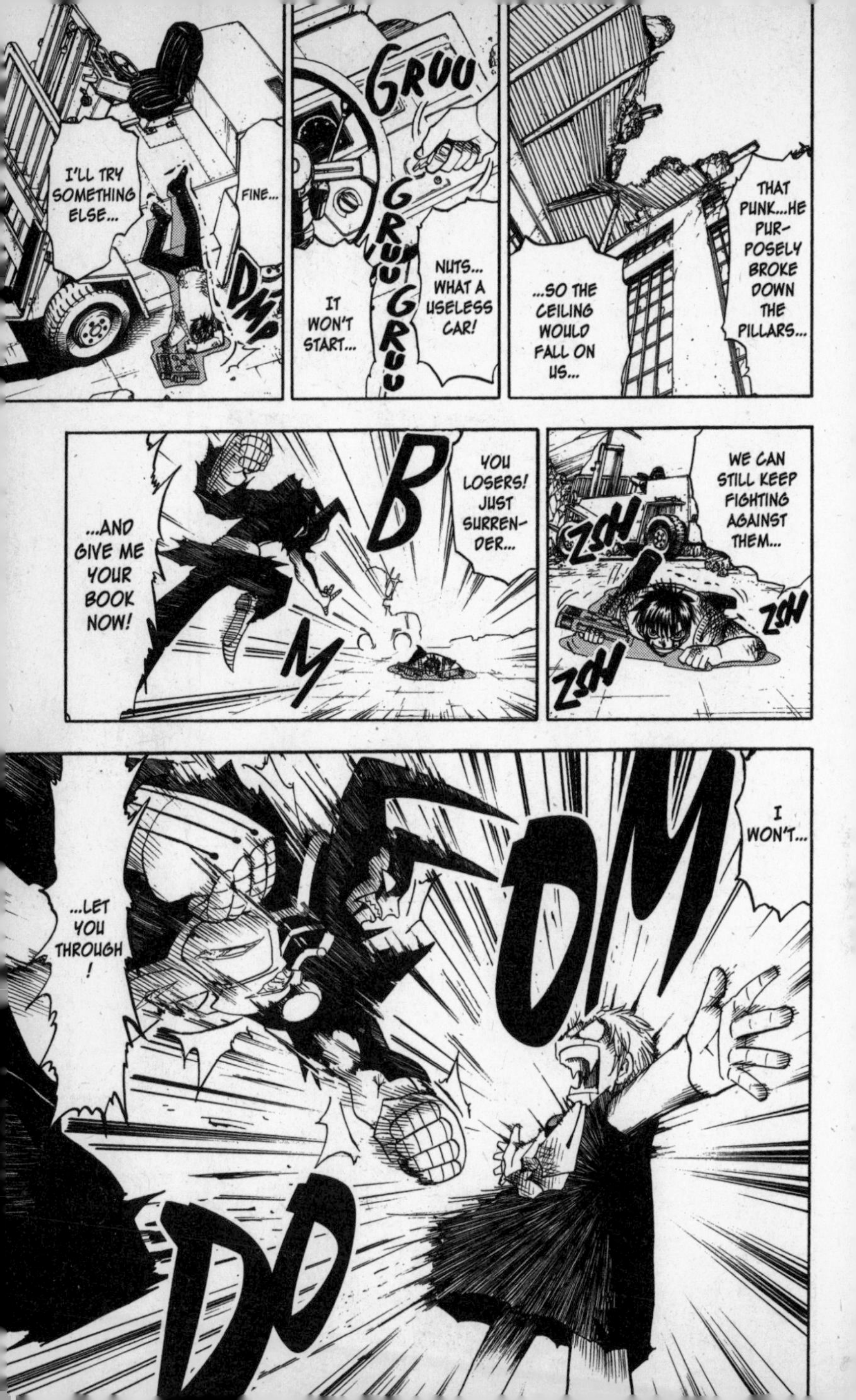
THAT PUNK...HE PUR-POSELY BROKE DOWN THE PILLARS...
...SO THE CEILING WOULD FALL ON US...
GRUU
NUTS... WHAT A USELESS CAR!
GRUU GRUU GRUU
IT WON'T START...
FINE...
I'LL TRY SOMETHING ELSE...
DMP
WE CAN STILL KEEP FIGHTING AGAINST THEM...
ZSH
ZSH
ZSH
YOU LOSERS! JUST SURREN-DER...
B
M
...AND GIVE ME YOUR BOOK NOW!
I WON'T...
DM
...LET YOU THROUGH!
DD

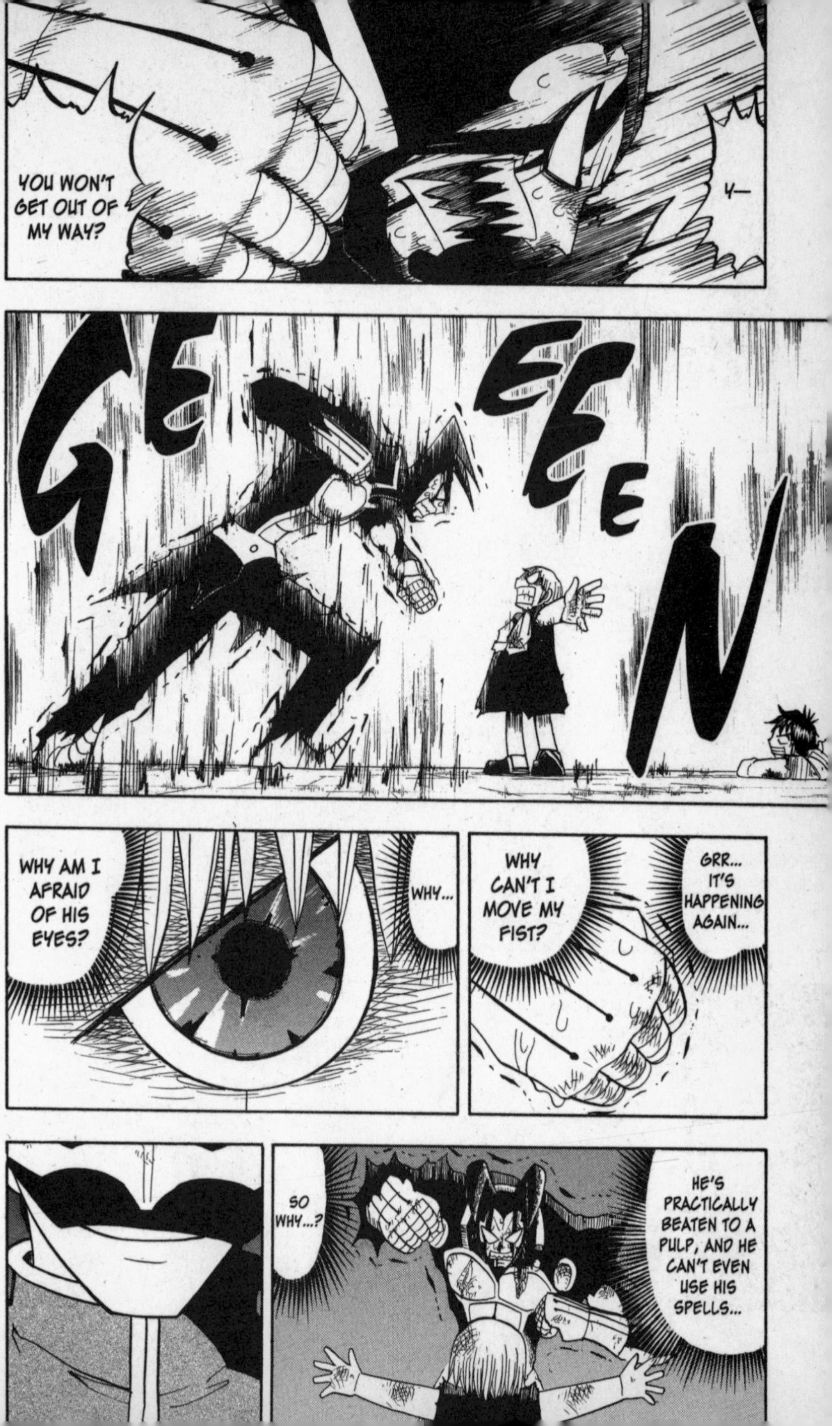
Y—
YOU WON'T GET OUT OF MY WAY?
GEEEEN
GRR... IT'S HAPPENING AGAIN...
WHY CAN'T I MOVE MY FIST?
WHY...
WHY AM I AFRAID OF HIS EYES?
HE'S PRACTICALLY BEATEN TO A PULP, AND HE CAN'T EVEN USE HIS SPELLS...
SO WHY...?

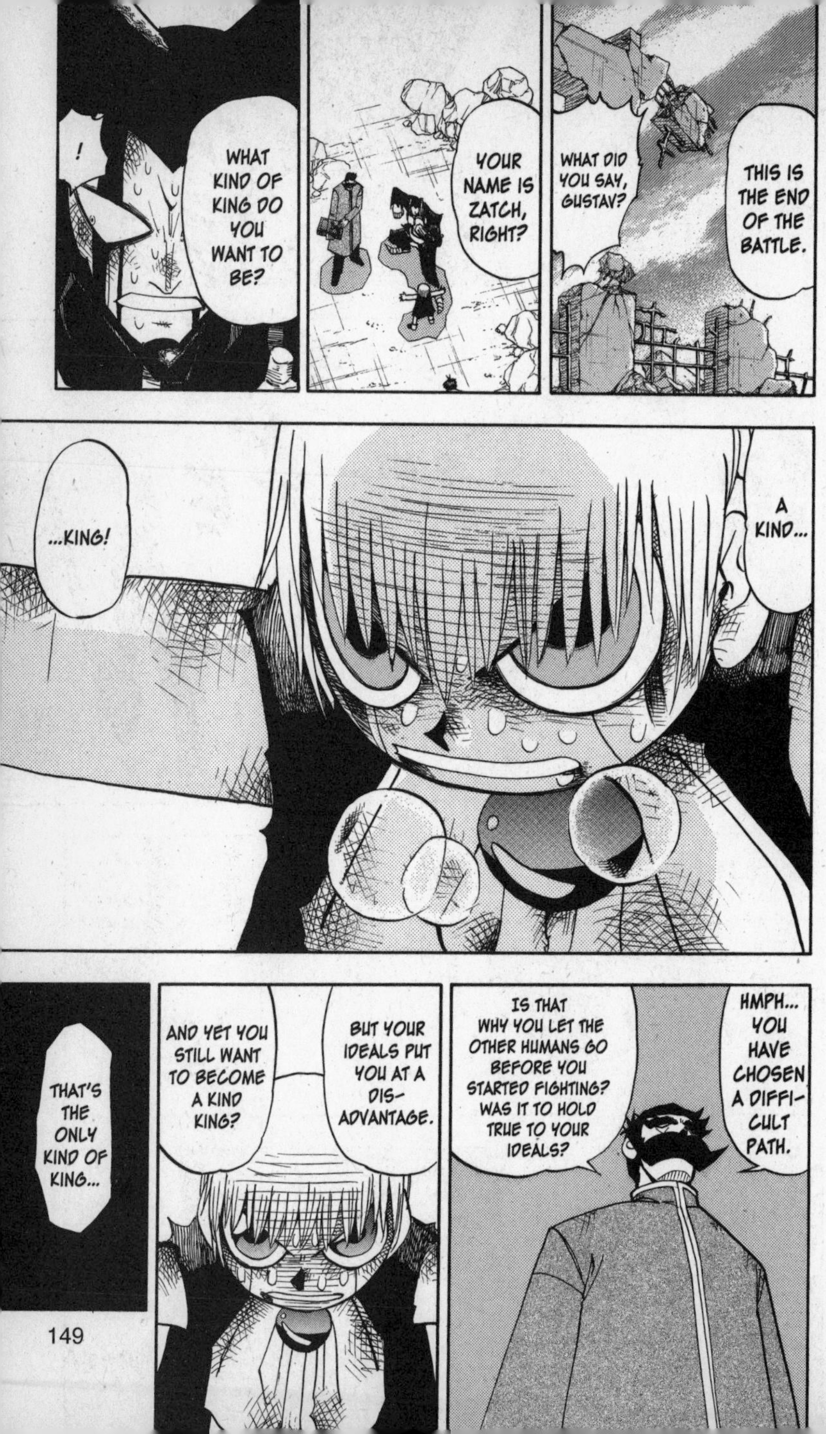
THIS IS THE END OF THE BATTLE.
WHAT DID YOU SAY, GUSTAV?
YOUR NAME IS ZATCH, RIGHT?
!
WHAT KIND OF KING DO YOU WANT TO BE?
A KIND...
...KING!
HMPH... YOU HAVE CHOSEN A DIFFI-CULT PATH.
IS THAT WHY YOU LET THE OTHER HUMANS GO BEFORE YOU STARTED FIGHTING? WAS IT TO HOLD TRUE TO YOUR IDEALS?
BUT YOUR IDEALS PUT YOU AT A DIS-ADVANTAGE.
AND YET YOU STILL WANT TO BECOME A KIND KING?
THAT'S THE ONLY KIND OF KING...

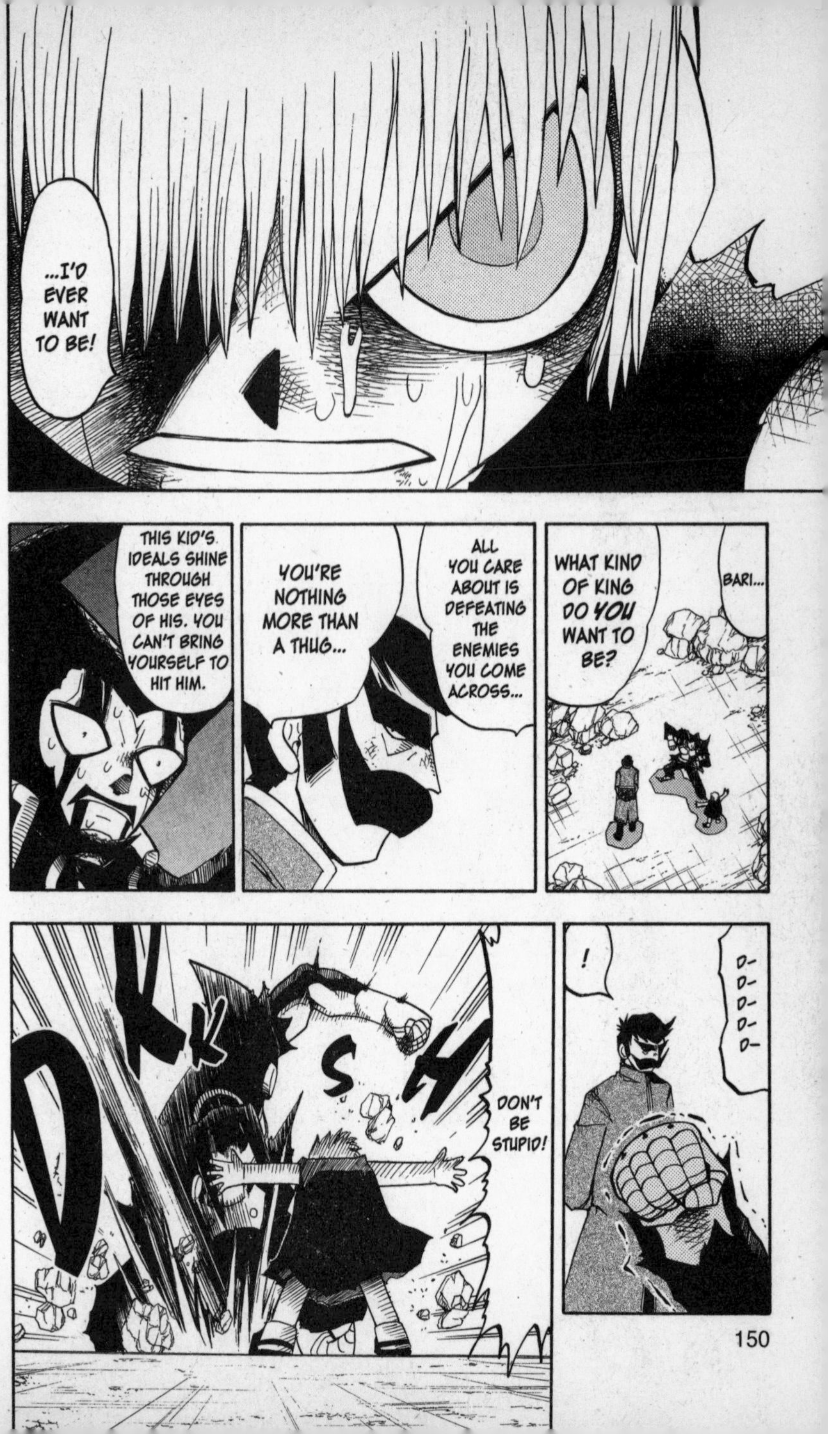
...I'D EVER WANT TO BE!
BARI...
WHAT KIND OF KING DO YOU WANT TO BE?
ALL YOU CARE ABOUT IS DEFEATING THE ENEMIES YOU COME ACROSS...
YOU'RE NOTHING MORE THAN A THUG...
THIS KID'S IDEALS SHINE THROUGH THOSE EYES OF HIS. YOU CAN'T BRING YOURSELF TO HIT HIM.
D-D-D-D-D-
!
DON'T BE STUPID!

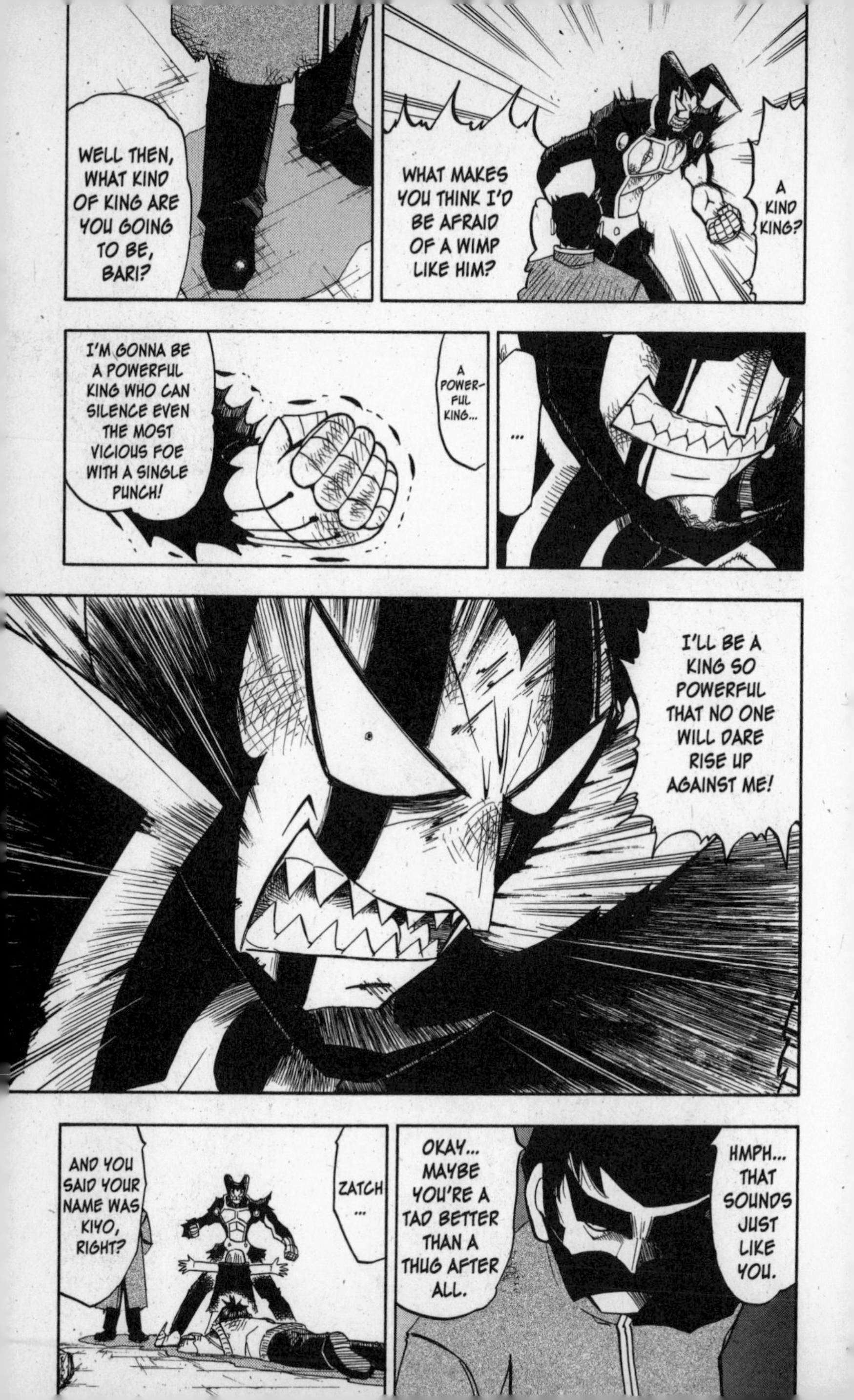
A KIND KING?
WHAT MAKES YOU THINK I'D BE AFRAID OF A WIMP LIKE HIM?
WELL THEN, WHAT KIND OF KING ARE YOU GOING TO BE, BARI?
...
A POWER-FUL KING...
I'M GONNA BE A POWERFUL KING WHO CAN SILENCE EVEN THE MOST VICIOUS FOE WITH A SINGLE PUNCH!
I'LL BE A KING SO POWERFUL THAT NO ONE WILL DARE RISE UP AGAINST ME!
HMPH... THAT SOUNDS JUST LIKE YOU.
OKAY... MAYBE YOU'RE A TAD BETTER THAN A THUG AFTER ALL.
ZATCH ...
AND YOU SAID YOUR NAME WAS KIYO, RIGHT?

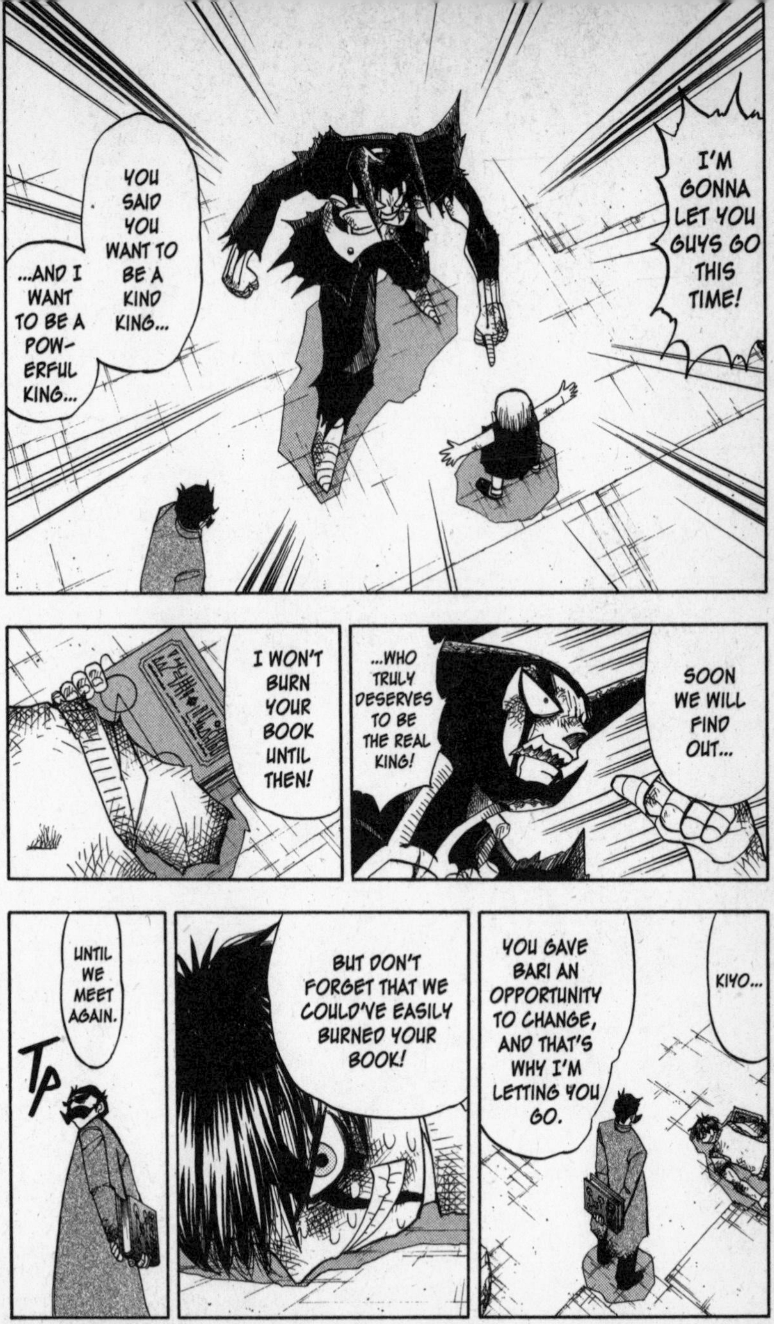
I'M GONNA LET YOU GUYS GO THIS TIME!
YOU SAID YOU WANT TO BE A KIND KING...
...AND I WANT TO BE A POWERFUL KING...
SOON WE WILL FIND OUT...
...WHO TRULY DESERVES TO BE THE REAL KING!
I WON'T BURN YOUR BOOK UNTIL THEN!
KIYO...
YOU GAVE BARI AN OPPORTUNITY TO CHANGE, AND THAT'S WHY I'M LETTING YOU GO.
BUT DON'T FORGET THAT WE COULD'VE EASILY BURNED YOUR BOOK!
UNTIL WE MEET AGAIN.
TP

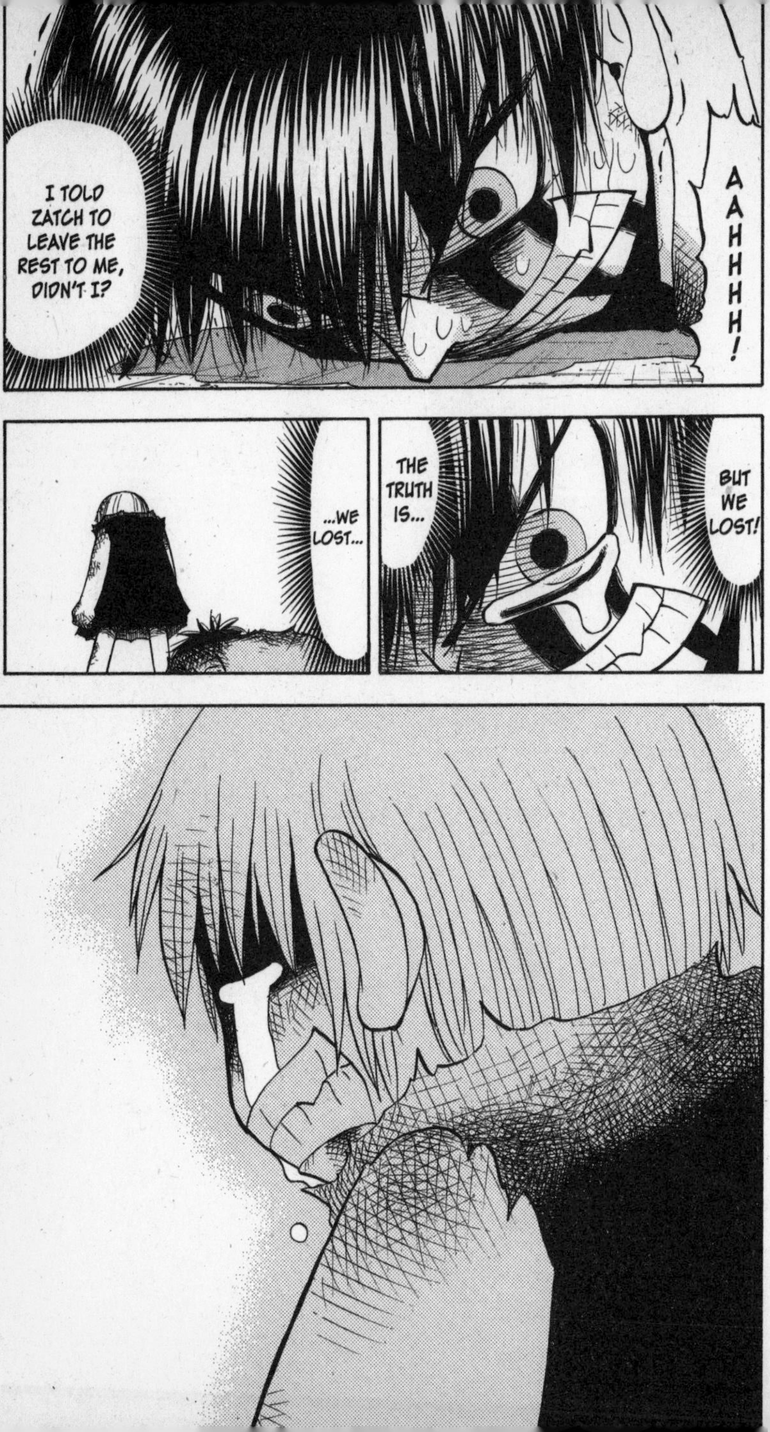
AAHHHH!
I TOLD ZATCH TO LEAVE THE REST TO ME, DIDN'T I?
BUT WE LOST!
THE TRUTH IS...
...WE LOST...

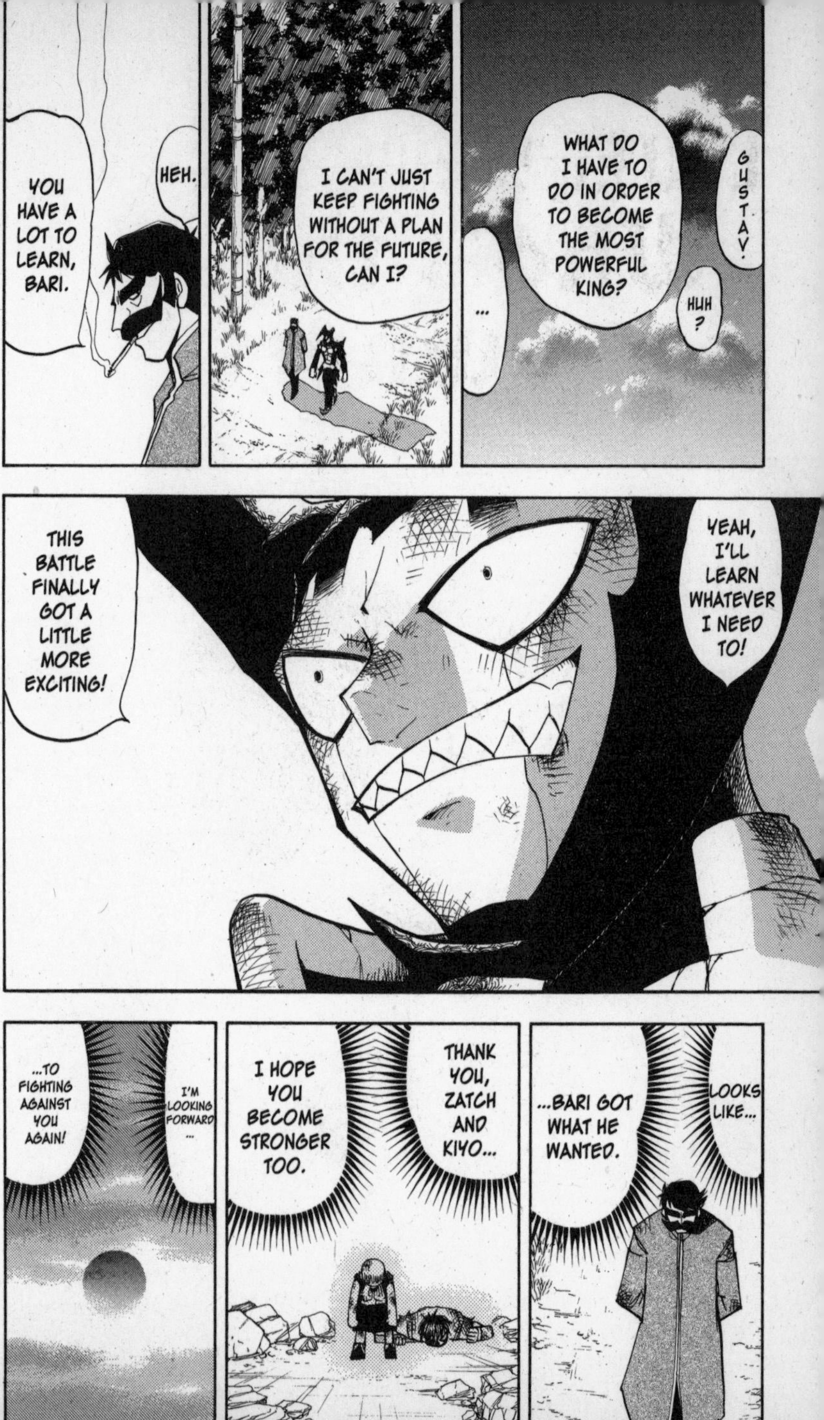
GUSTAV.
HUH?
WHAT DO I HAVE TO DO IN ORDER TO BECOME THE MOST POWERFUL KING?
...
I CAN'T JUST KEEP FIGHTING WITHOUT A PLAN FOR THE FUTURE, CAN I?
HEH.
YOU HAVE A LOT TO LEARN, BARI.
YEAH, I'LL LEARN WHATEVER I NEED TO!
THIS BATTLE FINALLY GOT A LITTLE MORE EXCITING!
LOOKS LIKE...
...BARI GOT WHAT HE WANTED.
THANK YOU, ZATCH AND KIYO...
I HOPE YOU BECOME STRONGER TOO.
I'M LOOKING FORWARD...
...TO FIGHTING AGAINST YOU AGAIN!

# LEVEL 93:
# Who's the
# Owner?

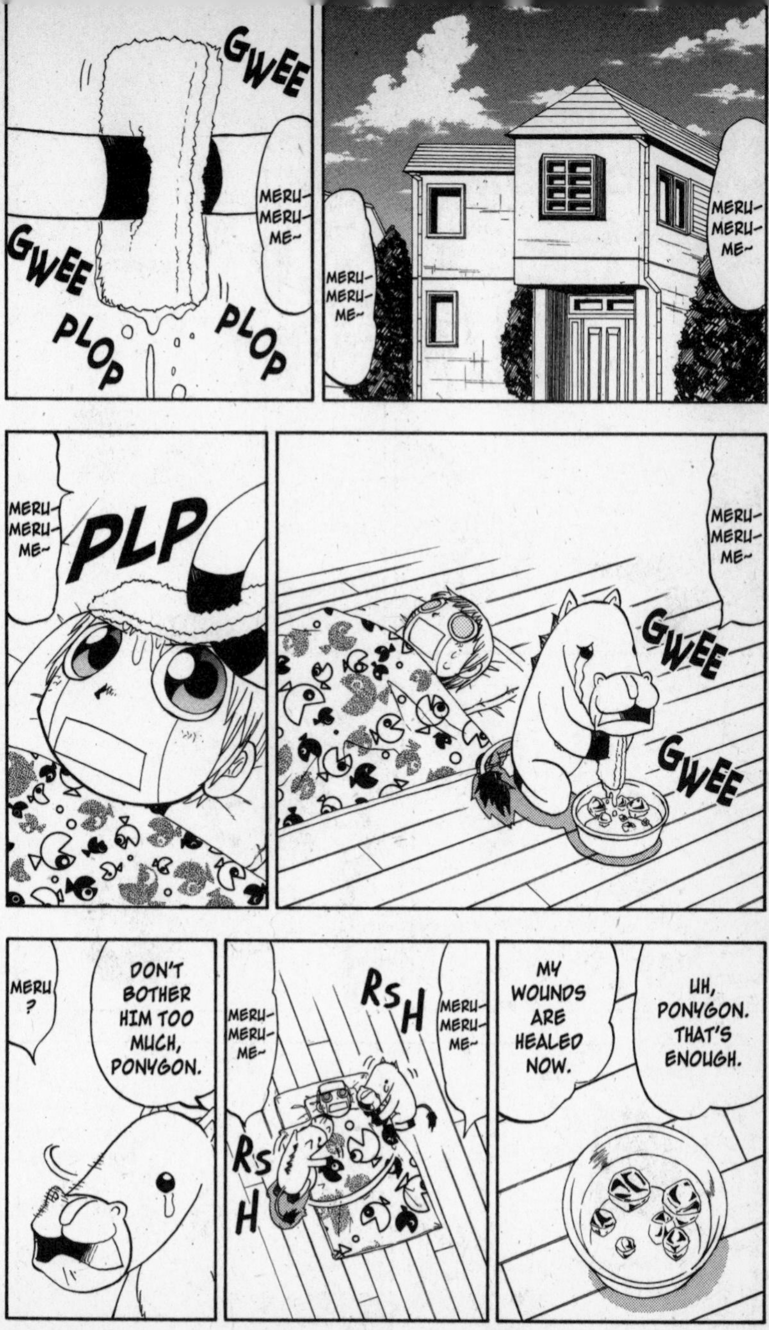
MERU-MERU-ME~
MERU-MERU-ME~
GWEE
MERU-MERU-ME~
GWEE
PLOP
PLOP
MERU-MERU-ME~
GWEE
GWEE
MERU-MERU-ME~
PLP
UH, PONYGON. THAT'S ENOUGH.
MY WOUNDS ARE HEALED NOW.
MERU-MERU-ME~
RSH
MERU-MERU-ME~
RSH
DON'T BOTHER HIM TOO MUCH, PONYGON.
MERU?

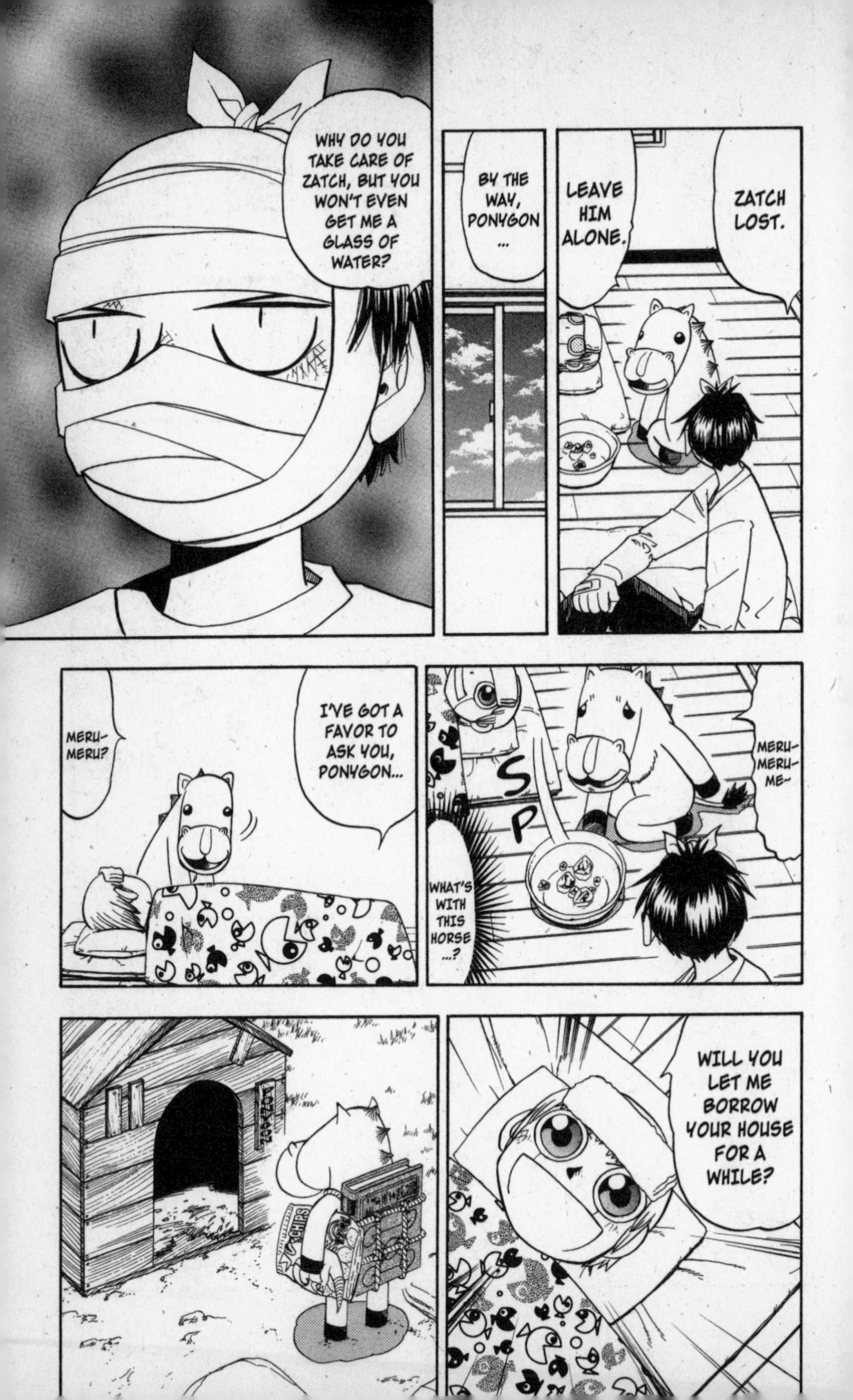
ZATCH LOST.
LEAVE HIM ALONE.
BY THE WAY, PONYGON ...
WHY DO YOU TAKE CARE OF ZATCH, BUT YOU WON'T EVEN GET ME A GLASS OF WATER?
MERU-MERU-ME~
SP
WHAT'S WITH THIS HORSE ...?
I'VE GOT A FAVOR TO ASK YOU, PONYGON...
MERU-MERU?
WILL YOU LET ME BORROW YOUR HOUSE FOR A WHILE?

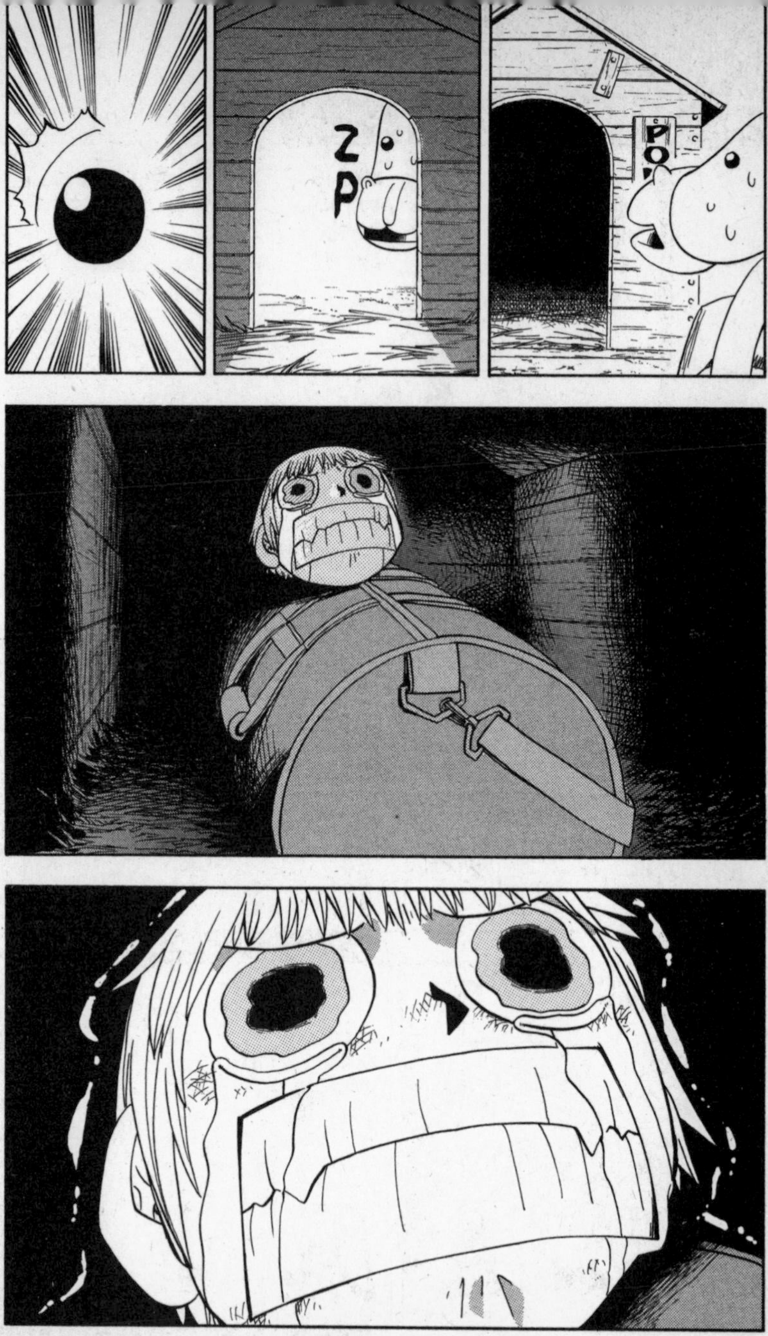
PO
ZP

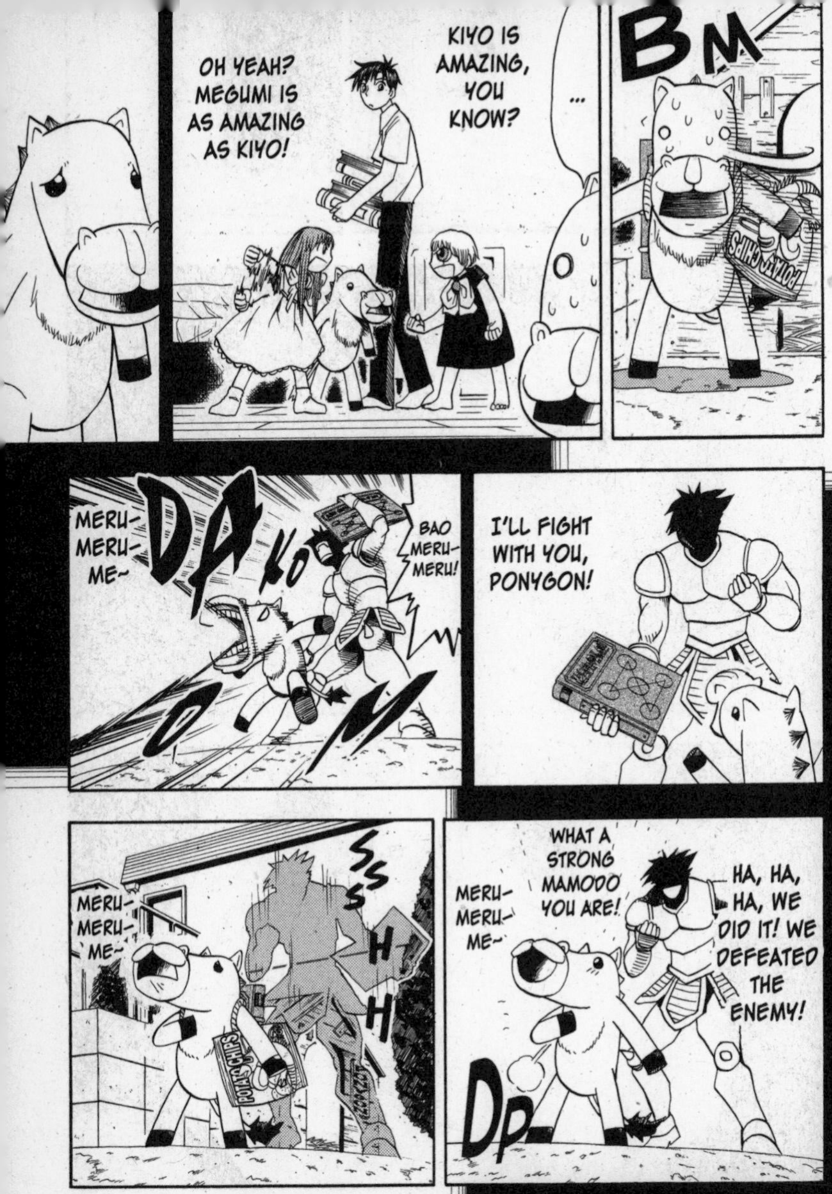
BM
...
KIYO IS AMAZING, YOU KNOW?
OH YEAH? MEGUMI IS AS AMAZING AS KIYO!
I'LL FIGHT WITH YOU, PONYGON!
BAO MERU-MERU!
MERU-MERU-ME~
DA
KO
O
M
HA, HA, HA, WE DID IT! WE DEFEATED THE ENEMY!
WHAT A STRONG MAMODO YOU ARE!
MERU-MERU-ME~
DP
S
S
S
H
H
MERU-MERU-ME~
POTATO CHIPS

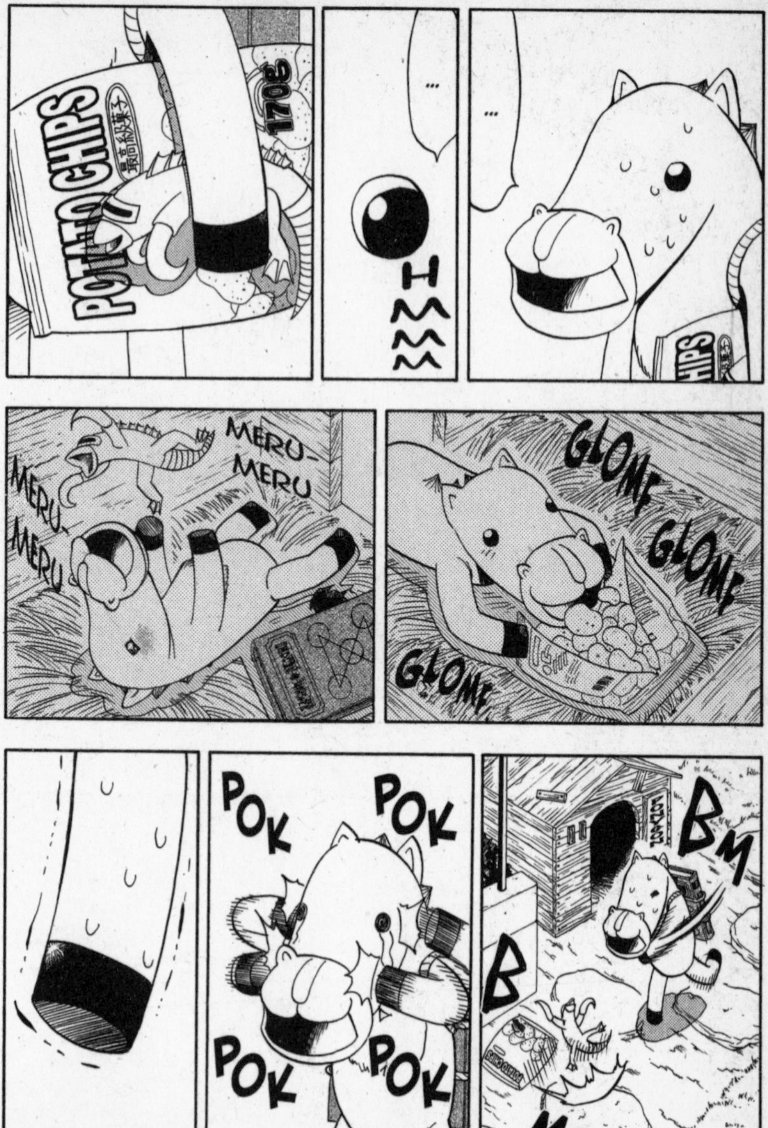
...
CHIPS
...
HMMM
POTATO CHIPS
最高級菓子
170円
GLOMF
GLOMF
GLOMF
MERU-
MERU
MERU-
MERU
BM
B
M
POK
POK
POK
POK

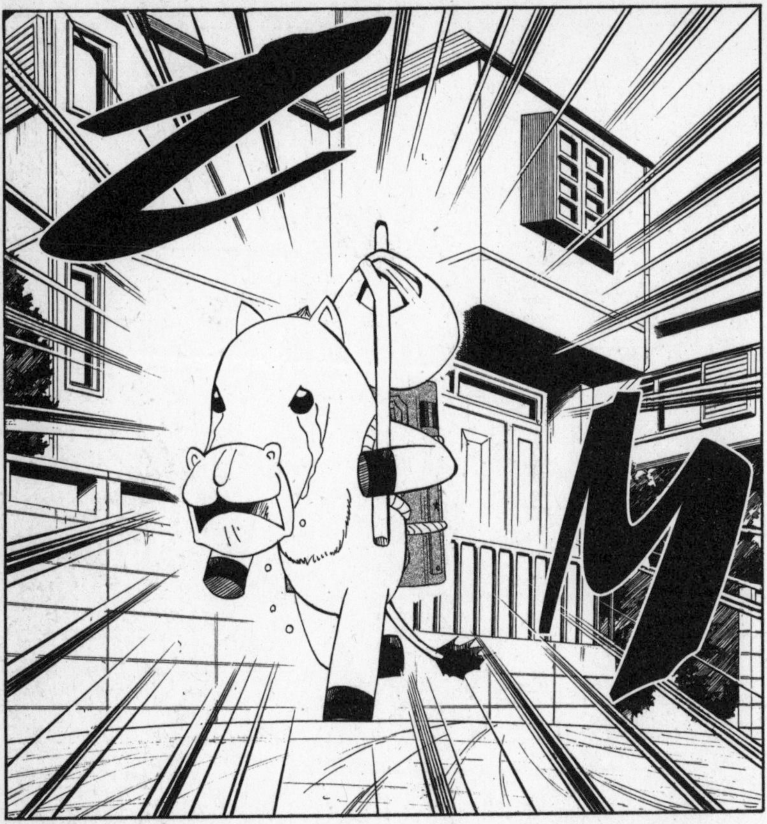
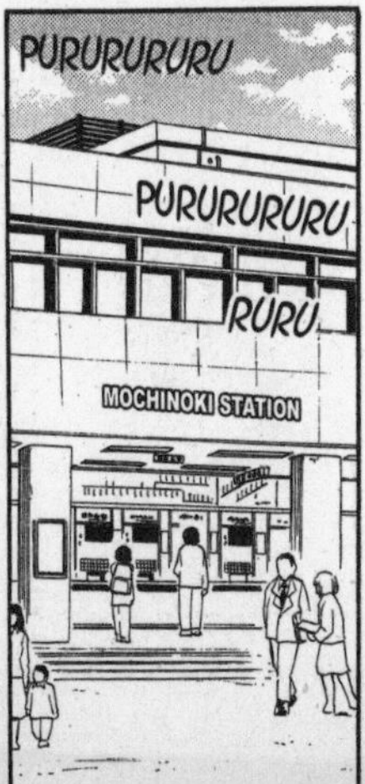
PURURURURU
PURURURURU
RURU
MOCHINOKI STATION
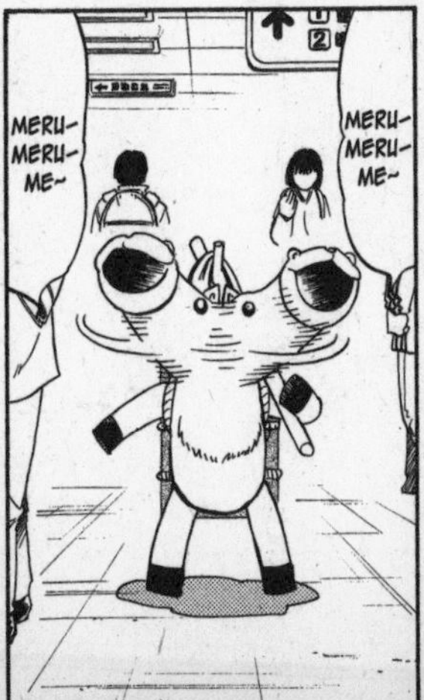
MERU-MERU-ME~
MERU-MERU-ME~
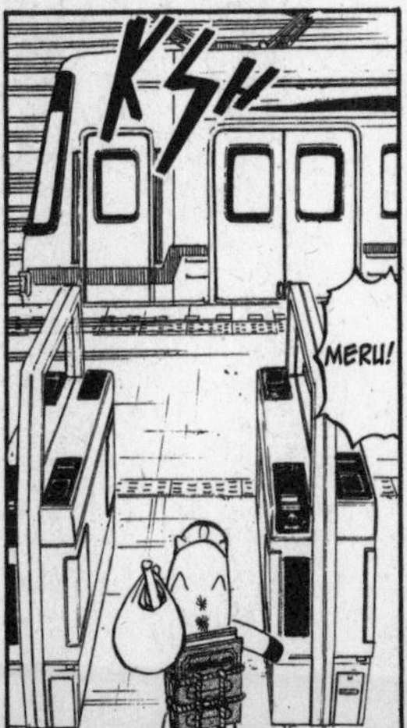
KSH
MERU!

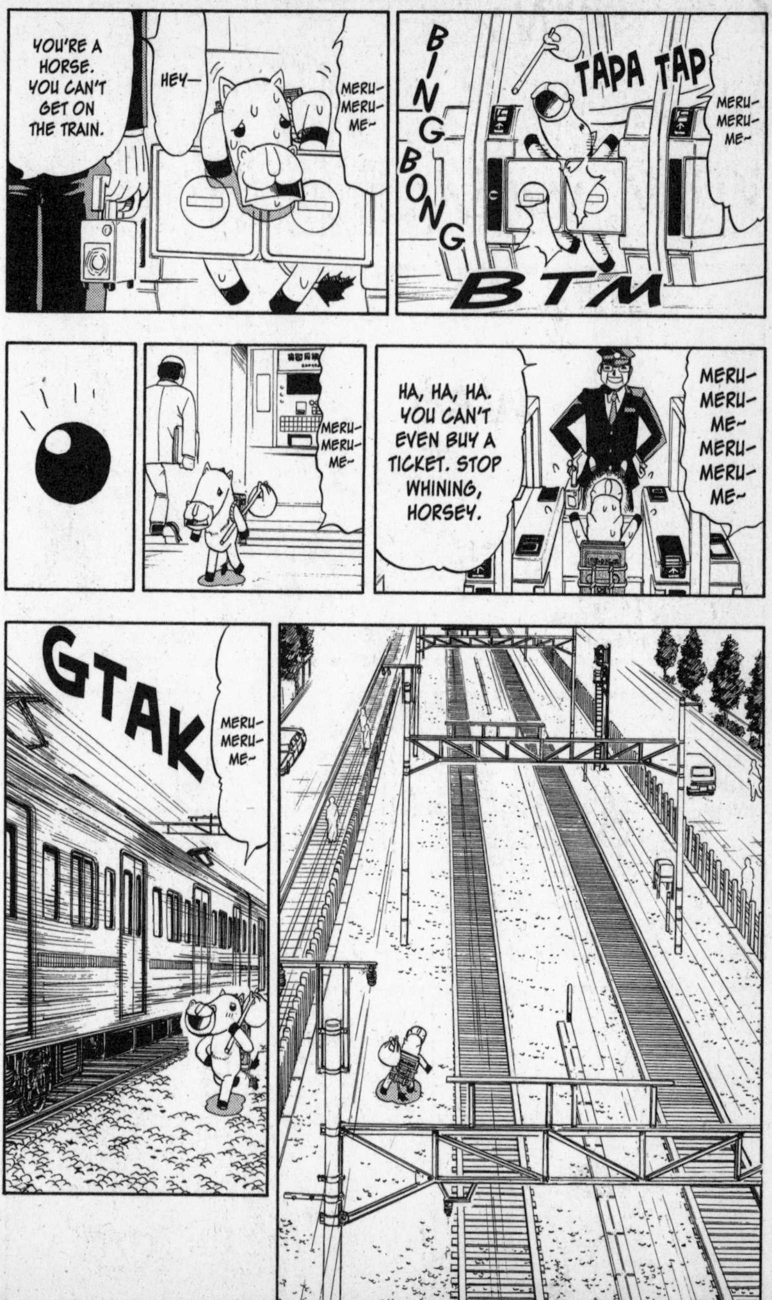
MERU-MERU-ME~
TAPA TAP
BING BONG
BTM
MERU-MERU-ME~
HEY—
YOU'RE A HORSE. YOU CAN'T GET ON THE TRAIN.
MERU-MERU-ME~ MERU-MERU-ME~
HA, HA, HA. YOU CAN'T EVEN BUY A TICKET. STOP WHINING, HORSEY.
MERU-MERU-ME~
MERU-MERU-ME~
GTAK

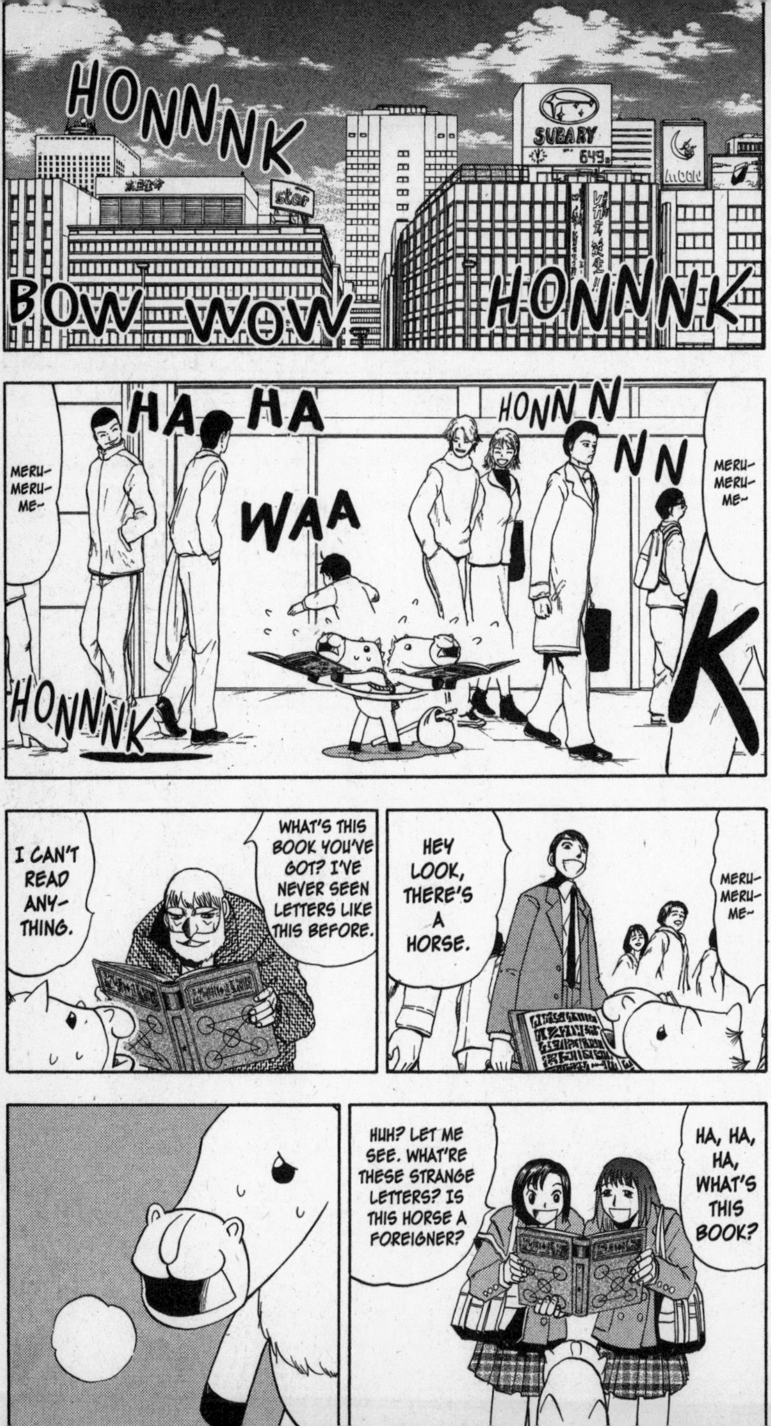
HONNNK
SUBARY
649
MOON
star
HONNNK
BOW WOW
MERU-MERU-ME~
HONNN NNN K
HA HA
WAA
MERU-MERU-ME~
HONNNK
MERU-MERU-ME~
HEY LOOK, THERE'S A HORSE.
WHAT'S THIS BOOK YOU'VE GOT? I'VE NEVER SEEN LETTERS LIKE THIS BEFORE.
I CAN'T READ ANYTHING.
HA, HA, HA, WHAT'S THIS BOOK?
HUH? LET ME SEE. WHAT'RE THESE STRANGE LETTERS? IS THIS HORSE A FOREIGNER?

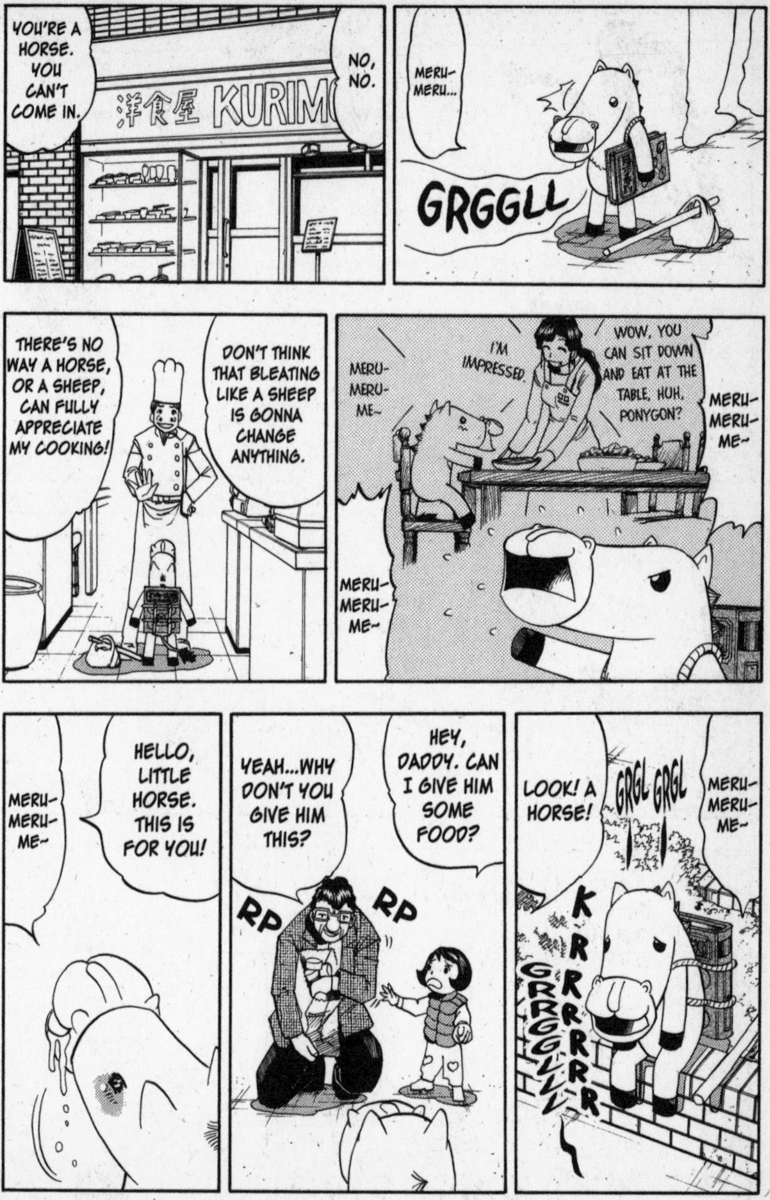
MERU-MERU...
GRGGLL
NO, NO.
YOU'RE A HORSE. YOU CAN'T COME IN.
洋食屋 KURIM
MERU-MERU-ME~
WOW, YOU CAN SIT DOWN AND EAT AT THE TABLE, HUH, PONYGON?
I'M IMPRESSED.
MERU-MERU-ME~
MERU-MERU-ME~
DON'T THINK THAT BLEATING LIKE A SHEEP IS GONNA CHANGE ANYTHING.
THERE'S NO WAY A HORSE, OR A SHEEP, CAN FULLY APPRECIATE MY COOKING!
MERU-MERU-ME~
GRGL GRGL
LOOK! A HORSE!
KRRRRRRR
GRRRGGLLL
HEY, DADDY. CAN I GIVE HIM SOME FOOD?
YEAH...WHY DON'T YOU GIVE HIM THIS?
RP
RP
HELLO, LITTLE HORSE. THIS IS FOR YOU!
MERU-MERU-ME~

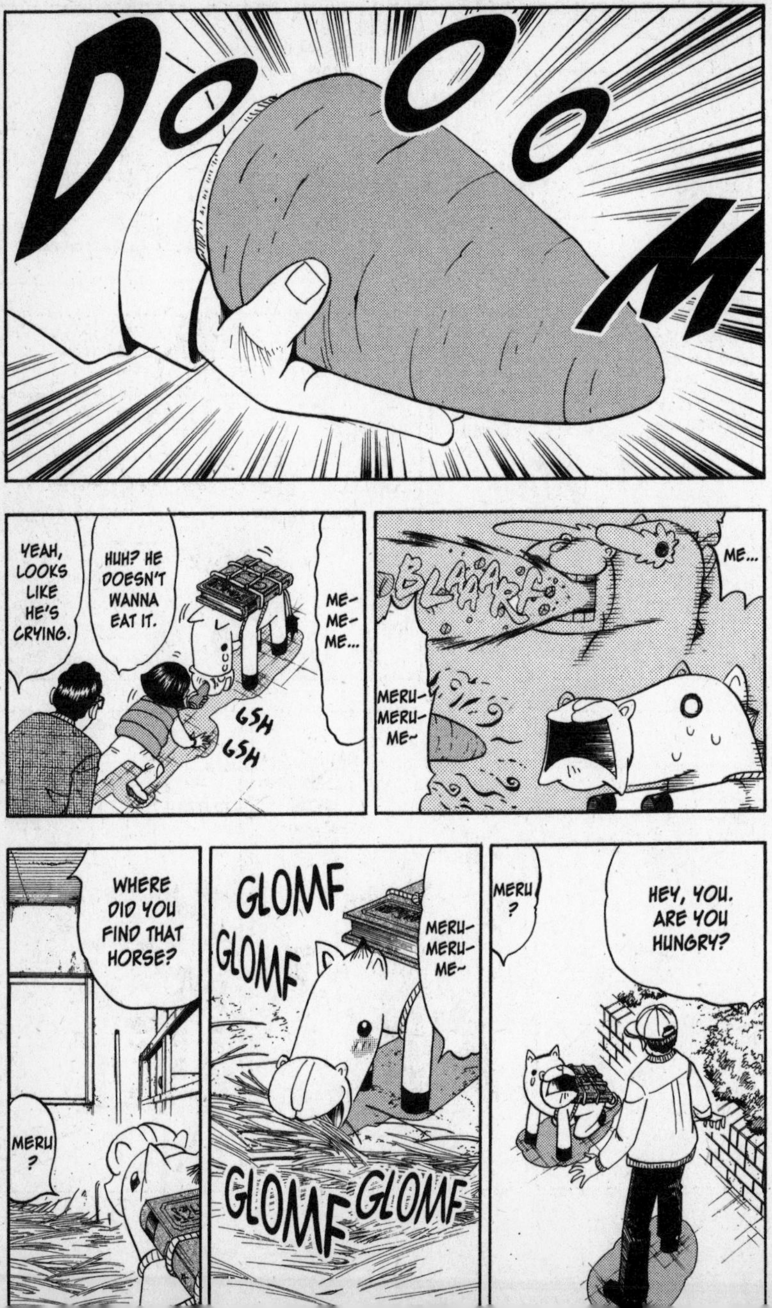
DOOOOM
ME...
BLAAARF
MERU-MERU-ME~
ME-ME-ME...
HUH? HE DOESN'T WANNA EAT IT.
YEAH, LOOKS LIKE HE'S CRYING.
GSH GSH
HEY, YOU. ARE YOU HUNGRY?
MERU ?
MERU-MERU-ME~
GLOMF GLOMF
GLOMF GLOMF
WHERE DID YOU FIND THAT HORSE?
MERU ?

I FOUND HIM IN THE CITY.
STARTING TODAY I'M GONNA TRAIN HIM REALLY HARD, AND...
...TURN HIM INTO THE FASTEST RACING HORSE THAT EVER EXISTED!
MERU?
AH, HE RAN AWAY!
MERU-MERU-ME~
AKA STABLES
ANNIVERSARY
DM
MERU-MERU-ME~
MERU-MERU-ME~
ME...
DP
ME...
FWMP
MERU-MERU-ME~
FLAP
FLAP
FLAP

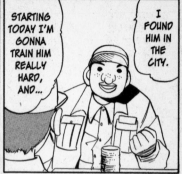

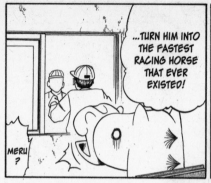

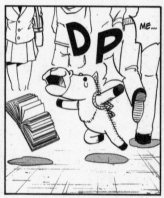

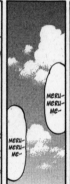

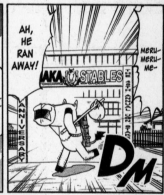

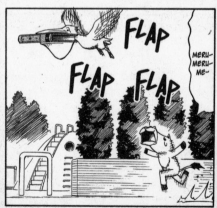

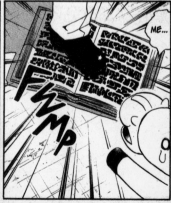

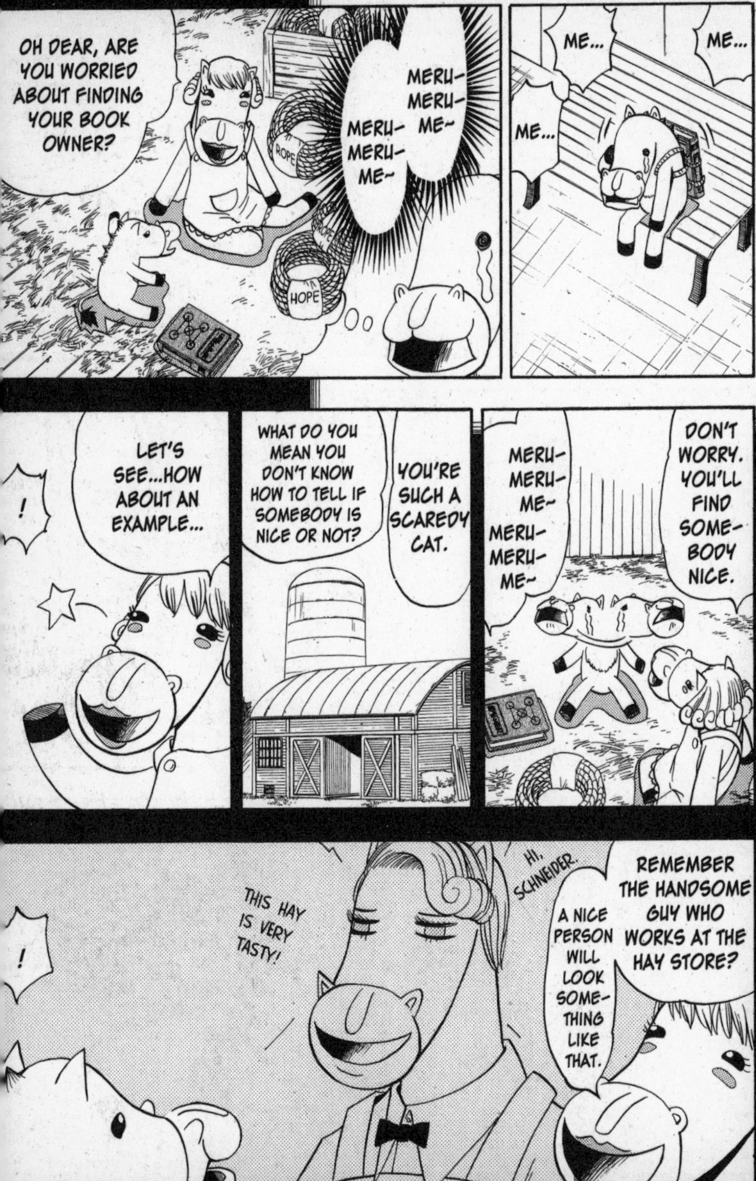
ME...
ME...
ME...
MERU-MERU-ME~
MERU-MERU-ME~
OH DEAR, ARE YOU WORRIED ABOUT FINDING YOUR BOOK OWNER?
HOPE
ROPE
ROPE
DON'T WORRY. YOU'LL FIND SOME-BODY NICE.
MERU-MERU-ME~
MERU-MERU-ME~
YOU'RE SUCH A SCAREDY CAT.
WHAT DO YOU MEAN YOU DON'T KNOW HOW TO TELL IF SOMEBODY IS NICE OR NOT?
LET'S SEE...HOW ABOUT AN EXAMPLE...
!
REMEMBER THE HANDSOME GUY WHO WORKS AT THE HAY STORE?
A NICE PERSON WILL LOOK SOME-THING LIKE THAT.
HI, SCHNEIDER.
THIS HAY IS VERY TASTY!
!

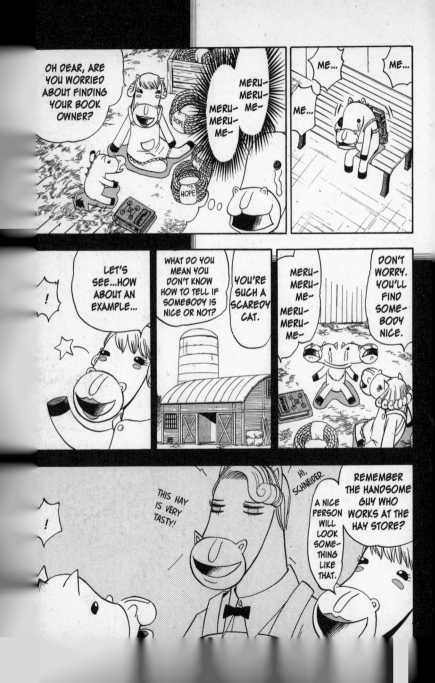

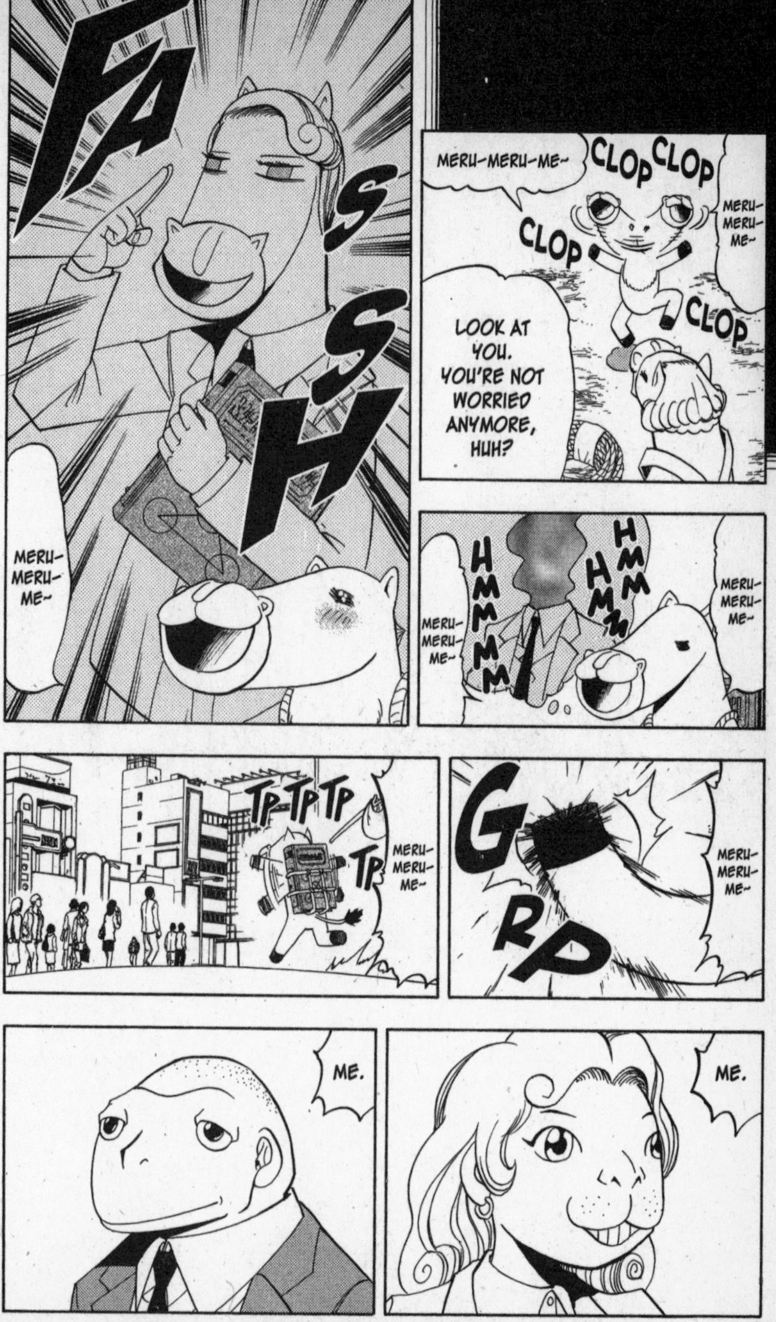
CLOP CLOP
MERU-MERU-ME~
MERU-MERU-ME~
CLOP
CLOP
LOOK AT YOU. YOU'RE NOT WORRIED ANYMORE, HUH?
HMMM
HMMM
MERU-MERU-ME~
HMMMMM
MERU-MERU-ME~
FASSH
MERU-MERU-ME~
MERU-MERU-ME~
GRP
MERU-MERU-ME~
TP TP TP TP
ME.
ME.

ME.

ME.

BMMM

MERU-
MERU-
ME~

ME.

ME.

ME.

ME.

BM

MERU
?

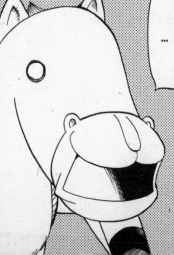

...

CLOP

MEE.

CLOP

CLOP

CLOP

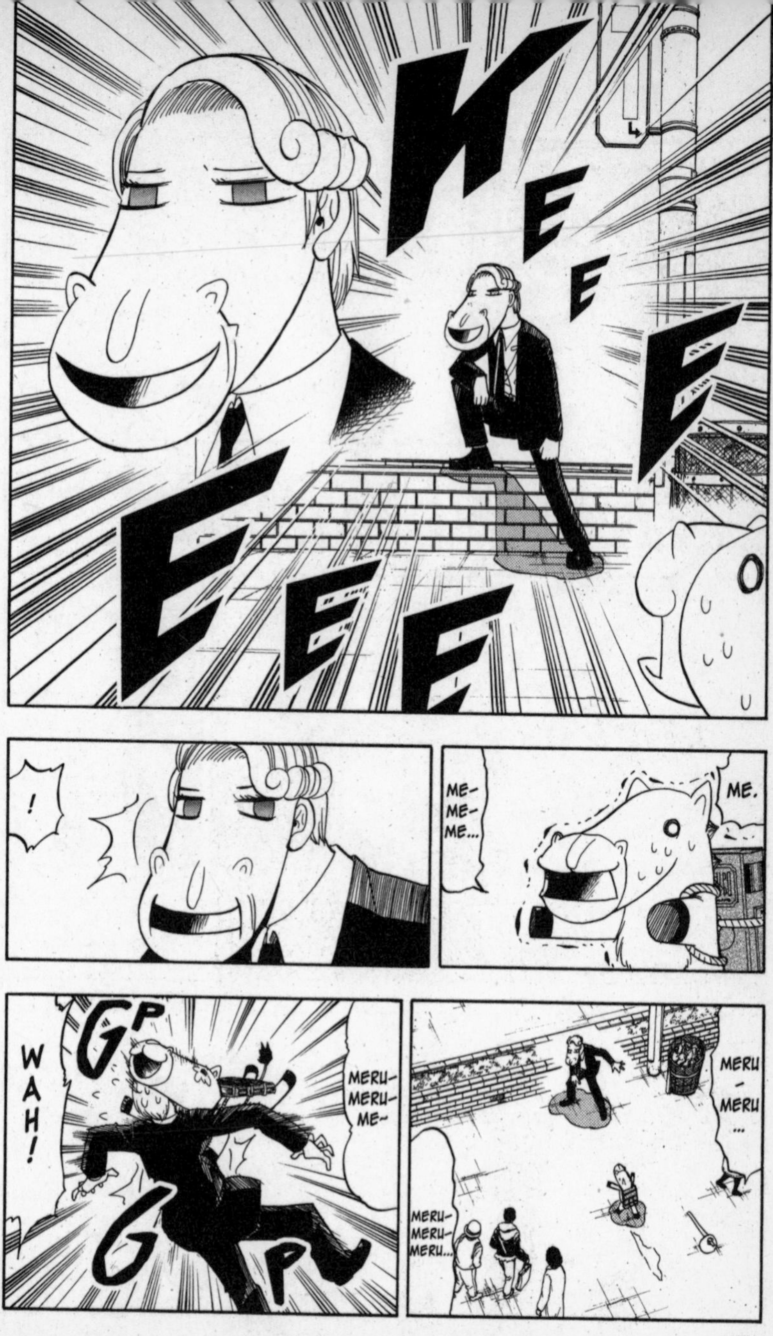
WEEEEEE
ME.
ME-ME-ME...
!
MERU-MERU...
MERU-MERU-MERU...
MERU-MERU-ME~
GP
WAH!
GP

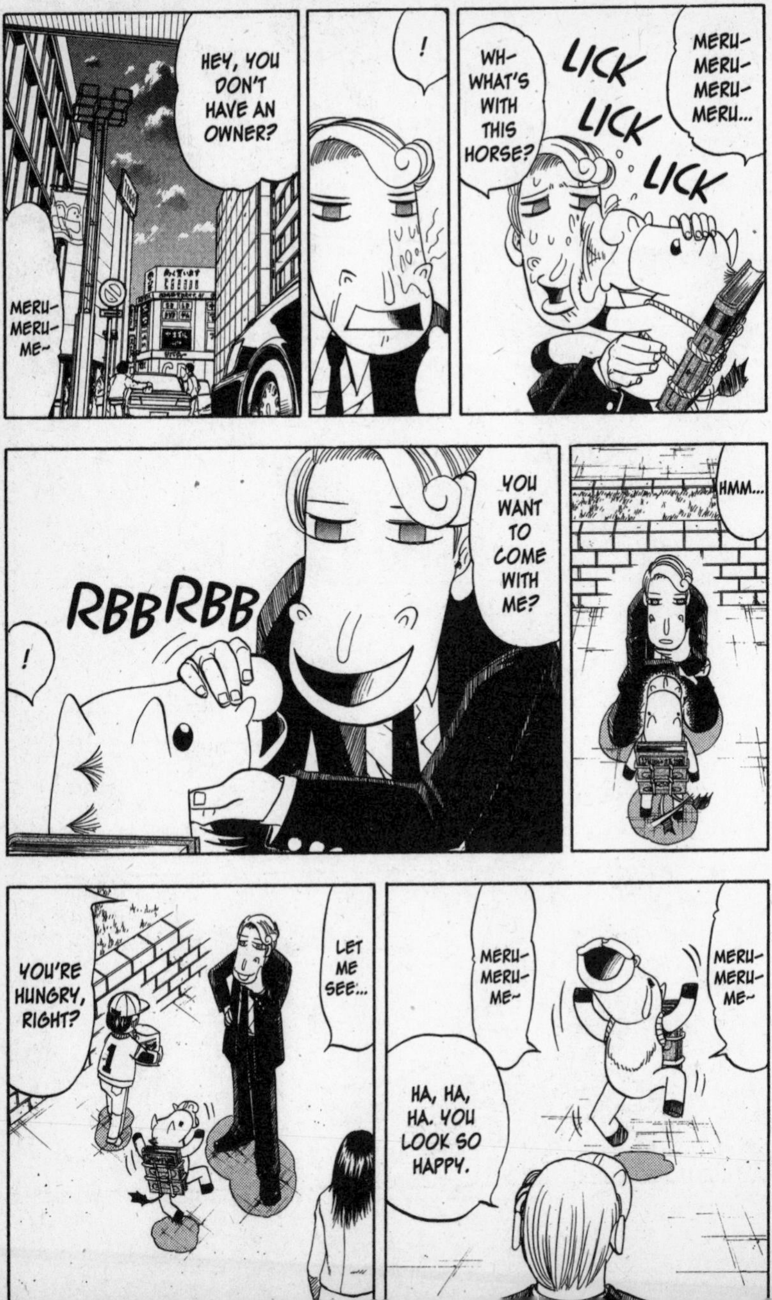
MERU-MERU-MERU-MERU...
LICK LICK LICK
WH-WHAT'S WITH THIS HORSE?
!
HEY, YOU DON'T HAVE AN OWNER?
MERU-MERU-ME~
HMM...
YOU WANT TO COME WITH ME?
RBBRBB
!
MERU-MERU-ME~
MERU-MERU-ME~
HA, HA, HA. YOU LOOK SO HAPPY.
LET ME SEE...
YOU'RE HUNGRY, RIGHT?

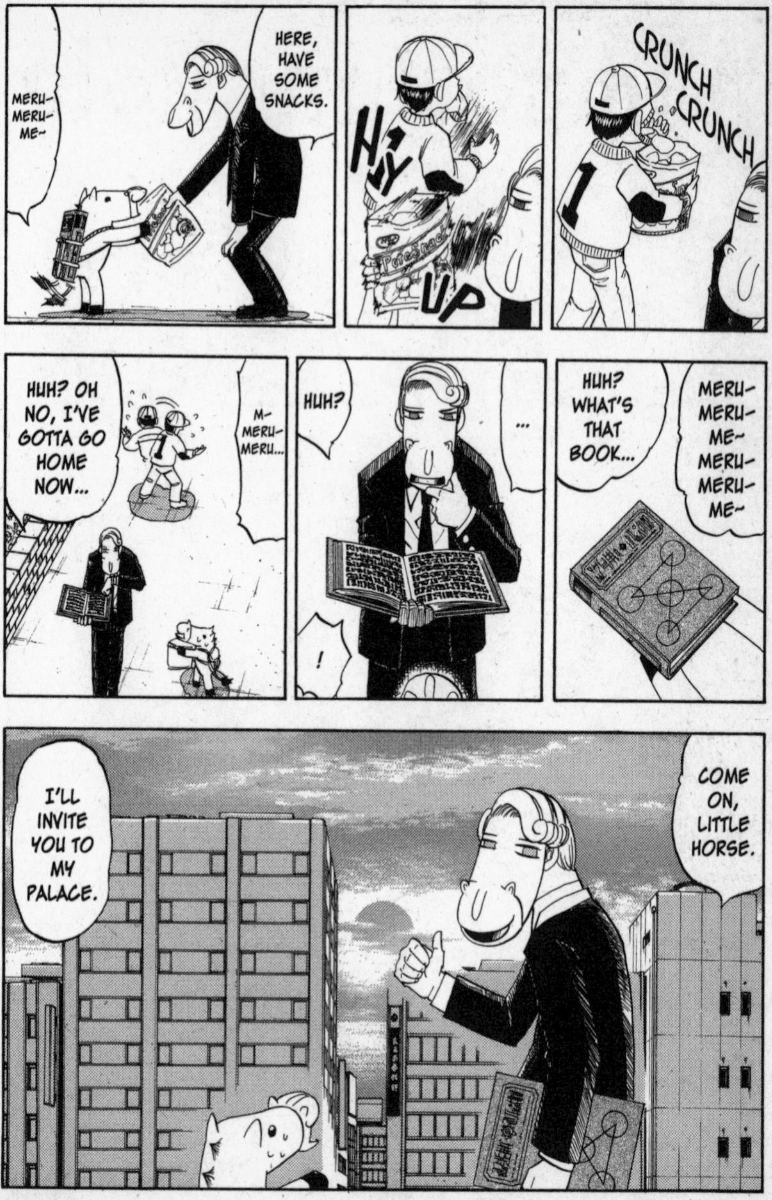
CRUNCH
CRUNCH
UP
HERE, HAVE SOME SNACKS.
MERU-MERU-ME~
MERU-MERU-ME~ MERU-MERU-ME~
HUH? WHAT'S THAT BOOK...
...
HUH?
!
M-MERU-MERU...
HUH? OH NO, I'VE GOTTA GO HOME NOW...
COME ON, LITTLE HORSE.
I'LL INVITE YOU TO MY PALACE.

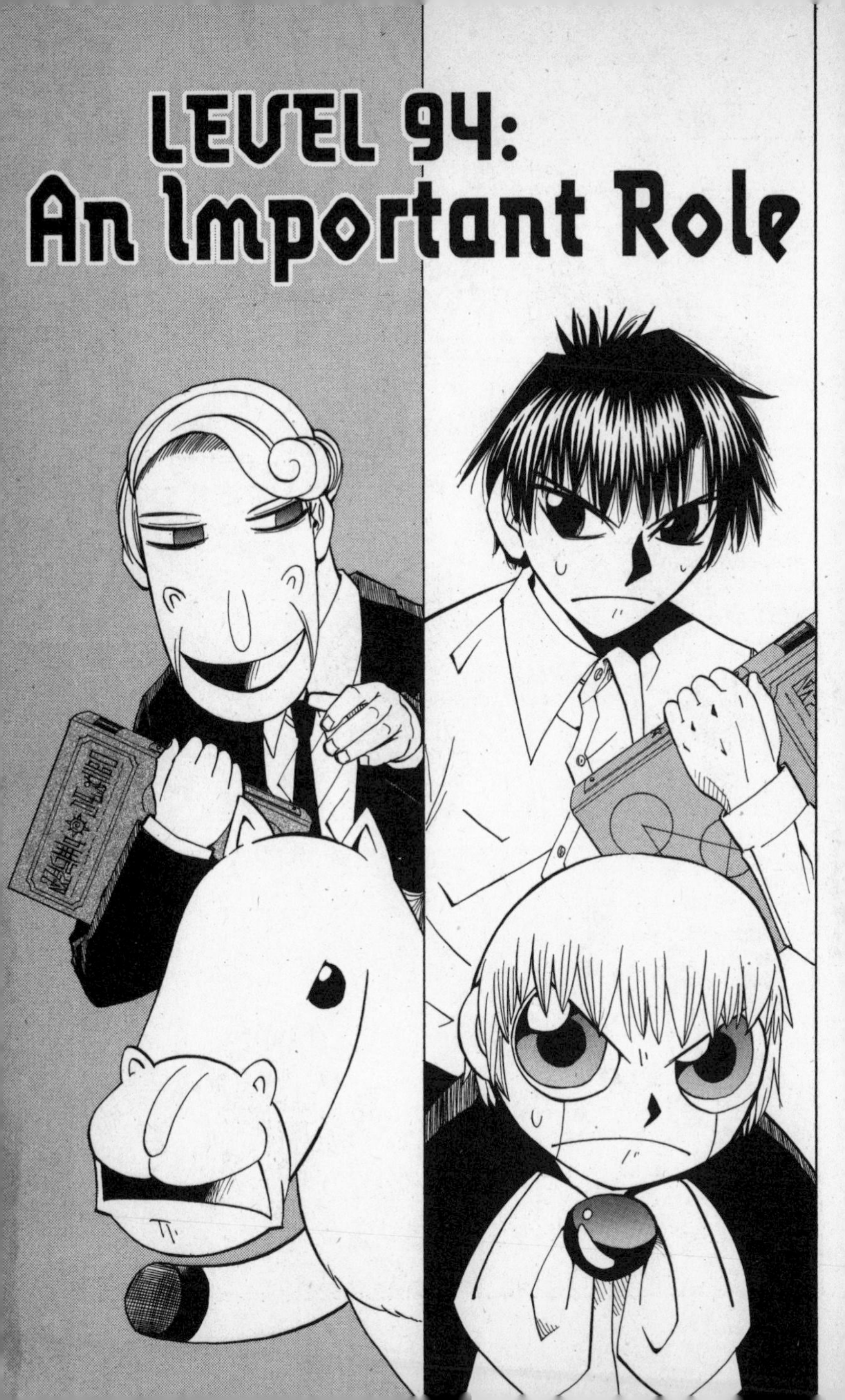
LEVEL 94:
An Important Role

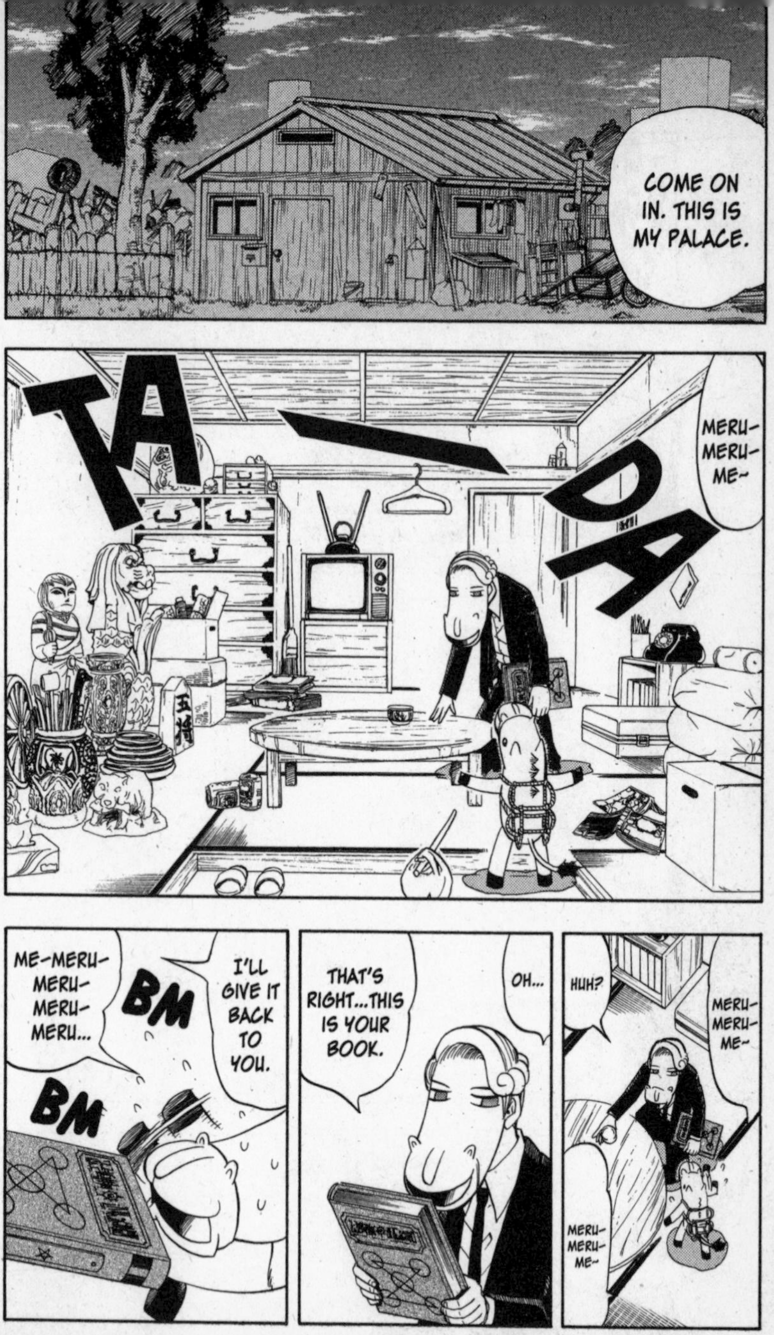
COME ON IN. THIS IS MY PALACE.
MERU-MERU-ME~
TA—DA
HUH?
MERU-MERU-ME~
MERU-MERU-ME~
OH...
THAT'S RIGHT...THIS IS YOUR BOOK.
I'LL GIVE IT BACK TO YOU.
ME-MERU-MERU-MERU-MERU...
BM
BM

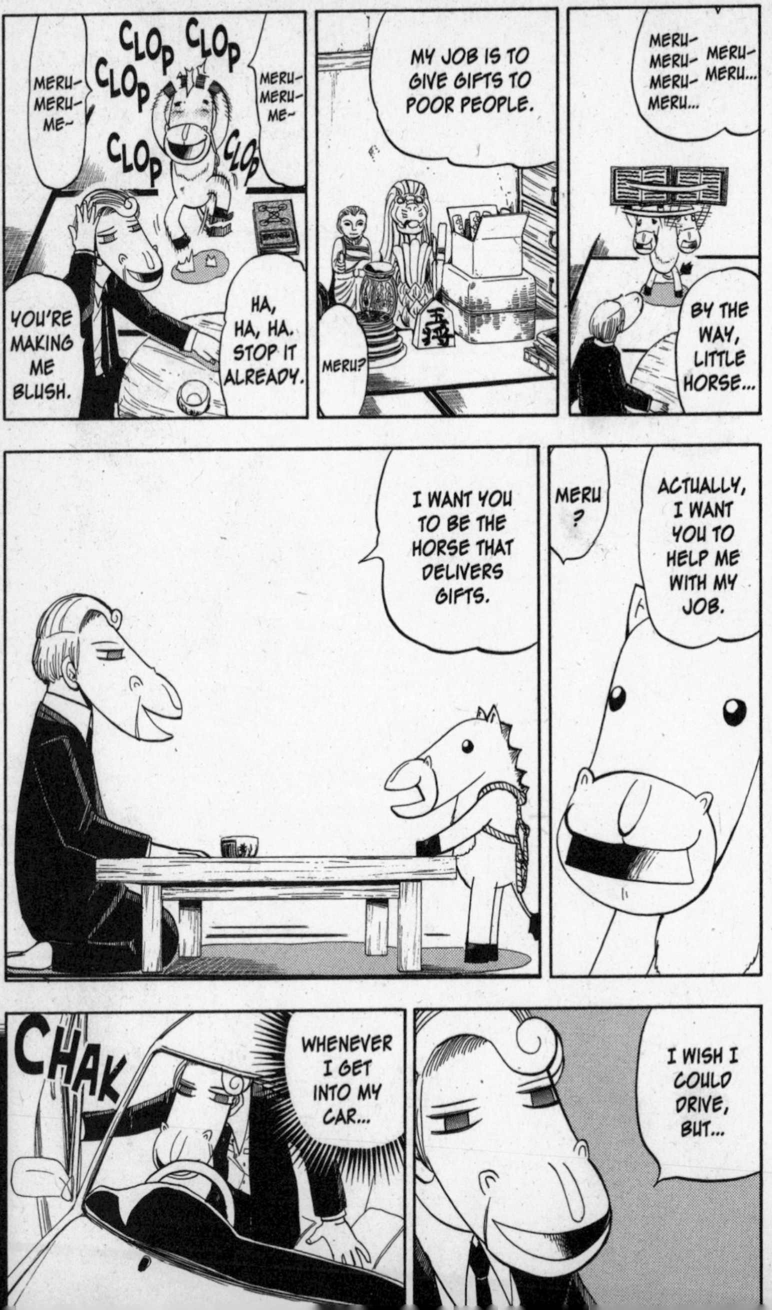
MERU-MERU...
MERU-MERU-MERU-MERU...
BY THE WAY, LITTLE HORSE...
MY JOB IS TO GIVE GIFTS TO POOR PEOPLE.
MERU?
MERU-MERU-ME~
CLOP CLOP CLOP CLOP CLOP
MERU-MERU-ME~
HA, HA, HA. STOP IT ALREADY.
YOU'RE MAKING ME BLUSH.
ACTUALLY, I WANT YOU TO HELP ME WITH MY JOB.
MERU ?
I WANT YOU TO BE THE HORSE THAT DELIVERS GIFTS.
I WISH I COULD DRIVE, BUT...
WHENEVER I GET INTO MY CAR...
CHAK

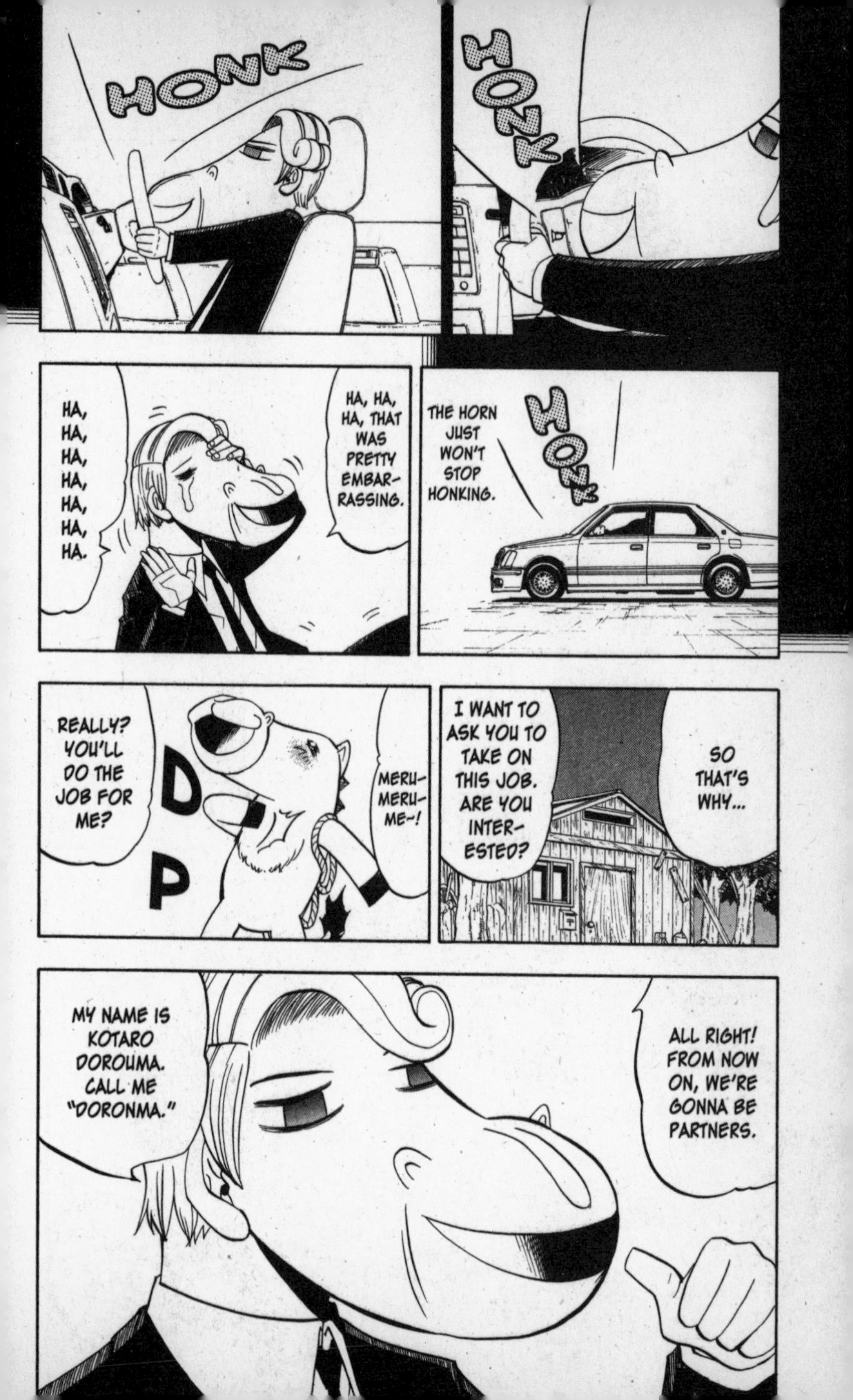
HONK
HONK
HONK
THE HORN JUST WON'T STOP HONKING.
HA, HA, HA, THAT WAS PRETTY EMBARRASSING.
HA, HA, HA, HA, HA, HA, HA.
SO THAT'S WHY...
I WANT TO ASK YOU TO TAKE ON THIS JOB. ARE YOU INTERESTED?
MERU-MERU-ME~!
DP
REALLY? YOU'LL DO THE JOB FOR ME?
ALL RIGHT! FROM NOW ON, WE'RE GONNA BE PARTNERS.
MY NAME IS KOTARO DOROUMA. CALL ME "DORONMA."

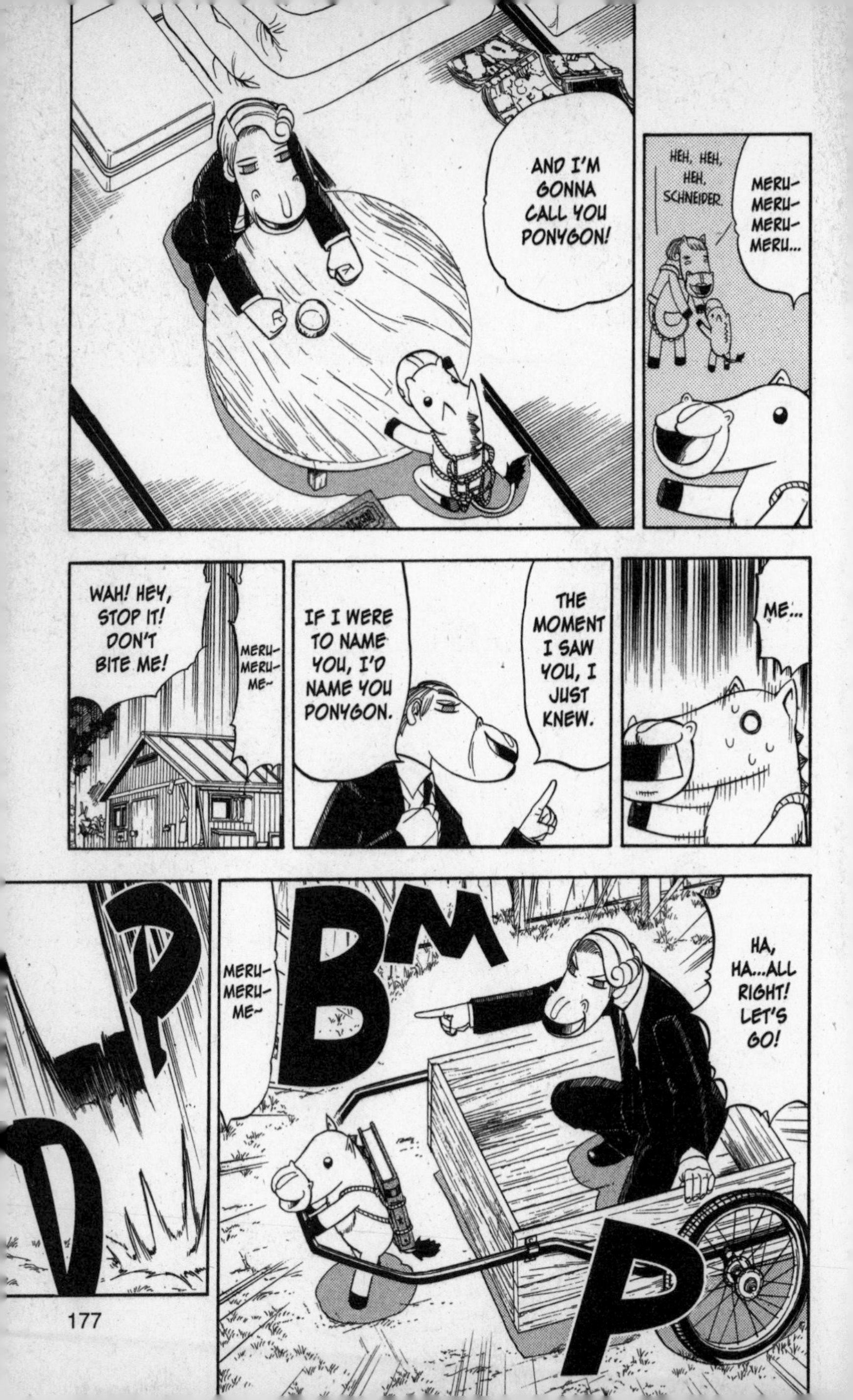
MERU-MERU-MERU-MERU...
HEH, HEH, HEH, SCHNEIDER.
AND I'M GONNA CALL YOU PONYGON!
ME...
THE MOMENT I SAW YOU, I JUST KNEW.
IF I WERE TO NAME YOU, I'D NAME YOU PONYGON.
MERU-MERU-ME~
WAH! HEY, STOP IT! DON'T BITE ME!
HA, HA...ALL RIGHT! LET'S GO!
BM
MERU-MERU-ME~
P
P
P

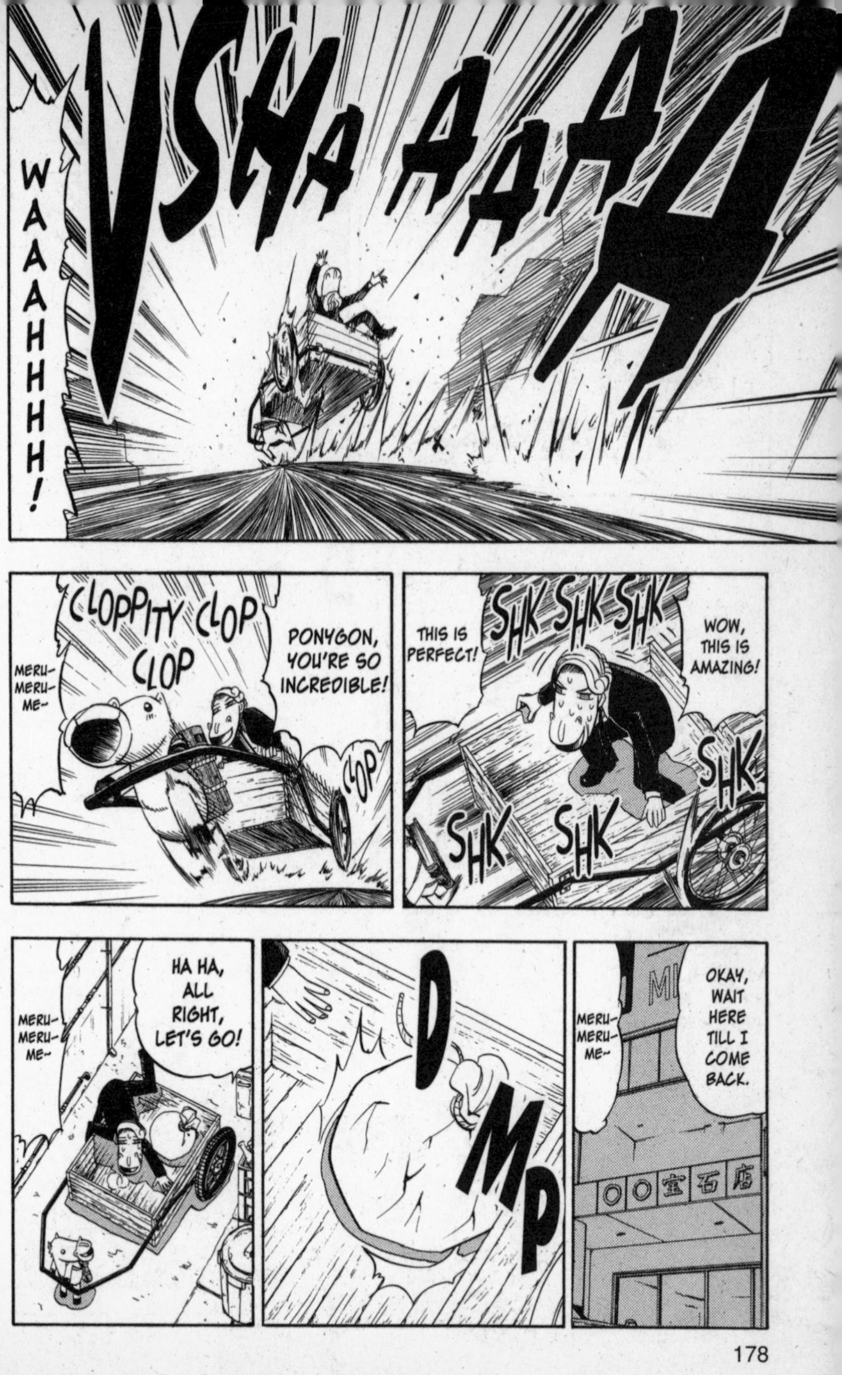
VSHAAAAA
WAAAAHHHHH!
WOW, THIS IS AMAZING!
SHK SHK SHK
THIS IS PERFECT!
SHK
SHK
SHK
PONYGON, YOU'RE SO INCREDIBLE!
CLOPPITY CLOP
CLOP
MERU-MERU-ME~
CLOP
OKAY, WAIT HERE TILL I COME BACK.
MERU-MERU-ME~
○○宝石店
DMP
HA HA, ALL RIGHT, LET'S GO!
MERU-MERU-ME~

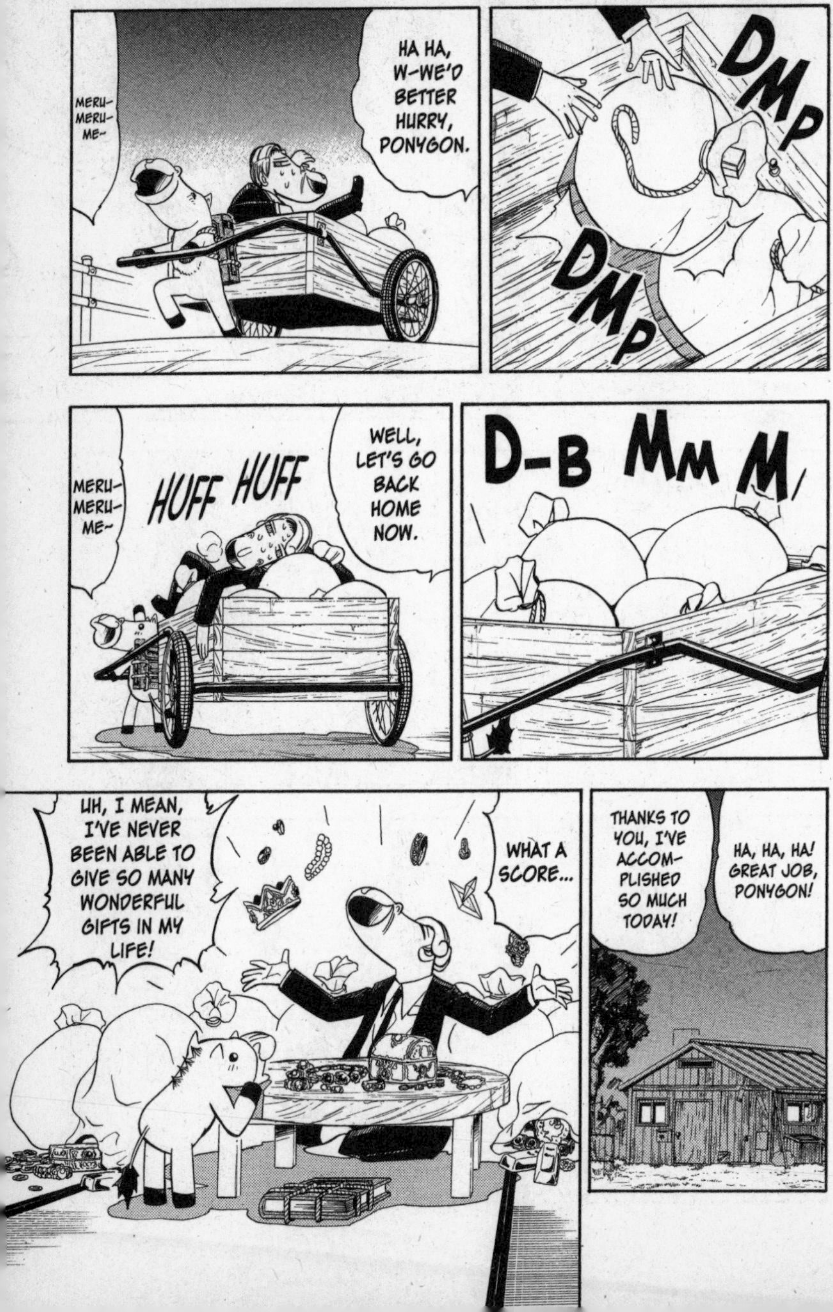
DMP
DMP
HA HA, W-WE'D BETTER HURRY, PONYGON.
MERU-MERU-ME~
D-B MM M
WELL, LET'S GO BACK HOME NOW.
HUFF HUFF
MERU-MERU-ME~
HA, HA, HA! GREAT JOB, PONYGON!
THANKS TO YOU, I'VE ACCOMPLISHED SO MUCH TODAY!
WHAT A SCORE...
UH, I MEAN, I'VE NEVER BEEN ABLE TO GIVE SO MANY WONDERFUL GIFTS IN MY LIFE!

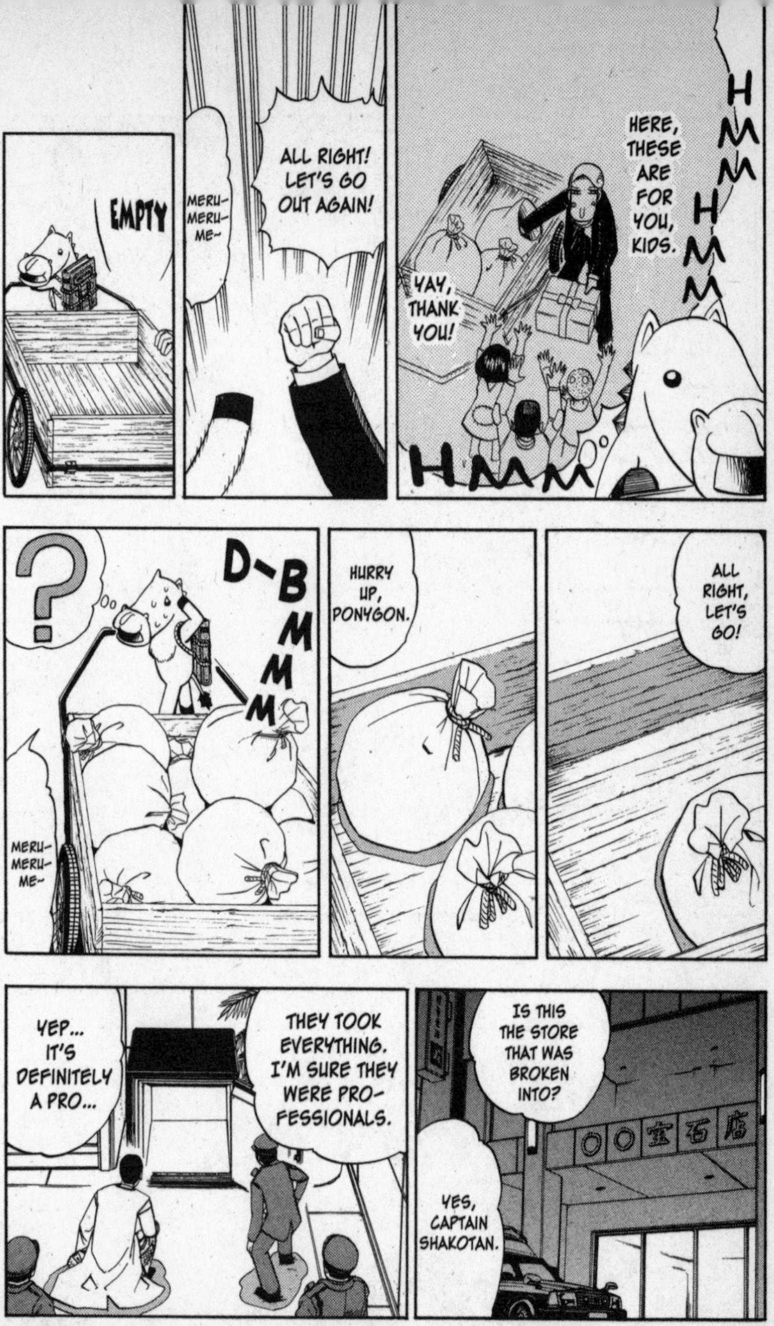
HERE, THESE ARE FOR YOU, KIDS.
HMM HMM
YAY, THANK YOU!
HMM
ALL RIGHT! LET'S GO OUT AGAIN!
MERU-MERU-ME~
EMPTY
ALL RIGHT, LET'S GO!
HURRY UP, PONYGON.
D-BMMM
?
MERU-MERU-ME~
IS THIS THE STORE THAT WAS BROKEN INTO?
○○宝石店
YES, CAPTAIN SHAKOTAN.
THEY TOOK EVERYTHING. I'M SURE THEY WERE PROFESSIONALS.
YEP... IT'S DEFINITELY A PRO...

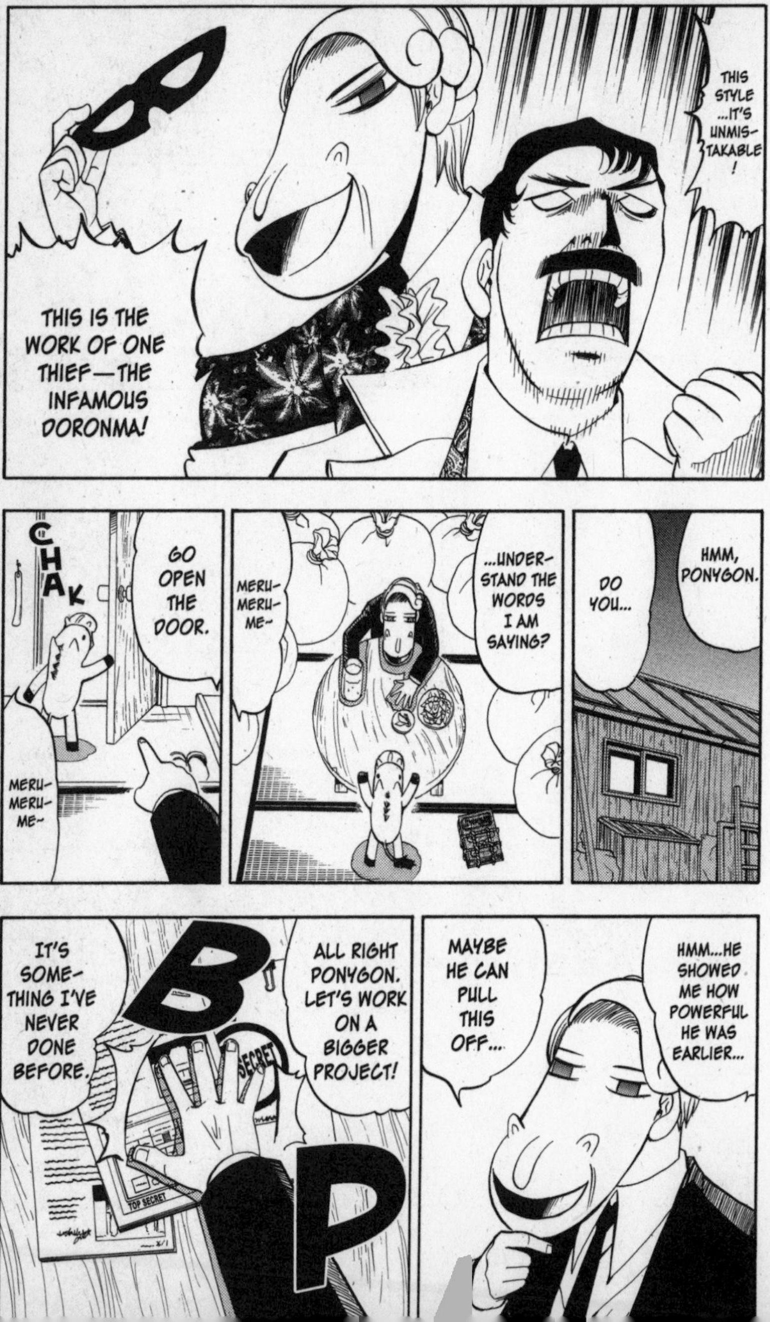
THIS STYLE ...IT'S UNMISTAKABLE!
THIS IS THE WORK OF ONE THIEF—THE INFAMOUS DORONMA!
HMM, PONYGON.
DO YOU...
...UNDERSTAND THE WORDS I AM SAYING?
MERU-MERU-ME~
GO OPEN THE DOOR.
CHAK
MERU-MERU-ME~
HMM...HE SHOWED ME HOW POWERFUL HE WAS EARLIER...
MAYBE HE CAN PULL THIS OFF...
ALL RIGHT PONYGON. LET'S WORK ON A BIGGER PROJECT!
BP
IT'S SOMETHING I'VE NEVER DONE BEFORE.
SECRET
TOP SECRET

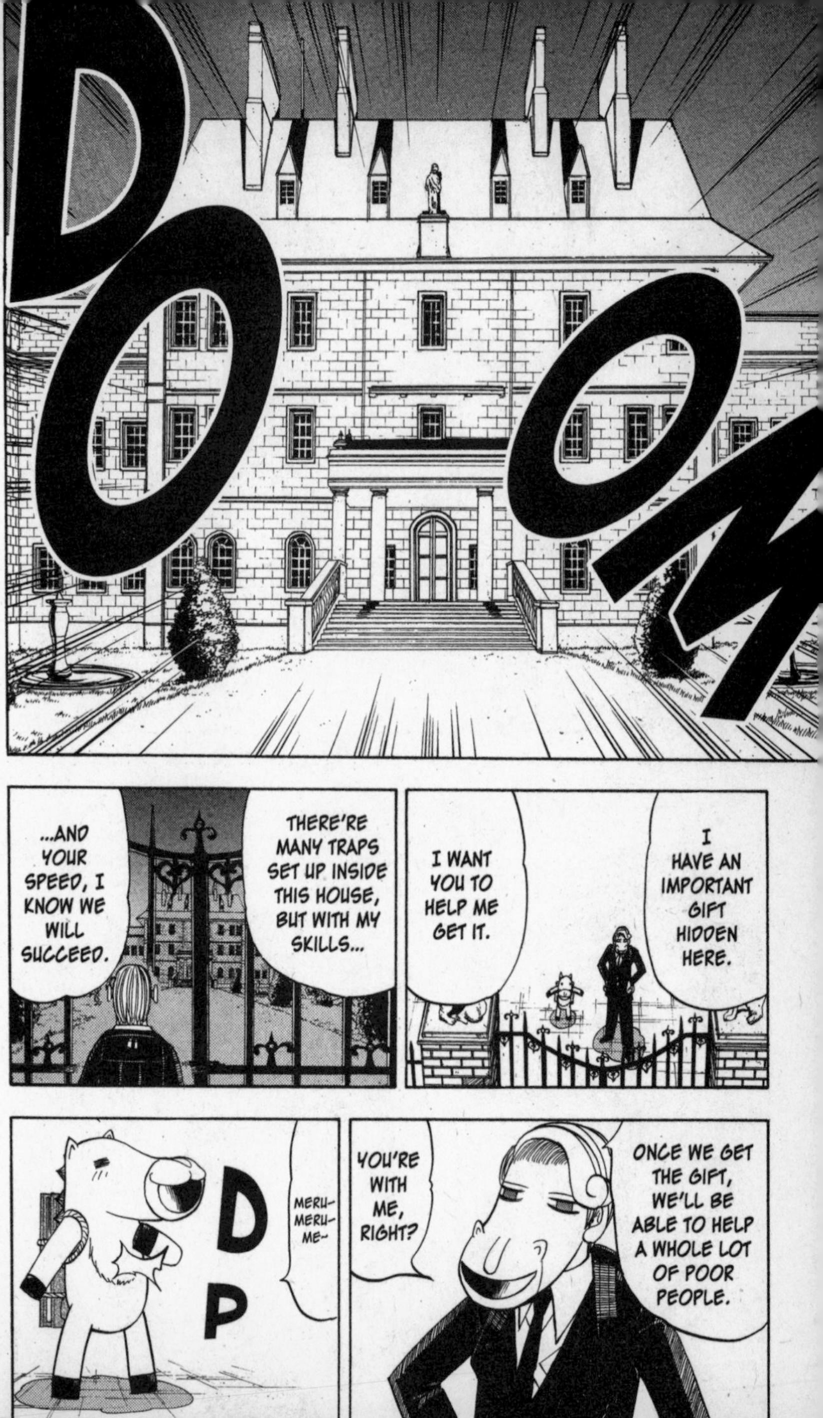
DOOM
I HAVE AN IMPORTANT GIFT HIDDEN HERE.
I WANT YOU TO HELP ME GET IT.
THERE'RE MANY TRAPS SET UP INSIDE THIS HOUSE, BUT WITH MY SKILLS...
...AND YOUR SPEED, I KNOW WE WILL SUCCEED.
ONCE WE GET THE GIFT, WE'LL BE ABLE TO HELP A WHOLE LOT OF POOR PEOPLE.
YOU'RE WITH ME, RIGHT?
MERU-MERU-ME~
DP

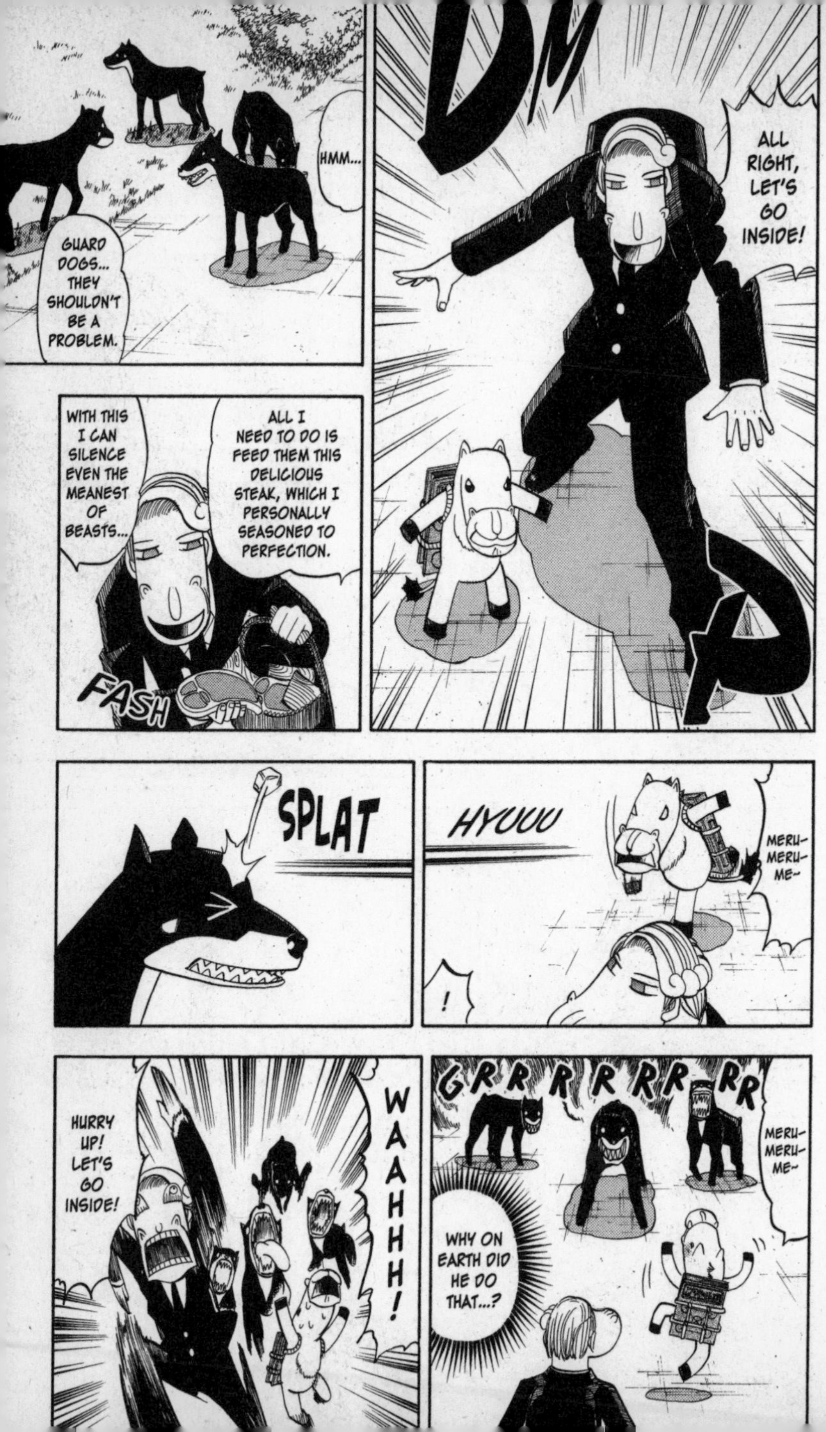
ALL RIGHT, LET'S GO INSIDE!
DM
HMM...
GUARD DOGS... THEY SHOULDN'T BE A PROBLEM.
ALL I NEED TO DO IS FEED THEM THIS DELICIOUS STEAK, WHICH I PERSONALLY SEASONED TO PERFECTION.
WITH THIS I CAN SILENCE EVEN THE MEANEST OF BEASTS...
FASH
MERU-MERU-ME~
HYUUU
!
SPLAT
GRRRRRRRR
MERU-MERU-ME~
WHY ON EARTH DID HE DO THAT...?
WAAHHH!
HURRY UP! LET'S GO INSIDE!

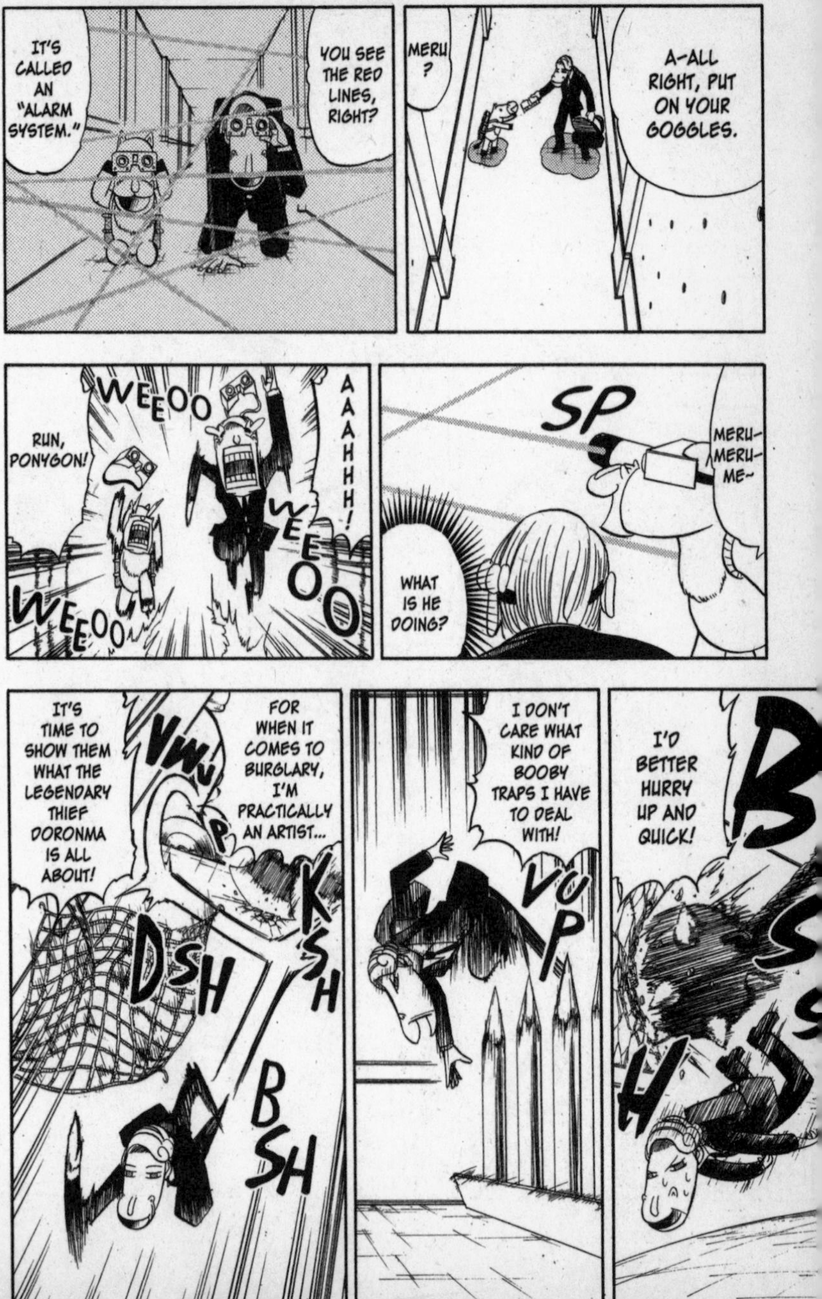
A-ALL RIGHT, PUT ON YOUR GOGGLES.
MERU?
YOU SEE THE RED LINES, RIGHT?
IT'S CALLED AN "ALARM SYSTEM."
SP
MERU-MERU-ME~
WHAT IS HE DOING?
AAAHHH!
WEEOO
WEEOO
RUN, PONYGON!
WEEOO
BSSH
I'D BETTER HURRY UP AND QUICK!
I DON'T CARE WHAT KIND OF BOOBY TRAPS I HAVE TO DEAL WITH!
VUP
FOR WHEN IT COMES TO BURGLARY, I'M PRACTICALLY AN ARTIST...
IT'S TIME TO SHOW THEM WHAT THE LEGENDARY THIEF DORONMA IS ALL ABOUT!
VWIP
KSH
DSH
BSH

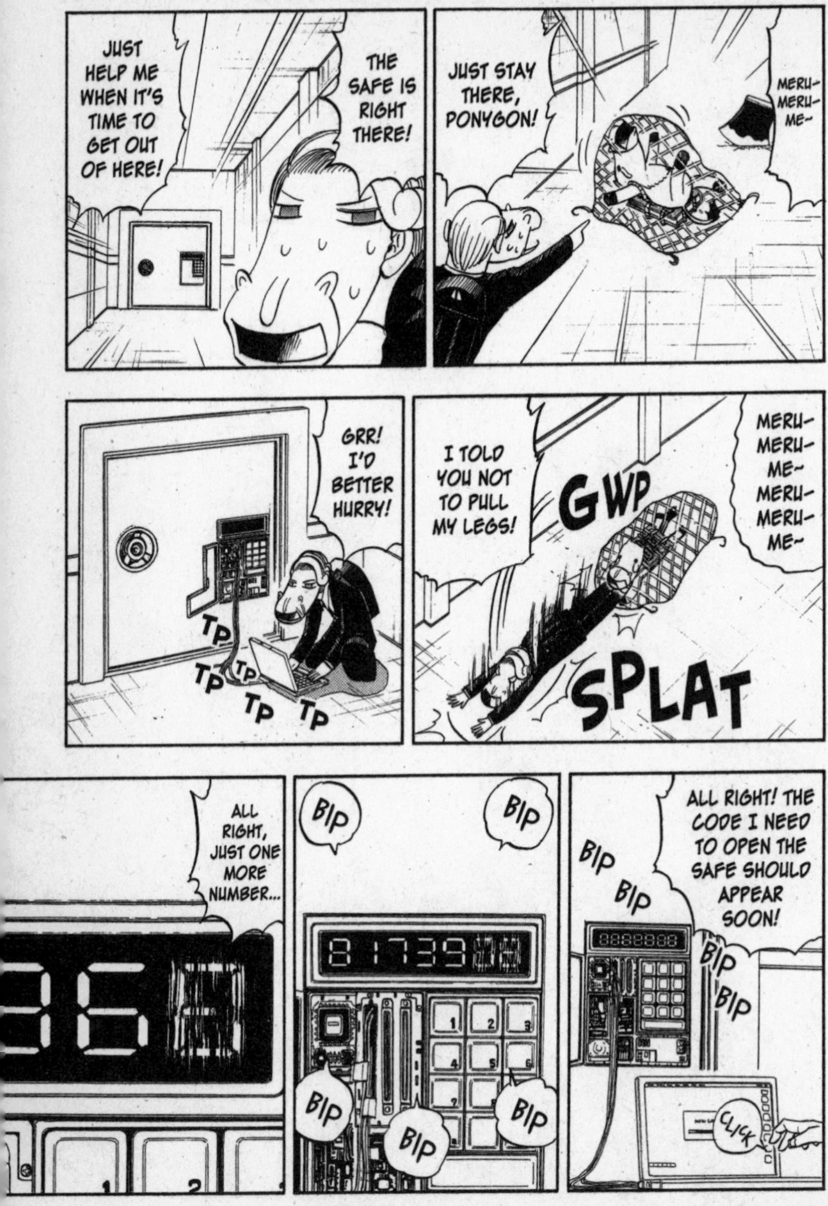
MERU-MERU-ME~
JUST STAY THERE, PONYGON!
THE SAFE IS RIGHT THERE!
JUST HELP ME WHEN IT'S TIME TO GET OUT OF HERE!
MERU-MERU-ME~ MERU-MERU-ME~
I TOLD YOU NOT TO PULL MY LEGS!
GWP
SPLAT
GRR! I'D BETTER HURRY!
TP TP TP TP TP
ALL RIGHT! THE CODE I NEED TO OPEN THE SAFE SHOULD APPEAR SOON!
BIP BIP
BIP BIP
CLICK
BIP BIP
BIP BIP BIP
ALL RIGHT, JUST ONE MORE NUMBER...

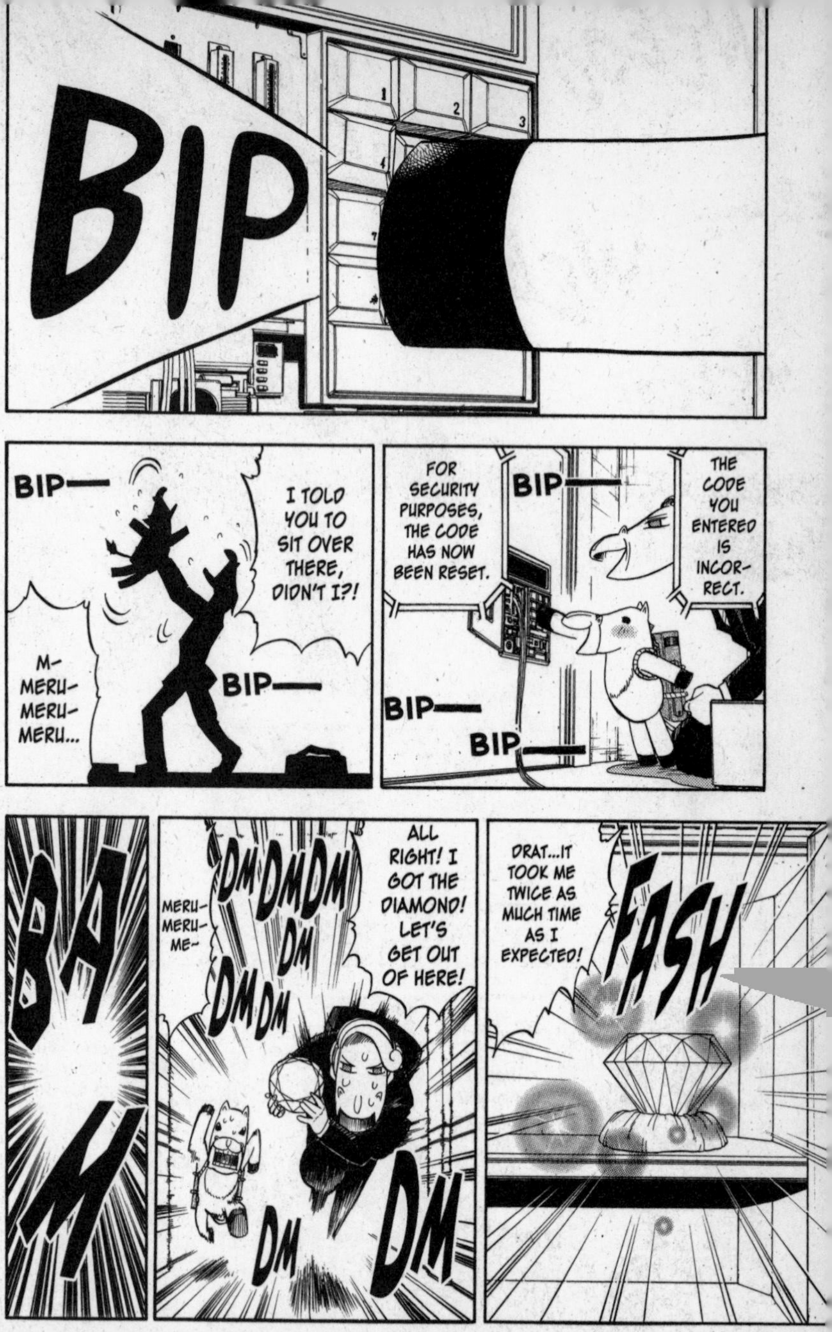
BIP
THE CODE YOU ENTERED IS INCORRECT.
BIP—
FOR SECURITY PURPOSES, THE CODE HAS NOW BEEN RESET.
BIP—
BIP—
I TOLD YOU TO SIT OVER THERE, DIDN'T I?!
BIP—
BIP—
M-MERU-MERU-MERU...
DRAT...IT TOOK ME TWICE AS MUCH TIME AS I EXPECTED!
FASH
ALL RIGHT! I GOT THE DIAMOND! LET'S GET OUT OF HERE!
DM DMDM DM DMDM
MERU-MERU-ME-
DM DM
BAM

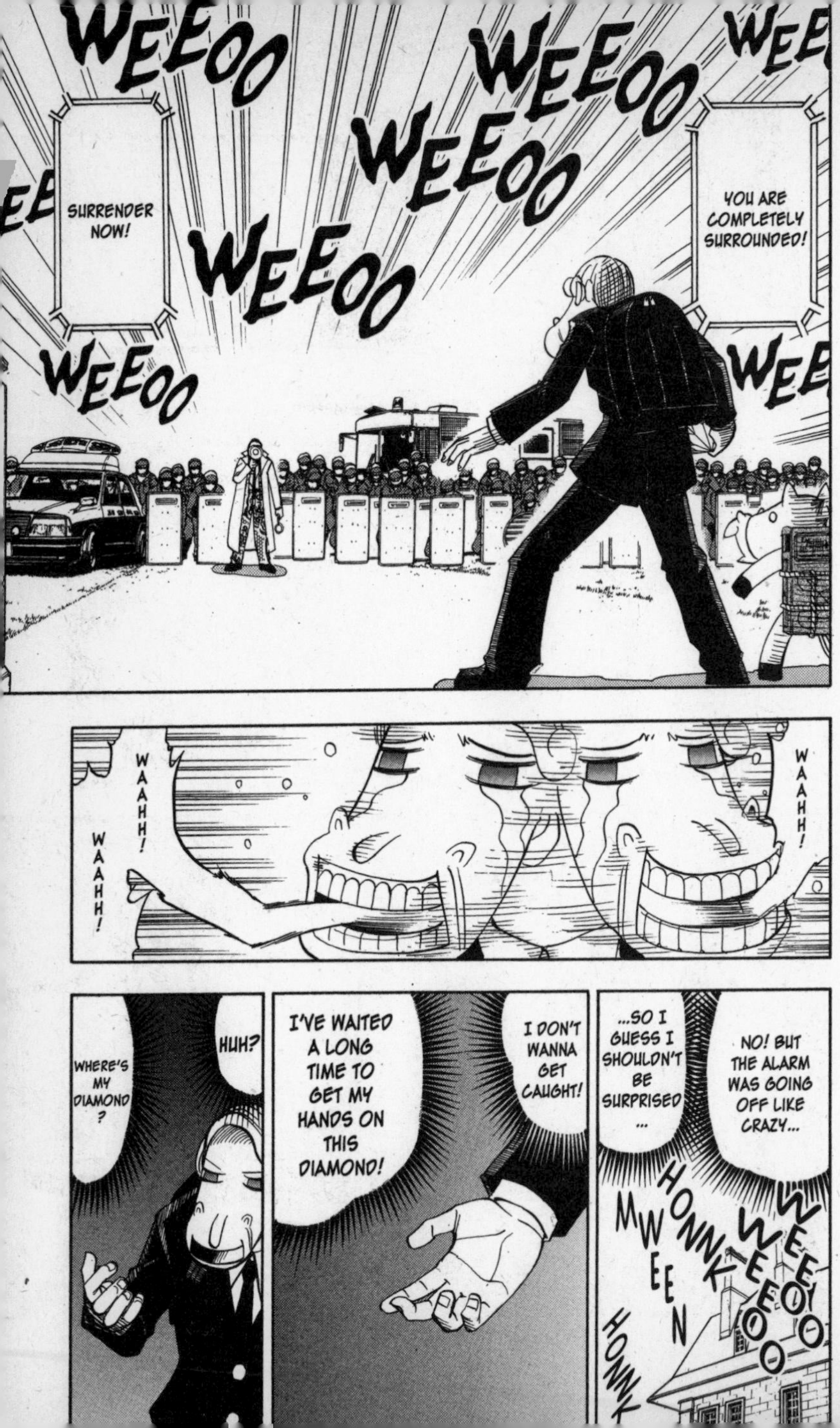
WEE
YOU ARE COMPLETELY SURROUNDED!
WEEOO
WEEOO
WEEOO
WEEOO
SURRENDER NOW!
WEEOO
WEE
WAAHH!
WAAHH!
WAAHH!
NO! BUT THE ALARM WAS GOING OFF LIKE CRAZY...
...SO I GUESS I SHOULDN'T BE SURPRISED...
WEEOO
WEEOO
HONNK
MWEEN
HONNK
I DON'T WANNA GET CAUGHT!
I'VE WAITED A LONG TIME TO GET MY HANDS ON THIS DIAMOND!
HUH?
WHERE'S MY DIAMOND?

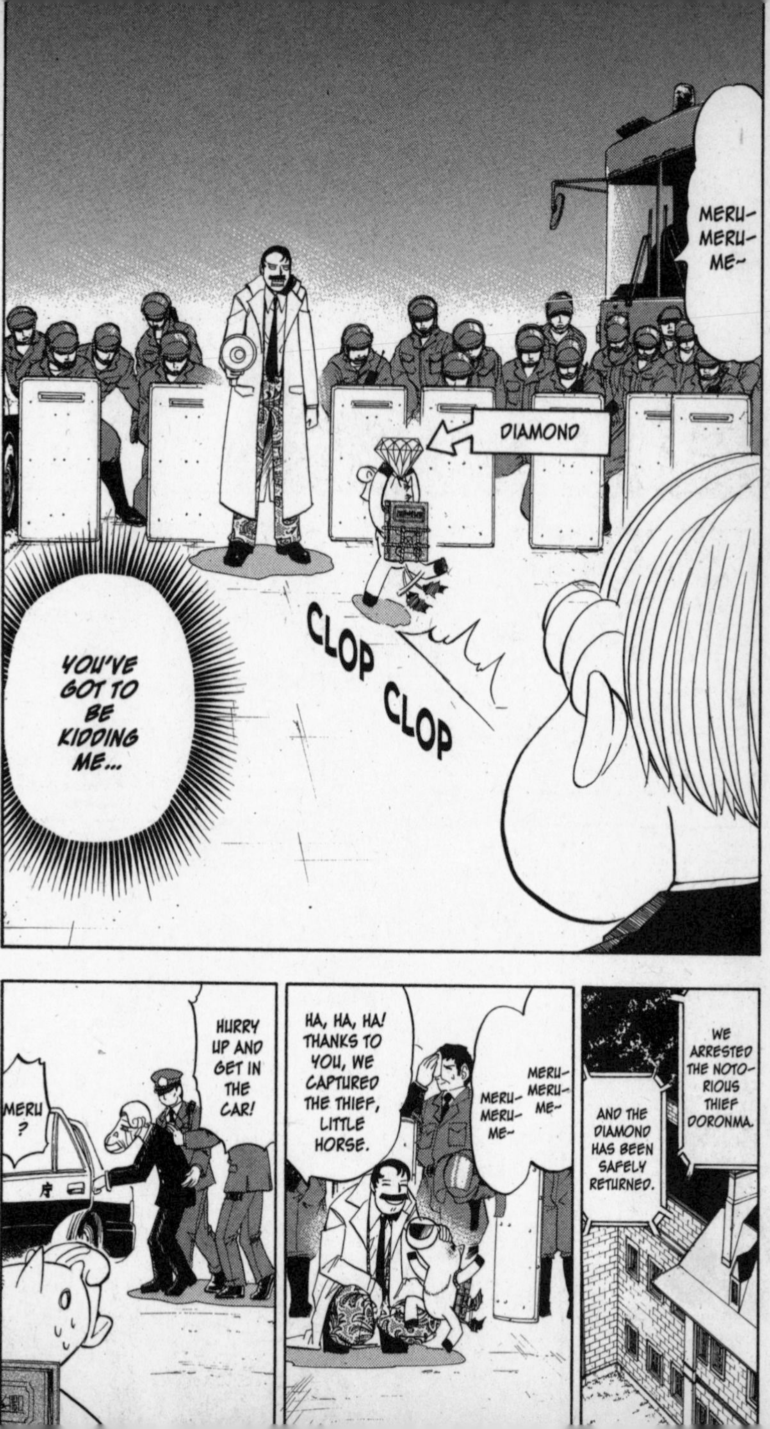
MERU-MERU-ME~
DIAMOND
CLOP CLOP
YOU'VE GOT TO BE KIDDING ME...
WE ARRESTED THE NOTORIOUS THIEF DORONMA.
AND THE DIAMOND HAS BEEN SAFELY RETURNED.
MERU-MERU-ME~
MERU-MERU-ME~
HA, HA, HA! THANKS TO YOU, WE CAPTURED THE THIEF, LITTLE HORSE.
HURRY UP AND GET IN THE CAR!
MERU?

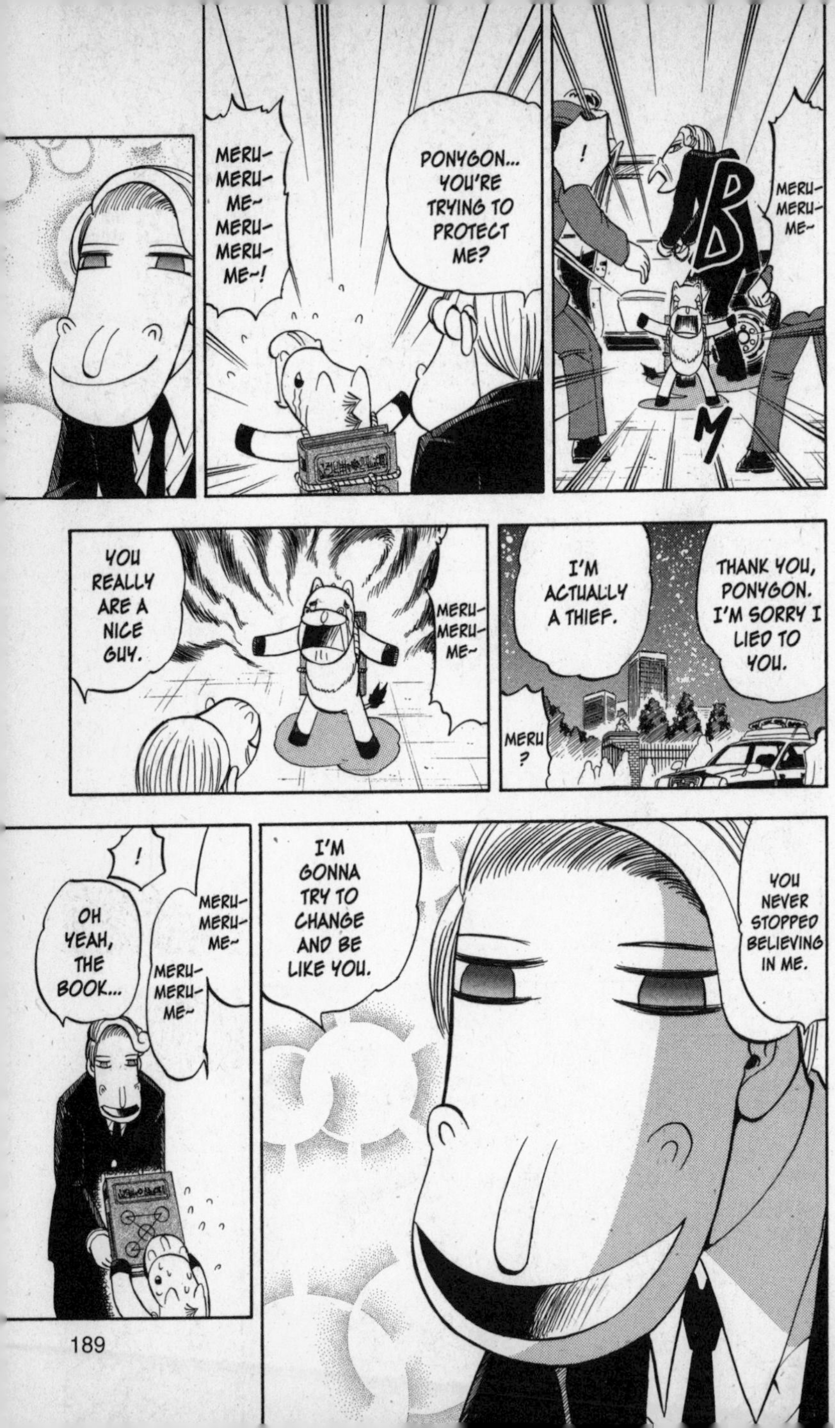
MERU-MERU-ME~
B
M
PONYGON... YOU'RE TRYING TO PROTECT ME?
MERU-MERU-ME~MERU-MERU-ME~!
THANK YOU, PONYGON. I'M SORRY I LIED TO YOU.
I'M ACTUALLY A THIEF.
MERU?
MERU-MERU-ME~
YOU REALLY ARE A NICE GUY.
YOU NEVER STOPPED BELIEVING IN ME.
I'M GONNA TRY TO CHANGE AND BE LIKE YOU.
!
MERU-MERU-ME~
OH YEAH, THE BOOK...
MERU-MERU-ME~

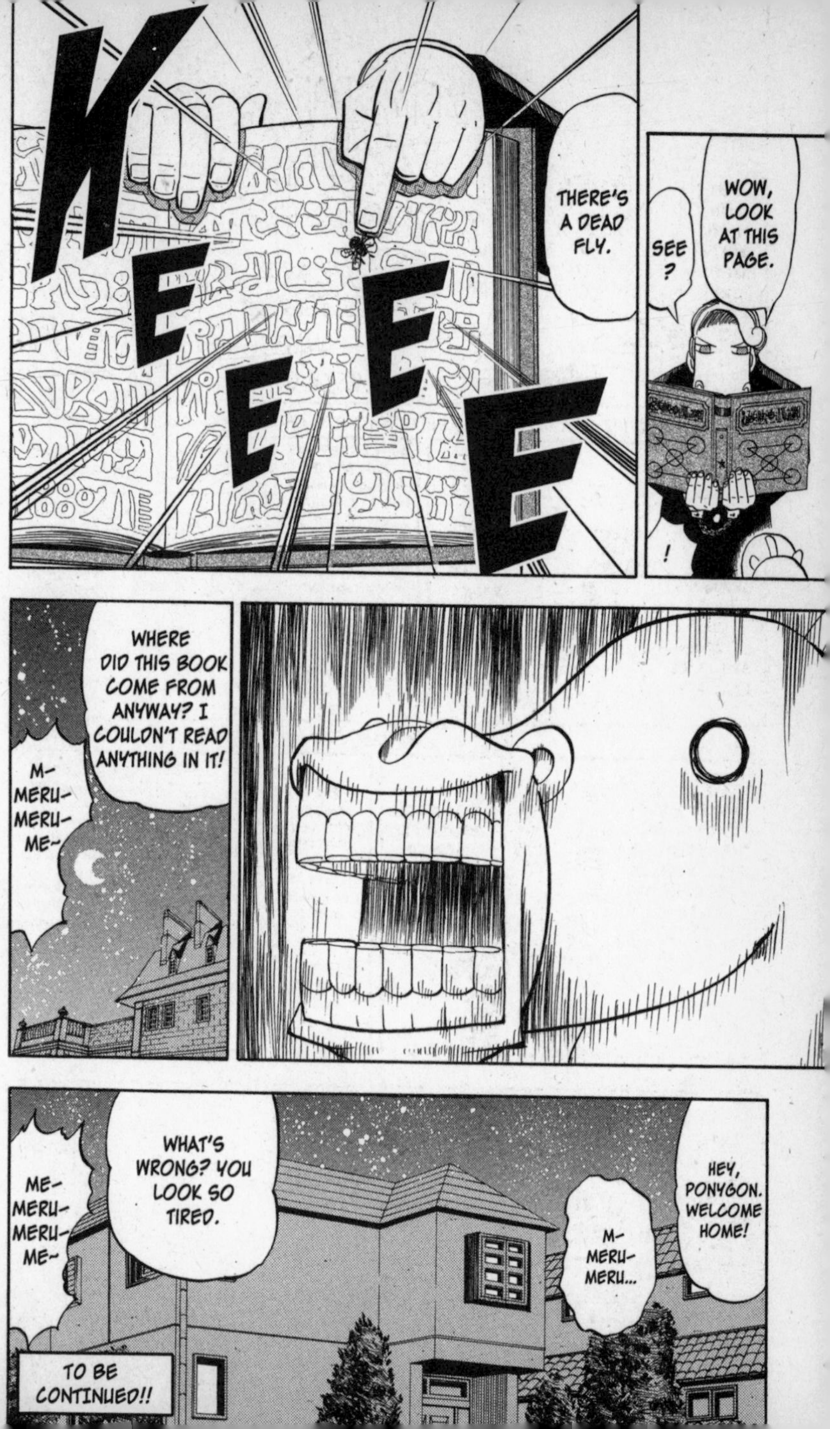
WOW, LOOK AT THIS PAGE.
SEE?
!
THERE'S A DEAD FLY.
KEEEEE
WHERE DID THIS BOOK COME FROM ANYWAY? I COULDN'T READ ANYTHING IN IT!
M-MERU-MERU-ME~
HEY, PONYGON. WELCOME HOME!
M-MERU-MERU...
WHAT'S WRONG? YOU LOOK SO TIRED.
ME-MERU-MERU-ME~
TO BE CONTINUED!!

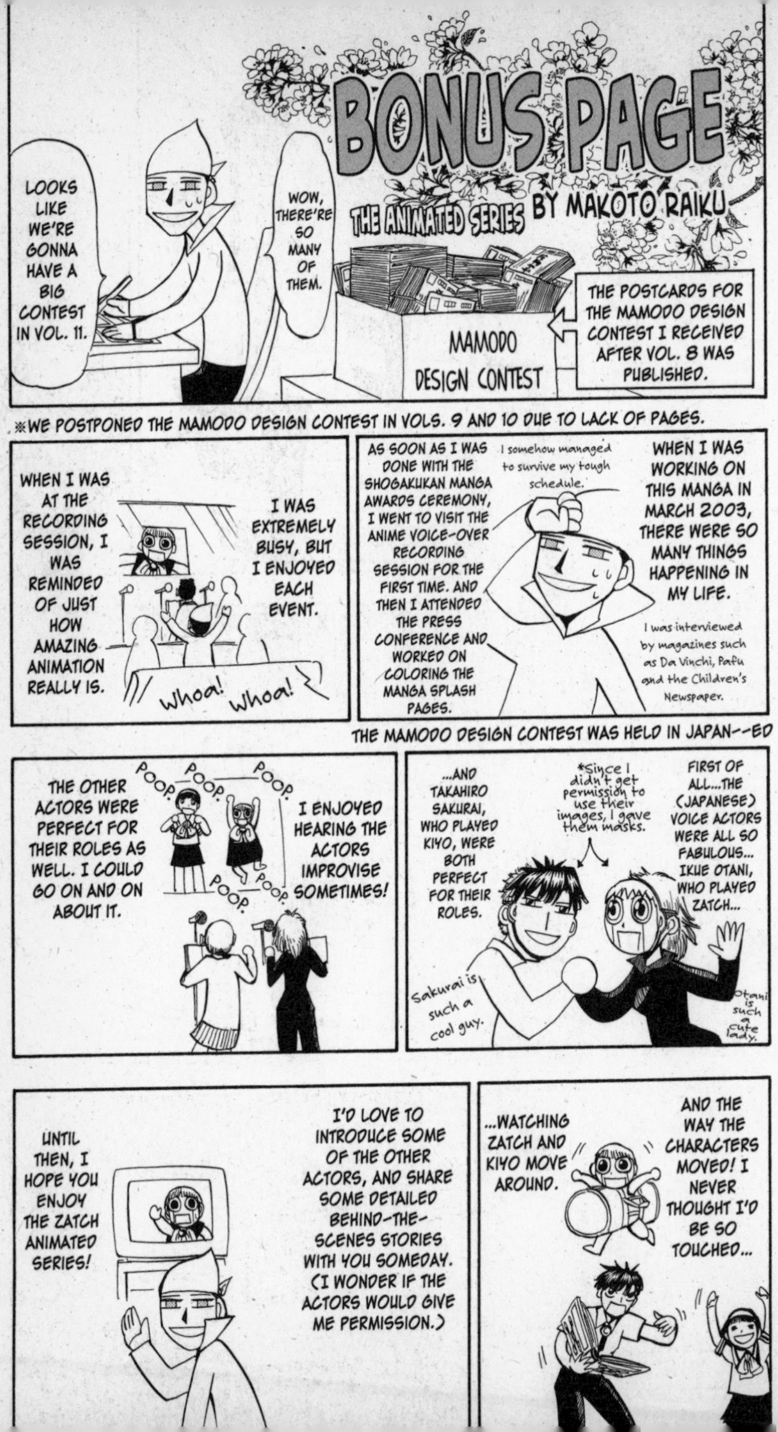
BONUS PAGE
THE ANIMATED SERIES BY MAKOTO RAIKU
THE POSTCARDS FOR THE MAMODO DESIGN CONTEST I RECEIVED AFTER VOL. 8 WAS PUBLISHED.
MAMODO DESIGN CONTEST
WOW, THERE'RE SO MANY OF THEM.
LOOKS LIKE WE'RE GONNA HAVE A BIG CONTEST IN VOL. 11.
※WE POSTPONED THE MAMODO DESIGN CONTEST IN VOLS. 9 AND 10 DUE TO LACK OF PAGES.
WHEN I WAS WORKING ON THIS MANGA IN MARCH 2003, THERE WERE SO MANY THINGS HAPPENING IN MY LIFE.
I somehow managed to survive my tough schedule.
AS SOON AS I WAS DONE WITH THE SHOGAKUKAN MANGA AWARDS CEREMONY, I WENT TO VISIT THE ANIME VOICE-OVER RECORDING SESSION FOR THE FIRST TIME. AND THEN I ATTENDED THE PRESS CONFERENCE AND WORKED ON COLORING THE MANGA SPLASH PAGES.
I was interviewed by magazines such as Da Vinchi, Pafu and the Children's Newspaper.
I WAS EXTREMELY BUSY, BUT I ENJOYED EACH EVENT.
WHEN I WAS AT THE RECORDING SESSION, I WAS REMINDED OF JUST HOW AMAZING ANIMATION REALLY IS.
Whoa! Whoa!
THE MAMODO DESIGN CONTEST WAS HELD IN JAPAN--ED
FIRST OF ALL...THE (JAPANESE) VOICE ACTORS WERE ALL SO FABULOUS... IKUE OTANI, WHO PLAYED ZATCH...
*Since I didn't get permission to use their images, I gave them masks.
...AND TAKAHIRO SAKURAI, WHO PLAYED KIYO, WERE BOTH PERFECT FOR THEIR ROLES.
Otani is such a cute lady.
Sakurai is such a cool guy.
I ENJOYED HEARING THE ACTORS IMPROVISE SOMETIMES!
POOP. POOP. POOP.
POOP. POOP.
THE OTHER ACTORS WERE PERFECT FOR THEIR ROLES AS WELL. I COULD GO ON AND ON ABOUT IT.
AND THE WAY THE CHARACTERS MOVED! I NEVER THOUGHT I'D BE SO TOUCHED...
...WATCHING ZATCH AND KIYO MOVE AROUND.
I'D LOVE TO INTRODUCE SOME OF THE OTHER ACTORS, AND SHARE SOME DETAILED BEHIND-THE-SCENES STORIES WITH YOU SOMEDAY. (I WONDER IF THE ACTORS WOULD GIVE ME PERMISSION.)
UNTIL THEN, I HOPE YOU ENJOY THE ZATCH ANIMATED SERIES!

# ZATCH & SUZY

BY MAKOTO RAIKU

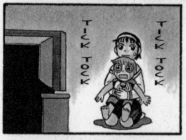

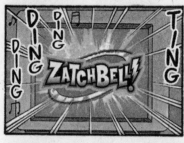

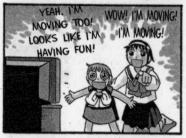

TICK TOCK
TICK TOCK
TING
DING
DING
DING
ZATCHBELL!
WOW! I'M MOVING! I'M MOVING!
YEAH, I'M MOVING TOO! LOOKS LIKE I'M HAVING FUN!
KYAA! IT'S TAKAMINE! I'VE GOTTA TAPE THE SHOW!
WHOA! WHAT A FRESH, TASTY-LOOKING YELLOWTAIL I'VE GOT!

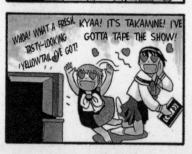

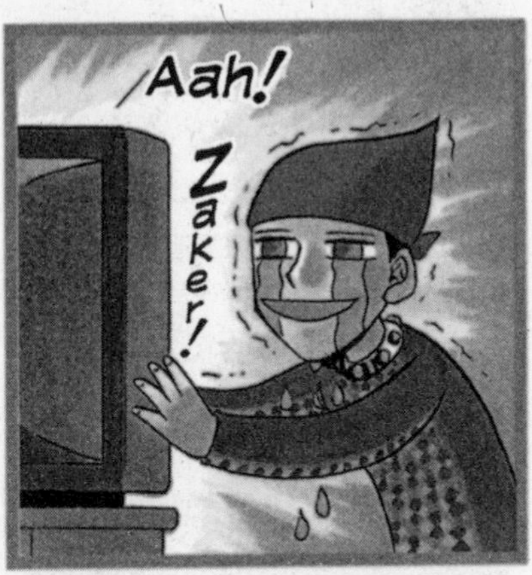
Aah!
Zaker!

**MAKOTO RAIKU**

The *Zatch* TV animation series started. I was deeply moved when I saw Zatch jumping around on TV for 30 minutes. I actually surprised myself. I want to thank the staff and everybody else who's been a part of the series. I'm so thrilled!

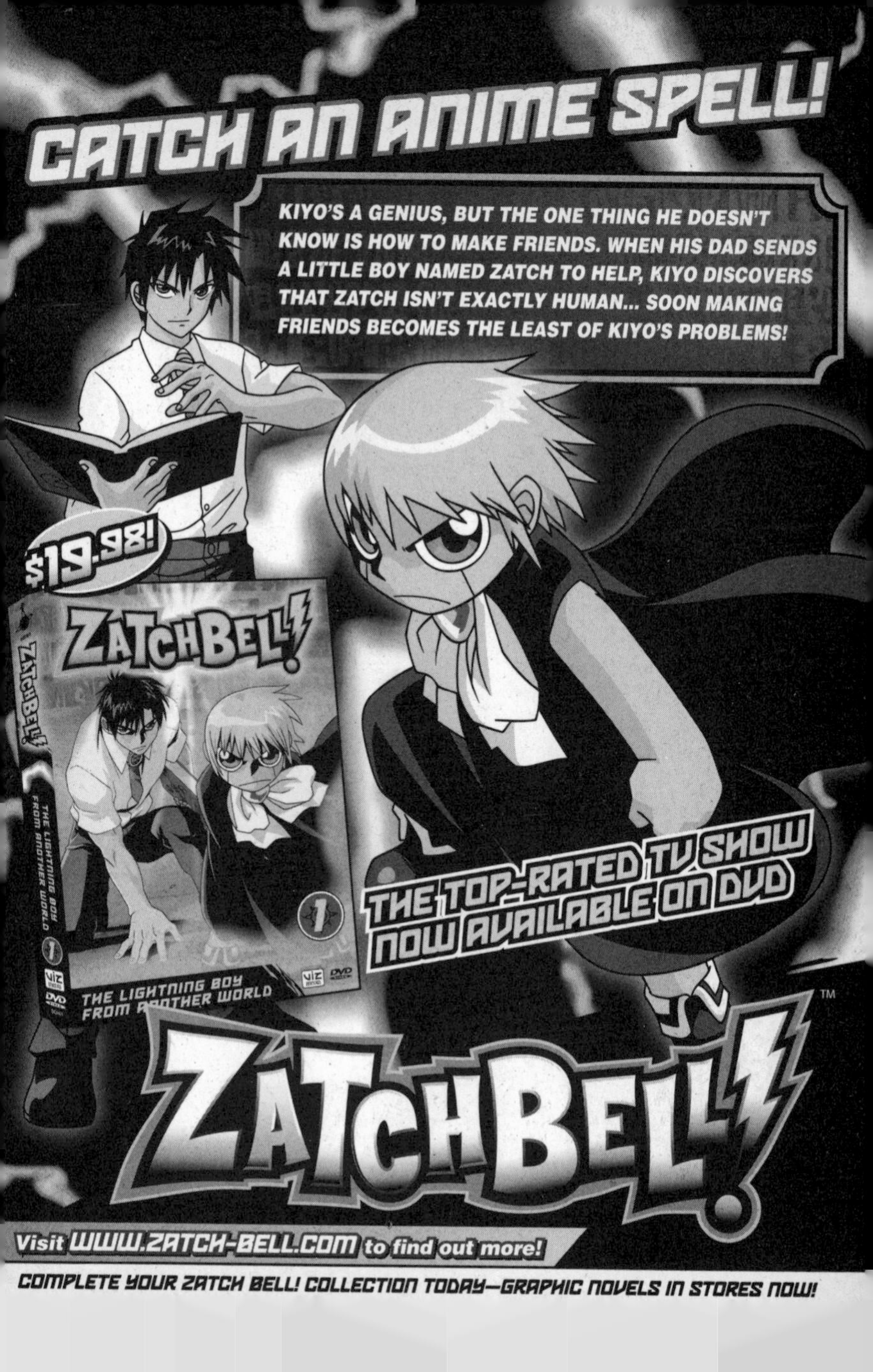
CATCH AN ANIME SPELL!
KIYO'S A GENIUS, BUT THE ONE THING HE DOESN'T KNOW IS HOW TO MAKE FRIENDS. WHEN HIS DAD SENDS A LITTLE BOY NAMED ZATCH TO HELP, KIYO DISCOVERS THAT ZATCH ISN'T EXACTLY HUMAN... SOON MAKING FRIENDS BECOMES THE LEAST OF KIYO'S PROBLEMS!
$19.98!
ZATCH BELL!
THE LIGHTNING BOY FROM ANOTHER WORLD
THE TOP-RATED TV SHOW NOW AVAILABLE ON DVD
ZATCH BELL!™
Visit WWW.ZATCH-BELL.COM to find out more!

# INUYASHA
## THE THRILLING THIRD SEASON!

Includes **FREE** exclusive Kagome collector coin!*

**Inuyasha Season 3 DVD Box Set**

Kagome continues her double life as present-day schoolgirl and feudal-era demon-slayer. With the threat of archenemy Naraku lurking at every turn, can she work with half-demon Inuyasha and friends to collect all the shards of the Sacred Jewel?

**Buy yours today at store.viz.com**

www.viz.com
inuyasha.viz.com

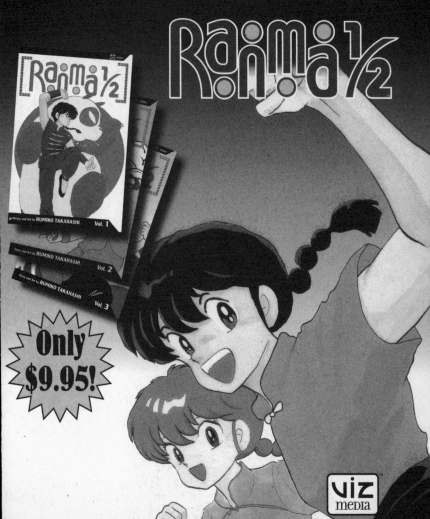

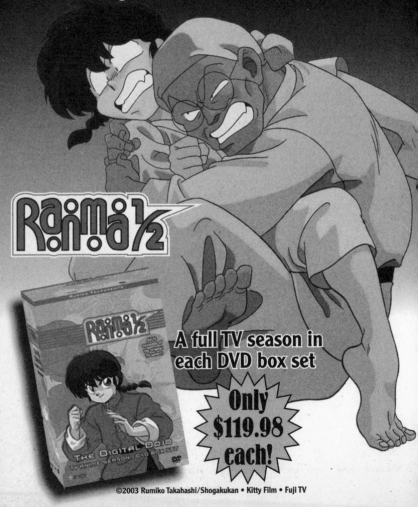

## Fullmetal Alchemist Profiles

Get the background story and world history of the manga, plus:

- Character bios
- New, original artwork
- Interview with creator Hiromu Arakawa
- Bonus manga episode only available in this book

## Fullmetal Alchemist Anime Profiles

Stay on top of your favorite episodes and characters with:

- Actual cel artwork from the TV series
- Summaries of all 51 TV episodes
- Definitive cast biographies
- Exclusive poster for your wall

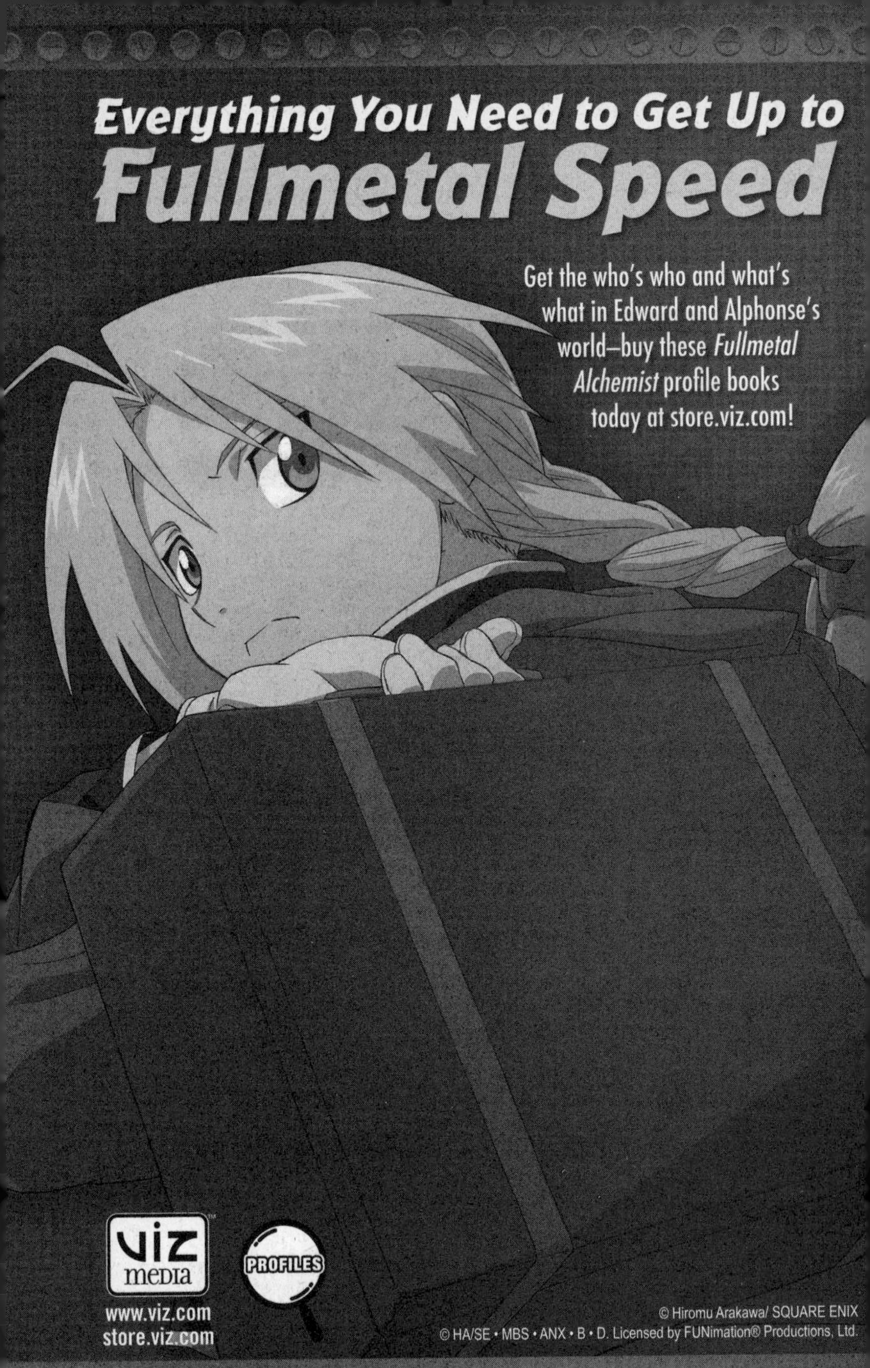
Everything You Need to Get Up to
Fullmetal Speed
Get the who's who and what's what in Edward and Alphonse's world—buy these Fullmetal Alchemist profile books today at store.viz.com!
viz media
PROFILES
www.viz.com
store.viz.com
© Hiromu Arakawa/ SQUARE ENIX
© HA/SE • MBS • ANX • B • D. Licensed by FUNimation® Productions, Ltd.

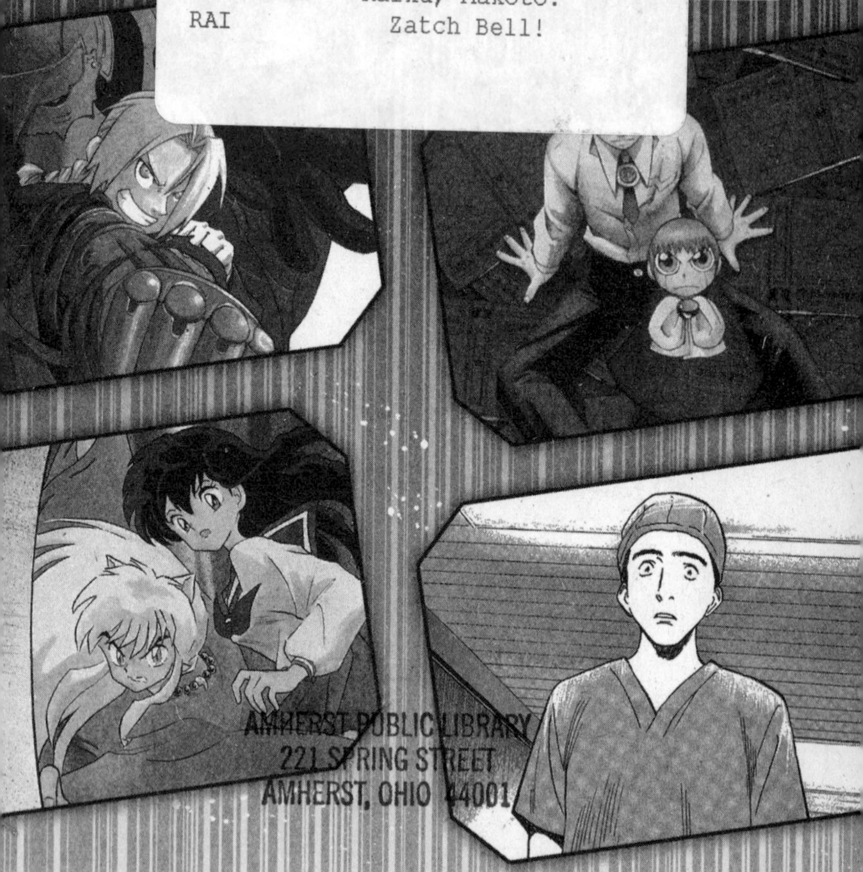